Studies in the Political and Administrative Systems in Ancient and Medieval India

Studies in the Political and Administrative Systems in Ancient and Medieval India

D. C. SIRCAR

Director of the Centre of Advanced Study in Ancient Indian History and Culture, Calcutta University; formerly Carmichael Professor and Head of the Department of Ancient Indian History and Culture, Calcutta University, and Government Epigraphist for India

MOTILAL BANARSIDASS
Delhi :: Varanasi :: Patna

Head Office : BUNGALOW ROAD, JAWAHARNAGAR, DELHI-7
Branches : 1. CHOWK, VARANASI-1 (U.P.)
2. ASHOK RAJPATH, PATNA-4 (BIHAR)

ISBN 0—8426—0579—7

First Edition : *Delhi*, 1974

Printed in India
BY SHANTILAL JAIN, AT SHRI JAINENDRA PRESS, BUNGALOW ROAD, JAWAHAR NAGAR, DELHI-7 AND PUBLISHED BY SUNDARLAL JAIN FOR MOTILAL BANARSIDASS, BUNGALOW ROAD, JAWAHARNAGAR, DELHI-7

PREFACE

Some time ago, I arranged for the publication of a volume in which it was my intention to include most of my studies in the social life and administration in ancient and medieval India. The grouping of Society and Administration together was suggested by the fact that a few studies could be placed under both. Unfortunately, certain unpleasant experiences compelled me to give up the original idea and my papers on social life only were published as *Studies in the Society and Administration of Ancient and Medieval India*, Vol. I—*Society* (Firma K.L. Mukhopadhyay, Calcutta, 1967). The papers on Administration, originally intended to be incorporated in the same volume, were therefore arranged to be published separately under the title *Studies in the Administration of Ancient and Medieval India*. Finally, however, 'Political and Administrative Systems' appeared to me more suitable than 'Administration' in the title, for the topics discussed in the volume.

The plan of this book is the same as in the other volume as well as in my *Studies in the Geography of Ancient and Medieval India* (1960, 1971) and *Studies in Indian Coins* (1968). I am thankful to the authorities of the publications in which the studies originally appeared. A few of them have also been utilised in my other works.

The matter of nearly forty papers has been arranged in the present volume in twenty-one Chapters and Appendices, the sources of which are indicated below.

I.—*Land System and Feudalism in Ancient India*, ed. D.C. Sircar, Calcutta, 1966, pp. 11ff.

II.—*Ibid.*, 57 ff., 124ff.; *Journ. Or. Inst.*, Baroda, Vol. XVI, 1966, pp. 166ff.; *Journ. Ind. Hist.*, Trivandrum, Vol. XLIV, 1966, pp. 351 ff.

III.—*Journ.* [*R.*] *As. Soc.* [*Beng.*], Calcutta, Letters, Vol. XII, 1946, pp. 71 ff.; Vol. XIII, 1947, pp. 75 ff.; *Ind. Cult.*, Calcutta, Vol. VII, 1941, pp. 364-65; *Ep. Ind.*, Delhi, Vol. XXXIV, 1961-1962, pp. 135-40.

IV.—*Ep. Ind.*, Vol. XXXIII, 1959-1960, pp. 50ff.; Vol. XXXV, 1963-1964, pp. 287ff.

V.—*Journ. R. As. Soc.*, London, 1952, pp. 4ff.; *Ind. Hist. Quart.*, Vol. XXIX, 1953, pp. 298ff.; *Ep. Ind.*, Vol. XXXIII, 1959-1960, pp. 150ff.; Vol. XXXIV, 1961-1962, pp. 137ff.

VI.—*Journ. Univ. Gau.*, Gauhati, Vol. VI, 1955, pp.81ff.; *Ep. Ind.*, Vol. XXXII, 1957-1958, pp. 305ff.

VII.—*Ep. Ind.*, Vol. XXXV, 1963-1964, pp. 95-96; *Gopalakrishnamacharya Book of Commemoration*, pp. 4.37 ff.; *Purāṇa*, Varanasi, Vol. VI, 1964, pp. 445ff.

VIII.—*Cal. Police Journ.*, Vol. I, 1953, pp. 6ff.; *Journ. Or. Inst.*, Vol. XV, 1966, pp. 378ff.

IX.—*Journ. Andh. Hist. Res. Soc.*, Rajahmundry, Vol. VII, 1933, pp. 195ff.

X.—*Bhārata-Kaumudī* (R. K. Mookerji Presentation Volume), Part II, Allahabad, 1947, pp. 943ff.; *Ind. Hist. Quart.*, Vol. XXVI, 1950, pp. 309ff.; *Ep. Ind.*, Vol. XXVIII, 1949-1950, pp. 244-45.

XI.—*Ep. Ind.*, Vol. XXXIII, 1959-1960, pp. 167ff.; *Nalinīkānta Bhaṭṭaśālī Memorial Volume*, Dacca, 1966, pp. 8ff.

XII.—*Ep. Ind.*, Vol. XXXIII, 1959-1960, pp. 54ff.; *Quart. Journ. Myth. Soc.*, Bangalore, Vol. LI, 1960, pp. 1 ff.

XIII.—*Ep. Ind.*, Vol. XXX, 1953-1954, pp. 166ff.

XIV.—*Journ. As. Soc.*, Calcutta, Letters, Vol. XX, 1954, pp. 201ff., 209ff.

XV.—*Ep. Ind.*, Vol. XXX, 1953-1954, pp.51 ff.

App. I.—*Journ. Ind. Hist.*, Trivandrum, Vol. XLIX, December, 1971, pp. 125-34.

App. II.—*Early Indian Political and Administrative Systems*, ed. Sircar, Calcutta, 1972, pp. 50-61.

App. III—*Indian Museum Bulletin*, Calcutta, Vol. IV, No. 2, July, 1969, pp. 7-9.

App. IV.—*Ind. Stud. Past & Pres.*, Calcutta, Vol. V, No. 1, October-December, 1963, pp. 89-92; cf. *Proc. XXVI Intern. Cong. Or.*, New Delhi, 1964, Vol. III, Part II, pp. 786-88.

App. V.—*Journ. Anc. Ind. Hist.*, Calcutta, Vol. III, 1969-70, pp. 137-41.

App. VI.—*Early Indian Trade and Industry*, ed. Sircar, Calcutta, 1972, pp. 92-100.

For the blemishes that may have crept into the present volume in spite of my best efforts, I crave the indulgence of the sympathetic readers. Any suggestion for the betterment of the work will be carefully considered.

D.C. SIRCAR

645, New Alipore,
Calcutta-53.
July 7, 1973.

CONTENTS

Addenda et Corrigenda

Page	32, note 2, line 4.	*Add*—See James Legge, *The Travels of Fahien*, Delhi, 1971, pp. 42-43.
,,	,, last line.	*Add*—About ancient Indian warriors, Arrian says, "the pay which they receive from the state being so liberal that they can with ease maintain themselves and others besides" (Majumdar, *Class. Ac. Ind.*, pp. 225-26).
,,	53, line 4.	*Read*—Malaysia
,,	90, line 24.	*Read*—Mithilā
,,	98, line 17.	*Read*—Nārāyaṇ-opādhyāya
,,	129, line 20.	*Read*—Kashmir
,,	180, line 19.	*Read*—Sarsavani
,,	223, note, lines 5-6.	*Read*—Amgachhi
,,	230, lines 16-17.	*Read*—Madanpāḍā
,,	239, note 15, line 1	*Add*—The number 7707 reminds us of 6666 supposed to be mentioned in the *Ṛgveda*, VII. 18. 14.

CHAPTER I

THE LANDLORD AND TENANT

Some scholars have expressed their views on the early Indian land system, though their writings appear to be based on a rather inadequate study of the epigraphical material. This is easily explained by the fact that the inscriptions in the various Indian languages are too many and their interpretation is difficult in many cases.

The Indian king was theoretically the lord of all land in his kingdom. There was difference of opinion between two groups of early Indian writers on the ownership of land. According to one of these schools, represented by Jaimini and Śabara and correctly understood by the author of the *Vyavahāra-mayūkha*, the king was not the owner of the land, but that he was only entitled to levy taxes from the holders of land.[1] It is indicated that the king could acquire proprietary right on a plot of land under a tenant if only he purchased it from the latter. While the *Ṛgveda* (VIII. 91.5) represents one's field as a personal possession like his head of hair, the *Kauṭilīya Artha-śāstra*[2] refers to an old legend, according to which people suffering from the effects of anarchy first elected Vaivasvata Manu as their king and allotted to him $\frac{1}{6}$ share of the grains grown (*dhānya-ṣaḍbhāga*), $\frac{1}{10}$ of the merchandise (*paṇya-daśabhāga*) and a tax in cash (*hiraṇya*). Thus, in the opinion of the above school, the king collected taxes in exchange for the protection he offered to the subjects.

The other school represented by Manu (VIII. 39) and others acknowledges the king's responsibility for the subjects' protection, but regards him as a god in human form and the lord of all land. According to Megasthenes as well as a commentator on the *Kauṭilīya Arthaśāstra*, land was the property of the king, and private persons were not entitled to own it.[3] But the theoretical nature of the king's ownership of land under

1. Cf. Kane, *Hist. Dharm.*, Vol. II, pp. 865-66.
2. Shama Sastry's ed., pp. 22-23.
3. Majumdar, *Class. Ac. Ind.*, p. 237; Shama Sastry, *Arthaśāstra*, trans., p. 129.

permanent tenants is clearly demonstrated by the reluctance of Indian monarchs to dispossess the subjects from their landed property. The Kārkoṭa section of Kalhaṇa's chronicle, which is believed to be based on authentic information, tells us how, about the beginning of the 8th century A. D., king Candrāpīḍa was reluctant to take away a plot of land in the possession of a tanner because it was 'other's land' and how ultimately he purchased the plot at the tanner's terms.[1]

Land may be variously classified as cultivable, cultivated, uncultivable, fallow, barren, jungly, hilly, marshy, low, high, etc. But from the king's point of view, it was of three classes, viz. (1) State land, (2) land in the occupation of tenants who paid the king's dues according to agreed rates, and (3) land in more or less uninhabited and uncultivated areas over which State control varied under different circumstances. Each of these classes has its sub-divisions. Thus State land can be divided into (1) land attached to the king personally, (2) fiefs allotted to officers, subordinates and members of the royal family, (3) land cultivated by State farms, (4) land cultivated by temporary tenants receiving half the share of the produce for their labour, and (5) uncultivated and waste land of various types. New villages were usually founded in areas which were more or less uninhabited and uncultivated. As regards State land in newly formed villages, Kauṭilya says (1) that the land prepared for cultivation should be allotted to tax-payers only for life, (2) that unprepared land should not be taken away from people who were preparing them for cultivation, (3) that land could be taken away from those who were not cultivating it and could be allotted to others, and (4) that those who did not cultivate the land should pay for the loss of the State.[2]

The State was eager to get its uncultivated fields cultivated and to keep them continuously under cultivation. The tenant, who cultivated the land and paid the king's dues regularly, had therefore little chance of being dispossessed of his field, because it was not easy for the State to cultivate all land freshly acquired or reclaimed. On the death of the tenant, his heirs could easily get a fresh lease, and when the land would be thus enjoyed by a

1. *Op. cit.*, IV. 55 ff.
2. *Op. cit.*, II. 1.

family for a few generations, it would have to be regarded as its permanent property according to the well-known principle—

> *adbhir = dattaṁ tribhir = bhuktaṁ sadbhiś = ca paripālitam /*
> *etāni na nivartante pūrvarāja-kṛtāni ca //*[1]

The stanza states that a plot of land could not be confiscated by the State under the following circumstances: (i) when it was ceremonially granted by the king, (2) when it was in the possession of a family for three generations. (3) when care is taken for it by good tenants, and (4) when it is enjoyed by a tenant by virtue of the charter of an earlier king.

Many copper-plate grants state that land was granted to the gods and Brāhmaṇas according to the *bhūmicchidra-nyāya*, which means that the gift land had to be enjoyed as a free-holding just as a person would enjoy a plot of land, brought by him under cultivation for the first time, without payment of taxes.[2] The said *nyāya* refers to an interesting tenure, the principle being logical since the State does not pay anything for the reclamation of the land though it expects taxes on its reallotment after the first tenant's death.

When a governor or vassal wanted to create a free-holding in his fief or estate in favour of a god or a Brāhmaṇa, he applied to the king and apparently paid the price of the land at least on a theoretical basis. According to an old convention, $\frac{5}{6}$ of the religious merit accruing to the pious act of donation in such cases would go to the purchaser of the land, i. e. the real donor of the grant, and $\frac{1}{6}$ of it to the king whose government alone could really create a rent-free holding.[3] The king's share of the merit was equal to his share of the produce of the tenant's fields. If the State did not get any compensation for the loss of revenue, the merit accruing to the donation would not go to anybody other than the king. The royal charters, however, do not usually refer to the acceptance of compensation, but say that the free-holding was created by the king at the request of a subordinate whose name was mentioned in the document only when he was of sufficient importance. When he became

1. Sircar, *Indian Epigraphy*, p. 176; *Ep. Ind.*, Vol. XXXIII, p. 92; Viṣṇu, V. 183.
2. Sircar, *op. cit.*, pp. 397-98.
3. Cf. *ibid.*, pp. 114ff.; *Ep. Ind.*, Vol. XXXIII, pp. 50 ff.

more powerful, he would himself issue charters with the king's permission, and, when still more powerful, his charter would not even mention the name of the overlord. The next stage would of course be represented by his charters issued as an independent monarch. Thus a landlord became a king. As to the creation of a free-holding in a fief or estate, it has to be noticed that the holder of the fief or estate would lose the revenue income of the gift land so long as he would be in its occupation, while the State's loss was practically permanent. That is why compensation was paid, and it is made fairly clear by certain East Indian epigraphs of the Gupta age.

There are cases which represent the king as ratifying the creation of rent-free holdings by his subordinates in their fiefs. But the State was usually reluctant to mention in the charters the fact that the king was not the real donor of the grant. Sometimes the real donors are mentioned in the records without indicating their association with the grant while, in the Paramāra inscriptions, they are called *dāpaka*, i. e. 'one who has caused the gift'.[1] But some East Indian inscriptions of the Gupta age, referred to above, record the sale of big plots of fallow land to applicants paying the usual price and the State's acceptance of their proposal for the creation of free-holdings in favour of gods or Brāhmaṇas.[2] The State's interest in such transactions is sometimes stated to be the king getting $\frac{1}{6}$ of the religious merit accruing to the pious act. Actually, however, the donees, who now became landlords, were expected to develop the area by founding habitations, etc., so that the contiguous areas would be automatically developed at least partially and it would be easier for the State to complete the process of reclamation. Moreover, if a Brāhmaṇa donee died without leaving an heir or if he committed treason, the estate would be taken away by the State. Large areas of fallow and jungle land in Bengal were reclaimed by Brāhmaṇas and temple authorities in the way indicated above.

Besides escheat and a rebel's estate reverting to the donor, there were other recognised ways of confiscating donated lands without blemish. Thus, in a few charters of the Vākāṭakas

1. Sircar, *Ind. Ep. Gloss.*, p. 83; below, p. 57.
2. Sircar, *Sel. Ins.*, pp. 337 note, 342ff., etc.

and Yādavas, there are some specific conditions along with the statement that their violation would lead to the confiscation of the property granted to the Brāhmaṇa donees.[1]

It is clear from epigraphic and literary records that pious kings generally respected the free-hodings created by earlier rulers. But, at the same time, the charters exhibit a persistent fear of the donors that their gifts might be resumed by the future kings.[2] This shows that unscrupulous rulers sometimes transformed free-holdings into rent-paying property on flimsy grounds. Sometimes inscriptions recording sale of land and fixation of annual revenue also quoted old stanzas praising the gift of land and denouncing its resumption. This refers to the well-known convention that the sale of land should also be represented as a gift.[3]

We have referred to the legend of Vaivasvata Manu, the first king who was allotted by the people $\frac{1}{6}$ share of the grains, $\frac{1}{10}$ share of the articles for sale and a tax in cash. According to Megasthenes, the king received $\frac{1}{4}$ of the produce of land and a tribute apparently in cash besides other dues from traders, herdsmen, etc.[4] Manu (VII. 130) speaks of $\frac{1}{6}$, $\frac{1}{8}$ and $\frac{1}{12}$ of the grains as the king's share, of which $\frac{1}{6}$ seems to be the king's normal share of the principal crop of an area. This is supported by the official designation *Ṣaṣṭhādhikṛta*,[5] i. e. the Superintendent of the $\frac{1}{6}$ share, in the records of the Pālas. The Collector of the king's grain-share was called *Dhruvādhikaraṇika*,[6] i. e. Superintendent of the office in charge of 'the fixed', in the Gujarat region. This seems to suggest that, in the said area, different rates were fixed for different types of fields, crops or tenants.

Although the lexicons recognise the words *kara*, *bali* and *bhāga* or *bhāgadheya* as synonyms, once *bali* and *bhāga* must have been regarded as different types of *kara* or revenue in general. Early epigraphic records make a clear distinction between *bali* and *bhāga*. Thus an inscription[7] of Aśoka says how he

1. Sircar, *Ind. Ep.*, pp. 140-41; also *Ep. Ind.*, Vol. XI, pp. 184 ff.; Vol. XV, pp. 286 ff.
2. Cf. Sircar, *op. cit.*, pp. 141ff.
3. *Ibid.*, p. 111 and note 1.
4. Majumdar, *Class. Ac. Ind.*, p. 237; Sircar, *Landl. Ten.*, pp. 2, 13.
5. Sircar, *Ind. Ep. Gloss.*, p. 305.
6. *Ibid.*, p. 96.
7. Sircar, *Sel. Ins.*, p. 70.

visited a pilgrim spot which was made, on that occasion, *udbalika*, i. e. exempted from *bali*, the same as Tamil *umbalika*, *umbaḷam* or *umbaḷikkai*, and also *aṣṭabhāgika*, i. e. entitled to pay only ⅛ of the produce as *bhāga* or the king's share. *Bali* here apparently means the land tax in cash mentioned by Megasthenes as also probably by Kauṭilya in the legend of Vaivasvata Manu. In a second-century inscription[1] of Rudradāman, we have two interesting passages, one enumerating the State's dues from the subjects as *kara* (levies in general), *viṣṭi* (unpaid labour) and *praṇayakriyā* (benevolence or emergency impost), and the other mentioning the king's revenue income as consisting of *bali* (land-tax in cash), *śulka* (tolls, etc.) and *bhāga* (share of the produce of the tenants' fields). The word *kara* is conspicuous by its absence from the second passage apparently because *bali*, *śulka* and *bhāga* were regarded as three kinds of *kara*.

Bali originally meant the offerings to a deity as well as the tribute to a king. It was therefore at first whatever the king received from the subjects and the subdued rulers and peoples, the contributions from the subjects gradually developing into fixed taxes payable regularly for a definite period. At the same time, the word *bhāga* was becoming popular in the sense of the share of the crops payable by the tenants to the king, the proportion being soon standardised. *Bhāga* was thus originally the principal part of *bali*, though the latter gradually developed a distinct meaning. This is the reason why *bali* and *bhāga* were regarded as synonymous even in later works.

A Śātavāhana epigraph[2] mentions the king's levies as *deya* (what has to be offered or paid in cash) and *meya* (what has to be paid after measurement). *Meya* here seems to be the same as *bhāga* while *deya* is the same as either *bali* or the periodical offerings of fruits, etc., payable to the king, which were later called *bhoga*.

The charters[3] of the Śarabhapura kings of the 6th century A. D. mention the royal dues as *bhoga-bhāga*. The

1. *Ibid.*, pp. 173-74.
2. *Ibid.*, p. 195.
3. *CII*, Vol. III, pp. 194, 198.

records[1] of the Uccakalpa kings of the same age have (1) *kara-pratyāya* or income in the shape of *kara*, (2) *bhāgabhogakara-pratyāya* or income in the form of *kara* levied as *bhāga* and *bhoga*, (3) *bhāgabhogakara- hirany-ādi-pratyāya* or income including *bhāga-bhogakara* and *hiraṇya* which means tax payable in cash, (4) *śu-lkabhāgabhogakara-hirany-ādi-pratyāya* in which *śulka* or tolls is added to the list, and (5) *bhāgabhogakara- hirany- āvātāy- ādi-pratyāya* which includes *āvāt-āya* or income resulting from storms. There is really no question of a gradual increase in the number of the levies since the records cover only a few decades. The difference in the lists is due to the difference in the extent of the king's favour to the various donees or to special circumstances.

In the expression *dhānya-hiranya* found in records like those of the Maitrakas,[2] *dhānya* or 'grains' means either *bhāga* or the small contributions in grains often made for the maintenance of local officials like the village watchman. When *tulya-meya* (what has to be weighed and what has to be measured) is mentioned along with *bhāgabhogakarahiraṇya*, it may mean tolls on commodities sold in the markets.[3]

Firewood, shrubs and particular trees in the land under unprivileged tenants could not be owned by the latter. There is evidence to show that even the branch of a tree brought down by storms could not be appropriated by an ordinary tenant. In one case,[4] a person purchasing a plot of land from ordinary tenants is known to have acquired the right to own certain trees only when the king made the property a rent-free holding in his favour. Whether he paid some money to the State for this purpose is not clearly stated; but any such right could be purchased. There is clear mention in one record that even *aṣṭabhoga-tejaḥsvāmya* or complete control involving all the eight kinds of enjoyment of landed property could be secured by means of purchase.[5] This *aṣṭa-bhoga* is sometimes enumerated as (1) treasure-trove, (2) deposits or accumulations on the soil, (3) fishing rights in waters, (4) quarrying rights in

1. *Ibid.*, pp. 118, 122, 127, 131, 133, 137.
2. *Ibid.*, p. 179.
3. Sircar, *Ind. Ep.*, p. 394.
4. *Journ. As. Soc.*, Letters, Vol. XXI, p. 205.
5. Sircar, *Ind. Ep. Gloss.*, p. 31.

hills, (5) actual income, (6) future income, (7) income from land already under cultivation, and (8) income from land that may be brought under cultivation in future.

In some cases (as in the Semra plates),[1] the donees were empowered to sell or mortgage the gift land while, in others (as in the Purushottampuri plates),[2] such a right was withheld from them. Some grants are stated to have been made in accordance with the custom governing permanent endowments, which means that the donees were entitled to enjoy only the income from the gift land, but had no power to sell it. The same thing is indicated in some Orissan records as 'the condition of no employment of the pen [for writing out a fresh deed concerning the land]'.[3]

A Sena inscription shows that, when a free-holding was sold, it became rent-paying property, and the same must have been the case when such land was given in mortgage.[4] That the smaller tenants were also entitled to sell their landed property is clear from the Sena and Maitraka records. The Maitraka charters often mention the gift land as the *pratyāya* or property of a tenant such as a carpenter or an agriculturist householder, and it is apparent that the king purchased the land from them in order to gain religious merit by granting it in favour of gods and Brāhmaṇas.[5] A Śaka ruler of the Nasik-Poona region is known to have visited the Puṣkara-tīrtha where he purchased a plot of land from its Brāhmaṇa holder, at the cost of a large sum of money, for making a free gift after taking his bath in the holy waters of the Puṣkara lakes.[6]

The rights of the donees were not the same in different charters especially of different regions and ages. Of course the vague indication of 'all exemptions or customary privileges'[7] often found in the documents suggests that there was a general agreement on the nature of the privileges at least in an area or a kingdom in a particular age.

1. *Ep. Ind.*, Vol. IV, pp. 153ff.
2. *Ibid.*, Vol. XXV, pp. 199ff.
3. *Ibid.*, Vol. XXVIII, p. 216; Vol. XXIX, p. 89.
4. *Journ. As. Soc.*, Letters, Vol. XX, pp. 206-07.
5. *CII*, Vol. III, pp. 164ff.
6. Sircar, *Sel. Ins.*, p. 162.
7. Sircar, *Ind. Ep. Gloss.*, pp. 403-04.

Sometimes the gift land enjoyed complete freedom from the entry of *Bhaṭas* and *Cāṭas* or *Chātras*, i. e. Pāiks and Barkandāzes, who were, however, entitled to enter into the freeholding, according to some charters, only to deal with cases of theft or of theft and treason.[1] In many records, the power to deal with cases involving 'the 10 offences' was granted to the donee.[2] According to the *tribhog-ābhyantara-siddhi*, the donee was entitled to enjoy only $\frac{1}{8}$ of the income from the gift land while, under the *pannāsa* tenure, he could enjoy $\frac{1}{2}$ of it.[3] Likewise, the *brāhmaṇa-viṁśati*[4] tenure would allow the donee to enjoy $\frac{1}{5}$ of the income. Sometimes a small rent of about 200 *paṇas* (equivalent to about 16,000 cowrie-shells or a little over 12½ silver coins) was fixed for free-holdings per annum.[5]

Persons of non-Brāhmaṇa communities also sometimes received free-holdings from the king either as a reward for their services or by purchase. Grants made for the maintenance of the families of warriors of different communal groups, who died fighting on the king's behalf, were called *mṛtyuka-vṛtti*, *rakta-mānya*, etc.[6] A Gaṅga king of Orissa is known to have created a *vaiśy-āgrahāra*, i. e. a free-holding in favour of the mercantile class, after receiving 150 silver coins from the donees.[7] Late medieval epigraphs of the Vijayanagara kings speak of a tenure according to which a person enjoyed royal land on condition that he would help the king with forces whenever required.[8]

When a village was granted, the tenants belonging to it were generally advised by the donor to pay to the donee whatever was so long been paid to the king; in a few cases, certain tenants, artisans and traders were specially attached to the gift village.[9] The tenants and others were often asked to be obedient to the donee and not to cause any obstruction to his enjoyment of the gift land. Thus a landlord was created by

1. *Ibid.*, p. 394.
2. *Ibid.*, p. 398.
3. *Ibid.*, pp. 334, 343.
4. *Ibid.*, p. 61.
5. Sircar, *Ind. Ep.*, p. 113.
6. Sircar, *Ind. Ep. Gloss.*, pp. 203, 275.
7. *Ibid.*, p. 360.
8. *Ibid.*, p. 17, s. v. *Amara* and *Amara-nāyaka*; below, p. 15 and note 3.
9. See below, pp. 23-24.

relegating the king's rights over the village to the donee. The charters suggest the existence of several kinds of such landlords; e. g., (1) those who enjoyed complete freedom from taxes and obligations, (2) those whose estates were partially exempted from obligations and paid a nominal tax, and (3) those who were not exempted from obligations. When the charter creating the free-holding was lost and the estate fell into the rent-paying category, the king issued a fresh document after an official investigation.[1]

The boundaries of the free-holdings were often clearly mentioned or demarcated; but sometimes it was considered unnecessary to mention them in detail because they were well marked and also well known to the people of the locality.

Some of the following are mentioned in certain charters in connection with the free-holdings:[2] (1) boundaries, grass land and pasture land, (2) the surface with the space above and the region under the ground, (3) what is above and under the ground, (4) approaches, ingress and egress. (5) movable and immovable belongings, (6) land and waters, (7) pits and barren spots, (8) mines of salt and metals, (9) fallow land and cultivated plots of land, (10) market places and landing stations, (11) trees, creepers, shrubs, branches, hemp, sugar-cane, etc., (12) orchards, wells, step-wells, springs and water-falls, (13) temples and ramparts, (14) ponds, tanks, rivers and hills, (15) woods, bricks and stones, (16) domestic and wild animals, birds, aquatic beings, fish and tortoise, (17) mounds and waste land attached to the village, (18) platforms for collection of tolls and records in the custody of local officials, (19) houses, house-sites, threshing floors and their sites, etc., (20) dwellings or households of artisans, cultivators and traders, (21) areas producing fish and betel-vines, etc., etc. But all these are never specifically mentioned together in one record or a group of records. There is some regional element in the specification. Thus tortoise is only known from Orissan documents while springs and waterfalls are mentioned in the epigraphs of the Himalayan region.[3]

The tax burden and obligations of the tenants were heavy.

1. *Ep. Ind.*, Vol. XXXI, pp. 267.
2. Cf. Sircar, *Ind. Ep.*, pp. 388ff.
3. *Ibid.* p. 402, note 1; *Ep. Ind.*, Vol. XXXI, p. 281, text line 22.

An 8th-century king is known to have held the view that villagers should not be left with more food than required for one year's consumption, nor more oxen than are required for the tillage of their fields; because, if they were allowed to accumulate wealth, they would become, in a single year, formidable landlords strong enough to disregard the king's commands.[1] This shows that the tenants, at least in some parts of the country, had the opportunity of becoming rent-paying landlords if the kings were not oppressive.

The privileges going with rent-free holdings indirectly refer to a large number of taxes and obligations of both the landlords and the tenants.[2] All of them are never mentioned together in a single record. Even in the early inscriptions of the Śātavāhanas and the Pallavas, only some of them are enumerated with the phrase 'and all kinds of exemptions' and 'the 18 kinds of exemptions beginning with...' Some charters merely state that the grants were made together with all the usual privileges, without specifying them. But, in spite of certain regional variations and modifications due to change of time, the obligations are more or less of the same type.

The following are some of the numerous items noticed in various epigraphical records:[3] (1) obligation to supply to the king or landlord on occasions and to the touring officers or local officials such articles as rice, cooking pot, firewood, accommodation, servants, milk, curds, gruel, myrobalan, vegetables, flowers, bullocks and cows, hide-seats, charcoal, etc., (2) taxes in general, (3) profession tax on artisans, (4) tax for producing salt, sugar, toddy, etc., (5) supply of unpaid labour, (6) surrender of treasure-troves and deposits, (7) fixed taxes and occasional levies including the tax on temporary tenants, (8) supply of sacrificial animals, (9) tax on shopkeepers and shops of metal and leather workers, (10) tax on the outcastes, masked actors, water-diviners, weavers and barbers, (11) tax on marriage and gambling, (12) tax for the maintenance of spies, surveyors, gate-keepers or toll-collectors, etc., (13) tax on artisans enjoying free-holdings, (14) presents of various kinds to be made on different occasions, (15) payment of small

1. *Rājataraṅgiṇī*, IV. 347-52; also see below, p. 13.
2. See Sircar, *Ind. Ep. Gloss.*, pp. 388ff.
3. See *loc. cit.*: *Ind. Ep.*, pp. 388ff.

quantities of grains per month, (16) two handfuls per *puṭṭi* measure of grains payable to the village officials, (17) tax on uncultivated land, (18) surrender of half the produce of the fields, (19) levy for the supervision of partition of land and other property, (20) taxes in kind and cash, (21) income from changes caused by natural agencies and cyclones, (22) fines for the ten offences, (23) all fines and exactions, (24) restriction on the production of certain crops, (25) confiscation of the property of one dying without leaving an heir, (26) income from the bees such as honey and wax, (27) power to deal with cases of abduction of unmarried girls, (28) appropriation of all sources of income, (29) appropriation of all internal revenue incomes, (30) power to deal with the recovery of stolen goods, (31) power to assess taxes afresh, (32) obligation relating to the supply of free labour, (33) tax on the merchants, (34) taxes relating to the Turuṣkas, Andhras and Tiguḷas (Tamils), (35) profession tax on the wrestlers, (36) payment of one silver coin on the occasion of the birth of a prince, (37) water-tax for fishing rights, (38) cattle-tax for grazing rights, (39) tax for the possession of race bullocks, (40) fixed or regular taxes and occasional or irregular taxes, (41) perquisites for hereditary officers, (42) quarrying rights in the hills, (43) dues payable for the maintenance of armed constables, (44) income from the receipts of the examiner of coins, (45) tax for the maintenance of elephants, (46) levy on amounts lent out by the money-lenders, (47) levy on amounts realised by the money-lenders, (48) levy on the arrears of taxes or fines, (49) levy for the maintenance of or profession tax on snake-charmers, (50) levy for the medical treatment of the king when he is sick, (51) fine in lieu of imprisonment, (52) presents to be made to the king especially when he returns from a military campaign, (53) tax for the maintenance of swordsmen, (54) tax for the maintenance of Pāiks, (55) transit duties, (56) profession tax on goldsmiths, (57) tax for the grazing and watering of cattle, (58) obligation to supply uncooked food, (59) collective tax for land partitioned among cultivators, etc., etc.[1]

1. See also Sircar, *Landlordism and Tenancy in Ancient and Medieval India*, pp. 78-79. Some topics discussed in these pages have been dealt with in that book in greater detail.

CHAPTER II

INDIAN LANDLORDISM AND EUROPEAN FEUDALISM

I

As Hallam long ago pointed out, "It is easy to find partial resemblance to the feudal system. The relation of patron and client in the Republic of Rome has been deemed to resemble it, as well as the barbarians and veterans who held frontier lands on the tenure of defending them and the frontier; but they were bound not to an individual, but to the State. Such a resemblance of fiefs may be found in the Zamindārs of Hindūstān and the Timariots of Turkey. The clans of the Highlanders and Irish followed their chieftain into the field; but their tie was that of imagined kindred and birth, not the spontaneous compact of vassalage."[1]

In spite of Hallam's warning, Tod, in the first half of the last century, was tempted to believe in the existence of most of the characteristics of feudalism in late medieval Rajasthan.[2] Fortunately, however, later writers on the subject have exposed Tod's 'obvious anxiety to discover elements of European Feudalism in the Rajput States'.[3] Sometimes even more careful writers also made similar mistakes. Thus Stein, in the latter half of the last century, explains the word *Ḍāmara*, as found in Kalhaṇa's *Rājataraṅgiṇī*, as a feudal baron. But the *Ḍāmaras* of Kashmir were rural landholders and not feudal barons in the European sense. This is quite clear from several references in the *Rājataraṅgiṇī*. It is said that king Lalitāditya (8th century A. D.) warned his successors not to leave with the cultivators of the land more than what was necessary for their bare sustenance and the cultivation of their fields, because, it was argued, if they were allowed to keep more wealth, they would, in a single year, become formidable *Ḍāmaras* strong enough to defy the king's command (IV. 347-48). Jayyaka,

1. *Middle Ages*, Vol. I, p. 200.
2. *Annals and Antiquities of Rajasthan*, ed. Crooke, Vol. I, pp. 153 ff.
3. Cf. A. C. Banerjee, *The Rajput States and the East India Company*, pp. 239 ff.
4. *Kalhaṇa's Rājataraṅgiṇī*, Vol. II, pp. 304 ff.

the clever son of a householder of Selyapura, is stated to have succeeded in becoming a *Ḍāmara* by means of accumulating the income derived from his lands and from trading with foreign countries in foodgrains (VII. 494 ff.). One could therefore become a *Ḍāmara* without any contact or contract with the king. On the execution of Lakkanacandra, a *Ḍāmara* in possession of the fort of Dugdhaghāta and the surrounding lands, by order of king Kalaśa, the *Ḍāmara's* window offered the fort to the king apparently for protection from the inroads of the Daradas, though the king refused the offer, so that the Dugdhaghāta region, which looks like the hereditary property of the *Ḍāmara*, fell into the hands of the Darada ruler (VII. 1171 ff.). Considereing the above cases, it is impossible to agree with Stein's hesitant conjecture that 'a kind of service tenure, the grant of land in return for military or other services, may have been the original foundation of the system'.[1] It is interesting to note that, in the 16th century, the designation *Ḍāmara* was applied to local grandees, both Hindu and Muhammadan.

The servants (both military and civil) of ancient Indian kings, besides slaves, were generally of two kinds, viz. *Maula* (those who enjoyed land, etc., hereditarily in lieu of wages) and *Bhṛtaka* (those who enjoyed regular pay).[2] The evidence of the Arab writers shows that the Rāṣṭrakūṭa king of Mānyakheṭa used to give 'regular pay to his troops', but, at the same time, also had soldiers who did not receive any wages.[3] There is, however, no doubt that the *maula* type of civil and military servants were entitled to surrender the land of the State and adopt any other profession of their choice. The *Rājataraṅgiṇī* speaks of an additional allowance paid to the soldiers when they were sent on an expedition.[4]

With the growth of communism, a new conception of history developed, and a socio-economic approach to historiography became popular with a section of Western historians who conceived the existence of four successive stages through

1. *Op. cit.*, p. 307.
2. Cf. *Mbh.*, V. 165-68; see for *bhakta* and *vetana* to soldiers, also II. 100. 23; III. 15.21: cf. below, p. 29; also p. 32, note 3.
3. See *The Age of Imperial Kanauj*, ed. Majumdar, p. 17; Altekar, *The Rāṣṭrakūṭas and Their Times*, pp. 250-51.
4. VII. 1457; VIII, 757, 808-10.

which the history of a country has to pass. These are: (1) the primitive community and the system of slavery, (2) the feudal period, (3) the capitalist period, and (4) the epoch of socialism.[1] This approach is apparently dogmatic and uncritical; but it exercised considerable influence on some Indian historians about the middle of the present century, and we have seen, as a result, attempts to prove the existence of a feudal period in early Indian history. It is not that different writers of this category interpret the data in the same way. Often they differ widely in this respect, one finding traces of the system only in one period and another only in a second.[2] Really however, the views of all these writers appear to us to be based on misunderstanding and wrong interpretation of the evidence at our disposal as well as on the study only of a part of it. Like the Zamindari system of late medieval Hindustan, the early Indian land system may exhibit some superficial resemblance with European feudalism; but none of the essential characteristics of the feudal system can be traced in India.

We fully agree with a recent writer on the subject who has rightly pointed out, "the class-, caste- and clan-ridden society, as it was and still is in India, led to the development of certain social, economic, and political concepts, not at all in keeping with those in Europe. Here the Pañcāyat system, in one form or another, took deep root, and a proper investigation of different castes, classes and clans would reveal that they were organised in close groups with different social regulations. The loyalty of the individual member was as much, if not more, to his social group as it was to the sovereign."[3]

II

With the exception of certain late medieval records of Vijayanagara speaking of the Amara tenure[4] involving enjoy-

1. Cf. *Outline History of the USSR*, Moscow, 1960.

2. See *Land System and Feudalism in Ancient India*, ed. Sircar, pp. 62ff., 72ff., 96ff., etc.

3. See D. R. Das in *JAIH*, Vol. I, 1967-68, p. 211.

4. Cf. Sircar, *Ind. Ep. Gloss.*, *s. v. amara* and *Amara-nāyaka*. The difference between the Amara-nāyakas of Vijayanagara and the feudal Barons of medieval England is quite clear. For this difference between the two systems, see Mahalingam, *Adm. Soc. L. Vijayan.*, pp. 195 ff.

ment of royal land by persons on the condition of supplying soldiers to the king or landlord when necessary, there is no trace, in ancient and medieval India, of any tenure even remotely resembling any aspect of the socio-economic system called feudalism that was prevalent in much of Western Europe in the Middle Ages. But some writers, as we have seen, are inclined to confuse Indian landlordism with European feudalism. They should note that even the Amara-nāyakas of Vijayanagara and the *Maula* servants of the king were not tied to the soil in the fedual sense.

In the feudal system of Europe, the king was regarded as the holder of all the land of the kingdom, much of the land being let out by him to the barons or tenants-in-chief who, in return for the land, agreed to perform certain services for the king and were under the obligation of making some payments and supplies on occasions. They had usually to provide the king with a specified number of soldiers in times of war. The barons, in their turn, let out land to others on similar conditions, and thus the process was continued down the scale. When a tenant died, it was usual for his successor to pay a fine to the overlord before he could succeed to his estate. Fines were also paid when the tenant sold or gave any part of his land to a stranger. Payments and supplies of articles had again to be made to the master on other recognised occasions such as the knighting of the latter's eldest son and the marriage of his eldest daughter and when he himself required to pay ransom.[1] None of these characteristic features is especially noticed in the landlordism known from the ancient and early medieval records of India.

In India, as we have seen, the king's ownership of all land was only theoretical at least in respect of land under the possession of permanent tenants whose property could not be confiscated by the king. As we have pointed out, there is evidence that kings often purchased land under permanent tenants in order to obtain proprietary right over them.

The majority of the numerous charters discovered all over the country record grants of land to gods and Brāhmaṇas

1. See *Encyclopaedia Britannica*, s. v. *Feudalism*, and references cited therein.

without stipulating any obligation of the donees to the donors. Obviously the priestly class was the most unsuitable for rendering services of the feudal type. On the other hand, it is generally stated in the grants in clear terms that the donees were exempted from all kinds of obligations including the supply of unpaid labour. In some cases, it is stated that the donees were entitled to sell and mortgage the donated land. It is significant that not even a single charter records the creation of a great baron. The charters generally created small privileged estates.[1]

The object of the grants is often clearly stated in the charters. It was the desire of attaining religious merit by the donors and their parents. There are only a few early Indian charters recording grants of land to people of the warrior class, sometimes for services rendered to the king.[2] But there is generally no mention of obligations of the feudal type even in such records.

The successors of the donees of free-holdings were not required to pay any money or to offer presents to the king, and it is often mentioned that the estate would automatically pass to the donees' heirs.[3]

In the feudal system, the man who held land from another was considered to be the dependant and subordinate of the latter. But, in India, the social position of the Brāhmaṇa donees and the temple authorities was exceptionally high, and they were never looked upon as the king's vassals.

It is sometimes supposed that feudalism involving the payment for services in land instead of money developed in an economy characterised by dearth of coins and absence of trade and that India also exhibited the same characteristics after the fall of the Guptas in the 6th century A. D. Nothing can be more erroneous.

Of course, early Indian rulers often granted *jā'gīrs* for the maintenance of their officers and dependants.[4] But the latter were not under the feudal type of obligations, and there

1. See Sircar, *Ind. Ep.*, pp. 135ff.
2. *Ibid.*, p. 136
3. *Ibid.*, p. 140; *Ind. Ep. Gloss.*, p. 397 (*putra-pautr-ādi-santati-kramena*, etc.).
4. Cf. Manu, VII. 118-19; Watters, *On Yuan Chwang's Travels in India*, Vol. I, p. 177; etc.

was always plenty of coins in the market. A large number of kings and other agencies belonging to the post-Gupta period issued coins, and such coins have been discovered in all parts of the country.[1] Moreover, numerous records, both literary and epigraphical, mention various coins of gold, silver and copper prevalent in those days, e. g., *Purāṇa* (also called *Kārṣāpaṇa*, *Dharaṇa*, *Dramma*, *Rūpaka* and *Cūrṇī*), *Dīnāra*, *Niṣka* or *Suvarṇa*, *Kaḻañju*, *Accu*, *Varāha*, *Māḍa*, *Gadyāṇa*, etc., etc.[2] Over and above these, there was never any real dearth of cowrie-shells which were extensively used as coined money in India in the Gupta and post-Gupta ages.[3] The *Rājataraṅgiṇī* often speaks of payment of salaries in cowrie-shells, the word used for it being *Dinnāra*.[4]

It has of course to be admitted that many of the rulers and ruling families of the early and medieval ages do not appear to have issued coins. But the reason apparently is that the kings and the traders did not feel any necessity for fresh coins owing to the plenty of old coins and also of cowrie-shells in the market.[5] There is enough evidence to show that coins circulated in the market never went out of use in early and medieval India, and cowries were there to make up the scarcity even if coins were not occasionally available in particular areas for some reason or other. In the 5th century A. D., Buddhaghoṣa mentions the *Kārṣāpaṇas* issued by Rudradāman I in the 2nd century A. D. as current coins, while the Anjaneri plates of the 8th century refer to the currency of the *Rūpakas* issued by Kalacuri Kṛṣṇarāja in the 6th century. Even during the Muslim rule, coins of all ages and countries were current in the Indian market.[6]

There is again some reason to believe that the right of minting coins was usually leased to the goldsmiths who made coins according to the demand of traders and bankers, and that it was these latter who determined whether they required more coins at a particular time. They had to pay a commission

1. See L. Gopal, *Early Medieval Coin Types of North India*, 1966; W. Elliot, *Coins of Southern India*, 1886; etc.
2. See Sircar, *Ind. Ep. Gloss.*, pp. 428ff.
3. Sircar, *Studies in Indian Coins*, pp. 279 ff.
4. Stein, *Kalhaṇa's Rājataraṅgiṇī*, Vol. II, pp. 309, 324.
5. Sircar, *Stud. Ind. Coins*, pp. 273 ff., 279ff.
6. *Ibid.*, pp. 289 ff.

for getting their bullion minted into coins. Buddhagoṣa's writings suggest that silver punch-marked coins were manufactured as late as the 5th century A. D. apparently by private agencies.[1]

A flourishing internal trade is indicated by the discovery of hoards of coins of one part of the country in another, as in the case of the Petluripalem (Guntur District, A. P.) find of Śaka coins.[2] As regards foreign trade and commerce, India's contact with the Arabs by sea and with the Chinese by both land and sea, in the post-Gupta period, is well established. The Arabs were already in the possession of Sind about the beginning of the 8th century, and we know of Arab officers in the service of the Rāṣṭrakūṭas and the Kadambas as well as of Arab settlements at Cambay and Veraval, both in the present Gujarat State.[3] The Veraval inscription[4] of Arjuna points to brisk trade between Gujarat and ports like Ormuz on the Persian Gulf. The Buddhist missionaries travelled from India to China and from China to India along the trade routes and often in merchants' vessels. A number of Indian kings sent embassies to the Chinese emperors. The relations, friendly or hostile, between the Śailendras of Malaysia and Indonesia and the Pālas and Coḷas of India[5] presuppose brisk maritime trade between India and the land beyond the Bay of Bengal as far as China. The shortness of the period between the application of the name of the Śakas to the era of 78 A. D. in India and the beginning of the use of the 'Śaka era' in Indonesia and Indochina points to the very close relation of those lands with the West Indian ports during the rule of the Cālukyas of Bādāmi.[6] Indian scholars at the courts of South-East Asian kings must have travelled from their countries in merchants' vessels.

The wealth exacted by the early Muslim invaders from

1. *Ibid.*, pp 101 ff.
2. *Ibid.*, pp. 150 ff.
3. Sircar, *Stud. Soc. Adm. Anc. Med. Ind.*, Vol. I, p. 77.
4. Cf. *Ep. Ind.*, Vol. XXXIV, pp. 143ff.
5. *The Age of Imperial Kanauj*, ed. Majumdar, p. 414; *The Struggle for Empire*, ed. Majumdar, pp. 730ff.
6. Sircar, *Stud. Soc. Adm. Anc. Med. Ind.*, Vol. I, pp. 145-46.

the defeated Indian kings and the plundered temples[1] as well as the high salaries in cash paid by Kashmir kings to their officers (one lakh *Dinnāras* paid by Jayāpīḍa daily to his court Pandit and 1½ lakhs and 80,000 by Ananta daily to two of his officers)[2] undoubtedly point to the great prosperity of the country, which must have been due, at least partially, to flourishing internal and external trade. As regards, internal trade, we may also refer to the *Rājataraṅgiṇī* indicating Kashmir's commercial relations with Malwa and the Deccan in the 11th century,[3] while India's contact (by both sea and land) with the Arab world and with China and the countries beyond the Bay of Bengal can be easily proved as already noted.

It is sometimes supposed that the king or landlord had often right over the person of the tenants who were tied to the soil in more or less the feudal sense. This view appears to be wrong. 'To give a village' is really the same as 'to give a village along with the villagers' which means that the king's rent-paying subjects in the village should henceforth pay taxes to the donee. Indeed the grant of a village without giving the donee the power of tax collection from the inhabitants was never meant by any early Indian document. As regards the occasional mention of the gift of a village together with this or that person or class of people, the reference to vintners, etc., being attached to the village, no doubt means that the revenue income from particular classes was State monopoly in some areas exactly as the income from mango and some other trees. Professionals like the priests, barbers, carpenters, washermen, etc., often enjoyed State land or common village land on the condition of offering their services regularly to the villagers, and such people could be attached to a grant without the State having any right over their person. Some of the attached persons were no doubt slaves; but agriculturist householders attached to a grant must have been enjoying state land or favours for working in the State farms or for ploughing State land on the condition of receiving a share of the crops. Such people were free from their obligations as soon as they gave up the enjoyment of the State land or favours.

1. Cf. Ray, *DHNI*, Vol. I, pp. 21, 65-68, 82, 86, 91, etc.
2. *Rājataraṅginī*, IV. 495; VII. 145-46.
3. *Ibid.*, VII. 190-93, 1119ff.

Particular merchants of different markets were often attached to a gift village by the Eastern Gaṅga kings apparently because the king was willing to augment the donee's income by transferring his revenue income from them in favour of the donee. Often people of one State migrated to and settled in another, so that tenants were never tied to the land in India as in the European feudal system.[1]

Feudalism is thus a misnomer in the early Indian context.

III

A recent writer points out that the ancient Indian cultivators were not tied to the soil like the European serfs and were in a position to settle in a different State and that this right is indicated by such medieval texts as the *Bṛhannāradīya Purāṇa* (assigned to c. 750-900 A. D.), Vidyākara's *Subhāṣitaratnakoṣa* (12th century) and the *Bāburnāma* (16th century).[2] We fully agree with this view and may quote various other texts in its favour.

But the writer then thinks that the *Upamitibhavaprapañcakathā* of Siddharṣi (906 A. D.) and a number of early medieval inscriptions indicate the existence of feudal serfdom and manorial villages in some parts of Northern India. In our opinion, this is due to misunderstanding of the evidence at our disposal. If this contention would have been correct, we would have found reference to the system in some other works 'in the entire range of Sanskrit Literature'.

According to a story in the *Upamitibhavaprapañcakathā*,[2] the entire population of a city, which was the *bhukti* of a ruler named Karmapariṇāma, was thrown by the latter into cells and kept there for a long time. Another ruler named Sadāgama liberated some of the wretched people and settled them else-

1. For the above points, see below. That the donees received only the dues previously collected by the king is clear from many documents; e. g., the Sungal plate (*ASI*, *AR*, 1902-03, pp. 251ff.) of Vidagdha (lines 21-22) speaks of *yathā-samucita-bhāgabhoga-kara-hirany-ādi-samasta-rājabhāvya-pratyāyam=asy=opadeyam*. See also below, p. 31.
2. Lallanji Gopal, 'Quasi-manorial Rights in Ancient India' in the *Journal of Economic and Social History of the Orient*, Vol. VI, Part iii, 1963, pp. 296-308.
3. XXXVIII. 87.

where, while Karmapariṇāma's sister brought some people from a different town to occupy the places vacated by those liberated citizens. Two things have to be noticed in this story. Firstly, Karmapariṇāma was an oppressive ruler and his tyranny, like that of such Kashmirian monarchs as Śaṅkaravarman and Harṣa, cannot be regarded as the normal behaviour of ancient Indian rulers. Secondly, Karmapariṇāma's sister brought some citizens for settling them in another city not by compulsion, but by persuasion and allurement. It can be easily done even today. Muḥammad bin Tughluq Shāh had apparently no proprietary right over the person of those citizens of Delhi, whom he took to his new capital at Daulatābād (Devagiri).[1]

The Nirmand plate of Samudrasena (8th century) records the grant of a village to a body of Brāhmaṇas together with its inhabitants (*prativāsi-jana*);[2] but the reference, as we have seen, is no doubt to the fact that the villagers, who so long paid taxes to the donor, would henceforth have to pay them to the donees. The grant of a village really means the transfer of the donor's revenue income, etc., from the villagers to the donees. The gift of a village without such income would be useless to the donee. 'Granting a village' and 'granting a village together with the villagers' really mean the same thing, and the latter certainly does not refer to the king's or landlord's proprietary right over the villagers' person. Because the donated land could be either with or without inhabitants, 'together with inhabitants' (i. e. the right to collect taxes, etc., from them) was mentioned specifically.

A Nanana plate of the 12th century records the grant or permanent allotment of certain persons (including songstresses, musicians and cultivators) to a deity,[3] and it has been supposed that these people were not slaves, but independent persons. There is, however, little doubt that most of them were slaves belonging to the well-known classes of Devadāsa and Devadāsī. There was (and still is at least in some parts of the country) another class of professional people, e. g., the priests, barbers, washermen, carpenters, etc., who enjoyed

1. For some of the Sulṭān's unnatural acts and the transfer of his capital, see *Camb. Hist. Ind.*, Vol. III, pp. 136 ff.

2. *Corp. Ins. Ind.*, Vol. III, pp. 286 ff.

3. *Ep. Ind.*, Vol. XXXII, pp. 244ff.

village land on the condition of rendering service to the villagers. Such people enjoying State land or common land of a village could of course be allotted to the donee, and the transfer would not indicate any right of the king or landlord over the person of the people since the families would cease to be under the obligation of rendering service whenever they gave up the enjoyment of the property. They were therefore not tied to the soil in the feudal sense, as we have already seen above.

Sometimes agriculturist householders must have enjoyed State land or favours on the condition of working in the State farms or of cultivating State land on the basis of a share of the produce. Such cultivators could be allotted to the gift land since the State had a right over their services so long as they were enjoying the State's property or favours. There is no question of the State having any right over their person if they did not sell themselves to the State and become slaves of the latter. This question has also been touched above.

In the charters of the Bhauma-Karas of Orissa, the grant of a village includes such subjects (*prakṛti*) as the weavers, milkmen, vintners, etc.[1] It has been supposed that these records point to the king's right over the persons belonging to certain occupations and crafts. But, in our opinion, the revenue income from the weavers, etc., was a State monopoly and was not enjoyed by the non-privileged rent-paying landlords. That is why the State generally transferred its right in the cases of the donees who were privileged landlords. This is exactly similar to the transfer of the right over mango and some other trees in favour of the privileged tenants and landlords, as we have also seen.[2]

The grants of the Eastern Gaṅga king Narasiṁha II generally allot to a gift village a few persons called *prajā* or subject. In one such case, we have reference to the following persons attached to the village: a conch-shell worker, a banker or merchant (*śreṣṭhin*), a goldsmith, two oilmen, a milkman and a potter belonging to this market or that.[3] It is difficult to believe that the king could have any right over the person

1. Cf. p. 215; Vol. XXIX, p. 89.
2. See, e. g., *ibid.*, Vol. XXIX, p. 8, text line 42.
3. *Ibid.*, Vol. XXVIII, pp. 190-91.

of the bankers and merchants. Apparently, the revenue income of the said persons, who were not inhabitants of the gift village, was transferred to the donee in order to augment his income; otherwise, the merchants received certain concessions from the State and, in return, allowed themselves to be attached to the gift village or settled therein.

The Assam plate[1] of Vallabharāja records the grant of seven villages to an almshouse together with the inhabitants (called *jana*) as well as with five persons (called *sahāya* or assistant) who were given along with their wives and children. If the king had equal right over the person of all the inhabitants of the villages, it would be difficult to explain the separate mention of the two classes. It appears that the assistants were slaves or that their families were enjoying State land for rendering particular services.

The expression *sa-kāru-karṣaka-vaṇig-vāstavya* occurring in the Candella grants[2] means 'together with the houses or households of the artisans, agriculturists and merchants' and refers to the transference of the king's right over the revenue income of the said classes of people in the donee's favour. Apparently, certain classes of people, such as the Brāhmaṇas, were excluded from such a special transfer.

One set of the Anjaneri plates (8th century) states that a ruler first peopled a township and a few localities and then granted them in favour of a mercantile guild (*nagara*) headed by certain *Śreṣṭhins.*[3] Likewise, an Eastern Gaṅga king of the 13th century granted to a Brāhmaṇa a township containing four palatial buildings and thirty houses inhabited by various citizens who included a number of merchants and people of different professions.[4] It is hardly possible to think that the rulers, in these cases, gave to the donees anything more than their income from the townships. The mention of the personal names of the merchants and professionals in the Gaṅga record suggests that they were recently and specially brought from other places to people the township in question.

1. *Ibid.*, Vol. V, pp. 183 ff.
2. *Ibid.*, Vol. XXXII, pp. 121 ff.
3. *Ibid.*, Vol. XXV, p. 237.
4. *Ibid.*, Vol. XXVIII, p. 244.

The above discussion is expected to cover the various inscriptions cited in the paper in question. Its author further says, "As regards the status of the men said to have been attached to the donee as a religious grant, it is clear that they were not slaves, but independent persons. They have also to be distinguished alike from serfs, if serfdom is conceived as a perpetual adherence to the soil of an estate owned by a lord. If performance of services for other persons is taken as the essence of the status of a serf, the men of our inscriptions may be described as serfs, but only in a restricted sense. The comparison is probably closed with the villeins of the European manorial system which is associated with dependence of a population on a ruler consisting not in ownership extending over persons nor in contractual agreements, but in various forms and degrees of subjection, chiefly regulated by custom." We are not inclined to agree with this view.

In our opinion, the persons in question, in most cases, enjoyed State land on the basis of a contract and were not compelled to serve the king or landlords when they were pleased to give up the possession of the property. Their obligation and status were not the same as those of the serfs or villeins.

The Indian king or landlord of the early period demanded free labour from the subjects, and the charters creating rent-free holdings specifically state that the right to unpaid labour from the tenants was transferred to the donee who was himself exempted from all obstructions or troubles no doubt including the supply of free labour to the king. But the obligation was not of the feudal type, since nobody was tied to the soil. Even in the late medieval cases, in which the kings of a particular area donated land on the condition that the donee would supply forces at the time of war, the latter seems to have been under no obligation when he relinquished the property.

Indian landlordism is sometimes confused with European feudalism. While, in the feudal system, the king as the lord of all land gave big estates to the barons on the condition of receiving service and help from the latter on particular occasions, the Indian kings, whose claim of ownership over the land under permanent tenants was never real, mostly created small estates in favour of Brāhmaṇas and religious institutions, and it was usually stated in clear terms in the charters that the donees were exempt from all obligations. Indeed, the donees of the majority of the Indian land grants were utterly unsuitable for offering military assistance to the donors who avowedly created the free-holdings only for religious merit and fame. These points have also been touched above.

IV

Workers in the field of Indian historical research generally attach considerable importance to the early accounts of foreign writers, even though they are often found to be demonstrably defective. It is well known as to how the statements of Megasthenes regarding the absence of slavery in ancient India and the freedom of the country from famines[1] influenced some students of Indian history and how they are now usually believed to be on account of insufficient study or misunderstanding of the socio-economic life of ancient India.[2]

Recently our attention has been drawn to a Chinese account of India,[3] which belongs to 732 A. D. and runs as follows :

"(1). According to the law of the Five Indies, from the King, the royal consort and the princes down to the chiefs and their wives, all build monasteries separately in accordance with their respective capacities and abilities. Each of them builds his own temple, but does not construct it jointly. They say, 'When each person has one's own meritorious virtues, what is the necessity of a joint effort ?'

"(II). Whenever a monastery is built, a village and its folk are immediately offered to support the Three Precious Ones. Merely building a monastery without making any donation of a village and its folk is not done.

"(III). This is followed as an example by foreign countries.

1. Cf. R. C. Majumdar, *The Classical Accounts of India*, pp. 224, 233.
2. See, e. g., *Camb. Hist. Ind.*, Vol. I, pp. 203, 416; A. N. Bose, *Social and Rural Economy of Northern India*, 600 *B. C.*-200 *A. D.*, Vol. I, 1942, pp. 129ff.
3. See Jan Yun-Hua, 'Hui Chao's Record on Kashmir' in *Kashmir Research Biannual*, No. 2 (1962), pp. 119-20; cf. R. S. Sharma, *Indian Feudalism* : *C.* 300-1200, p. 58-59.

"(IV) The king, the queen and the royal consorts have their respective villages and their folk.

"(V) Donation is free and the king is not asked for that. This also applies in the case of building a temple. When it is necessary to build a temple, they build it and the king is not asked. The king dare not obstruct. He is afraid lest it should infect him with sins.

"(VI) As to rich commoners, though they have no village to donate, they try their best to build temples and manage these by themselves. Whenever they obtain things, they offer them to the Three Precious Ones.

"(VII) As in the Five Indies no human being is sold, so there are no female slaves.

"(VIII) Villages and their inhabitants could be donated if wanted and necessary."

This account contains statements characterised by misunderstanding and half-truths as will be clear from the following analysis.

I. Of course the Indians were never miserly as regards expenditure for the purpose of securing religious merit and often built temples, monasteries, etc., individually when they could afford it; but the impression created is that the Indians always built religious establishments individually and were never inclined to share the merit accruing to a pious deed with any body else. This is certainly wrong since collective performance of deeds for the sake of religious merit has been an important feature of Indian religious life throughout the ages. We have many instances of Caityas and cave-dwellings for monks made by the inhabitants of an entire village, or all the members of a family or a guild or a group of people.[1]

There are innumerable similar other cases of meritorious deeds jointly performed by a group of persons.[2] It is well known that grants of land were made by early Indian kings often for the religious merit of their own as well as that of

1. Cf., e. g., Lüder's List of Inscriptions, Nos. 1037, 1045, 1048, 1107, 1121, 1127, 1140, 1153, 1169, 1180, 1185.

2. See *ibid.*, Nos. 925-926, 931, 1006, 1020, 1024, 1041, 1121, 1127, 1181, 1210, 1239, 1248, 1250-52, 1254-55, 1262, 1271, 1272, 1280, 1281, 1287, 1291-92, 1294, 1303, 1329-30.

their parents or families,[1] while Buddhist images were dedicated to temples for the merit of the donors and their parents, teachers, etc., as well as for the benefit of the whole world.[2] A Nagarjunikonda inscription says how Queen Rudradharabhaṭṭārikā, besides donating a pillar, contributed a sum of 170 *dināri-māṣakas* towards the expenses incurred for building a Stūpa by her husband's paternal aunt.[3]

II. That a village and its folk were granted in favour of a monastery as soon as it was founded by the kings, etc., is a half-truth since often rent-free plots of land were granted for the maintenance of religious establishments instead of rent-free villages[4] and permanent endowments (*akṣaya-nīvī*) were created for their maintenance by depositing a sum of money in a guild.[5]

III. That the custom of granting land for the maintenance of religious establishments was emulated by some foreign rulers is corroborated by the Nālandā plate of Devapāla recording the grant of five villages of the Patna-Gaya region for the maintenance of the monastery built at Nālandā by the Śailendra king Bālaputradeva of Indonesia and Malaysia and that of one village by the Coḷa king Rājarāja I in favour of another monastery built at Nagapattanam by another Śailendra king named Māravijayottuṅgavarman.[6] The gift villages in question were apparently purchased, at least theoretically, by the builders of the monasteries from the Pāla and Coḷa kings respectively.[7] It seems, however, that such establishments, founded by rich foreigners, were often maintained by grants of money and rent-paying landed property purchased by them for the purpose.

1. See, e. g., *Select Inscriptions*, 2nd ed., pp. 395, 467, 487, 492, etc.
2. See, e. g., *JBRS*, Vol. XXXVII, Parts 3-4, 1951 (Some Inscriptions from Bihar, p. 10); Vol. XLI, Part 2, 1955 (Jayanagar Image Inscriptions of Year 35), p. 9; etc.
3. *Ep. Ind.*, Vol. XX, p. 19 and note.
4. Cf. *Select Inscriptions*, 2nd ed., pp. 197ff., 200-01.
5. Cf. *ibid.*, pp. 164ff.
6. See *The History and Culture of the Indian People*, ed. Majumdar, Vol. IV, p. 52; Vol. V, p. 236 (cf. p. 239).
7. Cf. Sircar, *Indian Epigraphy*, pp. 114ff.,; *Ep. Ind.*, Vol. XXXIII, pp. 50 ff.

IV. This refers to the king's Khās Mahāl and the *jā'gīrs* or rent-free holdings in the possession of his dependants, officers and favourites. Creation of such holdings in favour of temples, monks, learned Brāhmaṇas, etc., are well known from the Śaka-Śātavāhana age down to recent times. There is evidence to show that the early Indian kings paid for the services of their officers and servants in several ways. The *Kauṭilīya Arthaśāstra*[1] speaks of payment of *vetana* in cash and *bhakta* in foodgrains to the various grades of officers, while the *Manusmṛiti*[2] prescribes payment of wages in foodgrains, cash and clothing in the case of menial workers and by *jā'gīr* in the case of high officers. Hiuen-tsang's *Si-yu-ki*[3] also refers to payment by means of *jā'gīrs* in the case of high officers and the *Rājataraṅgiṇī*[4] speaks of payment of wages by money or *khārīs* of crops, although Stein believes that the Kashmirian officers, etc., were usually paid in crops. There is likewise reference in the epigraphic records to the kings' Khās Mahāl[5] and the *jā'gīrs* in the possession of the king's officers and the members of the royal family.[6]

It has to be noticed that, in the rent-free holdings and *jā'gīrs*, the obligations of the inhabitants towards the king were transferred to the landlord. The lower class of tenants (such as temporary tenants) in such holdings had to offer *viṣṭi* or unpaid labour to the master. This has been somewhat misuderstood in the Chinese account as the grant of villages together with their folk.

V. The impression created by the statement that all kinds of donations and the building of temples, etc., could be undertaken by anybody without the sanction of the Government is no doubt wrong. Donation of money from one's own pocket and of rent-paying land out of one's landed property apparently did not require the king's special consent, although the trans-

1. Cf. Shama Sastry, trans., pp. 276 ff.
2. See VII. 118-119, 126.
3. Watters, *On Yuan Chwang's Travels in India*, Vol. I, p. 177.
4. Cf. Stein, *Kalhaṇa's Rājataraṅgiṇi*, Vol. II, pp. 327-28.
5. See *Select Inscriptions*, 2nd ed., p. 200, text line 4: *rājakaṁ kṣetram = asmat-svatvakam*.
6. See *JAS*, Letters, Vol. XX, p. 206, for the grant of land out of their respective *jā'gīrs* by the king's dependants.

fer of the ownership of landed property must have required the recognition of the State. But the creation of a rent-free holding out of one's *jā'gīr* was not possible without the State's permission and that is why the Vaṅgīya Sāhitya Pariṣad plate of Viśvarūpasena ratifies the grants made out of the *jā'gīrs* of the kings's mother, of his two sons and of one of his ministers.[1]

The specific mention of temple-building in the passage *devakula-puṣkariṇy-ādikaṁ kārayitvā* in the above-mentioned Vaṅgīya Sāhitya Pariṣad plate of Viśvarūpasena makes it clear that temples could be built by the privileged tenants without Government sanction, but that the ordinary tenants were not entitled to do so.[2]

VI. There is evidence to show that a rich commoner paid some money to the State for creating a rent-free holding in favour of a temple and that the Government approved of his proposal.[3]

VII. This of course reminds us of similar wrong statements of Megasthenes, to which reference has been made above.

VIII. That rent-paying villages could be granted without the king's special permission (probably on payment of fees required for the transfer of landlordship) and that rent-free holdings could be created by requisite payments made to the Government is to be admitted. But the implication that the inhabitants of the gift village served as serfs to the donees is certainly wrong. A village was normally inhabited by people of different communities including Brāhmaṇas, Mahattaras, Karaṇas, merchants, artisans, etc., its permanent tenants enoying privileges of various grades, and it is only the obligations of the villagers to the king that could be transferred to the donees of the royal grants. Priests, carpenters, barbers, fishermen and others who enjoyed village-land in lieu of service had to offer their services to the new landlord while temporary tenants had to offer to the latter their *viṣṭi* or unpaid labour according to rules. It is, however, absurd to think that high class people including Brāhmaṇas, village-elders and big merchants, served as serfs.

1. *Loc. cit.* See below, p. 53.
2. *JAS*, Letters, Vol. XX, p. 207.
3. See *Select Inscriptions*, pp. 338, 348-49, 357-58, 360-61.

Let us take up a specific case. The Khoh copper-plate grant of *Mahārāja* Śarvanātha, dated in the Gupta year 193 (512 A. D.) records a grant as follows : *Mahārāja* Śarvanātha informs the cultivators including the Brāhmaṇas as well as the aritsans at the villages of Āśramaka on the northern banks of the Tamasā : 'Be it known to you that this village is allotted by me, in four shares, permanently, together with the taxes on permanent and temporary tenants and freedom from the entry of royal agents and policemen. Two of the four shares belong to Viṣṇunandin, and the third and fourth respectively to Skandanāga's son Śaktināga and to Kumāranāga and Skandanāga. The gift village is to be enjoyed by themselves and their descendants. It is moreover agreed by them and by myself that the village is given for the repairs, by the donees and their descendants, for the increase of their religious merit, of whatever may be broken or torn in the shrine of the Bhagavat (Viṣṇu) established by them and in that of Āditya-bhaṭṭāraka as well as for the maintenance of *bali*, *caru*, *sattra*, perfumes, incense, garlands and lamps. You yourselves should render to the donees the offering of the customary dues including taxes in the shape of the grain-share and periodical offerings and tax payable in cash and shall be obedient to their commands."

It is quite clear from the language of the record, which is not dissimilar to that of numerous other documents of the kind, that the king relegated to the donee landlords what he himself expected and realised from the villagers. It is indeed impossible to think that the tenants including the Brāhmaṇas, artisans and other inhabitants, who are clearly stated to have paid taxes in kind and cash, were mere serfs. It is a significant fact that, even when land is specifically stated to have been granted along with *jana* and *dhana* (i. e., tenants and revenue income), the inhabitants were advised by the king to pay to the donee whatever dues they were previously paying to the State (*yat-kiñcid=rāja-pratyāy-ādikaṁ tad=asy=opanetavyam*).[2]

We therefore find it difficult to agree with the view that the said Chinese account of 732 A. D. 'establishes a significant link between the breakdown of slavery and emergence of serf-

1. Cf. *Corp. Ins. Ind.*, Vol. III, pp. 128-29; *Select Inscriptions*, pp. 391-92.
2. See *Ep. Ind.*, Vol. XXXV, pp. 135, 139. See also above, p. 21, note 1.

dom' and that 'obviously the inhabitants were bound to serve the donors as long as they lived under them and to serve the beneficiaries when they were transferred to the latter'.[1] Since the pattern of the donation of villages in favour of temples does not exhibit any change in the Indian royal documents from the Śaka-Śātavāhana age to recent times, there is no justification for postulating the breakdown of slavery and emergence of serfdom on the basis of the Chinese account of 732 A. D. When rent-free land and villages were granted by Indian rulers in favour of Buddhist monks dwelling in the excavated caves of Western India as early as the 2nd century A. D. and when even the pre-Gupta work called *Manusmṛti* speaks of the *jā'gīrs* enjoyed by the different grades of the king's governors,[3] it is indeed absurd to speak of the emergence of serfdom about 732 A. D. on the basis of the Chinese account of the said date.[3]

1. R. S. Sharma, *Indian Feudalism* : *C.* 300-1200, p. 59.

2. Manu (VIII. 188-89) says that the ruler of a village should enjoy whatever the villagers have to pay to the king in the shape of *anna*, *pāna*, *indhana*, etc., while the rulers of ten, twenty, hundred and thousand villages should enjoy respectively one *kula* (two *halas*, one *hala* being the area that can be cultivated by one plough in a year) of land, five *kulas* (10 *halas*) of land, one village and one township (*daśī kulan = tu bhuñjīta viṁśī pañca kulāni ca/ grāmaṁ grāma-śat-ādhyakṣaḥ sahasr-ādhipatiḥ puram*).

3. On the qustion whether ancient Indian tenants were tied to the soil, note also that Fa-hien says, "Only those who cultivate the royal land have to pay [to the State] a portion of the gain from it. If they want to go, they go; if they want to stay, they stay." Cf. Raychandhuri, *PHAI*, 1938, p.469. The ancient Indian rulers were very particular about the payment of both *bhakta* (allowances) and *vetana* (wages) to their soldiers. Cf. *Early Indian Political and Administrative Systems*, ed. Sircar, p. 57; above, p. 14 and note 2.

CHAPTER III

SOME ASPECTS OF KINGSHIP

I

On the death of the Vākāṭaka king Rudrasena II, his queen Prabhāvatiguptā, who was the daughter of the Gupta emperor Candragupta II (376-413 A. D.), ruled her husband's kingdom for at least about thirteen years, even though she is known to have had three sons. Prabhāvatī issued the Poona copper-plate inscription[1] in the 13th year of her rule as 'the mother of the *Yuvarāja*' (cf. *jananyā Yuvarājasya* on the seal) and is mentioned in the record also specifically as 'the mother of *Yuvarāja* Divākarasena' (*Yuvarāja-Divākarasena-jananī*). In her Rithpur copper-plate inscription[2] issued in the 19th regnal year of her son Pravarasena II, Prabhāvatī is represented as the mother of the *Mahārājas* Dāmodarasena and Pravarasena (II)' (*Mahārāja- Dāmodarasena- Pravarasena- jananī*). It also states that, at this time, Prabhāvatī was more than 100 years in age (*s-āgra-varṣa-śatā*). It appears that Divākarasena never ruled as *Mahārāja* and that Prabhāvatī's rule was followed by the fairly long reigns of Dāmondarasena and his younger brother and successor Pravarasena II.

The writers on Vākāṭaka history generally believe that Divākarasena was not raised to the throne as *Mahārāja* because he was a minor at the time of the death of his father Rudrasena II. This contention appears to be wrong while the suggestion that Divākara could not ascend the throne because he was less than 21 years of age is palpably untenable.[3]

R. C. Majumdar thinks that a person became 'major' in ancient India at the age of about 21 years. This view, however, goes against the opinion[4] of old writers on Indian law that 'one who has not reached his sixteenth year is called a

1. Sircar, *Select Inscriptions*, 1965, pp. 435 ff.
2. *Ibid.*, pp. 439ff.
3. See, e.g., A. S. Altekar in *N. Hist. Ind. Peop.*, Vol. VI, pp. 110ff.; R. C. Majumdar in *JRASB*, Letters, Vol. XII, 1946, pp. 1ff.; etc.
4. Medhātithi on Manu, VIII. 148; Jhā, *Manusmṛti*, Vol. IV. i, p. 176.

minor'. The *Kauṭilīya Arthaśāstra* (III.3) has : *dvādaśa-varṣā strī prāpta- vyavahārā bhavati, ṣoḍaśa- varṣaḥ pumān*; cf. also *aprāpta-vyavahāro='sau yāvat- ṣoḍaśa- vārṣikaḥ*, quoted from Dakṣa in Apte's Sanskrit-English Dictionary, s. v. *a-prāpta*. The *Śabdakalpadruma- pariśiṣṭa*, s. v. *a-prāpta- vyavahāra*, has: *bāla ā ṣoḍaśād-varṣāt paugaṇḍo='pi nigadyate/ parato vyavahārajñaḥ sva-tantraḥ pitarāv=ṛte //* quoted from Nārada in the *Vyavahāratattva*.

If Divākarasena was the eldest of the three sons of the Vākāṭaka king Rudrasena II, as he seems to have been (Divākarasena, Dāmodarasena and Pravarasena II, there being no reason to believe that two of the three names indicated a single individual), it is not unnatural to believe that he was about four or five years old when his father died.[1] Consequently, it is probable that he had already attained majority before the time when the Poona copper-plate grant was issued about 13 years after the death of his father. This would suggest that the cause of Divākarasena not being installed as *Mahārāja* even as late as the 13th year of his *Yauvarājya* was probably something other than his minority. It may have been due to his mother's love of power, or to some defect or deformity of the prince, or to some unknown political problem. While we know that Pallava Viṣṇugopavarman probably remained a *Yuvamahārāja* even during the reign of his son, *Mahārāja* Siṁhavarman,[2] the Ajanta inscription[3] speaks of a Vākāṭaka prince, only eight years old, ascending the throne of Vatsagulma apparently as *Mahārāja*. Minority of a prince, therefore, was not regarded as bar to his attainment to the status of *Mahārāja* at least among the Vākāṭakas. We have seen that Prabhāvatiguptā styled herself 'mother of the *Yuvarāja*' instead of 'mother of the *Mahārāja* who is a minor'; but, considering the cases of minor *Mahārājas* in Indian history, it is not easy to accept the usual theory about the regency of Prabhāvatiguptā during the minority of her eldest son as perfectly satisfactory.

A question difficult to answer is whether Rudrasena II had other queens older than Prabhāvatiguptā and other sons from

1. Cf. Altekar, *op. cit.*, p. 111.
2. Sircar, *Suc. Sāt.*, p. 205. There are several cases of a *Yuvarāja* issuing a charter in his own name. Cf. *Ep. Ind.*, Vol. XXXII, pp. 201ff.
3. *Select Inscriptions*, 1965, p. 451, verse 10.

them older than Divākarasena and whether the installation of Prabhāvatiguptā as the *agra-mahiṣī* of Rudrasena II and of Divākarasena as the crown-prince was due to their relationship with Candragupta II whose subordinate ally the Vākāṭaka king seems to have been. As regards the age of Prabhāvatiguptā when her husband died, it is unknown if the queen's first conception was late, or if her earlier children were all daughters, or if her earlier sons predeceased their father.

Majumdar suggests that Vindhyaśakti I, founder of the Vākāṭaka dynasty, began his career about 250 A. D. and that Pṛthivīsena II, ninth in descent from Vindhyaśakti I, ascended the throne about 505 A. D. and ended his rule about 530 A. D. or 'somewhat later, say about 540 A. D.' Thus a period of 290 years between 250 and 540 A. D. has been assigned to nine generations of the Vākāṭakas from Vindhyaśakti I to Pṛthivīsena II. This would give an average reign-period of more than 32 years per generation. The average length of a generation, however, does not appear to be more than 25 years, so that it is difficult to believe that nine generations of the Vākāṭakas ruled for much more than 225 years. Rudrasena II, son-in-law and contemporary of Candragupta II Vikramāditya (376-414 A. D.) was sixth in descent from Vindhyaśakti I who, therefore, may be assigned to the second half of the third century A. D. Thus Pṛthivīsena II may not have ended his rule very considerably after 500 A. D.

II

We have stated above—

(1) that, according to ancient Indian law, one attained to majority at the age of sixteen and not at that of twenty-one;

(2) that one could ascend the throne as king even when he was a minor; and

(3) that an average reign-period of more than thirty-two years per ruler appears to be too long.[1]

As regards the first point, it has to be noted that there is absolute unanimity amongst writers on Indian law—ancient, medieval and modern—that boys attained to majority at the age of sixteen, while there is not a single evidence in support of the conjecture about the age of majority at twenty-one. It was

1. On these points, cf. R.C. Majumdar in *JRASB*, Letters, Vol. XII, pp. 71ff.

only in 1875 that, under the Indian Majority Act (Act IX of 1875), year eighteen (twenty-one only in certain cases) was made the age of majority except in matters of marriage, dower, divorce and adoption. We refrain from quoting further authorities as the views of Kauṭilya, Medhātithi, Dakṣa and Nārada have been cited above and refer our readers to a good discussion on the topic by P. V. Kane in his *Hisory of Dharmaśāstra*, Vol. III, pp. 573-74, where the authority of Aṅgiras, Kātyāyana, Haradatta, Vijñāneśvara and others has been quoted.[1] Jayaswal's conjecture that in ancient India 'for obtaining royal *abhiṣeka*, the age of 25 was a condition precedent' not only goes against the theory of the age of majority at twenty-one, but its utterly unconvincing nature was, it may be pointed out, long ago demonstrated by a more well-informed writer who quotes the *Mahābhārata* (1. 101. 12) to show that the *rājyābhiṣeka* of the Kuru king Vicitravīrya took place when he was a mere child and had not yet reached the period of youth—*Vicitravīryañ=ca tadā bālam=aprāpta-yauvanam / Kuru-rājye mahābāhur=abhyasiñcat tad-antaram.*[2] The minor king is said to have ruled his paternal kingdom according to the instructions of his guardian Bhīṣma.[3] That Vicitravīrya was a king in spite of Bhīṣma's guardianship and not merely a *Yuvarāja* is quite clear from other passages of the *Mahābhārata.*[4] Another competent scholar points out that the *Bārahaspatyasūtra*, the only authority referred to by Jayaswal, 'says not a word about the age of coronation.'[5] The epigraphic passage *siri-Khāravelena paṁdarasa-vasāni... kiḍitā kumāra-kiḍikā... tato nava-vasāni yovarajaṁ pasāsitam* (i. e. Khāravela passed the first fifteen years of his life

1. There is another discussion on the subject in Mayne's *Hindu Law and Usage* (1938 ed.), Ch. VI, where it has been shown that 'minority under Hindu law terminates at the age of sixteen' on the authority of the *Dāyabhāga*, Vol. III. 1, p. 17, note; *Dattakamīmāṁsā*, Vol. IV, p. 47; Colebrooke's *Digest*, Vol. I, p. 202; Nārada, 1. 35-36; Kullūka's gloss on Manu, VIII. 227; *Vyavasthādarpaṇa*, Vol. I, p. 591; *Vyavasthācandrikā*, Vol. II, p. 590; cf. *SBE*, Vol. XXXIII, p. 51, and Kullūka on Manu, VIII. 148.
2. Raychaudhuri, *PHAI*, 4th ed., p. 249.
3. *Op. cit.* verse 13: *Vicitravīryaḥ sa tadā Bhīsmasya vacane sthitaḥ/anvaśāsan=mahārāja paitra-paitāmahaṁ padam //*
4. Cf. I. 102. 53: *prayayau Hastināpuraṁ yatra rājā sa kauravaḥ/ Vicitravīryo dharmātmā praśāsti vasudhām=imām //*
5. Kane, *op. cit.*, p. 80.

in playing juvenile games whereafter he was installed as crown-prince and held that position for the following nine years) apparently suggests that Khāravela was made *Yuvarāja* as soon as he attained to majority at the age of sixteen before which he had been a *kumāra* or minor. Of course, there was a controversy as to whether one became major by just stepping in the sixteenth year or after completing that year of one's age. But that is not quite material in our enquiry, because the age of majority had really nothing to do with one's accession to the throne. The statement of the Hathigumpha inscription that Khāravela received installation as *Mahārāja* after completing his twenty-fourth year only shows that his predecessor (probably his father) died about that time. As regards the intervening period between the death of a king and the formal coronation of his successor, the *Viṣṇudharmottara* (II. 18.2-4), an old work repeatedly quoted by Al Bīrūnī in the first half of the eleventh century and used by Brahmagupta in 628 A. D.,[1] says that there was no waiting for an auspicious time, while the *Rājanītiprakāśa* (included in the *Vīramitrodaya* written by Mitramiśra in the first half of the seventeenth century) notes that on the death of a king his successor should be ceremonially crowned one year thereafter, but that when a king abdicates, his successor may be formally crowned on any auspicious day without waiting for a year.[2] There is absolutely no authority in support of Jayaswal's conjecture about princes waiting for their *rājy-ābhiṣeka* till they reached the twenty-fifth year of their age.

In regard to the second point, we referred to the cases of minor kings in ancient Indian history, especially to the Vākāṭaka king of Vatsagulma who obtained *rājya* and ruled when he was only eight years old, according to the Ajanta inscription.[3] Now the point is not whether the minor king (not to be confused with the *Yuvarāja* or crown-prince) actually ruled or a regent or regency council ruled in his name. The real point at issue is whether, in ancient India, a dead monarch could be succeeded as king on the throne by his minor heir-apparent or the kingdom remained without a king, the heir-apparent enjoying merely the status of the *Yuvarāja*. In our

1. Jolly, *Hindu Law and Custom*, p. 65.
2. Cf. Kane. *op. cit.*, pp. 79-80.
3. *Sel. Ins.*, Vol. I, p. 428: *avāpya rājyam=aṣṭābdako yaḥ praśaśāsa samyak.*

opinion, the second alternative is not only unsupported by any evidence worth the name, but goes actually against known facts of history. That Vicitravīrya had been installed in *rājya* and was a *rājā* before he attained majority and that a Vākāṭaka king aged eight years obtained *rājya* and duly ruled show that these were kings and not crown-princes or heirs-apparent, even if the word *rājya* is taken in the sense of 'kingdom' and not in that of 'sovereignty'. Reference may also be made to the Ikṣvāku prince Sudarśana who ascended the *siṁhāsana* of his forefathers as *Mahārāja* at the age of six only.[1] Of numerous other instances, a few may be quoted in support of the suggestion. Gopālavarman became *rājan* of Kashmir when he was *anatikrānta-bālya*.[2] Pārtha became a *bhūpati* when he was a *bāla* and his father Paṅgu ruled Kashmir in the name of the minor king.[3] Cakravarman was installed in *rājya* when he was a *śiśu* and had not passed his *bālya*;[4] but he was soon deposed and Śūravarman was made *nṛpa* instead.[5] Another *śiśu* named Śūravarman was installed as *rājan* on the *nṛpāsana* of Kashmir;[6] when a general revolted against the authority of the *śiśu-bhūpati* and entered the *rājadhānī* at the head of his victorious army, the child king's soldiers fled away and the king was carried to a hiding place by his mother.[7] The above instances are quoted only from Book V of the *Rāja-taraṅgiṇī*. Of the instances of minor kings in the annals of Rajasthan, we refer only to Mokaljī who became king, according to Rajput chronicles, at the age of five.[8] Of the many other instances of minor kings in ancient Indian history, the most celebrated appear to be the cases of Rāṣṭrakūṭa Amoghavarṣa I and Pallava Nandivarman II Pallavamalla. Verse 26 of the Sanjan plates seems to suggest that Amoghavarṣa was born about 802 A. D.[9] while he is known to have ascended

1. Cf. *Raghuvaṁśa*, XVIII. 39-44.
2. *Rājatar.*, V. 229, 235, 237.
3. *Ibid.*, 264, 280.
4. *Ibid.*, 288, 290-91.
5. *Ibid.*, 292.
6. *Ibid.*, 446, 449.
7. *Ibid.*, 455.
8. Tod, *An. Ant. Raj.*, Calcutta ed., Vol. 1, p. 296; Ojha, *Udaypur Rājyakā Itihās*, p. 583.
9. His birth was formerly assigned to 808 A.D. Cf. Altekar, *The Rāṣṭrakūṭas and their Times*, p. 68.

the *simhāsana* after his father's death (cf. Sanjan pletes, verses 35-36) about 814 A. D. More explicit and uncontrovertible is the case of Nandivarman who became sovereign ruler of the Pallavas at the age of twelve only. According to one of the Vaikunthaperumal temple epigraphs,[1] the Pallava throne of Kāñcī fell vacant after the death of king Parameśvaravarman II, and the officials and citizens of the kingdom approached a Pallava chief named Hiraṇyavarman for the selection of a sovereign for the Pallava throne. Thereupon Hiraṇyavarman held consultations with the chief potentates as well as his own sons. Ultimately Pallavamalla, twelve year old son of Hiraṇyavarman, was selected by common consent and was 'crowned king under the name Nandivarman and with the insignia of *viḍelviḍugu, samudraghoṣa, khaṭvāṅga-dhvaja* and *vṛṣabha-lāñchana* (which are the well-known marks of Pallava sovereignty)' by the ministers, feudatories and others. It is also known that Vijayāditya V, minor son (*kaṇṭhikā-kram-āyāta-paṭṭ-ābhiṣekaṁ bālam*) of Amma I of the Eastern Cālukya dynasty, reigned for fifteen days as king about 925 A. D. when he was ousted by Tālapa.[2] That, in ancient India, princes were often crowned even when they were in the mother's womb seems to be suggested by Minhāj-uddīn's description of the coronation of Rāī Lakhmaniā or king Lakṣaṇasena of Bengal.[3] The above instances will show that, in ancient India, boys often ascended the throne as king even when they were far below the age of majority[4] which was, again, the sixteenth and not the twenty-first or twenty-fifth year of one's age.

As regards the third point, the usually respected view is that 'in India the duration of a generation amounts, as the statistical tables of the Life Insurance Companies show, at the outside to only 26 years'.[5] It should also be remembered in this connection that members of the royal families usually married earlier than the common people. Now the above

1. *SII*, Vol. IV, pp. 10ff.; *Ep. Ind.*, Vol. XVIII, p. 117.
2. See *Ep. Ind.*, Vol. XXIV, p. 275 (text line 15); *SII*, Vol. I, p. 45 (text line 14); p. 54 (text line 40-41).
3. *Tab. Nas.*, pp. 554ff.
4. Manu (VII, 8 : *bālo = pi n = āvamantavyo manuṣya iti bhūmipah*) refers to *bāla* (minor) kings. Cf. also the well-known adage *lālayet pañca-varṣāṇi daśa-varṣāṇi tāḍayet| prāpte tu ṣodaśe varṣe putre mitravad = ācaret||*
4. *Ind. Ant.*, Vol. XXIII, p. 417.

statement has never been challenged with reference to any definitely known genealogy and chronology of any Indian ruling family representing many generations and belonging to historical times. The observation that six generations of Gupta kings from Candragupta I to Budhagupta and Narasiṁhagupta 'ruled more, perhaps considerably more than 180 years, giving an average of more than 30 years' is an unconvincing conclusion in view of the indefinite character of the premises, viz. (1) that the accession of Candragupta I is placed by 'many scholars' before 320 A. D., (2) that Budhagupta died 'about' 500 A. D. and (3) that Budhagupta was 'probably' succeeded by Narasiṁhagupta. There is certainly a differencc between theories of earlier writers and definitely established facts of history. As a matter of fact, there is no definite and stisfactory evidence to show that Candragupta I became king before 320 A. D., that Budhagupta lived after 495 A.D. and that Narasiṁhagupta was a successor and not a predecessor of Budhagupta. Although therefore the duration of the rule of six generations of Gupta kings may be supposed to have been more than 180 years by many writers, the real duration is unknown. This theory, not based on definite evidence, can hardly be upheld as an argument strong enough to nullify the conclusion, based on statistical tables of the Insurance Companies, that the average duration of a generation in India is less than twenty-six years.

We suggested the possibility of Rudrasena II having had other queens older than Prabhāvatiguptā and other sons from them older than Divākarasena and also of Prabhāvatiguptā's installation as Rudrasena's *agra-mahiṣī* and Divākarasena's position as *Yuvarāja* having been due to their relationship with Candragupta II whose subordinate ally Rudrasena II seems to have been. It appears that there is some support in favour of the suggestion in the Ceylonese chronicles and in certain Indian documents. In Ceylon, as also probably in India, the *mahiṣī* was the chief consort of the king in contrast to the large number of the king's wives or concubines, collectively styled *avarodha* or *antaḥpura*, and only the sons of the *mahiṣī* had the right to succession. When there were several *mahiṣīs*, one (in rare cases, possibly two) of them was raised to the dignity of *agra-mahiṣī*.[1] That Kāśyapa I was an elder step-

1. Cf. Geiger, *Cūlavaṁsa*, trans., Vol. I, p. xv.

brother of Maudgalyāyana I, who, however, was the legal heir to the throne (as he was the son of the chief queen of Dhātusena), was the cause of the former's rebellion against king Dhātusena, father of both Kāśyapa and Maudgalyāyana.[1] That Amma II of the Eastern Cālukya dynasty succeeded his father, while his elder step-brother Dānārṇava (who later succeeded Amma II) served under him faithfully seems really to be due to the position of the former's mother. Ancient Indian writers on law usually speak of succession passing to the eldest son of the king; but the part played in this matter by the position of the successor's mother does not appear to be quite clear.[2] We know that Candragupta I selected, as his successor, Samudragupta who was apparently one of his younger sons, and that Govinda III was installed as *Yuvarāja* and successor by Rāṣṭrakūṭa Dhruva in supersession of his elder son Stambha. But these selections are said to have been due to the superior qualities of the princes in question.

III

H. C. Raychaudhuri wrote an interesting note on Jahāngīr's 'Chain of Justice'.[3] During the early years of this Mughul king's reign, he gave orders to fasten one end of a gold chain, 30 gaz in length and 4 maunds in weight and containing 60 bells, to battlements of the Shāh Burj of the Agra fort and the

1. Mendis, *Early History of Ceylon*, p. 49.

2. Cf. Kane, *op. cit.*, p. 41ff.

3. *Ind. Cult.*, Vol. VII, pp. 1-2; *Studies in Indian Antiquities*, 2nd ed., pp. 249 ff. The *Tuzuk-i-Jahāngīrī* (trans. Rogers and Beveridge, Vol. I, p. 7) says, "After my accession, the first order that I gave was for the fastening up of the Chain of Justice, so that if those engaged in the administration of justice should delay or practise hypocrisy in the matter of those seeking justice, the oppressed might come to this chain and shake it so that its noise might attract attention. Its fashion was this: I ordered them to make a chain of pure gold, 30 gaz in length and containing 60 bells. Its weight was four Indian maunds, equal to 42 Iraqi maunds. One end of it they made fast to the battlements of the Shāh Burj of the fort at Agra and the other to a stone-post fixed on the bank of the river (i. e. the Yamunā)." Du Javnic says that the conception of the Chain of Justice was borrowed by Jahāngīr, from Persia (Rogers and Beveridge, *op. cit.*, p. 7, note) while Elphinstone regards it to be an 'invention' (*The History of India*, p. 539).

other end to a stone post near the Yamunā. If the persons responsible for the administration of justice should delay or practise hypocrisy, the oppressed might go to shake the chain, so that its noise would attract the emperor's attention.

Ibn Batūta speaks of an analogous device adopted by Iltumish who is said to have ordered that any man who suffered from injustice should wear a coloured dress in place of the white clothes in general use. But he was not satisfied with this plan. "So he placed at the door of his palace two marble lions upon two pedestals which were there. These lions had an iron chain round their necks from which hung a great bell. The victim of injustice came at night and rang the bell, and when the Sulṭān heard it, he immediately inquired into the case and gave satisfaction to the complainant."[1]

It is very interesting to note in this connection that an Indo-Chinese contemporary of Jahāngīr, who reigned in the period between 1605 and 1627 A. D., adopted the same practice. This is Anaukpetlun who ruled from 1605 to 1628 A. D. and belonged to the famous Toungoo royal dynasty of Burma. It is known that, in 1622 A. D., Anaukpetlun 'set up at his palace [at Pegu] a great bell with an inscription in Burmese and Talaing which says that it was placed under a double roof where the sound could reach his ears and all who had a grievance could strike it and claim his attention'.[2] It may be noticed that both Jahāngīr and Anaukpetlun ascended the throne in 1605, but the latter hung up the Bell of Justice about 17 years later than the former.

There was always brisk communication between India and Burma. The Buddhist monks of Burma often visited the Bodhgayā temple on behalf of the Burmese kings. Anaukpetlun's celebrated predecessor, the great Bayinnaung (1551-81 A. D.), is reported to have sent to Bengal several missions, one of which, according to the Burmese chronicles, met a little before 1579 A. D. Emperor Akbar (father of Jahāngīr) in his palace at Fatehpur Sikri. It is therefore not improbable that the Burmese king Anaukpetlun got the idea of the Bell of Justice from the example set by his Mughul contemporary.

1. Elliot and Dowson, *History of India as told by its own Historians*, Vol. III, p 591.

2. G. E. Harvey, *History of Burma*, 1925, p. 191.

It must, however, be admitted that the idea reached Indo-China from India or Ceylon much earlier than the 17th century. Rāmarāja or king Ram Khamhaeng (end of the 13th century and beginning of the 14th) of the Sukhothai (Sukhodaya) dynasty of Siam is also known to have hung up a Bell of Justice with the same purpose.[1]

When Thirithudamma, i.e. Śrīsudharman (1622-38 A.D.), king of Arakan, raided Moulmein and Pegu, he took away Anaukpetlun's Bell of Justice and set it up at a pagoda near Mrohaung, his capital. During the First Burmese War in 1824-26 A. D., a Hindu officer of irregular horse is said to have taken it to Aligarh, U. P.[2]

But the Bell of Justice often appears in Pāli and Sanskrit in reference to much earlier periods.

The *Mahāvaṁsa*, the Pāli chronicle of Ceylon composed about the close of the 5th or the beginning of the 6th century A. D., narrates an interesting legend about an ancient king named Eḷāra.[3] This pious king had a bell fixed to his bed, rope of the bell hanging in the open so that anybody suffering some wrong could ring it. The first to pull the rope was a cow whose calf had been run over by the chariot of the king's only son. King Eḷāra had then his son crushed under the wheels of the same chariot. The king's aid was next sought by a bird whose young one had been killed by a serpent. That serpent was now killed by the king. The third time the bell rang when an old woman pulled the rope. Her complaint was that she had laid some rice out to dry and an unseasonal shower spoilt it. The king considered it to be due to a sin which he had himself recently committed. He therefore performed penance by fasting, and Śakra thereupon ordered the rain-god Parjanya to rain only once a week at a certain hour of the night.

A similar tale has been traced in the *Pañcatantra*,[4] while E. Hultzsch noticed a Tamil version of the story and cited other parallels noted by Th. Zachariae.[5]

1. *Journ. Siam Soc.*, Vol. VI. i, p. 26.
2. *JASB*, 1838; Harvey *op. cit.*, pp. 145, 174.
3. XXI. 15ff.; cf. Winternitz. *Hist. Ind.Lit.*, Vol. II, p. 215 and note 1.
4. Benfey, *Pantschatantra*, Vol. I, pp. 168f.
5. *JRAS*, 1913, p. 529; cf. Grimm, *Deutsche Sagen*, Vol. II, No. 453—"when the emperor Chalemagne...lived at Zuerich, he had a pillar erected with a bell attached to it, so that any one who desired administration of justice

According to Kalhaṇa's *Rājataraṅgiṇī*,[1] the chronicle of ancient Kashmir composed about 1150 A. D., king Harṣa (1089-1101 A. D.) hung up great bells in all four directions, at the *siṁha-dvāra* (palace gate) 'to be informed, by their sound, of those who had come with the desire of making representations'. The Jain chronicler Merutuṅga (14th century) narrates, in his *Prabandhacintāmaṇi*,[2] a similar tale about king Govardhana of the country of Cauḍa (i. e. Coḍa or Coḷa). This king had, in front of his council-house, a gong of justice fastened to an iron pillar, which sounded when struck by a person demanding justice. Once the king's only son while driving his chariot on the road, accidentally killed a calf. The mother of the calf, the cow, with a desire to avenge the outrage done to her, struck the gong of justice by the point of her horn and made it sound. The king heard the sound of the gong and thoroughly enquired into the case of the cow. In order to do justice, he himself sat in a chariot next morning, placed his beloved son on the road and drove the chariot over him in the presence of the cow. But, owing to the virtue of the king and the good fortune of his son, the wheel of the chariot was held up and the prince was not killed.

Indeed the story as given in the *Prabandhacintāmaṇi* is the same as that found in the *Mahāvaṁsa*, with but a little difference. Of course such devices could hardly be effective.

IV

P. L. Gupta edited in the *Epigraphia Indica*, Vol. XXXIV, pp. 123 ff., the Nesarikā grant issued by the Rāṣṭrakūṭa king Govinda III in Śaka 727 (805 A. D.). The inscription was previously published by G. H. Khare in his *Sources of the Medieval History of the Dekkan* (Marāṭhī), Vol. I, pp. 15-26, and was commented on by R. C. Majumdar and G. S. Gai in the *Journal of the Asiatic Society*, Letters, Vol. XXII, pp. 133-34 and Vol. XXIV, No. 1. Khare's transcript at pp. 18-23 of his work contains some lacunae; but he suggested the readings for these gaps in an appendix at pp. 83-84. Majumdar was interested in the reference in the record to king Dharma of Vaṅgāla and

could pull it whenever the emperor was seated at his midday meal." There is a similar legend about the sage Theodosius (*Gesta Romanorum,* 105). In both these cases, it is a serpent which demands, and gets justice against a toad.

1. VII. 879.
2. Tawney's trans., p. 179.

suggested the reading of the letters in the gaps of the stanza in question. He did not notice that some of his readings had been suggested by Khare himself in the appendix referred to above. This fact was pointed out by Gai.

The importance of the inscription lies in verses 21-24 which mention the *cihnas* snatched away by king Govinda III from thirteen different rulers apparently defeated by him. Gupta has taken them to be the insignia of the particular families, to which the kings in question belonged, as found on the seals attached to their copper-plate grants. But, in regard to two of the thirteen rulers, he offers a different suggestion and thinks that Govinda III took away an image each from the kings of Siṁhala and Vaṅgāla. Majumdar is right when he says, "Most probably the reference is to royal banners with these emblems, which were surrendered by their owners and carried by Govinda III as trophies of victory or tokens of suzerainty." He concludes, "The fact... that the kings were forced to surrender what was obviously their *lāñchanas* or royal insignia seems to imply that Govinda III claimed suzerainty over them." But, as regards king Dharma of Vaṅgāla, Majumdar says, "It is of great importance to note... that what was taken from Dharmapāla was not the *lāñchana* or royal emblem, but the image of a goddess. This seems to put him in a different category." He then comes to the following conclusion: "The present .... of an image of Bhagavatī Tārā... presumably a Buddhist deity, to Govinda III, a staunch follower of Purāṇic religion, is also of great interest. But as we know, Amoghavarṣa, son of Govinda III, had great leanings towards Jainism. Govinda III might have been attracted to Buddhism by his contact with the Buddhist Pāla ruler, Dharmapāla."

Unfortunately the suggestion of Majumdar and Gupta that Govinda III took away the royal insignia from most of the defeated kings but an image from a few of them is not supported by the language of the inscription which very clearly refers to the objects taken away from all the thirteen rulers as their *cihnas* or insignia (verse 24). This has been pointed out by Gai. The error of both Majumdar and Gupta lies in that they have no clear idea about the royal insignia of ancient Indian rulers and fail to distinguish between the crest represented on the seals of the kings and the emblem appearing on their banners.[1] Majumdar's conclusions based on the said faulty premise are of course equally unwarranted.

The emblem on the seal of a family of rulers represented its crest or coat of arms, often called the *lāñchana*. In some cases, the same emblem is also found on the coins issued by the kings in question, both seals and coins being called *mudrā*. But, although in many cases the same emblem is found on the seal and the banner of a royal family, often the banner of rulers of a particular dynasty, generally called *dhvaja*, bore a different emblem. Thus the *Raṭṭas* of Saundatti and Belgaum had the *Sindhura-lāñchana* or elephant crest, but the *Suvarṇa-Garuḍa-dhvaja* (i. e., the banner of the golden or gold-coloured Garuḍa), while the Kadambas of Banavasi and Goa, who had the *Siṁha-lāñchana* or lion crest, had besides the *Śākhācarendra-dhvaja* or *Vānara-mahādhvaja*, i. e. the monkey (i. e. Hanumat) banner.[2] The seal attached to the copper-plate grants of the Nanda or Nandodbhava family of Orissa has the representation of a bull along with those of the sun and the moon and a conch-shell; but the kings of the family are described in their charters as having the *Sitadhātumaya- godhā- śikharīkṛta-lohita- locan- āmbara-dhvaja* probably meaning a piece of cloth bearing the representation of a silver alligator above that of a snake or of two eyes in red colour.[3] Although, in the case of the Nanda or Nandodbhava kings, some emblems seem to have been painted on a piece of cloth, it is difficult to determine whether the Garuḍa emblem of the Raṭṭas and the Hanumat emblem of the Kadambas were painted on cloth or were really images fixed to the top of poles for the convenience of carrying them. That the *dhvaja* was sometimes an image fixed to a pole seems to be indicated by the statement of Curtius that an image of Heracles (i. e. Vāsudeva-Kṛṣṇa) was being carried in front of the infantry of Porus (i. e. the Paurava king) as it advanced against the Greeks led by Alexander the Great.[4] In this connection, it is interesting to

1. Even today the emblems on the seal and the flag of the Government of India are not the same, the former being the lion-capital of an Aśokan pillar and the latter a Carkhā wheel.

2. *CII*, Vol. III, p. 151, note 4.

3. Cf. *Ep. Ind.*, Vol. XXVII, pp. 326-27.

4. J. W. Mc'Crindle, *The Invasion of India by Alexander the Great*, p. 208.

note that some coins of the Imperial Guptas, who had the Garuḍa emblem on their *dhvaja* and seal and on several types of their coins, bear the representation of a standard surmounted by the figure of Garuḍa.[1] The epic and Purāṇic literature suggests that the image of the individual emblems of particular archers were fixed at the top of their chariots. In an excellent survey of this evidence, Hopkins has shown that *dhvaja* is sometimes used as a synonym of *ketu*, but that sometimes the former means the whole arrangement including the staff and image or banner while the latter means only the symbol or banner. *Ketu* is also sometimes synonymous with *patākā* or flag, while *dhvaja* is the metallic top-piece of the staff, or that together with the staff. It has also been shown that the staff bore flags beneath the emblem.[2]

Another interesting fact is that sometimes a royal family had its *dhvaja* and *ketu* clearly distinguished or had more than one emblem for its *dhvaja*. Thus the Imperial Rāṣṭrakūṭas claimed to have had the *Pāli-dhvaja* and the *Oka- ketu* besides the *Garuḍa-lāñchana*.[3] The bull-banner of the Pallava kings is referred to in Tamil literature, although in their inscriptions the Pallavas are sometimes stated to have had the *Khaṭvāṅga-dhvaja*, *Khaṭvāṅga* being 'a club with a skull at the top'.[4] Hopkins has shown that such was sometimes also the case with the individual emblems of particular charioteers according to epic and Purāṇic evidence. Thus Bhīṣma had sometimes the *tāla-dhvaja* (banner of the palmyra tree) and sometimes the ensign of five yellow stars and a blue silk flag. Similarly Droṇa had sometimes a *kamaṇḍalu* (pot) and sometimes a *vedi* of gold for his ensign.[5]

Verses 21-24 of the Nesarikā grant read as follows :

Pāṇḍya- deś- ādhipān=matsyaṁ varāhaṁ Pallaveśvarāt |

1. See Allan, *A Catalogue of Indian Coins* (Gupta), pp. 1 ff., Plate I, Nos. 1ff.; cf. *CII*, Vol. III, p. 255.

2. See 'The Social and Military Position of the Ruling Caste in Ancient India' in *Journ. Am. Or. Soc.*, Vol. XIII, pp. 243 ff.

3. *Bomb. Gaz.*, Vol.I, Part ii, pp. 387, 402.

4. See *The Successors of the Sātavāhanas*, p. 188, note 2; *Bomb. Gaz.*, *op. cit.*, p. 319, note; T.V. Mahalingam, *South Indian Polity*, pp. 85-86. The Guttas of Guttal had both the *vaṭavṛkṣa-dhvaja* and *Garuḍa-dhvaja* (*Bomb. Gaz.*, *op. cit.*, p. 578).

5. Hopkins, *op. cit.*, p. 245.

Colād=vyāghraṁ gajaṁ Gaṅgāc=cāpa-yaṣṭiṁ ca Keralāt ||
Andhra-Cālukya- Mauryebhyo varāhaṁ Gurjareśvarāt |
phalakaṁ prātipad- dhāryaṁ vṛṣabhaṁ Pallaveśvarāt ||
Kosal- Āvanti-nāthābhyāṁ Siṁhalād=api nāmakakam ||
Tārāṁ bhagavatīṁ khyātāṁ Dharmād=Vaṅgāla-bhūmipāt ||
Ittham=etāny=ath=ānyāni cihnāny=ādāya bhūbhujām |
Garuḍ-āṁko Jagattuṁgo vyādhatta sakalaṁ jagat ||

The passage *vṛṣabhaṁ Pallaveśvarāt* may have been repeated unnecessarily, although it is possible that the defeat of two different Pallava rulers or of the same king on two different occasions is referred to. It may be noted that the Pallava king is mentioned twice elsewhere in verses 7 and 8 of the inscription.

It is stated in these stanzas that Govinda III carried away the following *cihnas* or insignia of his enemies : (1) the fish from the Pāṇḍya king; (2) the bull from the Pallava ruler; (3) the tiger from the Cola king; (4) the elephant from the [Western] Gaṅga ruler; (5) the bow from the Kerala king; (6-8) the boar from the Andhra (Eastern Cālukya), Cālukya and Maurya rulers; (9) a *phalaka* or board, bearing [the figures of] the *prātipad* or kettle-drum and the *hārya* or snake, from the Gurjara king; (10) the bull from the Pallava ruler; (11-13) the *nāmaka* (i. e. the names of the individual rulers) from the Kosala, Avanti and Siṁhala kings and (14) the celebrated goddess Tārā from Dharma, the king of Vaṅgāla.

There are several interesting features of this list. In the first place, the banners of the kings of Kosala, Avanti and Siṁhala appear to have borne the names of the rulers in question. Secondly, the fish and the tiger are found on the seals respectively of the Pāṇḍyas and the Colas, though they appear along with other symbols, and it is uncertain whether the *dhvajas* of the Pāṇḍyas and Colas represented only the fish or tiger with the exclusion of the associate symbols on the seal. Thirdly, although the seal of the Pālas of Bengal and Bihar bore the representation of the Dharma-cakra and has been mentioned in their records as the *Dharmacakra-mudrā*, we find from the Nesarikā grant that the *dhvaja* of king Dharma, i. e. Dharmapāla, bore the figure of the goddess Tārā. Of course, as indicated above, it is difficult to say whether the figure of the goddess was fixed to the top of a pole or was painted on the flag cloth. But the idea that not the ensign but merely an image was carried away by Govinda III from Dharmapāla is unwarranted. Lastly, verse 4 of the Sagartal (Gwalior) inscription of Bhoja represents the Pratīhāra family as *Pratīhāra-ketana-bhṛt* (i.e. having the banner bearing the figure of the Pratīhāra, probably meaning Lakṣmaṇa who once acted as the door-keeper of Rāma), and, if it is believed that the same emblem was referred to in our record, we have to correct the passage in question as *phalakaṁ pratīhār-āṅkam*. Since, however, such an emendation would look rather arbitrary and since a royal family could have more than one emblem for their banners, it is difficult to be sure on this point. The claim of the Rāṣṭrakūṭa king to have defeated the kings mentioned and carried away their respective banners may be exaggerated; but his court poet, who composed the above verses of the *praśasti*, seems to have possessed accurate knowldge as regards the *dhvajas* of the different contemporary rulers.

The importance of the mention of Dharmapāla as the king of the Vaṅgāla country or of the Vaṅgāla people has been rightly stressed by Majumdar. The reference, as he points out, certainly indicates that the home territory of the Pālas lay in Vaṅgāla. Dharmapāla's dominions comprised a number of territories lying in the present Bengal, Bihar and Uttar Pradesh. It was rather difficult to designate his empire by a single territorial name. We know that he is sometimes called *Vaṅga-pati*, 'the lord of Vaṅga', as in the Sagartal inscription[1] of Bhoja, and sometimes 'the king of Gauḍa' as in the Sanjan plates[2] of Amoghavarṣa I, because Vaṅga and Gauḍa forming parts of his empire were both well-known geographical names and the latter name was sometimes actually used to indicate wide areas of Eastern India since the 7th century when Daṇḍin, in his *Kāvyādarśa*, named the East Indian style of Sanskrit composition after Gauḍa. This was no doubt the result of the expansion of the Gauḍa kingdom under rulers like Śaśāṅka (first quarter of the 7th century) whose dominions included parts of Bengal, Bihar and Orissa and for sometime also of U.P.[3]

1. *Ibid.*, Vol. XVIII, p. 108, verse 10.
2. *Ibid.*, p. 214, verse 14.
3. Cf. *IHQ*, Vol. XXVIII, pp. 129ff.

Gauḍa was thus a more appropriate name for the Pāla empire and not only are the Pāla kings called 'the lord of Gauḍa' very often in the records of their contemporaries, but there is reason to believe that they themselves preferred the designation.[1] It is interesting to note that the tradition about 'the five Gauḍas', referred to in an inscription of 926 A. D. and in Kalhaṇa's *Rājataraṅgiṇī* (c. 1150 A. D.), developed in the early medieval period.[2] The extensive conquests of kings like Śaśāṅka and Dharmapāla appear to have contributed to its development.

The representation of Dharmapāla in the present record as the king of Vaṅgāla, which was a small tract of land in his vast empire, has to be regarded as a sort of sneer at the Pāla monarch who was one of the mightiest Indian rulers of his age. The personal name of the enemy king has been mentioned only in this case apparently because Vaṅgāla as a geographical name was more or less unknown at the time while the name of Dharmapāla was famous. Its mention in the record incidentally shows that Vaṅga and Gauḍa were later annexations to the Pāla dominions.

There is another interesting aspect of this question. Vaṅgāla became famous in the political geography of India with the rise of the Candras in the 10th century. These Candras originally ruled over Candra-dvīpa, i.e. Bāklā Candra-dvīp in the Buckergunge District of South Bengal. In the 10th century, they conquered Vaṅga, a name then often applied particularly to the territory around the Vikramapura region covering the Munshiganj Sub-Division of the Dacca District and the Madaripur region of the Faridpur District, although, in a general sense, the name was applied to the whole of South-Eastern Bengal. About the 11th century, the Candra king Govindachandra is called the lord of Vaṅgāla-deśa which was apparently the original name of Candra-dvīpa or the land around it. This is suggested by the fact that Abul Fazal's *'Ain-i-Akbarī* explains the derivation of the name Bangāl (Vaṅgāla) from Bang (Vaṅga) as follows: "Its former rulers raised mounds measuring ten yards in height and twenty in breadth throughout the province, which were called *āl*." Although the suggested derivation may be

1. Cf., e. g., verse 13 of the Badal pillar inscription (*Gauḍalekhamālā*, p. 74).

2. Cf. *Ep. Ind.*, Vol. XXXII, p. 46; *Rājataraṅgiṇī*, IV. 468.

wrong and *Vaṅgāla* may have sprung from *Vaṅga* + Prakrit *āla* in the sense of 'a notable region in Vaṅga', the mention of the earthen mounds, no doubt meant for keeping off the encroachment of sea-water from the corn-fields, certainly refers to a condition prevailing in the southernmost areas of Bengal, including the Buckergunge region, even today.[1] With the Candra (i. e. Vaṅgāla) conquest of Vaṅga, the name Vaṅgāla became applied to Vaṅga (i. e. the expanded Candra kingdom), although the name originally indicated merely a southern district of Vaṅga. That is why the Muslim authors sometimes referred to East and West Bengal together as Gaur-Bangāl (Gauḍa-Vaṅgāla). The solitary mention of Vaṅgāla in the pre-Candra inscription of Govinda III shows, however, that the name Vaṅgāla was not entirely unknown in earlier times since the Early Pālas appear to have been sometimes regarded by their contemporaries as primarily the rulers of that tract. But it is interesting to note that the Pāla conquest of Vaṅga and Gauḍa did not popularise the name Vaṅgāla in the sense of the whole of Bengal. This is probably because the Pāla kings became well known as 'the lord of Gauḍa', a designation which was obviously more suitable to them and which they apparently chose in preference to 'the lord of Vaṅgāla'. The Candras did not rule over any part of Gauḍa in the western half of Bengal.

[1]See *IHQ*, Vol. XXXIII, p. 63.

Chapter IV

PROBLEMS OF THE RĀJAŚĀSANA

I

There are some copper-plate charters (*śāsana* or *rāja-śāsana*)[1] which record the sale of Government land to an applicant paying the usual price and the Government's acceptance of his proposal to create a rent-free holding out of the purchased land in favour of Brāhamaṇas or religious institutions. In such a transaction, it was believed, according to an ancient Indian convention, that five-sixths of the religious merit for the creation of the revenue-free holding would go to the purchaser of the land and one-sixth of it to the king of the country, whose government alone could create such a holding.[2]

There is another kind of charters which, instead of speaking of the sale of land that had been created a rent-free holding by the king in favour of Brāhmaṇas or religious institutions, merely state that the particular holding was created at the request of a certain officer or feudatory of the king or some other persons.[3] Inspite of the absence of any reference to sale in such records, some of them appear to be based on

1. *Select Inscriptions*, pp. 337 ff., 342ff., 346ff., 359ff.

2. Cf. *ibid.*, p. 344, text line 13; p. 348, text line 16; p. 352, text line 13; p. 362, text line 11. See also *Manusmṛti*, VIII. 304; *Viṣṇusmṛti*, III. 13-14. The same idea is also referred to in other records like the Damodarpur plates, No. 3, line 7 (*Ep. Ind.*, Vol. XV, p. 136), and No. 5, line 12 (*op. cit.*, p. 143), though the texts of most of the inscriptions have often been misunderstood. Cf. *Select Inscriptions*, p. 352, note 5.

3. See *Select Inscriptions*, pp. 331, 375, 421, etc. It may be pointed out that the feudatory's name was mentioned in royal charters in this fashion only when he was regarded as of some importance. When he grew more powerful, he issued charters himself with the permission of his master (cf. *Ep. Ind.*, Vol. XXXII, pp. 139ff.). With further growth in his power, his charters were issued without reference to his master's permission, but without concealing his subordinate position or indicating it somewhat vaguely (cf. *ibid.*, Vol XXVIII, pp. 201, 266, 332 ; Vol. XXX, p. 139; etc.). When still more powerful, he issued his grants without any reference to his master and endowing himself with a combination of subordinate and imperial titles which could in some

transactions involving sale.[1] Thus the Nālandā plate[2] of Devapāla records a grant of five villages by the Pāla king to a Buddhist monastery at Nālandā at the request of *Mahārāja* Bālaputradeva who was the lord of Suvarṇadvīpa (Malayasia and Indonesia) and was responsible for establishing the monastery. The five villages were apparently purchased by Bālaputradeva from Devapāla as, otherwise, the whole of the religious merit accruing to the pious act of endowing the monastery with a rent-free holding for its maintenance would go to Devapāla and nothing at all to Bālaputradeva.[3] This was no doubt an undesirable position for the king of Suvarṇadvīpa. If he really purchased the villages, as he no doubt did, five-sixths of the merit would be his and only one-sixth would go to Devapāla according to the convention referred to above.

But as regards the land made a rent-free holding at the request of an officer or feudatory of the king, it was no doubt in many cases lying within his *jā'gīr*, i.e. fief or estate. In the case of land forming part of *jā'gīrs* which royal officers of ancient India enjoyed temporarily,[4] their occupants lost the rent of the land in question so long as they were in their possession. But the king's loss of revenue was greater as the land remained rent-free even when the fief reverted to him or was subsequently allotted to some other officer. It therefore seems that the occupants of *jā'gīrs* had to compensate the king's loss, at least partially, for the creation of revenue-free holdings within their fiefs, as otherwise they could scarcely expect the full religious merit accruing to the pious act. We have also cases where a king is found to ratify the rent-free holdings created in their *jā'gīrs* by members of the royal family.[5]

cases be so interpreted as to indicate either his subordinate position or independent status (cf. *ibid.*, Vol. XXVII, p. 329; Vol. XXVIII, pp. 109, 264; Vol. XXIX, p. 186). The next stage of course is represented by his charters issued as a full-fledged independent ruler. See above, pp. 3-4.

1. The sale of land was generally represented in ancient India as a gift. See *ibid.*, Vol. XXVIII, p. 48, note 2; above, p. 5.
2. Bhandarkar's List, No. 1613.
3. Cf. R. D. Banerji, *Bāṅgālār Itihās*, Vol. I, B. S. 1330, p. 210.
4. Cf. Watters, *On Yuan Chwang's Travels in India*, Vol. I, p. 177.
5. See the cases of such holdings created by Princes Sūryasena and Puruṣottamasena and ratified by king Viśvarūpasena in his Vaṅgīya Sāhitya Pariṣad plate (N. G. Majumdar, *Inscriptions of Bengal*, Vol. III, p. 147; see *JAS*, Letters, Vol. XX, pp. 206-07). Cf. above, p. 30.

But it appears to us that a number of grants of rent-free lands issued by the kings were really made on behalf of persons whose names are not mentioned in the documents. This seems to be suggested by the fact that, in a few cases, even though the grants are recorded in the king's name, an endorsement at the end of the documents says that they were made by others, and in reality there is a contradiction between the facts as stated in the charter proper and in the endorsement. An important document of this type is the Bangaon plate[1] of Vigrahapāla, which purports to record the grant of a village by the Pāla king in favour of a Brāhmaṇa, although in an endorsement at the end it is summarily stated that the grant was made by an officer of the king, named Ghaṇṭīśa, out of his own *jā'gīr*.

Another interesting fact is that the indication of a particular grant being actually made by one of the king's officers or feudatories, but represented as one made by the king, is not clear in the documents though some of them appear to suggest the fact vaguely. There are many records which introduce a person without any ostensible relation with the charter stated to have been granted by the king. Such an introduction is often found at the end of the documents exactly in the position of the endorsement in the Bangaon plate of Vigrahapāla III, referred to above. In a few cases, such an enigmatic name is also met with in the body of the charter without any justification for its introduction. Since it is inexplicable why persons without anything to do with the grants should be mentioned in royal charters at all, we suspect that they might have been the real donors of the grants in question and that the fact was intended to be rather vaguely indicated in the said way. It also appears that there was an amount of reluctance on the part of the Government to admit such a fact.

The Mehar plate[2] of Dāmodara records a grant of lands in favour of a number of Brāhmaṇas. But at the end of the king's description in verse, there is one stanza introducing Gaṅgādharadeva who was the officer in charge of the royal elephant force. The introduction of this person cannot be explained unless it is supposed that he was the real donor of the

1. *Ep. Ind.*, Vol. XXIX. pp. 48ff.
2. *Ibid.*, Vol. XXVII, pp. 182 ff.

grant although the king was not eager to mention the fact explicitly in the document.[1] It seems that verses 8 and 12 mention the same officer respectively as *Dviradapati* and *Gajapati*, i.e. 'the lord of elephants'.

The Andhavaram plates[2] of the Eastern Gaṅga king Indravarman record the grant of a village as an *agrahāra* or rent-free holding in favour of several Brāhmaṇas. The king is mentioned as the donor. But, at the end, the record is stated to have been written under orders of Śrī-Lokārṇavadeva who vanquished many foes. The editor of the inscription says, "These plates furnish us with a new Gaṅga name—Lokārṇava." But he admits that the indentity of this person cannot be determined without further evidence.

The charter was issued in the Gaṅga year 133. But, instead of describing it as the *pravardhamāna- vijaya-rājya-saṁvatsara* or *Gāṅgeya- vaṁśa- pravardhamāna- vijaya- rājya-saṁvatsara* as we find in other Gaṅga records, the inscription in question calls it *Tumburu-vaṁśa-rājya-saṁvatsara*. This reminds us of the Santa-Bommali plates[3] issued by a Kadamba feudatory of a Gaṅga king, which describe the Gaṅga era as *Gaṅga-Kadamba-vaṁśa-pravardhamāna-vijaya-rājya-saṁvatsara* even though the Kadambas had nothing to do with the establishment of the era. It appears that the grant recorded in the Andhavaram plates of Gaṅga Indravarman was really made by his feudatory Lokārṇava of the Tumburu dynasty. Unless such was the case, it is difficult to explain why he was introduced as ordering for the writing of the document and the Gaṅga era is described only in this record as associated with the Tumburu dynasty.[4]

There is a stanza about the end of a charter issued by the Śailodbhava king Sainyabhīta Mādhavavarman II Śrīnivāsa.[5] The inscription was edited by N. G. Majumdar who believed that the date of the grant, viz., year 50, should be referred to the Harṣa era so as to yield 656 A. D. There is, however, little doubt that the inscription is dated in the regnal reckoning of the Śailodbhava king. The stanza in question has been read by Majumdar as follows:

1. *Ibid.*, Vol. XXX, pp. 52-53.
2. *Ibid.*, pp. 37ff.
3. Bhandarkar's List, No. 2053.
4. *A. R. Ep.*, 1951-52, p. 5.
5. *Ep. Ind.*, Vol. XXIV, pp. 148ff.

jayati Jayanta-pratimaḥ prasabha-samākṛṣṭa-ripu-nṛpa-śrīkaḥ|
Śrīdharapo(pau)raḥ kṣitipo varadīkṛta-lokanātha-sakhaḥ ||

Since another verse in the inscription states that king Mādhavavarman made the grant from his camp at Mādhavapura (probably named after himself), Majumdar suggests that the expression *Śrīdharapaura* refers to the king's stay, at the time of making the grant, at Śrīdharapura which is identical with Mādhavapura. He also says, "It further describes him (i.e. king Mādhavavarman) as a friend of the *lokanātha* who was graciously disposed towards him. By the term *lokanātha* we are probably to understand the paramount sovereign to whom Mādhavavarman owed allegiance." We are sorry that we cannot agree either with Majumdar's reading or with his interpretation. In the first place, what has been read as *Śrīdharaporaḥ* and corrected to *Śrīdharapauraḥ* has been read by S. N. Rajaguru, who has recently edited the inscription without noticing that it was previously published, as *Śrīvaramoraḥ*.[1] In regard to the reading of *va* for *dha*, Rajaguru seems to be right since the *akṣara* has a clear top *mātrā* which is expected in *v* and not in *dh*. The other disputed *akṣara* looks more like *mo* or *ṇa* than *po*. The reading of the expression thus seems to be *śrī-Varamoraḥ* or *śrī-Varaṇa(na)raḥ*. Secondly, the reference in the verse can hardly be to the Śailodbhava king as the feudatory of a certain *lokanātha*, i.e. 'king'. He was no doubt a feudatory of king Śaśāṅka of Gauḍa in the Gupta year 300 (619 A. D.). But his later records including the said epigraph are dated in his regnal reckoning and most of them (including the inscription in question) describe him as the performer of the *Aśvamedha* sacrifice.[2] There is thus little doubt that these charters were issued after Sainyabhīta Mādhavavarman II Śrīnivāsa had thrown off the yoke of the Gauḍa king. In our opinion, *lokanātha* mentioned in the stanza quoted above is no other than the Śailodbhava king himself and the illustrious Varamora or Varanara was his feudatory who was the real donor of the grant. The word *varadīkṛta* refers to the favour shown by the king to the feudatory by agreeing to the creation of the rent-

1. *Or. Hist. Res. Journ.*, Vol. II, Parts 3-4, p. 19.
2. See *IHQ*, Vol XXVII, pp. 166ff.

free holding recorded in the inscription no doubt at the feudatory's request.

While re-editing the Balangir Museum plates[1] of the 8th regnal year of Mahāśivagupta Yayāti I, we did not fully realise the implication of the endorsement at the end of it, referring to Prince Durgarāja, described as the son of Svabhāvatuṅga whom we identified with Mahāśivagupta Yayāti I himself. The introduction of the prince is really inexplicable, and it now appears to us that he was the real donor of the grant which was ratified by his father.

Similarly, the correct implication of the enigmatic endorsement at the end of the Mahada plates[2] escaped us while re-editing the inscription. It appears to us now that Yaśogaja, who seems to be described in the endorsement as a ruling chief born in the family of the issuer of the charter, i. e. king Someśvaradevavarman III, was the real donor of the grant which was ratified by the king. If this was not the case, the endorsement is quite meaningless.

The word *dāpaka* occurring in the records of the Imperial Paramāras is generally regarded as the same as *Dūtaka* or the executor of a copper-plate charter. But *Dāpaka* and *Dūta* are sometimes found in the same context. In our opinion, *Dāpaka* really means 'one who has caused the gift', i.e. the real donor whose gift was ratified by the king.[3]

II

Different versions of Minor Rock Edict I of Aśoka contain the Prakrit words corresponding to Sanskrit *yāta*, *upagata*, *upayāta* and *upeta* (respectively from *yā*, *upa-gam*, *upa-yā* and *upa-i*) in the same sense[4] which has been variously understood. Elsewhere we have suggested that *yāta-upagata-upayāta-upeta* in this context means *saṅgata*, 'intimately associated'.[5] In our opinion, the passages in question indicates Aśoka's intimate

1. *JAS*, Letters, Vol. XIX. pp. 117ff.
2. *Ep. Ind.*, Vol. XXVIII, pp. 283ff.
3. See Sircar, *Ind. Ep.*, p. 118; above, p. 4.
4. *CII*, Vol. I, p. 228.
5. *Maski Inscription of Aśoka*, p. 24; *Ep. Ind.*, Vol. XXXI, p. 209, text line 1; Vol. XXXII, p. 9, note 1.

association with the Buddhist Saṅgha. The lexicons, however, do not bear out this meaning quite clearly. In this connection, a study of similar words, often used in copper-plate grants to indicate the relation of the subordinates and officers of a king with the gift land or the district in which it was situated may be of interest. These words are generally understood in the sense of 'assembled',[1] though really some of them appear to support our interpretation suggested above.

From the standpoint of the recording of grants of land, copper-plate charters can be primarily divided into two classes, viz. (1) those that merely announce that some land or village was granted by the donor, and (2) those that contain an order of the donor in respect of the grant addressed to certain people. Among the records of the first category, mention may be made of a number of charters issued by the Imperial Gaṅgas of Orissa.[2] Copper-plate grants written in verse (e. g. many of the charters issued by the Vijayanagara kings)[3] and those written mostly in verse[4] generally fall in the same class. The passage *s-ānunayaṁ prāha bhūpālān* occurring in the versified part of a charter[5] from Orissa is one of the few exceptions.

The second category of copper-plate grants, in which the donor's order is addressed to certain people, is important for our enquiry as it is some of these that contain the words in which we are interested. Such records can be broadly subdivided into five classes: (1) those in which the addressees are vaguely and generally indicated: (2) those in which the order is primarily addressed to the inhabitants of the gift village or the village wherein the gift land was situated or the district wherein the gift land or village was situated; (3) those in which

1. Cf. *Ep. Ind.*, Vol. XXVI, p. 12 and note 3; see Vol. XII, p. 42 and note; Majumdar, *Ins. Beng.*, Vol. III, p. 190.

2. See *Ep. Ind.*, Vol. XXXI, p. 21, lines 181ff.; p. 260, lines 125-27; Vol. XXVIII, p. 190, lines 179-81; p. 194, line 179; p. 256, lines 122-26. For such records belonging to other dynasties or kings, see *ibid.*, Vol. XXXI, p. 15, lines 8-16; p. 190, lines 14-16; p. 312, lines 6-9; Vol. XXX, p. 140, lines 11-16; p. 187, lines 17-18; Vol. XXVIII, p. 75, lines 3-6; p. 210, verses 17-21; p. 266, lines 17ff.; Vol. XXVII, p. 77, lines 17-22.

3. See *ibid.*, Vol. XXXI, p. 144. For such records belonging to other families, see *ibid.*, Vol. XXX, p. 75; also Vol. XXIX, pp. 103, 198; cf. Vol. XXVIII, pp. 153-54.

4. *Ibid.*, Vol. XXIX, p. 32; Vol. XXX, p. 304.

5. *Ibid.*, Vol. XXX, p. 225, text lines 15-16. In these pages, we have quoted the epigraphic passages after removing scribal errors, etc.

the order is primarily addressed to the royal officers or agents including also the subordinate rulers, *jā'gīrdārs*, etc., in some cases; (4) those in which both the inhabitants of the locality in question and the royal officers or agents, etc., are mentioned; and (5) those in which the donor addresses neither the inhabitants nor his officers, but only the future kings.

The first and last of these subdivisions are simple. The first of the two is illustrated by the charters of the Cālukyas of Badami, in which we have the passage *sarvān = evam = ājñāpayati.*[1] The other, which is rare, is likewise illustrated by the passage *sarvān = eva bhāvi-bhūmipālān samanubodhayati* sometimes occurring in the grants of the Rāṣṭrakūṭas of the Gujarat region.[2] The other cases are complicated.

The order addressed to the inhabitants of a locality is simpler in passages like the following: (1) *śrī-Skandavarmaṇo vacanena Kudrāhāra-Kompāre grāmeyakā vaktavyāḥ;*[3] (2) °*grāme sarva-samavetān kuṭumbinaḥ samājñāpayati;*[4] (3) *Goṣṭhavāḍa-nivāsinaḥ kuṭumbinaḥ samājñāpayati;*[5] (4) *Sunikāyāṁ prativāsinaḥ samājñāpayati;*[6] (5) *Prastaravāṭa-vāsinaḥ sarva-samavetān kuṭumbinaḥ samājñāpayati;*[7] (6) *Reyūru-grāme grāmeyakān = ittham = ājñāpayati;*[8] (7) *Pherava-grāme yathā-nivāsi- janapadaṁ samājñāpayati;*[9] (8) *Andoreppa-grāme sarva- samanvāgatān kuṭumbinas = samājñāpayati;*[10] (9) *Pratiṣṭhāpura- nivāsinaḥ sarva-samupetān kuṭumbinaḥ samājñāpayati;*[11] etc.

But slight elaboration is noticed in such passages as follows: (1) *Brāhmaṇa-purogān grāmāñ = chārīr-ādi-kuśalaṁ pṛṣṭvā likhati;*[12] (2) *Kontinika-grāme Brāhamaṇān sampūjya prativāsinaḥ samājñāpayati;*[13] (3) *Keśavake Brāhmaṇa- purassarān prativāsi-kuṭumbinas =*

1. *Ibid.*, Vol. XXVII, p. 118, note 2; p. 130, text line 34.
2. *Ibid.*, Vol. XXVI, p. 253, text lines 29-30.
3. *Ibid.*, Vol. XXXI, p. 9, text lines 8-9.
4. *Ibid.*, p. 200, text lines 9-10; Vol XXX, p. 27, text lines 13-14; p. 117, text line 5.
5. *Ibid.*, Vol. XXXI, p. 203, text lines 24-25.
6. *Ibid.*, p. 315, text lines 4-5.
7. *Ibid.*, Vol. XXX, p. 277, text lines 2-3 (on first plate, second side).
8. *Ibid.*. Vol. XXIX, p. 96, text lines 12-13.
9. *Ibid.*, Vol. XXVII, p. 113, text lines 8-9.
10. *Ibid.*, Vol. XXVIII, p. 178, text lines 5-6.
11. *Ibid.*, Vol. XXVII, p. 219, text lines 8-9.
12. *Ibid.*, Vol. XXXI, p. 92, text lines 5-6.
13. *Ibid.*, p. 221, text lines 10-11.

samājñāpayati;[1] (4) *uktavāṁś=ca rājā tad-grāma-nivāsino mahattama-janapadān*;[2] (5) *Keselaka-grāme Brāhmaṇ-ottarān kuṭumbinaś=śīrṣakañ=c=ājñāpayati*;[3] (6) *sarva-samavetān kuṭumbino bhojakāṁś=ca samājñāpayati*;[4] (7) *Gudravāra-viṣaya-nivāsino rāṣṭrakūṭa-pramukhān kuṭumbinas=samāhūy=ettham=ājñāpayati*;[5] (8) *viṣaye Vardhamānake grāmakūṭa-droṇāgraka-nāyaka-devavārika-gaṇḍaka-pramukhān sarvān=eva yathā-prativāṣinaḥ samājñāpayati*;[6] (9) *Mehāra-grāma-nivāsi-yathā-pradhāna-janapadān mahattarāṁś=ca samādiśanti*;[7] etc.

In the first group of these passages, the inhabitants of a village (*grāmeyaka, kuṭumbin, prativāsin, janapada,* etc.; cf. *grāma, jānapada,* etc., in the second group) are referred to while, in the second group, they are mentioned along with their social or administrative leaders and with certain village officials in a few cases. Rarely, the villagers of a whole district are stated to have been ordered after having been summoned (*samāhūya*). The word used in some cases in respect of the villagers is *sarva-samaveta* which may mean 'assembled from all sides'. This seems to be supported by the expression *sarva-samanvāgata* rarely used in place of *sarva-samaveta.* As will be seen below, the expression *samupasthita* is used in some cases in a similar context in respect of the villagers and local officials. Sometimes *sarva-samupeta* is also found in place of *sarva-samaveta.* The reference may be to an announcement to the people summoned by the beat of drums in respect of the grant in the gift village or the village containing the gift land or at the headquarters of the district in which the gift land or village was situated.

There are some charters in which the order is addressed not to the villagers, but to others such as the subordinates, officers and agents of the king often with reference to a district. Cf. (1) *Śrī-Kapālivarmaṇo vacanena Śivapura-viṣaye vartamāna- bhaviṣyad-bhojak-āyuktaka-sthāyy-ādayo vaktavyāḥ*;[8] (2) *sarvān=eva svān=āyuktaka- mahattara- drāṅgika- cāṭa-bhaṭa- dhruvasthānādhikaraṇa-*

1. *Ibid.*, p. 265, text lines 3-4.
2. *Ibid.*, Vol. XXX, p. 149, text line 18.
3. *Ibid.*, Vol. XXVIII, p. 16, text line 3.
4. *Ibid.*, Vol. XXVII, p. 35, text lines 2-3.
5. *Ibid.*, pp. 45-46, text lines 15-16.
6. *Ibid.*, p. 142, text lines 35-36.
7. *Ibid.*, p. 188, text lines 15-16.
8. *Ibid.*, Vol. XXXI, p. 233, text lines 1-3.

daṇḍapāśik-ādīn = anyāṁś = ca yathā-sambadhyamānakān = anudarśayati;[1] (3) *asmin Koṅgoda- maṇḍale śrīsāmanta- mahāsāmanta- mahārāja-rājaputr-āntaraṅga- daṇḍapāśik- oparika- viṣayapati- tadāniyuktaka-vartamāna- bhaviṣya- vyavahāriṇaḥ sa-karaṇān yathārhaṁ pūjayati mānayati ca*;[2] (4) *sarvān = ev = āgāmi-vartamāna-nṛpati-sāmanta-viṣayapati-bhogika- rāṣṭragrāmakūṭa-deśillaka-mahattar- ādhikārikādīn samanudarśayati*;[3] (5) *sarvān = eva samupagata-viṣayapati-rāṣṭragrāma-mahattar- ādhikārikān samanudarśayati*;[4] (6) *Uttamālokaviṣaye samupāgatān vartamāna-bhaviṣyan-mahāsāmanta-mahārāja-rājaputrakumārāmāty oparika-viṣayapati- tadāyuktaka-dāṇḍapāśika-sthānāntarikān = anyāṁś = ca cāṭa-bhaṭ-ādīn = adhikaraṇāṁś = ca pūjayati*;[5] (7) *yato = ' smat-santakāḥ sarv-ādhyakṣa-niyoga-niyuktā ājñāsañcāri-kulaputr-ādhikṛtāḥ bhaṭāś = chātrāś = ca viśruta-pūrvay = ājñay = ājñāpayitavyāḥ*;[6] etc. In these, the expressions *vartamāna-bhaviṣyat* and *yathā-sambadhya-mānaka*, used in several cases, show that the order was meant for the king's officers, etc., who were associated with the administration of the area containing the gift village or land for the time being and also those who would be so associated in future.[7] Sometimes the word *samupāgata* has been used in relation to the 'present and future' subordinates and officers of the donor in the district containing the gift village (No. 6). It is difficult

1. *Ibid.*, p. 300, text lines 11-12; p. 303, text lines 16-18.
2. *Ibid.*, Vol. XXX, p. 268, text lines 31-34; cf. p. 272, text lines 23-26.
3. *Ibid.*, Vol. XXVIII, p. 21, text lines 15-17.
4. *Ibid.*, p. 201, text lines 12-13.
5. *Ibid.*, p. 334, text lines 3-6. Cf. *Kārttikeyapura-viṣaye samupāgatān sarvān = eva niyogasthān rājanaka*, etc. (*ibid.*, Vol. XXXI, p. 280, text line 11; cf. p. 287, text line 10; p. 294, text line 13).
6. *Ibid.*, Vol. XXVI, p. 160, text lines 20-22.
7. For *sambadhyamānaka*, see *Lalitapuravāla-sambadhyamānaka-Tauḍā-grāme* (*ibid.*, Vol. XXXI, p. 312, text line 8.). In the charters of the Bhauma-Karas of Orissa, a distinction is generally made between the subordinates and officers of the district or province and those of a village or a group of villages; e. g., *Dakṣiṇa-Tosalāyāṁ vartamāna-bhaviṣya-mahāsāmanta- rājasatka-rājaputra-kumārāmāty-auparika- viṣayapati- tadāyutaka- dāṇḍapāśika-sthānāntarikān = anyān = api rājaprasādinaś = cāṭa- vallabha- jātīyān Tamura- viṣaya- paścima- khaṇḍe mahāmahattara- bṛhadbhogi- pustakapāla- kūṭakolas-ādy- adhikaraṇaṁ yathārhaṁ mānayati bodhyatis amājñāpayati ca* (see *ibid.*, Vol. XXIX, pp. 88-89, text lines 26-30; cf. p. 217, text lines 23-26; p. 219, text lines 25-27; Vol. XXVIII, pp. 215-16, text lines 213-16). Here the local officers of the western subdivision of the Tamura district have been mentioned separately from the subordinates and officers associated with the province of South Tosalā in which the Tamura-viṣaya was situated.

to take *samupāgata* here in the sense of 'assembled' since the whole district seems to be too big a place for an assemblage, while it is not easy to understand how the 'future' subordinates and officers also assembled.

In a large number of copper-plate charters, the order regarding the grant is addressed to both the local people or people in general and the royal officers, etc. This is simply indicated in the records of some dynasties while the charters of certain areas have it in a somewhat elaborate form. But it is the most elaborate in the records of some of the early medieval ruling families of Northern India, especially those of its eastern regions. The simple and semi-elaborate forms of indication are illustrated in the following quotations.

For simple indication, cf. (1) *Pḷaki-viṣaya-vṛddhān = adhikāriṇaḥ Kundūra-grāma-kuṭumbinaś = ca samājñāpayati*;[1] (2) *Kaliṅganagarāt ....samast-āmātya-pramukha-janapadān samāhūya samājñāpayati*:[2] (3) *sarvān = eva svān = āyuktaka-viniyutaka-cāṭa-bhaṭa-kuṭumbi-mahattara-draṅgikān bodhayati*;[3] (4) *Ramalava- viṣaya- paścima-khaṇḍe yathā-nivāsi-sa-karaṇa-sāmanta-bhogy-ādi-janapadān yatharhaṁ mānayati bodhayati samādiśati ca*;[4] etc.

For semi-elaborate indication, see (1) *Nātavāḍi-viṣaya-nivāsino rāṣṭrakūṭa-pramukhān kuṭumbinas = samāhūya-mantri-purohita-senāpati-yuvarāj- ādy-aṣṭādaśa-tīrth-ādhyakṣam = ittham = ājñāpayati*;[5] (2) *Maṁḍāura-grām-opagatān Brāhmaṇān = anyāṁś = ca mānyān = adhikṛtān kuṭumbi-kāyastha-dūta-vaidya-mahattarān meda-caṇḍāla-paryantān sarnvān sambodhayati samājñāpayati ca*;[6] (3) *grāmeyakān rājapuruṣa-talavara- daṇḍanāyaka- rāṣṭrika-dūta- bhaṭa-naṭa-ceṭaka- paricāraka-niyukt-ādhyakṣa-praśāstṛ- samāhartṛ- nāyakāṁś = c = ājñāpayati*;[7] (4) °*bhūmau yathāyathaṁ samupasthita- viṣayakaraṇa- vyavahārika-pramukha- janapadān rāja- rājñī- rāṇak- ādhikṛtān = anyān = api rājanyaka- rājaputra- rājavallabha-prabhṛtīn yathā- kāla- bhāvino = pi*

1. *Ibid.*, Vol. XXXI, p. 135, text lines 12-13.
2. *Ibid.*, p. 196, text lines 44-47; p. 308, text lines 40-41.
3. *Ibid.*, Vol. XXX, p. 4, text line 1.
4. *Ibid.*, Vol. XXIX, pp. 192-93, text lines 13-15.
5. *Ibid.*, Vol. XXXI, p. 42, text lines 31-34.
6. *Ibid.*, p. 72, text lines, 7-9.
7. *Ibid.*, p. 78, text lines 22-24.

sarvān mānanā- pūrvakaṁ samādiśanti;[1] (5) *Jiloṇḍā- viṣaye bhaviṣyad-yathākāla-bhāvino rājanakān rājaputrān Brāhmaṇa-purogān sāmanta-nivāsi-janapadān = adhikāriṇaḥ sa-karaṇān = anyāṁś = ca cāṭa-bhaṭa-vallabha-jātīyān rāja-pād- opajīvinaḥ sarvān yathārhaṁ mānayati bodhayati kuśalayaty = ādiśati c = ānyat*;[2] (6) *Vaṭapadrake Brāhmaṇān sampūjya sa-pradhānān prativāsino yathā-kāl- ādhyāsinas = samāhartṛ-sannidhātṛ- pramukhān = adhikāriṇas = sa-karaṇān = anyāṁś = c = āsmat-pād-opajīvinas = sarva-rājapuruṣān samājñāpayti*;[3] (7) *Māṇḍiḍḍā-viṣaye rāja- rājanaka-rājaputrān viṣayapati-daṇḍapāśikān yathākāl-ādhyāsino vyavahāriṇo Brāhmaṇān Karaṇa-purogān nivāsi-janapadāṁś = ca yathārhaṁ mānayati bodhayati samādiśati ca sarvataḥ śivam = amākam = anyat*;[4] etc.

In these instances, the word *upagata* has been used once in relation to the inhabitants and local officials of the gift village (No. 2 of Group II). In one case (No. 4 of Group II), the local people and officials are stated to have been *samupasthita* at the gift land while the subordinates, etc., are separated from the said class by the epithet *yathākāla-bhāvin*. The same distinction is also made in another case (No. 5 of Group II) by using the expressions *bhaviṣyad-yathā-kālabhāvin* and *sāmanta-nivāsin*. Similar use of the expressions *prativāsin* and *yathākāl-ādhyāsin* is noticed in one case (No. 6 of Goup II) and *yathākāl-ādhyāsin* and *nivāsin* in another (No. 7 of Group II). This distinction is made clear in the Gāhaḍavāla records in which, in the course of an elaborate indication, we have *grāma-nivāsino nikhila-janapadān = upagatān = api ca rāja-rājñī*, etc. Here the relation of the subordinates and officers of the king with the gift village is indicated by the word *upagata*.[5] Some charters signify the same distinction by enumerating the two classes as *sarvān = ātmīyān mantri-purohita*, etc., and *tan-nivāsi-Brāhmaṇ-ottarān*, etc.[6]

1. *Ibid.*, Vol. XXX, p. 207, text lines 30-32.

2. *Ibid.*, Vol. XXIX, p. 188, text lines 27-29; cf. Vol. XXVI, p. 79, text lines 24-27; also Vol. XXVII, p. 330, text lines 25-27, where we have *yathākāl-ādhyāsin* for *yathākāla-bhāvin*.

3. *Ibid.*, Vol. XXII, p. 290, text lines 6-91; cf. p. 323, text lines 6-8.

4. *Ibid.*, Vol. XXVII, p. 339, text lines 11-14.

5. *Ibid.*, Vol. XXVI, p. 73, text lines 12-14.

6. *Ibid.*, p. 202, text lines 28-30. A stanza ascribed to Vyāsa says—*sthānaṁ vaṁś-ānupurvi ca deśaṁ grāma = upagatān/Brāhmaṇāṁś = ca tathā c = ānyān mānyān = adhikṛtān likhet* //

The word found in the Gāhaḍavāla records as *upagata* is often found in the form *samupagata* or *samupāgata* in the same context in many other charters, especially in the elaborate indication in the grants of the Pālas and Senas of Eastern India. We have seen above how the 'present' and 'future' subordinates, etc., of a ruler are described as *samupāgata* with reference to a *viṣaya* or district. The question now is what *upagata, samupagata* or *samupāgata* in this context really means. In our opinion, it means the same thing as *sambadhyamānaka, yathākāla-bhāvin* and *yathākāl-ādhyāsin* as found in the same context in many records. This may be clear from the study of a few corresponding passages from the charters of the Gāhaḍavālas, Pālas and Senas.

The Gāhaḍavāla grant referred to above has: *upagatān=api ca rāja-rājñī- yuvarāja-mantri-purohita-pratīhāra- senāpati-bhāṇḍāgārik-ākṣapaṭalika-bhiṣag-naimittik-āntaḥpurika-dūta-kariturагapattanākarasthānagokulādhikāri-puruṣān=ājñāpayati bodhayaty=ādiśati ca.* It is difficult to believe that all the said kinds of subordinates and officers of the king would have assembled in a gift land or village whenever he made a grant especially in view of the fact that the Gāhaḍavāla kings are known to have often issued such charters. The number of these classes of people is much higher in the Pāla and Sena charters. It has also to be noticed that often the subject of the gift was a plot or several plots of land including tanks, etc., and the assemblage of subordinate rulers, their queens and sons and of all the officers (*aśeṣa-rājapuruṣān*) therein becomes inconceivable. The list sometimes includes, besides others, the mercenary soldiers of various nationalities such as Gauḍa, Mālava, Khaśa, Kulika, Hūṇa, Karṇāṭa and Lāṭa and also people performing menial services such as Meda, Andhra and Caṇḍāla. An assemblage seems to be physically impossible in such cases. It should moreover be noted that different plots of the gift land sometimes lay in different districts.

Thus the Belwa plate of Mahīpāla has : *grāma- puṣkariṇīṣu samupāgat- āśeṣa- rājapuruṣān rāja-rājanyaka- rājaputra- rājāmātya- mahāsāndhivigrahika- mahākṣapaṭalika- mahāsāmanta- mahāsenāpati- mahāpratīhāra- dauḥsādhasādhanika- mahādaṇḍanāyaka- mahākumārāmātya- rājasthān- oparika- daśāparādhika- caurodharaṇika- dāṇḍika- dāṇḍapāśika- śaulkika- gaulmika- kṣetrapāla- prāntapāla- koṭṭapāl- āṅgarakṣa- tadāyuktaka- viniyuktaka- hastyaśvoṣṭranaubalavyāpṛtaka-*

kiśoravaḍavāgomahiṣyajāvikādhyakṣa- dūta- preṣaṇika- gamāgamik-ābhitvaramāṇa- viṣayapati-grāmapati-tarika-gauḍa-mālava-khaśa-hūṇa-kulika- karṇāṭa-lāṭa- cāṭa- bhaṭa- sevak-ādīn=anyāṁś=c=ākīrtitān rājapād- opajīvinaḥ prativāsino Brāhmaṇ-ottarān mahattam-ottama-kuṭumbi-puroga-med-āndhra- cāṇḍāla-paryantān yathārhaṁ mānayati bodhayati samādiśati ca.[1]

Thus, in the above context, the words *upagata*, etc., seem to refer to the intimate relation of the king's officers and subordinates with an area as administrators or fief-holders.[2]

1. *Ibid.*, Vol. XXIX, pp. 7-8, text lines 31-41. Some records make it clear that the grant was made at the donor's capital in the presence of officers, etc. See *ibid.*, Vol. XXXIV, p. 222; cf. Vol. XXVIII, p. 309.

2. Cf. *yathākāla-bhāvi-bhogapatibhiḥ* in the Paschimbhag plate, text line 57; *samupasthita-kālaṁ (ye bhavanti*) ye='py=anye viṣayapatayaḥ ...vyava-hāriṇo bhaviṣyanti tair=api...akṣayanīvy=anupālanīyā* in the Jagadishpur plate, text lines 22-24. See Sircar, *Epigraphic Discoveries in East Pakistan*, p. 68 and pp. 62-63.

CAPTER V

KRAYA-ŚĀSANA AND KARA-ŚĀSANA

The word *śāsana* means 'a royal charter' and *tāmra śāsana* 'a royal charter engraved on a plate or plates of copper'. Revenue-free gifts, granted by ancient Indian rulers in favour of persons, deities or religious establishments were usually endowed with a deed engraved on durable *tāmra-paṭṭa*, i. e. 'a plate or plates of copper'.[1] By *lakṣaṇā*, a *tāmra-śāsana* was sometimes called *tāmra-paṭṭa*.[2] Often, again, the word indicating the deed or charter was applied, by *lakṣaṇā*, to signify the land granted.[3] But the expression *tāmra-śāsana*, in this modified sense of a gift of revenue-free land, was often indicated either by *tāmra*[4] or by *śāsana*.[4] The word *śāsana* in this sense is used not only in the medieval records of Orissa, but even in modern Oriya. Numerous villages in Orissa still bear names ending with the word *śāsana*, indicating that originally they were gift villages. Besides the word *tāmra-śāsana*, early Orissan epigraphy knows two other types of *śāsanas*. These are the deeds called *kraya-śāsana* and *kara-śāsana*, even though these two expressions are actually noticed in a small number of inscriptions. Similar epigraphs have also been found in a few other parts of India.

The Madras Museum plates of the time of king Narendradhavala of Orissa, published in the *Epigraphia Indica*, Vol. XXVIII, pp. 44ff., is a *kraya-śāsana* which literally means 'a deed of purchase' and is the same as 'a sale deed'. The ex-

1. The document was written usually on a piece of birch bark (*bhurja-patra*) by a high official and later copied on copper by an engraver. Cf. *Proc. I H C*, Lahore, 1940, pp. 52-56. Often the official would write on the copper plate (or stone) with some point or ink to facilitate the work of engraving (*Bul. Dec. Col. Res. Inst.*, Vol. XI, December, 1950, p. 120). See Sircar, *Indian Epigraphy*, p. 83.

2. Cf., e. g., *tāmra-paṭṭa- dharmeṇa* in *Select Inscriptions*, Vol. I, p. 352, etc.

3. Cf. *ibid.*, p. 353, text line 24, etc.

4. See, e. g., *IHQ*, Vol. XXIII, p. 240, text line 33, etc.

5. See, e. g., Majumdar, *Inscriptions of Bengal*, Vol. III, p. 74, text line 34, etc.

pression also indicates 'land sold or purchased by means of a *kraya-śāsana*'. The inscription does not record any royal charter, although it may have been issued with the king's permission. According to it, a person named Seḍā sold a village called Taḍeśvaragrāma to three other persons on receipt of an amount of *rūpyaka* or silver, specified as *pla* 10 *ā-mā* 2 *gu* 4. The syllable *pla* is a contraction of the well-known weight *pala* (equal to four *karṣas* = 320 *ratis* = 585½ grains), while *mā* stands for *māṣa* and *gu* for *guñjā* (or *rati*). The contraction *ā* apparently stands for *ādya* and, as is well known, the lexicons recognise *ādya-māṣa* weighing 5 *ratis*.[1] According to Manu[2] and other writers, two *guñjās* of silver make a *māṣa*, although five *guñjās* make a *māṣa* of other metals like gold and copper. Since in the above record 4 *guñjās* appear as a fraction of an *ā-mā*, the latter was heavier than the silver *māṣa* weighing two *guñjās* only.

The Srikakulam copper-plate inscription of the Gaṅga king Madhukāmārṇava was edited by C. Narayana Rao and R. Subba Rao in the *Journal of the Andhra Historical Research Society*, Vol. VIII, pp. 180ff. The inscription was re-edited by G. Ramadas in the *Journal of the Bihar and Orissa Research Society*, Vol. XVIII, pp. 293ff. Unfortunately the published transcripts of the record are full of mistakes and its correct interpretation has yet to be made. Line 32 of the inscription has the passage: *dātu(ḥ*) deḍha(dvyardha)-śata-ru(rū)pya(pyāṇi)* 150. This shows that the donor received from the donee 150 *rūpyas* or silver coins. The charter thus records what was actually a *kraya-śāsana*, although the *Vaiśy-āgrahāra* mentioned in the charter may have been made a rent-free holding.

There are some inscriptions which are *kara-śāsanas* created by the Somavaṁśī king Mahābhavagupta I Janamejaya (middle of the 10th century). The expression *kara-śāsana* of

1. *Amarakoṣa*, Vaiśya-varga, verse 85. Wilson in his *Glossary of Judicial and Revenue Terms*, s. v., says that a *māṣa* is variously regarded as equal to five, eight or ten *ratis*, while the *Śabdakalpadruma*, s. v., also quotes authorities speaking of *māṣa* of five, six, seven and eight *ratis*. According to Oriya lexicons (see *Pramoda Abhidhāna*, s. v. *māṣa*, *māṣā*) eight *ratis* make one *māṣā*, which is regarded as one-tenth of a *tolā* and one-fortieth of a *pala*.

2. VIII. 134-36: *pañca- kṛṣṇalako māṣas=te suvarṇas=tu ṣoḍaśa | palaṁ suvarṇāś=catvāraḥ palāni dharaṇaṁ daśa || dve kṛṣṇale samadhṛte vijñeyo raupya-māṣakaḥ | te ṣoḍaśa syād=dharaṇaṁ purāṇaś=c=aiva rājataḥ || kārṣāpaṇas=tu vijñeyas=tāmrikaḥ kārṣikaḥ paṇaḥ ||*

course means 'a charter recording a revenue-paying grant or the land granted by such a charter'. Thus it can refer to a piece of land either sold, the purchaser being allowed to enjoy some privileges, or given away, subject to the payment of the assessed rent regularly. A number of similar other cases in early Orissan epigraphs, some of them wrongly deciphered or misunderstood, have been traced. Several early examples of rent-paying charters are cited below.

I. The Bengal Asiatic Society's plate of Gayāḍatuṅga was edited by Nilmani Chakravarti. In lines 33-34 of the incription, we have: *Torogrāma(ḥ*) kara-śāsanaṁ kṛta(ḥ*) ru(rū)pya-pla-navena aṅken=āpi ru(rū)pya-pla* 9.[1] Thus Torogrāma was made a *kara-śāsana* with its [annual] rent fixed at 9 *palas* of silver. The village was divided among Brāhmaṇas, each of whom received a certain number (six or eighteen) of *mālas*. The word *māla* here seems to indicate a land measure known from a few other early Orissan records. Whether it is the same as *māṇa* (now regarded as equal to one acre of land) common in Orissa since the days of the later Imperial Gaṅgas, cannot be determined. In the passage quoted above, the word *pala* is used side by side with the contraction *pla*.

II. The Talcher plate of the same Gayāḍatuṅga was edited by N. N. Vasu and re-edited by R. D. Banerji. In lines 32-33 of this inscription, we have: *tṛṇodaka(ṁ*) ru(rū)pya-pla catvāri aṅke ru(rū)pya-pla* 4.[2] The expression *kara-śāsana* is not found in this record. Other cases discussed below would suggest that *tṛṇodaka* (literally, '[a tax for] grass and water') has here technically the sense of a cess due to the king even when the gift land was declared to be revenue-free. The word *tṛṇodaka* is actually mentioned in a list of taxes in line 17 of the Sonepur (Kelgam) plates of *Kumāra* Someśvara published in the *Epigraphia Indica*, Vol. XII, pp. 239ff., and recently re-edited in the same journal, Vol. XXVIII, pp. 322ff. There is no doubt that the village in question, which was granted to several

1. *JASB*, N. S., Vol. V, 1909, pp. 348ff. See *op. cit.*, p. 350. Chakravarti reads: *rupya-pañca- navena aṅken= āpi rupya* 40+5.

2. *Archaeological Survey of Mayurbhanj*, Vol. I, pp 152-54; *JASB*, N. S., Vol. XII, 1916, pp. 293-94. Vasu reads: *rupyaṣṭa -catvāri aṅke kapyaplat* (*op. cit.*, *p.* 154). Banerji reads: *rupya* 40 *catvāri aṅke rupya* 40+4 (*op. cit.*, p. 294).

Brāhmaṇas, was subject to the payment of an annual cess at the rate of four *palas* of silver. One-half (or a portion) of the village was given to a Brāhmaṇa hailing from a village in Varendra-maṇḍala, while the other half (or portion) was divided between two other Brāhmaṇas, each of whom recieved one-fourth *māla*. In the passage quoted, the contraction *pla* is used twice for *pala*; but the uncontracted form of the word is not used at all.

III. The Talcher plate of the Śulkī king Kulastambha was published by N. N. Vasu in his work cited above, pp. 157-60, and re-edited by R. D. Banerji in the *Epigraphia Indica*, Vol XII, pp. 156-59. Line 20 of the record says that a village called Siṅgagrāma was made a rent-free holding, while in lines 27-28 we have : *Siṅgagrāmaḥ tṛṇodaka(ṁ*) rūpya-pla* 2.[1] Thus, although the village was made a revenue-free holding, a cess styled *tṛṇodaka* was levied at the annual rate of two *palas* of silver. The use of this special term in preference to the usual *kara* points to the eagerness of ancient Indian rulers to represent even a rent-paying holding as a rent-free one.[2] It seems that the land was given away (and not sold) to the party and that this transaction had to be distinguished from an ordinary sale of land. This may explain the use of the word *tṛṇodaka* for *kara*.

IV. The Jurada grant of Neṭṭabhañja was edited by C. R. Krishnamacharlu in the *Epigraphia Indica*, Vol. XXIV, pp. 15-20. Lines 11-13 of the record show that a village was made a rent-free gift; but in lines 33-4 we have: *rājaki(kīya)-pratya(tyā)ya(yo) rūpya-pla* //4// *khaṇḍapāla- muṇḍamola rūpya-pla* // 4//[3] wherein it is clearly said that the [annual] royal dues

1. Vasu reads : *Siṅgigrāmaḥ pravantad=eva rup-āpta* 2 (*op. cit.*, p. 160); Banerji reads: *rupya* 40 + 4 (*op. cit.*, p. 158). In an editorial note, Sten Konow rightly pointed out that the last figure is 2 and not 4, although he apparently agreed with Banerji in reading *pla* as 40.

2. Cf. *Mitākṣarā* on Yājñavalkya, II. 114, quoted below.

1. Krishnamacharlu could not read either *pla* or 4. On his reading *pralaya rupya*, there is an editorial note of N. P. Chakravarti, which runs: "Reading seems to be *pratyaya rupya*. The symbol after *rupya* in this line and the next appears to represent a numerical sign and may have to be read as 70." He is silent about the figure 4 omitted by Krishnamacharlu. Moreover, the reading 70 is wrong. At p. 16, Krishnamacharlu says: "The symbol or ligature following the expression *rupya* is perhaps meant as an abbreviation for *rūpya*."

for the village were at the rate of four *palas* of silver, while another four *palas* of silver were also due for the taxes called *khaṇḍapāla-muṇḍamola* which is rather difficult to explain. *Khaṇḍapāla* of this record is no doubt the same as *khaṇḍapālīya* mentioned in the list of taxes in line 20 of the Sonepur (Kelgam) plates, referred to above, and may have been a cess payable to the officer in charge of a *khaṇḍa*, i. e. sub-division of a district. *Khaṇḍapāla* or *Khaṇḍapati* is sometimes mentioned in copper-plate charters in the usual list of royal officials. See, e. g., line 12 of the Sonepur (Kelgam) plates referred to above, and line 17 of the Ramganj plate of Īśvaraghoṣa in Majumdar's *Inscriptions of Bengal*, Vol III, p. 153. The contraction *pla* for *pala* is used twice in the passage quoted above.

V. The Angul plate of the Bhauma-Kara queen Dharma-mahādevī was edited by Binayak Misra in his *Orissa under the Bhauma Kings*, pp. 50ff. In lines 24-27 of the epigraphic text, we have: *śāsanaṁ* [*ni*]*kṛtya Sakembāgrāme* (*maḥ*) *tāmraśāsanaṁḥ* (*naṁ*) *Desalagra* (*grā*)*ma-dasa*(*śa*)*-ma* (*mā*)*la-vibhāgaḥ kara* (*ḥ**) *trīṇi-*(*tri*)*-pala-rukaḥ* (*rūpyakaḥ*)[1] *pratipāditaṁ* (*taḥ*) *dharma-gauravāyaḥ-*(*ya*) *Kehnava-khaṇḍeḥ* (*ṇḍe*).[2] The meaning seems to be that Dharma-mahādevī granted the village of Sakembā in favour of a Brāhmaṇa as a *tāmra-śāsana*, i.e. a revenue-free gift, and that she also gave to the same Brāhmaṇa a part of another village called Desala, which was ten *mālas* in area and subject to the annual payment of three *palas* of silver. Both the villages, Sakembā and Desala, were in the division called Kehnava-khaṇḍa.

VI. The Ganjam copper-plate inscription of Gaṅga Pṛthvīvarman of Śvetka (or Śvetaka) was edited by Kielhorn in the *Epigraphia Indica*, Vol. IV, pp. 198-201. In lines 20-21 of the inscription, we have: *sakarīkṛtya prativarṣaṁ ru* (*rū*)*pya-palāni catvāri deyaṁ* (sic). A village was thus given by the king as a *kara-śāsana* (although that expression is not used) with

1. The same word occurs in Telugu as *ruka* which is explained as 'a small coin called *Fanam* (Sanskrit *Paṇa*)' or 'money'. A *fanam* is regarded as equivalent to either one Anna and a quarter ($\frac{5}{64}$ Rupee) or two Annas and a half ($\frac{10}{64}$ Rupee). See Sankaranarayana's *Telugu-English Dictionary*, s. v.

2. *Op. cit.*, p. 54, Misra reads: *Desalagrāma-daśamaś=ca tribhāgaḥ karatrīṇiya laruka pratipāditaṁ dharmma- gauravāt Sakehava-khaṇḍaḥ.*

the fixed rate of four *palas* of silver to be paid every year by the donee as rent. Kielhorn, however, was inclined to correct the expression *sakarīkṛtya* to *akarīkṛtya* and thus to apply an altogether different meaning to the nature of the deed.

VII. The Patna plates of the Somavaṁśī king Mahābhavagupta I Janamejaya were edited by Fleet in the same journal, Vol III, pp. 340-44. In lines 19-20 of this record, there is the passage: *prativarṣa-dātavya-ru* (*rū*)*pyak-āṣṭa-pala-kara-dāna* (*ṁ**) *viniścitya.* Thus a village was granted by the king as a *kara-śāsana*, and its annual rent was fixed at eight *palas* of silver. Fleet, however, took *rupyak-āṣṭa-pala* as *rupya-kāṣṭa* (*ṣṭha*)*-pala*, although what he understood from the emended reading is uncertain.

VIII. Another set of plates of the same king from Patna was edited by Gangamohan Laskar in the *Journal and Proceedings of the Asiatic Society of Bengal*, Vol.1, 1905, pp. 1ff. This inscription records a grant with the following endorsement: *prativarṣa-dātavya-rūpyak-āṣṭa- pala-kara-dānaṁ viniścitya*[1] which is exactly the same as that found in the other record of Mahābhavagupta I Janamejaya noticed above.

IX. A third record of the Samavaṁśī king edited by Laskar in the same issue of the above journal has the following endorsement : *prativarṣe c=ātra śāsane kara* (*ṁ**) *pañca-rūpya-plāni niṣṭaṅkya kara-śāsanam=idaṁ dattaṁ yatra rū-pla* 5.[2] A village was thus granted by the king with the annual rent fixed at five *palas* of silver. The contraction *pla* is here used twice in place of *pala* which is used in the other two records of the same king discussed above.

X. The Srikakulam copper-plate inscription of the Gaṅga king Anantavarman, son of Devendravarman, was edited by C. Narayana Rao and R. Subba Rao in the *Journal of the Andhra Historical Research Society*, Vol. VIII, pp. 188ff. Unfortunately the inscription was not correctly read and interpreted. It has been re-edited in the *Journal of the Royal Asiatic Society of Bengal*, Vol. XVIII., pp. 47ff. Line 24 of the inscription has the passage : *samucita-pratya* (*tyā*)*ya* (*yo*) *daśa-māsa* (*ṣa*)*kā* (*ḥ**). The charter thus records a *kara-śāsana*, the dues for which

1. See *op. cit.*, p. 5.
2. See *op. cit.*, pp. 12-13.

payable to the king [apparently, annually], were ten *māṣakas*, i. e. one-fourth *pala*, probably of silver.

XI. The Adava-Kannayavalasa plates of the Māṭhara king Prabhañjanavarman, son of Śaktivarman and grandson of Śaṅkaravarman, were published by L. H. Jagadeb in the *Vaitaraṇī*, Vol. IV, June, 1930, pp. 293-98.[1] Jagadeb could not read and interpret the passage *sāṁvatsarika-kara-paṇ-āgra-śatau-(te) dvau (dve)* in the concluding portion of the record. It shows that the grant of Niṅgoṇḍi by king Prabhañjanavarman of Kaliṅga as an *agrahāra* to several Brāhmaṇas was subject to the payment of 200 *paṇas* (probably of cowries) in advance every year as *kara* or rent.[2]

XII. The Bobbili plates of Acaṇḍavarman, edited by R. K. Ghoshal in the *Epigraphia Indica*, Vol. XXVII, pp. 33ff., are of exactly the same nature as the Adava-Kannayavalasa plates noticed above, although the editor read the king's name as *Caṇḍavarman* and failed to interpret the record properly. In recording the grant of a rent-free *agrahāra* by king Acaṇḍavarman of Kaliṅga, the document says, *saṭṭṛṁśa-(triṁśa)d-agrahāra-sāmānyañ = c = āgrahāra-pardeyaṁ sāmba (sāṁva)-tsarikaṁ sa (pa)ṇ-āgraṁ (gra)-śa tab-bu (dva) yañ = c = ā (ṁ*) śaṁ c = opanibandhyaḥ (ndhya) Tiriṭṭhānavāṭak-āgrahara (ḥ*) Brāhmaṇānāṁ nānā-gā (go) tra-sabrahmacāriṇāṁ samprattaḥ.* It has been shown how numbers like 18 and 36 are used in the Indian languages in the sense of 'all'.[3] The number 36 has been used similarly to mean 'all' in the present record. Thus the inscription says that the grant of Tiriṭṭhānavāṭaka as a rent-free *agrahāra* in favour of some Brāhmaṇas was subject to the annual payment of 200 *paṇas* in advance as the *agrahāra-pradeya* payable by the donees of all *agrahāras*. As *agrahāras* were rent-free holdings and as the grant in question is declared to be revenue-free, the expression *agrahāra-pradeya* has been used here to indicate the nominal rent or cess instead of *kara*, just as *tṛṇ-odaka* is found used in similar context in some other records. The

1. See now *Ep. Ind.*, Vol. XXX, pp. 112ff.
2. In *JAHRS*, Vol. XIX, p. 127, S.N. Rajaguru suggests that this passage contains the date of the record in words which give 'the number 222, and it may be taken as the Gupta Saṁvat which was then current in this part of India'. The suggestion is, however, fantastic.
3 Cf. *Ep. Ind.*, Vol. XXVIII, p. 330; Vol. XXX, p. 115.

custom of collecting annually 200 *paṇas* from the *agrahāras* of ancient Kaliṅga seems also to be referred to in the passage *ṣaṭtriṁśad-agrahāra-sāmānyaṅ=kṛtvā* occurring in the Bṛhatproṣṭha grant of king Umāvarman of Kaliṅga.[1]

XIII. The Narsingpur plate of Devānanda was edited by myself in the *Epigraphia Indica*, Vol. XXVII, pp. 331ff. Lines 20-23 of the extremely corrupt text of this inscription record the grant of Dolosaragrāma situated in the Kaleda *khaṇḍa* (Pargana) of the Erāvaṭṭa *maṇḍala* (district) in favour of a Brāhmaṇa of the Dālbhya-gotra whose name is unfortunately not easily traceable in the text. As the passage *Viṭhusuta-Siharasau(su) ta- Naṭasuta* looked merely to give the names of the donee's father, grandfather and great-grandfather, it was suggested that the meaningless *tṛṇoka*, etc., following the reference to the Brāhmaṇa's *gotra* and *pravara*, may contain his personal name: "If the name of the donee is expected here, we may probably suggest *Trilokāya* in place of *tṛṇokapa*." It, however, appears that the passage *tṛṇokapañcapala* occurring in line 23 of the record really stands for *tṛṇodaka pañcapala* which no doubt speaks of the annual cess payable by the donee for the gift land as fixed at five *palas* probably of silver. As regards the name of the donee, it is either omitted through inadvertence or it was Naṭa the word *suta* being put after it inadvertently.

XIV. The Nesarikā grant of the Rāṣṭrakūṭa emperor Govinda III (794-814 A. D.) has been published by P. L. Gupta in the *Epigraphia Indica*, Vol. XXXIV, pp. 135ff.; but an interesting statement in lines 71-72 of the inscription has escaped Gupta's notice.[2] It says, *śrī-viṣaya-pate(ḥ*) pañca sahasrāṇi prati-variṣaṁ(varṣaṁ) deyāni*, "Five thousands are payable to the illustrious governor per annum." The charter therefore records a *kara-śāsana*, the annual rent for the gift village having been fixed at five thousand copper coins or cowrie-shells. In this case, the village was not made a fully rent-free holding in favour of the donee.

XV. The Panjim (Goa) copper-plate grant[3] issued in

1. *Ep. Ind.*, Vol. XII, p. 5.
2. Cf. *ibid.*, p. 140.
3. See *QJMS*, Vol. XLV, p. 66.

Śaka 981 (1059 A.D.) by the Kadamba king Jayakeśin I states that the donee had to pay *pāṅga* at a fixed rate every year for the village granted to him. According to Telugu lexicons, *paṅga* or *pāṅga* was a kind of tax, so that the charter was a *kara-śāsana.*

XVI. The Bhaturiya inscription of king Rājyapāla of the Pāla dynasty of Bengal and Bihar had been published by S.P. Lahiry in the *Indian Historical Quarterly*, Vol. XXXI, No. 3, September, 1953, pp. 215ff., and was re-edited in the *Epigraphia Indica*, Vol. XXXIII, pp. 150ff. Verse 12 of this epigraph reads as follows:

> *asmai Yaśodāsa-niveśitāya*
> *śrī-Rājyapālo Vṛṣabhadhvajāya* |
> *śataṁ purāṇān = nikaraṁ niyamya*
> *Madhusravaṁ grāmam = adāt kṣitiśaḥ* ||

It records that the king (i. e. Rājyapāla) dedicated the village of Madhusrava in favour of the god Vṛṣabhadhvaja (Śiva) installed by Yaśodāsa and fixed the *nikara* at one hundred *purāṇas* apparently per annum. The silver coin called *purāṇa* (also known as *kārṣāpaṇa, dharaṇa*, etc.) is well known, while the word *nikara* is recognised in Sanskrit lexicons in the sense of 'a suitable gift' and in Bengali, by an extention of that meaning, in that of 'an amount which is legitimately payable.' As wc have seen, when a small amount of rent was fixed for gift lands, it was often designated by some name other than *kara,* such as *tṛṇodaka*, *agrahāra-pradey-āṁśa*, etc. The word *nikara* has been employed in the present record in a similar sense. The inscription thus records a *kara-śāsana.*

It may be pointed out here that Lahiry failed to understand this interesting nature of the record and suggested that the word *nikara* should be corrected to *niṣkara*, 'rent-free'. But the emendation is unwarranted in view of the fact that *niṣkara* does not suit the metre of the stanza. In this connection, it may also be noted that there is nothing unusual in the Buddhist king Rājyapāla making a grant in favour of the Brāhmaṇical god Śiva since most of the grants of the Buddhist kings of the Pāla and other East Indian dynasties are known to have been made in favour of the Brāhmaṇas or the Brāhmaṇical deities or religious institutions.[1] It appears, however, that Yaśodāsa had to pay an amount of money to the royal treasury in order to get the partially rent-free holding created in favour of the deity installed by him.[2]

An interestinng fact is that the deeds called *kara-śāsana* and *kraya-śāsana* often quoted the usual imprecatory and benedictory verses meant for the *tāmra-śāsanas* or charters recording revenue-free gifts of land. Of course, a *kara-śāsana* could claim some merit when the land was given free of cost or at a reduced price and when the rent accepted was less than the usual rate of the age and locality. But no such claim seems to have been legitimately possible on behalf of a private *kraya-śāsana* except by a fiction. The attitude of the ancient Indian in this respect can be best explained by the following quotation from Vijñāneśvara's remarks in the *Mitākṣarā* on the *Yājñavalkya-smṛti*, II. 114: *sthāvarasya vikraya-pratiṣedhāt...dāna-praśaṁsāc=ca vikraye='pi kartavye sa-hiraṇyam=udakaṁ dattvā dāna-rūpeṇa sthāvara-vikrayaṁ kuryāt.* So, in ancient India, even a sale of land was represented in the form of a gift.

1. See *Ep. Ind.*, Vol. XXIX, p. 2 and note; Vol. XXX, p. 162, note 4. The real donors of most of the grants were really not the kings themselves as we have pointed out.

2. Cf. *ibid.*, Vol. XXXIII, pp. 50 ff.

Chapter VI

ASPECTS OF THE PANCĀYAT SYSTEM

I

It is well known to the students of Indian epigraphy that four Gupta inscriptions from Damodarpur in the old Dinajpur District of North Bengal mention, at the same time, the reigning Gupta emperor (*Paramabhaṭṭāraka Mahārājādhirāja*), his *Uparika* (viceroy, usually enjoying the title *Mahārāja*) in the *bhukti* (province) of Puṇḍravardhana (North Bengal), and the officer in charge of the *viṣaya* (district) of Koṭivarṣa (the Dinajpur region) who enjoyed an official rank or designation like *Kumār-āmātya* (officer of the rank of a prince of the royal blood), *Āyuktaka* (administrative officer) or *Viṣayapati* (governor of a district) and obtained his post not from the crown, but from the viceroy.[1] The seal of three of these documents is lost; but the extant seal attached to one of them bears the inscription: *Koṭivarṣ-ādhiṣṭhān-ādhikaraṇasya*, i.e., [the seal] of the *adhikaraṇa* (court and office of non-military administration) of the *adhiṣṭhāna* (city) of Koṭivarṣa (headquarters of the district of that name),[2] while the business of the *adhiṣṭhān-ādhikaraṇa* is stated in the records to have been conducted or transacted (cf. *saṁvyavaharati*) by a group including persons entitled (1) *Nagaraśreṣṭhin* or *Ārya-Nagara-śreṣṭhin*, (2) *Sārthavāha*, (3) *Prathama-Kulika*, and (4) *Prathama-Kāyastha*. Among other epigraphs of the same age, the Paharpur plate[3] records an order of the *Āyuktaka* or *Āyuktakas* stationed at Puṇḍravardhana (headquarters of the province of the same name) and the *adhiṣṭhān-ādhikaraṇa* headed by the *Ārya-Nagaraśreṣṭhin*, while the Baigram plate[4] records the order of a *Kumārāmātya*, stationed at Pañcanagarī, and the *adhikaraṇa* of the *viṣaya*. The Kalaikuri-Sultanpur plate[5]

1. See *Ep. Ind.*, Vol. XV, pp. 130 f.; 133 f., 138 f., 142 f.; *Select Inscriptions*, pp. 283 ff., 288 ff., 328 ff., 337 ff.
2. Cf. *Ep. Ind.*, *op. cit.*, p. 142; *Select Inscriptions*, p. 337.
3. *Ep. Ind.*, Vol. XX, pp. 61 ff.; *Select Inscriptions*, pp. 346 ff.
4. *Ep. Ind.*, Vol. XXI, pp. 31f.; *Select Insciptions*, pp. 342 ff.
5. *IHQ*, Vol. XIX, pp. 12 ff.; *Ep. Ind.*, Vol. XXXI, pp. 57ff.

similarly contains an order of the *Āyuktaka*, stationed at Pūrṇakauśikā in the Śṛṅgavera *vīthī* (sub-division) and the *adhikaraṇa* apparently of the *vīthī* in question. There are numerous other cases of the mention of the *adhikaraṇa* (rarely referred to as *karaṇa*) of an area, although the functionaries constituting such *adhikaraṇas* are not specifically mentioned as in some of the the cases referred to above.

The meaning of the designations of the *Nagaraśreṣṭhin* (*Ārya-Nagaraśreṣṭhin*)and his three colleagues and their functions have been the subject of speculation. R. G. Basak who edited the Damodarpur inscriptions in the *Epigraphia Indica*, Vol. XV, thinks that "The *Viṣayapati* as the head of the *viṣaya* was aided in his administrative work by a Board of Advisers, which seems to have been constituted by four members representing the different interests of those days, viz., (1) the *Nagaraśreṣṭhin* representing the various guilds or corporations of the town or the rich urban population, (2) the *Sārthavāha* (the chief merchant) representing the various trade-guilds and other mercantile professions of the *viṣaya*, (3) the *Prathama-Kulika* (the chief artisan) representing the craft guilds, and (4) the *Prathama-Kāyastha* (the chief scribe) representing either the *Kāyasthas* as a class or acting as a State official in the capacity of the Chief Secretary of the present day."[1] Elsewhere, the same scholar speaks of the Board of Advisers as having aided the *Viṣayapatis* of Koṭivarṣa in the administrative work of the *viṣay-ādhikaraṇa*[2] and having been formed by the four members, " (1) the *Nagaraśreṣṭhin* (the President of the town-guild of bankers), (2) the *Prathama-Sārthavāha*[3] (the representative of the merchant class), (3) the *Prathama-Kulika* (the representative of the artisan classes) and (4) the *Prathama-Kāyastha* (probably the chief scribe, the head of the government officials)."[4]

In his *Hindu Revenue System*, U. N. Ghoshal also says that the district officer was 'carrying on the administration of

1. Cf. *History of North-Eastern India*, 1st ed., pp. 309-10. The number of persons in the group is really many, of which only four are specified in the records.

2. The Damodarpur inscriptions speak of the *adhiṣṭhān- ādhikaraṇa* although the jurisdiction of the functionaries in question may have spread over an area much wider than the *adhiṣṭhāna* or city.

3. We have really *Sārthavāha* and not *Prathama-Sārthavāha* in the inscriptions.

4. *History of North-Eastern India*, p. 56.

the district town (*adhiṣṭhān-ādhikaraṇa*) with a guild-president, the leading merchant, the leading banker and the leading scribe at the top'.[1] As regards the expression *adhiṣṭhān-ādhikaraṇa*, he points out that it has been variously interpreted to mean 'an administrative board of the district' (R. G. Basak), 'the royal tribunal in a city' (R. C. Majumdar), and, with less justification, as 'the office and probably the court of a district officer' and 'a secretariat and advisory council' (Beni Prasad).[2] Ghoshal then draws our attention to the famous trial scene of the *Mṛcchakaṭika* which 'refers to the king's judges (called *Adhikaraṇika* and *Adnikaraṇa-bhojaka*) sitting in the court-house (*adhikaraṇa-maṇḍapa*), who are assisted by the guild president (*Śreṣṭhin*), the scribe (*Kāyastha*) and so forth,"[3] and concludes, "If it be supposed that the *adhikaraṇa* of the drama respresents the loosely organised institution of earlier times, that of the Gupta empire would be a development of the same with a well-defined organisation and with the addition of administrative functions as well. The reversion of the Gupta institution to the type of administrative boards described by Megasthenes for the Maurya empire is no doubt a witness to the enduring influence of the popular Pañcāyats."[4] The subject has also been discussed in some other publications,[5] although the real nature of the administrative institution referred to in the inscriptions discussed above still remains shrouded in mystery.

In this connection, the attention of scholars may be drawn to what James Tod says about the Pañcāyat system prevalent in Rajasthan in the first half of the nineteenth century. On this 'self-instituted tribunal', Tod observes, "Besides the resident ruler of the District, who was also a judicial functionary, there was.... a special officer of the Government in each frontier Thana or garrison post. He united the triple occupation of embodying the quotas, levying the transit duties and administering justice, in which he was aided at the Cabutrā or court, by assembling the Cauthiyā or Assessors of Justice. Each town

1. *Op cit.*, p. 202.
2. *Ibid.*, p. 203.
3. The *Mṛcchakaṭika* speaks of one *Adhikaraṇika* who was assisted in deciding the cases by one *Śreṣṭhin* and one *Kāyastha*.
4. *Op. cit.*, pp. 203-04.
5. Cf. *History of Bengal*, Dacca University, Vol. I, pp. 266 ff.

and village has its Cauthiyā, the members of which are elected by their fellow citizens, and remain as long as they conduct themselves impartially in disentangling the intricacies of complaints preferred to them. They are the aids to the *Nagarseṭh* or Chief Magistrate, an hereditary office in every large city in Rajasthan. Of this Cauthiyā, the *Paṭel* (headman)[1] and *Paṭwārī* (accountant)[2] are generally members....these are the special and fixed council of each town; the general Pañcāyats are formed from the respectable population at large and were formerly from all classes of society. The Cabutrās or terraces of justice, were always established in the Khalisa or crown demesne."[3] The Cauthiyās are described as 'the Town-Magistrates', and it is further said, 'In every town, there is an unpaid magistracy, of which the head is the *Nagarseṭh* or Chief Citizen, and the four Cauthiyās, tantamount to the Lord Mayor and Aldermen, who hold their courts and decide in all civil cases."[4] According to Tod, most of the *Nagarseṭhs* of Rajasthan in the first half of the nineteenth century were Jains.[5]

This institution of unpaid magistracy, viz., the Cauthiyā or council of 'four' members including the *Paṭel* and *Paṭwārī* and headed by the *Nagarseṭh*, as prevalent in Rajasthan and described by Tod, may be compared with both the council including the *Śreṣṭhin* and *Kāyastha* and headed by the *Adhikaraṇika* as known from the *Mṛcchakaṭika*, and the council including the *Sārthavāha*, *Prathama-Kulika* and *Prathama-Kāyastha* and headed by the *Nagaraśreṣṭhin* as found in the inscriptions referred to above. The resemblance among the said three councils is significant and, in our opinion, they are essentially the same institution.

1. According to Wilson's Glossary, the *Paṭel* is 'the headman of a village, who has the general control and management of the village affairs, is head of the police, and exercises, to a limited extent, the functions of a Magistrate : he is also the principal agent in the realization of the revenue, and the chief medium of communication with the officers of the Government'.

2. According to Wilson, the *Paṭwārī* is 'a village accountant, whose duty it is to keep and to produce, when required by the government revenue officers, all accounts relating to lands, produce, cultivation, changes, and past assessment of a village."

3. *Annals and Antiquities of Rajasthan*, ed. William Crooke, Vol. I, p. 171.

4. *Ibid.*, p. 231.

5. *Ibid.*, Vol. II, p. 682.

In the first place, the same designation,viz., *Nagarseṭh* or *Nagaraśreṣṭhin*, is applied to the president of two out of the three councils discussed above, although in one case he is called *Adhikaraṇika* or 'head of the *adhikaraṇa* or non-military administrative organisation'. Secondly, the *Kāyastha* or *Prathama-Kāyastha*, no doubt the same as the *Paṭwārī* of later times, figures in all the three councils. Thirdly, the representation of the mercantile class on the council is suggested by the mention of the *Śreṣṭhin* in the *Mṛicchakaṭika* and the *Sārthavāha* in the inscriptions, although we are not quite sure whether a merchant also figured in the Cauthiyā of Rajasthan.

The importance of the *Nagaraśreṣṭhin* in the council of the Gupta period seems to be clearly indicated by the epithet *ārya* applied to him. There is absolutely nothing in the inscriptions to show that the *Nagaraśreṣṭhin* and his colleagues formed a board of advisers or helpers to the Governor of a district. On the other hand, it is clearly stated that it was they that conducted the non-military administration of the *adhikaraṇa* of a city and often of a wider area under the jurisdiction of the city in question, although they must have been subordinate to the Governor. There is, again, no proof that the *Nagaraśreṣṭhin* represented the interests of certain guilds or corporations or of the rich urban population, as has been supposed by some writers.

II

The Modasa copper-plate inscription[1] of the Paramāra king Bhoja (1000-55 A. D.), dated 1011 A. D., records the grant of two *hala* measures of land in Śayanapāṭa-grāma made by a subordinate ruler named Vatsarāja in favour of the Brāhmaṇa Derda who is described as *Caturjātakīya*. The epithet *Caturjātakīya* is applied to the donee twice in the record (lines 7 and 12) and seems to mean 'member of the *Caturjātaka*'. The institution of the *Caturjātaka* is well known from the Cintra *praśasti*[2] and was probably an administrative board of 'four' like

1. *Ep. Ind.*, Vol. XXXIII, pp. 192ff.

2. *Ibid.*, Vol. I, pp. 271ff.; A. K. Majumdar, *Caulukyas of Gujarat*, pp. 250-51.

the Cauthiyā of Rajasthan (cf. the *Pañcakula* or Pañcāyat and *Aṣṭakula* which were similar boards of 'five' and 'eight' or more members).[1] It is stated in the *praśasti* that one Tripurāntaka procured some land for religious purposes with his self-acquired property and assigned it to the *śrī-Caturjātaka*, in exchange for which the *Caturjātaka* issued two grants. It is stated that Tripurāntaka caused the *Caturjātaka* to issue a charter whereby one *dramma* per day was assigned to the temple founded by himself and nine *drammas* monthly (from the same source) for the maintenance of a disciple. Tripurāntaka is also stated to have purchased from the *Caturjātaka* three shops which he converted into a temple endowment.

The expressions *aṣṭakul-ādhikaraṇa*, *grām-āṣṭakul-ādhikaraṇa*, *mahattarādy-aṣṭakul-ādhikaraṇa*, etc., occur in East Indian inscriptions of the Gupta and post-Gupta ages, and it is to be compared with Tamil *ūr-eṭṭu*, 'the committee of eight members of the village assembly (*ūr*)'.[2] The expressions *añjaṣṭa-sabha* and *añjaṣṭa-sattu-sabhai* mean 'the village committee of five or eight members' and is a combination of *Pañcakula* and *Aṣṭakula*.[3]

A. K. Majumdar has collected the references to *Pañcakula* in inscriptions and literary works mostly from Western India and has shown that sometimes the members of the body were nominated by the Government and that it was engaged to function in various capacities.[4] But there is little doubt that the *Pañcakula* was generally associated with the administration like the Cauthiyā. We may refer to the evidence of the Veraval inscription[5] of 1264 A. D. in this connection.

When *Parameśvara Paramabhaṭṭāraka Mahārājādhirāja* Arjuna of the Caulukya-Vāghelā dynasty was ruling from his capital Aṇahillapāṭaka, *Mahāmātya Rāṇaka* Māladeva was 'conducting all the business of the seal such as the making of *śrī-śrī* [at the beginning of documents]' (i. e. the drawing up of documents).[6] This was of course the usual style of early medieval documents for introducing the king's principal administrator of the kingdom or his viceroy of a province. Māladeva was either Arjuna's

1. See below.
2. See Sircar, *Ind. Ep. Gloss.*, p. 32.
3. *Ibid.*, p. 21.
4. *Op. cit.*, pp. 236ff.
5. *Ep. Ind.*, Vol. XXXIV, pp. 141 ff.
6. *Ibid.*, p. 142: *Śrīśrī- karaṇ- ādi- samasta-mudrā-vyāpārān paripanthayati*; cf. Vol. XXXII, p. 152 and note 2; p. 166.

Chief Minister or the Chief Administrator of his kingdom or, more probably, the king's Viceroy in charge of the administration of Kathiawar. The inscription next refers to the *pratipatti* or administration of the *Pañcakula* at Somanāthadevapattana (modern Somnāth Pāṭan near Veraval in the Junagarh District). The *Pañcakula* in charge of the administration of Somnāth Pāṭan is mentioned because the transaction of business recorded in the inscription (i. e. the transfer of ownership of some landed property) took place at the city and the epigraph was written and engraved there. The principal members of the *Pañcakula* were *Paramapāśupatācārya Mahāpaṇḍita Mahattara Para* (*Purohita*) Vīrabhadra *alias* Gaṇḍa and *Pāri* (*Pārīkṣika*) *Mahaṁ* (*Mahattara*) Abhayasiṁha. A later record of 1271 A. D. speaks of the *pratipatti* or administration of Abhayasiṁha who was probably the head of the local *Pañcakula* at the time.[1]

III

An inscription of the time of the Gāhaḍavāla king Jayaccandra and dated in Vikrama-saṁvat 1230 (1173 A. D.) is now preserved in the Bhārat Kalā Bhavan attached to the Hindu University at Varanasi, U. P. The internal evidence shows that it was raised at a place called Lāhaḍapura. It is difficult to say whether this place is the same as the modern town of Laharpur (lat. 27° 42′ 45″, long. 80° 56′ 25″), headquaters of a Pargana of the same name in the Sitapur District of U. P. since the inscribed stone is said to have been found at Barahpur near Nandganj in the Gazipur District.

The inscription is a private document. Its object is to record an ordinance issued by the Brāhmaṇas of a village in the Gāhaḍavāla kingdom without any reference to royal authority, though the heavy punishment stipulated is stated to have included not only some kind of harassment of the persons guilty of certain crimes, but even the death of some of the criminals. This throws some light on the responsibility of the public for the preservation of law and order and attaches a special interest to the inscription. Documents relating to this aspect of early Indian life have been discovered in large numbers in South India; but epigraphic evidence on the subject is meagre with reference to North India. The inscription under study

1. *Ibid.*, vol. XXXIV, p. 143, note 3.

shows that conditions in the North were practically similar to those prevailing in the South during the early medieval period. In this connection, it is also interesting to note the ancient Indian attitude towards theft and murder committed in a village, for which often the landlord or the villagers themselves were held responsible for tracing the thief or murderer or otherwise for compensating the aggrieved party.[1]

Verse 2 says that, on the date discussed above, the *Dvijas* or Brāhmaṇas assembled at Lāhaḍapura and drafted the *sthiti* recorded in the inscription and that they made the *saṁvid* in question because they were what is called *vaṭu-tuṇṭ-ābhibhūta*. Lāhaḍapura has been referred to as a *grāma* in verse 3 below; but whether the word *grāma* here indicates merely a village or a bigger area with its centre at Lāhaḍapura is difficult to determine. The word *sthiti* has been used in the verse apparently to indicate 'a fixed decision, ordinance or decree' and *saṁvid* in the sense of 'a mutual agreement or contract'. The nature of our document is thus that of what is called a *sthiti-patraka* in Smṛiti literature, which is a document recording the fixed decision of a corporate body.[2] But the calamity called *vaṭu-tuṇṭa* (or *tuṇṭā*), by which the *Dvijas* are stated to have been overwhelmed (*abhibhūta*) is difficult to explain. The word *vaṭu* or *baṭu* means a youngster especially of the Brāhmaṇa class, but is also contemptuously applied to adult persons; but the word *tuṇṭa* (or *tuṇṭā*) is not found in Sanskrit. The Hindi lexicons, however, recognise the word *ḍhuṇḍh* in the sense of 'a thief, robber or swindler', and it is not impossible that *tuṇṭa* in our inscription is a Sanskritised form of it. It may also be suggested that *tuṇṭa* is a mistake for *luṇṭa* used in the sense of a robber or robbery in the present context, although it is recognised in the lexicons in the adjectival sense of 'robbing'. Thus a gang of robbers seems to have been operating in the area around Lāhaḍapura and the local people were suffering from their depredations. The learned Brāhmaṇas of the area, probably being the leaders of the local society, therefore assembled

1. Cf. *Yājñavalkyasmṛti*, II. 271-72.

2. Cf. Kane, *Kātyāyanasāroddhāra*, v. 254 :
Cāturvidya-pura- śreṇi-gaṇa- paur- ādika- sthitiḥ /
tat- sidhy- arthe tu yal=lekhyaṁ tad=bhavet sthiti- patrakam //
See also Bṛhaspati in *SBE*, Vol. XXXIII, p. 305. For *saṁvid*, see the *Manusmṛti*, VIII. 19: *ye grāma- deśa-saṁghānāṁ kṛtvā satyena saṁvidam/ visaṁvaden=naro lobhāt taṁ rāṣṭrād=vinivāsayet* //

to find out a remedy for the menace and came to a decision which is quoted in the following stanzas of the inscription.

Verse 3 suggests that the unsocial activities were meant for the *parivāda* of the *Dvijas*. The word *parivāda* here appears to be used in the sense of 'ill-repute'. The idea seems to be that the depredations of the unsocial elements were considered by the leaders of the society as conceived in order to put them to shame. It is only another way of saying that the elders responsible for law and order in the village were discredited by the successful operations of the marauders.

Verses 3ff. contain the text of the *sthiti* or *saṁvid* referred to earlier in verse 2. Verses 3-4 state that the person who would plunder the *grāma* or village (apparently meaning Lāhaḍapura) or would be guilty of *droha* (mischief) of any other kind [to its inhabitants], such as the seizure of the cattle (*go-mahiṣy-ādi-veṣṭana*) [of the villagers], should be killed at once and his whole property should be confiscated, while his abettor (*upaṣṭambha-dāyaka*) should be expelled [from the village] and his house [in the village] should be demolished. This shows that the robbers referred to were among the inhabitants of Lāhaḍapura and its immediate neighbourhood. In verse 4, the instantaneous slaughter, as recommended for the culprit, has been indicated by the interesting expression *cakṣur-vadha* (i. e. 'slaughter at sight') in which the word *cakṣus* has been used in the sense of 'sight'. The confiscated property of the chief culprit was probably treated as pertaining to the whole village or was more probably assigned to the temple or temples of the locality. This is what was done in South India as we know from a number of inscriptions.[1]

While verses 3-4 speak of the punishment of the principal offender and his abettor, the first half of the next stanza (verse 5) prescribes the punishment for the instigator of the crime. It is stated that the *vimantṛ*, i. e. the adviser of the chief culprit, should be *vārita* (cf. *vārayan*) and should be treated as an equal of a dog or an ass or a Caṇḍāla. The causative form of the root *vṛ* may be taken to mean 'to hold captive' or 'to restrain'. But the injunction that the instigator of the crime should be

1. Cf. T. V. Mahalingam, *South Indian Polity*, p. 231. Considering the punishment prescribed for robbery by the law-givers (Jolly, *Hindu Law and Custom*, p. 273; Kane, *Hist. Dharm.*, Vol. III, pp. 519ff.), *cakṣur-vadha* does not appear to mean 'blinding the eyes'.

treated as a dog or ān ass or a Caṇḍāla seems to suggest that he was ostracised and that his movements were restricted. It has to be remembered in his connection that punishment by imprisonment was rather rare in aneient and early medieval India even in cases conducted in the kings courts.[1] Thus while the chief offender was killed and his whole property confiscated and his abettor was expelled from the locality, his counsellor was permitted to stay in the village though nobody was allowed to have any intercourse with him.

The second half of verse 5, with which the document ends, states that the god Dvādaśārka was the witness [of the *sthiti*] and prays for the success of the same. The name Dvādaś-ārka refers to the conception of the twelve Ādityas in a single Sun-god called Dvāda-ātman in the lexicons. Whether it was the name of the Sun-god worshipped at Lāhaḍapura cannot be determined. But the conception of the Sun as a witness of human deeds seems to be quite appropriate as he is called *Loka-locana* (literally, 'the eye of the world') and *Karma-sākṣin* (literally 'the witness of [all] acts') in the Sanskrit lexicons.

The question is now as to the capacity in which the Brāh-maṇas of Lāhaḍapura issued the decree contained in the document under review. Of course the Smṛti literature makes it abundantly clear that the particular jurisdiction of corporations of every kind was recognised by the ancient and medieval Hindu kings in the fullest measure and that the right of making laws for their corporations and composing disputes was often enjoyed by corporate bodies of farmers, craftsmen, cowherds, money-lenders, members of particular sects, robbers, actors, artisans, etc.[2] No doubt the king of the country was advised to recognise and support the arrangements of and punishment inflicted by the chief of a family or of a guild or of a corporation, and to interfere only when a dispute arose between a chief and his subordinates. But cases of grave crimes are stated to have been exclusively reserved for the king. This was, however, theoretical. In actual practice, inferior courts, such as those held by village assemblies, guilds, temple trustees and caste elders, appear to have been conducting criminal cases arising

1. Cf. Jolly, *op. cit.*, p. 282.
2. *Ibid.*, p. 293; N. C. Sengupta, *Evolution of Ancient Indian Law*, pp. 10-11, 259ff., 260.

within their jurisdiction side by side with the courts headed by the king and his governors and subordinates without interruption from the Government. A large number of South Indian inscriptions are known to prove that criminal cases including those involving homicide were decided by the village assembly, or the community to which the accused belonged, or the local people in general.[1]

In the present case, the Brāhmaṇas of Lāhaḍapura do not appear to have been members of a corporation of their own community nor do the unsocial elements seem to have belonged to the same community or corporation. The language of the inscription seems to suggest that the Brāhmaṇas were the members of the village corporation and the unsocial elements belonged to different classes of the local population. The former appear to have been the same sort of corporate body as is called the village *Mahājanas* in the Kannaḍa inscriptions and the village *Mahāsabha* in the Tamil epigraphs. These were generally composed of Brāhmaṇas. The organisation appears to be similar to the village court referred to by Pitāmaha, according to whom such courts could appeal to the city courts which could in their turn appeal to the king.[2]

It may be supposed that the Brāhmaṇas of Lāhaḍapura could not have undertaken the responsibility of preserving law and order in their locality without the king's permission and that, since there is no reference to any royal approval in the record, either the Gāhaḍavāla king specially empowered them to act in the manner described in the inscription or there prevailed a sort of anarchy resulting from maladministration in the region in question and the leaders of the local population had to make their own arrangement for the suppression of unsocial elements. The second of the two alternative sugestions seems to be improbable in view of the fact that, in such a case, the name of the reigning monarch may not have been prominently mentioned in the document. As regards the first alternative, it may be pointed out that, although in the early medieval

1. T. V. Mahalingam, *op. cit.*, pp. 225ff., 235. There is an interesting case, in which the village assembly and its officers as well as the local Government officers and the royal army failed to apprehend certain dacoits and ultimately the co-operation of the local people was sought.

2. Jolly, *op. cit.*, p. 290.

period the royal court was regarded as the highest institution for the dispensation of justice, the position of a court like the village assembly was recognised by convention. They automatically enjoyed a sort of relegated authority and did not require special authorisation. It seems that the Brāhmaṇas of Lāhaḍapura, who issued the ordinance, were also responsible for judging the criminals when caught by the people or the village officers and of inflicting the punishments stipulated in the document.

It may be asked why the Brāhmaṇas felt the necessity for prescribing the said drastic punishments for the crimes in question. The answer seems to be this. There was absence of uniformity and precision in the works of the ancient Indian law -givers in regard to the punishment for most crimes. Crimes were sometimes grouped in categories and a punishment was prescribed for a particular category. Even when various crimes and their punishments were specified, the specification was not exhaustive. Moreover, fines and *prāyaścitta* were often prescribed even for the most heinous crimes.[1] The Brāhmaṇas of Lāhaḍapura apparently felt the necessity to do away with this vagueness and prescribed exemplary punishments for the crimes concerned. This was probably done because the punishments then in vogue in the area were not sufficiently deterrent. Most of the ancient law-givers absolved a Brāhmaṇa from corporal punishment and some of them prescribed for the instigator of a crime double the penalty of the criminal himself.[2] The ordinance of the Brāhmaṇas of Lāhaḍapura shows that they did not find these prescriptions suitable for the preservation of law and order in their area under the prevailing conditions. Above all, the ordinance empowered any of the inhabitants of the village to kill a plunderer and cattle-lifter. This they could not ordinarily do without bringing trouble to themselves. The inscription under study draws our attention to one of the most interesting sources of criminal law in ancient and medieval India even in respect of some of the major crimes which are generally believed to have been dealt with by the kings and their feudatories and governors.

1. Sengupta, *op. cit.*, pp. 313ff.
2. *Ibid.*, pp. 314, 318.

CHAPTER VII

ŚARABHAṄGA, VARṢAVARA AND DHARMĀDHIKĀRIN

I

Some Magi priests of ancient Iran are known to have migrated to and settled in India and became known as Maga Brāhmaṇas, also called Śākadvīpīya, i.e. 'hailing from Śākadvīpa'.[1] This Śākadvīpa can be roughly identified with modern Seistān in Eastern Iran, which was known respectively as Sakastān and Sijistān in the ancient and medieval periods.[2] The said people and those who accompanied them to India introduced a few words in the Indian vocabulary, one of them being the well-known Sanskrit word *mihira* (i. e. the sun or the Sun-god) which is the same as Persian *mihr* derived from Avestic *mithr* = Vedic *mitra*.[3] On some coins of the Kuṣāṇa kings Kaṇiṣka and Huviṣka, the Sun-god is represented on the reverse and the name of the deity is spelt in Greek characters as *Miiro* (also as *Miuro* and *Miioro*), i.e. *Mihira*,[4] the Greek alphabet having no *h*. The alternative spellings suggest that the word was also pronounced as *mihura* and *mihara*.

Similarly, the Scytho-Parthian rulers of the north-western regions of Bhāratavarṣa and their Kuṣāṇa successors, who came to our country from the west, introduced certain official designations in the Indian administrative system, some of which became popular with the indigenous Indian kings of various parts of Northern India. A few such designations are (1) *Gañjavara* (cf. *Gañjapati*), (2) *Dibira* or *Divira* (cf. *Divirapati*), and (3) *Pīlūpati* (cf. *Mahāpīlūpati*).

The designation Gañjavara, occurring in a Mathurā inscription[5] of the Śaka chief Śoḍāśa (c. 15-25 A. D.) and in Kalhaṇa's Kashmirian Chronicle[6] written about the middle

1. R. G. Bhandarkar's *Collected Works*, Vol. IV, pp. 218 ff. Cf. 'Brakhmanoi Magoi' near Mt. Bettigo (Malaya) in Ptolemy's Geography, VII. 1.74.
2. *Camb. Hist. Ind.*, Vol. I, p. 564.
3. R. G. Bhandarkar, *loc. cit.*
4. See *Select Inscriptions*, p. 142, note 6; p. 155, note 5.
5. *Ep. Ind.*, Vol. IX, p. 247.
6. *Rājataraṅgiṇī*, V. 177.

of the twelfth century A. D., is the same as Persian *Ganjwar* meaning 'a treasurer', derived from *ganj*, 'treasury'. The same designation occurs as *Gañjapati* in the Taleswar (Almora District, U. P.) plate[1] of Dyutivarman who flourished about the sixth century A. D. About the middle of the tenth century A. D., Utpala, in his commentary on Varāhamihira's *Bṛhatsaṁhitā* (LII. 13), explains *gañjaḥ* as *koṣa-bhavanam* (i. e. treasury).[2] The designation *Dibira* or *Divira*, which is found in such an early record as the Khoh plates[3] of king Jayanātha of Uccakalpa, dated 496 A. D., was explained by Bühler as 'a clerk, writer or accountant' on the authority of the *Lokaprakāśa* ascribed to Kṣemendra.[4] It is the same as Persian *Dabir* meaning 'a writer, a secretary'.[5] *Divirapati* also occurs in the Taleswar plate referred to above and often in the records of the Maitrakas of Valabhī from the latter part of the sixth century A. D.[6] In the designation *Pīlūpati* or *Mahāpīlūpati*, which occurs in such early records as the Abhona plates[7] of the Kalacuri king Śaṅkaragaṇa, dated 595-96 A. D., and the Taleswar plate referred to above, as well as in a large number of copper-plate grants issued by North Indian kings of the early medieval period,[8] the word *pīlū* is the same as Arabic-Persian *fīl* meaning 'an elephant'.[9] An inscription of Kalacuri Śaṅkaragaṇa's time spells the designation as *Mahāpalūpati*.[10]

II

The official designation *Śarabhaṅga-Sarabhaṅga-Sarobhaṅga* often occurs in the list of subordinates and officers addressed by

1. *Ep. Ind.*, Vol. XIII, p. 115.
2. Bhaṭṭa Utpala wrote his commentary on Varāhamihira's *Bṛhajjātaka* in 966 A. D.
3. *CII*, Vol. III, p. 122.
4. *Ind. Ant.*, Vol. VI, p. 10.
5. Wilson's Glossary, s. v. The *Rājataraṅgiṇī* (VIII. 131) makes a distinction between *Divira* and *Kāyastha* probably because the Kashmirian *Kāyastha* was primarily a tax-collector.
6. Cf. Bhandarkar's List, No. 1326, dated 588 A. D. ; etc.
7. *Ep. Ind.*, Vol. IX, p. 298.
8. Cf. N. G. Majumdar, *Ins. Beng.*, Vol. III, p. 186.
9. Wilson's Glossary, s. v.
10. *Ep. Ind.*, Vol. II, p. 22.

some of the kings of Northern India in respect of the grants of land recorded in their copper-plate charters. The difference in the spelling of the word is sometimes noticed even in the records of the same king. Thus, while the Nalanda plate[1] of king Devapāla (c. 810-54 A.D.) of Bengal and Bihar has Śarabhaṅga, the Monghyr plate[2] of the same king has *Sarabhaṅga.* A tenth century copper-plate inscription[3] of king Vidagdha of Chamba in the Himalayas , on the other hand, spells the word as *Sarobhaṅga.* This confusion about the spelling seems to indicate that the word is of foreign origin.

The meaning of *Śarabhaṅga-Sarabhaṅga-Sarobhaṅga* has not been satisfactorily determined, though unsuccessful attempts have been made to explain it on the basis of Sanskrit *śara* meaning 'an arrow' probably regarding the spelling *sara* as a mere mistake for *śara* and ignoring *saras* altogether. Thus it has sometimes been suggested that *Śarabhaṅga* means a superior military officer equipped with bows and arrows, although the word *bhaṅga* remains unexplained in this interpretation.[4] While editing the Pandukesvar (Garhwal District, U. P.) plates of about the tenth century A. D., we ourselves observed, "*Śarabhaṅga* literally means 'wound and fracture'. He was probably the royal surgeon."[5] It has also been conjectured that *Śarabhaṅga* may have something to do with *śarayantra* or *Śarayantrin*, the latter being a title conferred in Mithila upon a very learned man who successfully faced an ordeal (called *śarayantra*) of answering satisfactorily all questions on any *śāstra* put to him by learned *ācāryas* and common people.[6] But, as indicated above, the spelling of the first part of the designation variously as *śara*, *sara* and *saras* seems to suggest that the writers of the epigraphic records were struggling to find out a suitable Sanskrit word for a foreign expression. Indeed it has also to be noticed that no word like *Śarabhaṅga*, *Sarabhaṅga* and *Sarobhaṅga* occurs in any of the Sanskrit lexicons

1. *Ep. Ind.*, Vol. XVII, p. 321, text line 29.
2. *Ibid.*, Vol. XVIII, p. 306, text line 32.
3. Vogel, *Antiquities of Chamba State*, Part I, p. 166, text line 7.
4. Cf. *Ind. Cult.*, Vol. VII, p. 309.
5. *Ep. Ind.*, Vol. XXXI, p. 282, note 6.
6. Kane, *Hist. Dharm.*, Vol. III, p. 1005.

in the sense of an official designation and that it is also not known from any epigraphic record of a South Indian monarch.

It now appears to us that *Śarabhaṅga-Sarabhaṅga-Sarobhaṅga* was introduced into India by the foreign rulers of North-Western Bhāratavarṣa just as *Gañjavara, Divira* and *Pīlūpati* and that it is really an Indian modification of Persian *Sarhang* meaning 'a commander of forces'. *Sarhang* is derived from *sar* (Sanskrit *śiras*), 'the head', and Old Persian *haṅga* (Sanskrit *saṅgha*), 'a company', in the sense of 'the head of a contingent of troops'. The same expression is used as *Sarāṅgha* in the official designation *Giligittā-sarāṅgha*, 'the chief of the army at Gilgit', occurring in the Hatun (Gilgit) inscription[1] of the Ṣāhī king Paṭoladeva who flourished about the seventh century A. D. The *Sarāṅgha* of the Hatun inscription may also have been a military governor. The same designation is still found in some of the Indian dialects in the form *Serāng*.[2] Wilson's Glossary recognises Persian *Sarhang* = Indian *Serāng* and explains the designation as follows: "a commander; but generally applied in India to the headman of a native crew whether on board a ship or boat; also to the headman of a gang of natives attached to artillery, dragging guns, or to the army in general, as tent-pitchers and the like, or to the head of gangs of a superior order of labourers employed in public or private works, in docks, buildings, etc."[3]

III

The vast Indian subcontinent is known to be equal to Europe with all its countries but Russia, and the Hindu population is made of numeroues tribes belonging to different grades of civilization and to alien ethnic types. Even the earliest authorities on Smṛti therefore had to recognise dissimilar customs for different parts and peoples of India; cf., as for intance, Bodhāyana's opinion on cross-cousin marriage amongst the peoples of the Deccan.[4] The factor of local or tribal variation in the development of customs, the cross-currents of

1. *Ep. Ind.*, Vol. XXX, p. 228.
2. The Bengali spelling of the word is *Sāreṅg*.
3. See also *Hobson-Jobson*, s. v. *Serang*.
4. Sircar, *The Successors of the Sātavāhanas*, p. 13.

different cultures and the lack of requisite data make a study of the evolution of Hindu society exceptionally difficult; but there is evidence to show that the position of women in Hindu civilization was not the same in different parts of India in any period of history.

While commenting on the theory that the Pardah system was beginning to be popular with some royal families in India only about 300 A. D.,[1] we had occasion to refer to a few points indicating its earlier existence.[2] The derivative meaning of the word *orodhana*=*avarodhana* (literally, 'restraint') to signify the women's apartments in the households of Aśoka's brothers and sisters,[3] Kauṭilya's description of the royal *antaḥpura*[4] and Patañjali's reference to the *asūryampaśyāni mukhāni*, i. e., faces that have never viewed the sun,[5] prove that Pardah, especially in royal households at least in some parts of India, is certainly much earlier. As we know, Aśoka flourished in the third century B. C. and the works of Kauṭilya and Patañjali, even in their present form, are not later than the second century A. D.[6] It has also been pointed out that Chapters III-IV of Book III of the *Arthaśāstra* definitely prove the existence of strict Pardah even in ordinary families.[7] The above suggestion

1. A.S. Altekar, *The Position of Women in Hindu Civilization*, p. 200.
2. *Science and Culture*, September, 1940, p. 183.
3. See Rock Edict V; Sircar, *Select Inscriptions*, Vol. I, p. 24.
4. *Arthaśāstra*, I. 20.
5. *Vyākaraṇa-Mahābhāṣya*, 1. 1.6; 2.1.6.
6. *The Successors of the Sātavāhanas*, p. 356, note; *Ind. Hist. Quart.*, 1939, pp. 633ff.
7. A woman shall pay a fine of 6 *paṇas* for going out at day time to sports or to see a woman or spectacles; a fine of 12 *paṇas* if she goes to see another man or for sports (cf. Manu, IX.84). For the same offences committed at night, the fine shall be doubled. If a woman goes out while the husband is asleep or under intoxication, she shall be fined 12 *paṇas*. For holding conversation in suspicious places, whipping may be substituted for fines. In the centre of the village, a Caṇḍāla may whip such a woman five times on each side of the body. See Shama Sastry's trans., p. 177. If, on any excuse other than danger, a woman gets out of her husband's house, the fine will be 6 *paṇas*; if against the husband's order, 12 *paṇas*; if beyond the neighbour's house, 6 *paṇas*; if a neighbour is allowed into the house, 12 *paṇas*; if she behaves as above, though expressly forbidden, she shall be punished with the first amercement. If she goes out beyond the surrounding houses, the fine will be 24 *paṇas* (*ibid.*, p. 178). If she goes out to another village,

is further supported by the *Mahābhārata* which offers passages like 'closely watched in my (i. e. of a princess) dwelling and my father, the king, is a man of severe rule',[1] 'a deposit and a woman ought to be kept watch of',[2] 'there is no such thing as women's independence, because women are not independent; it is the opinion of the lord of creation that a woman is not fit for independence'.[3] There is also a significant description of one who passes through three different inner rooms of the palace before coming to the garden where there was a playground for the women.[4] Hopkins, who has very ably scrutinized the epic data, seems to be right when he says, "It was already a second nature for women to be kept at home, girl and wife, all her life... We know from Vedic times that the women had separate apartments, and the seclusion of the royal dames is a carrying out of this exclusion from the home of the man."[5]

Reference may here be made to an interesting institution which is intimately related to the question of the freedom as well as the position and prestige of women. This is the employment of eunuchs or emasculated persons as guards of royal harems. The Khwājah (emasculated) slaves are so often heard in connection with the harems of Indo-Muslim rulers that it is sometimes doubted if they were also employed by any king in ancient India. There is, however, evidence to show that eunuchs were employed as guards of royal harems in some parts of India from long before 300 A. D. The words indicating an emasulated attendant of the royal harem are *Varṣavara* (literally, *retapātasya vārakaḥ*; also *Varṣadhara* and *Varṣadharṣa*), *Ṣaṇḍha*, *Kṣattṛ*, etc. A few references are cited below.

(1) Men of eighty and women of fifty under the guise of father and mother, and aged persons and eunuchs (*Varṣavara*)

she will pay a fine of 12 *paṇas* and also lose her endowment and jewels. If, on any other ground than receiving her subsistence or *tīrtha-gamana* (pilgrimage, or intercourse with the husband after menses), she goes to any other place even in the company of an associable man, she will pay a fine of 24 *paṇas* and lose all kinds of social privileges. See *ibid.*, p. 179.

1. 3. 55. 21.
2. 13.41.26ff.
3. 13.19.61ff.
4. 12. 326. 31ff.
5. 'Social and Military Position of the Ruling Caste in Ancient India' in *JAOS*, Vol. XIII, p. 350.

shall not only ascertain purity and impurity in the life of the inmates of the harem, but also regulate the affairs as to be conducive to the happiness of the king.'[1]

(2) In connection with the story of sage Saubhari, reference is made to the *Kany-āntaḥpura-varṣavara* of the Ikṣvāku king Māndhātṛ. The eunuch was in charge of the dwelling where the king's daughter lived. He allowed the sage entrance only under the king's orders.[2] The *Bhāgavata Purāṇa* refers to the same story, but uses the word *Kṣattṛ*.[3]

(3) According to the *Viṣṇusaṁhitā*, a king should employ eunuchs (*Ṣaṇḍha*) to guard the women of his harem.[4]

(4) The words *ṣaṇḍha* and *varṣavara* are recognised in early lexicons as indicating attendants in a royal harem.[5] The second word in its Pāli form is recognised by Moggallāna.[6]

(5) In a play of the 7th century A. D., a monkey frightens the females of the royal harem, and the eunuchs (*Varṣavara*), who were not counted amongst men, shamelessly fled.[7]

IV

Monier-Williams' *Sanskrit-English Dictionary* (2nd ed., 1899) explains *Dharm-ādhikaraṇa*, in the neuter, as 'administration' or 'a court of Justice' and, in the masculine, as 'a judge or magistrate', etc., and refers us to the *Matsya Purāṇa*. It also explains *dharm-ādhikāra* as 'administration of laws' with reference to the *Abhijñānaśākuntala*, while *Dharmādhikārika* is explained as 'an administrator of justice' or 'a judge' and *Dharmādhyakṣa* as 'a judge', 'a magistrate', 'a minister of justice'. No distinction is therefore made between *Dharm-ādhikaraṇa* and *Dharmādhikārika*, though there is some evidence to show that there was a difference in the meanings of the two expressions.

It seems that Monier-Williams' views were partly influenced by the *Śabdakalpadruma* (1822-58) which explains

1. *Arthaśāstra*, 1.20; cf. XII. 5.
2. *Viṣṇu Purāṇa* (Vaṅgavāsī ed.), 4. 2. 28-29.
3. 9. 6. 43.
4. *Viṣṇusaṁhitā* (Vaṅgavāsī ed.), 3. 9.
5. *Amarakoṣa*, Kṣatriya-varga, 9.
6. *Abhidhānasappadīpikā* (1153 A. D.), 242.
7. *Ratnāvalī*, 2. 3.

dharm-ādhikaraṇa as 'a court of law' (neuter) and 'a judge' (masculine). The first of the two meanings is supported in this work by quoting the following stanza of Kātyāyana as found in the *Vīramitrodaya*—

dharmaśāstr-ānusāreṇa arthaśāstra-nirūpaṇam/
yatr=ādhikriyate sthāne dharm-ādhikaraṇaṁ hi tat //

Another stanza, apparently from the *Matsya Purāṇa*, has also been quoted in the same connection, and the verse runs as follows—

puruṣ-āntara-tattvajñāḥ prāṁśavaś=c=āpy=a-lolupāḥ/
dharm-ādhikaraṇe kāryā jan-āhvāna-karā narāḥ //

"Those who are tall and not greedy and know the minds of others should be made callers of persons at the *dharmādhikaraṇa* or court of law." Unfortunately, it is difficult to understand why the caller of persons at the law-court was required to be capable of reading the minds of others and also be free from greediness. It seems therefore that there is some error in the quotation of the second half of the verse.

The *Śabdakalpadruma* further says that *Dharmādhikaraṇa* (masculine) or a judge is the same as *Dharmādhyakṣa* and quotes the following stanza from the *Matsya Purāṇa*, Chapter 189, enumerating the qualifications of the officer—

Samaḥ śatrau ca mitre ca sarva-śāstra-viśāradaḥ /
vipra-mukhyaḥ kulīnaś=ca Dharm-ādhikaraṇo bhavet //

"The *Dharmādhikaraṇa* (masculine) should be a prominent Brāhmaṇa of a respectable family, who is an adept in all the scriptures and is impartial to friend and foe."

This is verse 24 of Chapter 215 in the printed texts of the *Matsya Purāṇa*, in which we usually get the reading *Dharm-ādhikaraṇī* for *Dharmādhikaraṇo*, and that seems to be a better reading. Thus what has been said about *Dharmādhikaraṇa* in the *Śabdakalpadruma* (and Monier-Williams' *Sanskrit-English Dictionary*) on the strength of the above-quoted stanza may be due to misreading, and the qualifications enumerated may relate really to the *Dharmādhikaraṇin* and not to the *Dharmādhikaraṇa* (masculine). It is, however, not our plea that *Dharm-ādhikaraṇa* cannot be used as a synonym of *Dharmādhikaraṇin*.

What we mean is that the views of the *Śabdakalpadruma* and Monier-Williams' *Dictionary* may be based on the misreading of a word in the *Matsya Purāṇa*, 215. 24.

Moreover, the interpretation of *Dharmādhikārika* (*Dharmādhikārin*) as the same as *Dharmādhyakṣa*, *Dharmādhikaraṇika* (*Dharmādhikaraṇin*), etc., in the sense of 'an administrator of justice' or 'a judge' does not appear to be quite accurate.

In the *Abhijñānaśākuntala* (Act I), king Duṣyanta, in explaining his presence at Kaṇva's hermitage, represents himself to Śakuntalā and her friends as an officer of the Paurava king, who was employed in the *dharmādhikāra* and visited the holy forest inhabited by the hermits, in order to know if the religious rights of the sages were being performed without hindrance—*yaḥ Pauraveṇa rājñā dharmādhikāre niyuktaḥ so='ham=a-vighnakriy-opalambhāya dharmāraṇyam=idam=āyātaḥ*. On getting this information, a friend of Śakuntalā observes that the presence of the officer there indeed provided the performers of religious rites with a protector—*sa-nāthā idānīṁ dharmacāriṇaḥ*. This would suggest that the *Dharmādhikārin*, the same as *dharmādhikāre niyukta* of this text, was a superintendent of the Department of Religious Affairs rather than a judge.

That the *Dharmādhikaraṇin* (or *Dharmādhikaraṇa*) was different from the *Dharmādhikārin* is clearly indicated by the *Matsya Purāṇa* which not only deals with the qualifications of the two officers separately, but even enumerates other officers in an intervening section. Thus we have the following lines in the *Matsya Purāṇa*. 215, 24 ff.—

samaḥ śatrau ca mitre ca dharma-śāstra-viśāradaḥ |
vipra-mukhyaḥ kulīnaś=ca Dharmādhikaraṇī (or *ṇo*) *bhavet* ||
kāryās=tathāvidhās=tatra dvija-mukhyāḥ Sabhāsadaḥ ||
sarva-deś-ākṣar-ābhijñaḥ sarva-śāstra-viśāradaḥ |
Lekhakaḥ kathito rājñaḥ sarv-ādhikaraṇeṣu vai ||
Śīrṣ-opetān susampūrṇān sama-śreṇi-gatān samān |
āntarān vai likhed=yas=tu Lekhakaḥ sa varaḥ smṛtaḥ ||
upāya-vākya-kuśalaḥ sarva-śāstra-viśāradaḥ |
bahv-artha-vaktā c=ālpena Lekhakaḥ syān=nṛpottama ||
puruṣ-āntara-tattvajñāḥ prāṁśavaś=c=āpy=a-lolupāḥ |
Dharm-ādhikāriṇaḥ kāryā janā dānakarā narāḥ ||
evaṁvidhās=tathā kāryā rājñā Dauvārikā janāḥ ||

It will be seen that the qualifications of the *Dharmādhikaraṇin* (or *Dharmādhikaraṇa*) are separated from those of the *Dharmādhikārin* by the intervening description of the *Sabhāsad* and *Lekhaka*, so that they have to be regarded as separate officers. We have noticed that the *Śabda Kalpadruma* reads the line *Dharmādhikāriṇaḥ kāryā janā dānakarā narāḥ* as *dharmādhikaraṇe kāryā jan-āhvānakarā narāḥ* probably from a corrupt text of the Purāṇa. It may be pointed out that the qualifications of the *Dharmādhikārin* were the same as those of the *Dauvārika*, 'gatekeeper'. This, however, does not support the reading of the verse as quoted in the *Śabdakalpadruma*, because the *Dauvārika* or *Pratīhāra*, who was in charge of the gates of the royal palace or the capital or the cities and was often engaged in the collection of tolls, was not a petty official. The chief officer of this class, viz. the *Mahāpratīhāra*, who attended on the king even when the latter was relaxing, was not far below the Prime Minister or Commander-in- chief in rank. The occurrence of the expression *sarva-śāstra-viśāradaḥ* in two different stanzas in the description of the *Lekhaka* may be a copyists' error or due to the fact that the Purāṇa adopted the verses from two separate sources.

The epithet *dānakara* applied to the person qualified to become a *Dharmādhikārin* suggests that he was in charge of the king's *dāna-dharma* or charities, while we have seen above that he was a superintendent in the Department of Religious Affairs. Thus the king's charities formed a branch of the said Department; but whether the officer had any judicial function like the *Sadrus-Sudur* of the Muslim administration of medieval India is difficult to determine. The *Sadr,* whose function is understood as that of a civil judge, maintained the list of rent-free lands and the amounts of daily allowances to pious men, scholars and hermits, supervised the endowments created by the king and princes and saw that the money was rightly applied to the purposes for which the grants were made. He also noted the deaths of recipients and scrutinized the applications for fresh grants, and was sometimes empowered to try civil cases. The duty of the Chief *Sadr,* called *Sadr-us-Sudur*, *Sadr-i- jahān* or *Sadr-i-kul,* was to appoint *Sadrs* in the provinces. The Mughul emperors distributed their charities through this officer who was their chief almoner in charge of the distribution of large sums of money during court ceremonies and in the month of Ramadān and also tried civil suits and heard appeals when empowered to do so.[1]

The *Dharmādhikārin*, mentioned in some early records,[2] is apparently the same as the *Dharma-mahāmātra* of Aśoka's edicts[3] and *Dharmādhyakṣa*, *Dharmapradhāna*, *Dharmakarm-ādhikārin*, etc., of later inscriptions though sometimes the word *mahā* was prefixed to the official designations.[4] The epithet *dharm-ādhikār-ārpita*, applied to a royal officer in the Kamauli plate[5] of Vaidyadeva, refers apparently to the same officer and reminds us of the expression *dharm-ādhikāre niyukta* in the *Abhijñānaśākuntala* quoted above.

Halāyudha's *Brāhmaṇasarvasva* describes the author as the recipient of the *dharm-ādhikāra* from king Lakṣmaṇasena of Gauḍa and also as *Dharmādhyakṣa*, *Mahādharmādhyakṣa*, *Dharma-kośādhikārin*, *Dharmāgār-ādhikārin*, *Dharm-ādhikṛta* and *Mahā dharm-ādhikārin*, while his father is likewise described as *Dharmādhyakṣa* and *Dharm-ādhikārika*.[6] Nāryāyaṇ-opādhyāya's *Pariśiṣṭaprakāśa* speaks of the prosperity of the Brāhmaṇas when the author's father was in charge of the *dharm-ādhikāra*.[7]

As seen above, *dharm-ādhikāra* means the Department of Religious Affairs, of which the king's charities formed a branch. But there are a few cases where this meaning of the expression does not appear to be quite suitable. In the Nalanda plate of Devapāla, the illustrious Balavarman is stated to have served as the *Dūta* 'in the *dharm-ādhikāra* in question'— *dūtyaṁ śrī-Balavarmā vidadhe dharm-ādhikāre='smin.*[8] The use of the word *asmin* in relation to *dharmādhikāre* would suggest that the particular grant of the king, of which Balavarman acted as the *Dūtaka*, has been called here a *dharm-ādhikāra* or a subject relating to *dharma* (religious merit). Similarly, the passage *yuktatayā dharmādhikāra-buddhyā vijñāpitam* in one of the Dāmo-

1. See Wahed Husain, *Administration of Justice during the Muslim Rule in India*, pp. 64-65.
2. *Ep.*, *Ind.*, Vol. XXXIII, p. 151.
3. *CII*, Vol. I, 1925, pp. 8 ff., etc.
4. *Ep. Ind.*, Vol. XV, p. 283; *CII*, Vol. IV, pp. 326, 539, etc.
5. Maitreya, *Gauḍalekhamālā*, p. 136, line 68.
6. D. Bhattacharya, *Halāyudha's Brāhmaṇasarvasva*, pp. xviff.
7. *Loc. cit.*
8. *Ep. Ind.*, Vol. XVII, p. 323.
9. Sircar, *Select Inscriptions*, p. 339; *Ep. Ind.*, Vol. XV, p. 143.

darpur copper-plate grants seems to mean that an application was properly made with the intention of *dharm-ādhikāra*, i. e. for making a religious gift of the land purchased from the State. In both these cases, the expression *dharm-ādhikāra* appears to mean 'a ceremonial gift' which of course fell under the jurisdiction of the Department of Religious Affairs, also called *dharm-ādhikāra*.

Although most writers, excepting G. Bühler and D. Bhattacharya, appear to have misunderstood the function of the *Dharmādhikārin*,[1] some of them have even added to the confusion. Thus P. V. Kane's statement that the *Purohita's* function came to be exercised by the *Dharmādhyakṣa* or *Dharm-ādhikaraṇika*[2] not only regards *Dharmādhyakṣa* and *Dharmādhikaraṇika* as the same, but even considers the *Purohita* as identical with the said officer. We have seen above that the function of the *Dharmādhyakṣa* (*Dharmādhikārin*) was not really the same as that of the *Dharm-ādhikaraṇika*, while the *Purohita* (*Mahāpurohita*) and *Dharmādhyakṣa* (*Mahādharmādhyakṣa*) are known to occupy separate positions in the list of royal officers in numerous inscriptions.[3] V. V. Mirashi likewise regards the *Mahādharmādhikaraṇika* or *Mahāpurohita* as the Head of the Religious Department.[4]

1. *History of Bengal*, Vol. I, ed. R. C. Majumdar, pp. 278, 281; B. C. Sen, *Some Historical Aspects of the Inscriptions of Bengal*, pp. 548, 551; etc.

2. *History of Dharmaśāstra*, Vol III, p. 126.

3. Cf. the grants of the Candras and Senas in N.G. Majumdar's *Inscriptions of Bengal*, Vol. III.

4. *CII*, Vol. IV, p. cxlii.

CHAPTER VIII

THEFT AND ROBBERY

I

While discussing the condition of India during the age of Candragupta Maurya, Smith in his *Early History of India*, 1924, p. 137, observes, "The general honesty of the people and the efficient administration of the criminal law are both attested by the observation, recorded by Magasthenes, that while he resided in Candragupta's camp, containing 400,000 persons, the total of the thefts reported in any one day did not exceed two hundred Drachmai or about eight pounds sterling (roughly about Rs. 144 of the present time). When crime did occur, it was repressed with terrible severity."

The evidence of Megasthenes in regard to the severe punishment for theft is perfectly borne out by early Indian literature. It should, however, be noticed that the views of ancient Indian writers on law were not uniform on all points raised in this connection apparently because customs varied in different areas and possibly also in different ages. There was, again, the question of innovations introduced in the handling of cases. The story of Apahāravarman in Daṇḍin's *Daśakumāracarita* (Ch. II) records a tradition of such an innovation introduced by the Maurya kings. According to it, a king ordered the death of a merchant in a case of theft involving a prostitute; but it was pointed out that, according to a privilege granted by the Mauryas to the merchants, the punishment for the offence in question was not death (as must have originally been the case), but confiscation of property and banishment from the kingdom.[1]

Steya (theft including robbery) is regarded by Manu (XI.55) as one of the *pañca-mahāpātaka* or five great sins or heinous crimes, the other four being killing a Brāhmaṇa, drinking wine, adulterous intercourse with the wife of one's father,

1. Jivananda's ed., 1889, p. 135—*Maurya-datta eṣa varo vaṇijām=īdṛśeṣv=aparādheṣu n=āsti asubhir=abhiyogo yadi kupito='si hṛta-sarvasvo nirvāsanīyaḥ pāpa eṣa iti.* See below; also *Early Indian Trade and Industry*, ed. Sircar, pp. 92ff.

teacher, etc., and association with persons who have committed any of the above crimes. Nārada similarly includes theft in his list of the ten major crimes, viz., violation of a royal command, murder of a woman, mixing of castes, adultery, theft, pregnancy as the result of criminal intercourse, verbal injury, gross abuse, real injury and abortion of the embryo.[1]

Sometimes *steya* or theft is distinguished from *sāhasa* or violence;[2] but usually the former is included in the latter. Nārada (XVII.17), who defines *steya* as 'deprivation of wealth by various means from people who are asleep, careless or intoxicated', possibly means theft without violence; but Kātyāyana who defines it as 'depriving a man of his wealth either clandestinely or openly and either by night or by day' clearly includes cases of robbery.[3] Nārada (XIV.2-6) enumerates four kinds of *sāhasa* of which theft or robbery is one, the other three classes being man-slaughter, violence to the wives of others and abuse and assault. Theft is sometimes divided into three classes according to the value of the things stolen, viz. trifling, middling and grave or high.[4] Thieves are said to be either open or secret.[5] The open or patent thieves are described as traders employing false weights and balances, gamblers, quacks, bribers of the courtiers, prostitutes, manufacturers of imitation articles, false witnesses, people living on prognostication, magic or palmistry, and others.[6] Judges who

1 Cf. Jolly, *Hindu Law and Custom*, p. 268.

2 Cf. Manu, VIII. 332; Kauṭilya, III. 17; Nārada, XVII. 12; etc.

3 Cf. *pracchannaṁ vā prakāśaṁ vā niśāyām=athavā divā / yat=para-dravya-haraṇaṁ steyaṁ tat=parikīrtitam //*

See Kane, *History of Dharmaśāstra*, Vol. III, p. 519, note 948 b.

No difference is made between theft and robbery so far as punishment is concerned, while participation in the crime, abetting of every kind and refusing to render help are regarded as equally criminal. See Jolly, *op. cit.*, p. 273; Nārada, XIV.12, 19f.; Yājñavalkya, II. 276; etc.

4 See Nārada, XVII. 13-16; cf. Yājñavalkya, II. 275. When earthenware, seats, cots, wood, hides, grass, beans in pods and cooked food, etc., were stolen, the theft was regarded as trifling; it was middling when it related to clothes except silken ones, animals except cows and bulls, metals except gold, rice, barley, etc., and grave in cases involving gold, jewels, silken cloth, women, men, cattle, elephants, horses, property of Brāhmaṇas and temples; etc.

5 Manu, IX. 256; also Bṛhaspati quoted by Kane, *op. cit.*, p. 520, note 949.

6 Cf. Manu, IX. 258-60; also Nārada (Pariśiṣṭa, 2-3) and Bṛhaspati (*SBE.*, Vol. XXXIII, p. 360, verses 3-4).

take bribes and give wrong decisions and people deceiving others by betraying the trust imposed in them were also regarded as patent thieves. Thus cheating of all kinds is included in theft. The secret thieves are said to be those who move about with tools for house-breaking. They are classified as follows: those who quietly relieve one of his money when the latter is attending to something else, house-breakers, highway robbers, cut-purses and those who kidnap a woman or a man, cattle, horses and other animals.[1]

Although *steya* is thus included in *sāhasa*, often the two subjects are dealt with separately by ancient and medieval writers on Indian law, many of whom regarded theft with violence to be a greater sin or crime than theft without violence. Most of these writers enjoin upon the king not to tolerate, for a moment, a person guilty of violence.

II

It is interesting to note that theft was learnt by the professional thieves of ancient India as a science.[2] There were no doubt some text-books on the subject, although none of them has survived. But references in old works such as the *Mṛcchakaṭika* (sixth century), *Kādambarī* (seventh century), *Daśakumāracarita* (seventh century), etc., help us in forming an idea about them.

The goddess Kālī is known to have been the favourite deity worshipped by the dacoits, particularly of Eastern India, in the late medieval period.[3] But the thieves of ancient India were especially devoted to the god Skanda-Kārttikeya and regarded themselves as the god's sons. Some scholars think that there was a sage named Kanakaśakti who composed a work on the principles to be learnt by thieves and that he was an incarnation of the god Skanda-Kārttikeya and was especially venerated by the thieves of ancient India. There were

1 See Jolly, *op. cit.*, pp. 271-72.

2 Trained thieves were maintained by the kings for helping their army in harassing the enemies' territories in the company of the foresters. See below; *Mahābhārata*, XII. 59.48.

3 Cf. Bengali *Dākāte-Kālī* in J.M. Das's *Bāṅgālābhāṣār Abhidhān*, s.v. *Kālī*.

other teachers well-versed in the science of theft. Two such masters known to us were Bhāskaranandin and Yogācārya.[1] Bāṇa-bhaṭṭa's *Kādambarī* mentions Karṇīsuta, who was the famous author of a thieves' manual and was also called Karaṭaka, as having Vipula and Acala as his friends and Śaśa, as his advisor.[2]

The story of the *Daśakumāracarita* refers to the same Karṇīsuta and speaks of the following necessities and appliances of a thief: (1) an especially dark night, (2) dark-blue clothes including a covering piece of the same colour (3) a sharp sword, (4) an instrument called Phaṇimukha (literally 'snake-mouth') for digging purposes, (5) a knife, (6) a pair of tongs for taking out wedges, etc., strongly stuck up, (7) a 'man's head' made of wood or other materials to be pushed into a room through the hole made by the thief in its wall or foundation to determine whether the inmates were asleep,[3] (8) some magic powder believed to cause sound sleep if applied to a person, (9) a magic candle, (10) a measuring rope to determine the size of the hole to be made in the wall or foundation of a room, (11) an instrument called 'the crab', (12) a rope for climbing to or getting down from upper stories of buildings, (13) a lamp, (14) a small box containing black bees to be used for putting out lights, etc.[4] The *Mṛcchakaṭika* illustrates the use of some

1 See *Mṛcchakaṭika*, III. Cf. *namo varadāya Kumāra-Kārttikeyāya, namaḥ Kanakaśaktaye Brahmaṇyadevāya devavratāya, namo Bhāskaranandine, namo Yagācāryāya yasy=āhaṁ prathamaḥ śiṣyaḥ* (Haridas Siddhantavagisa's ed., p. 217, with commentary). Kanakaśakti and Brahmaṇyadeva, however, may be regarded as the names of Kārttikeya. But, in such a case, the passage *iha khalu bhagavatā Kanakaśaktinā caturvidhaḥ sandhy-upāyo darśitaḥ* would allude to a book ascribed to the god.

2 See Siddhantavagisa's ed., p. 63, with commentary. Cf. *Karṇīsutaḥ Karaṭakaḥ steyaśāstra-pravartakaḥ / tasya khyātau sakhāyau dvau Vipul-Ācala-saṁjñitau // Śaśo mantrivaras=tasya*, etc., ascribed to the *Bṛhatkathā*. Karṇīsuta Karaṭaka is said to have been a Kṣatriya.

3 It is mentioned in a medieval Telugu inscription as *poytala* or 'false head' which is stated to have been a thief's appliance (*JAHRS*, Vol. XXVII, p. 27).

4 Cf. *op. cit.*. pp. 109 ff. (p. 111—*Dhurjaṭi-kaṇṭha-kalmāṣa-kālatame tamasi nīla-nivasan-ārdhoruka-parihito baddha-tīkṣṇa-kaukṣeyakaḥ phaṇimukha-kākalī-sandaṁśaka-puruṣaśīrṣa-yogacūrṇa-yogavarttikā-mānasūtra-karkaṭaka-rajju-dīpa-bhājana-bhramarakaraṇḍaka-prabhṛty-anek-opakaraṇa-yukto*, etc.). Cf. *Karṇīsutaḥ Karaṭakaḥ steya-śāstrasya kārakaḥ* quoted from the *Vaijayantī* in Jivananda's commentary.

of the appliances in the description of a theft committed by an imaginary Brāhmaṇa thief named Śarvilaka.

Śarvilaka makes, with the help of 'his training and strength', a passage, wide enough to admit just the breadth of his body, in the outer wall of the house of the poor Brāhmaṇa merchant Cārudatta at a place where the wall is shaded by some trees. He then creeps through the passage like a snake and enters into the house. Just then the moon sets and Śarvilaka is very glad at the prospect of the darkness giving a hiding place for him, 'a unique warrior bent on despoiling other men's houses' and betraying by his movements 'a dread for the king's policemen'.

As to his profession, Śarvilaka thinks (apparently after some work on theft), "I admit that men call this a mean act and it is indeed theft, and no deed of valour, which thrives on another man's sleep and inflicts on a confiding person the calamity of loss of property. Condemnable as the position is, being independent, I prefer it to a servile submission to others and this after all was the course adopted by Droṇa's son Aśvatthāman in days gone by when the sleeping princes were assassinated."

Now Śarvilaka thinks of the place suitable for making a hole in Cārudatta's room. Here also he thinks after the teaching of the masters of the science of theft : "Which is the spot where the earth has become loose by falling water, so that it would make no sound ? What is the spot again where an opening in the walls will be large and yet not prominent in sight? Where has the house become dilapidated, the earth having been washed away and corroded by damp ? Where is it that I may not encounter a woman (so that I may think of nothing but stealing) and gain my purpose ?" Śarvilaka then feels the walls and finds a place where the earth has deteriorated and is eaten by damp 'being daily sprinkled with water in connection with the worship of the Sun-god'. He also finds there earth dug up by rats and thinks that his success is assured.

Śarvilaka now thinks of the kind of opening that he should make and remembers that *Bhagavat* Kanakaśakti speaks of four different ways of making a passage : "Thus, for instance, pulling out in the case of baked bricks, cutting to pieces in the case of unbaked ones, wetting in the case of blocks of earth, and splitting in the case of wooden ones." As the room in question is made of baked bricks, pulling them out is considered to be the appropriate procedure. Then Śarvilaka quotes an authority (possibly Kanakaśakti) saying, "The opening may be expansive like a lotus, or shaped like the sun or the crescent moon, or might be extensive like a well, or the *svastika* or the auspicious water-jar." The 'auspicious jar' type is considered suitable in the case of baked bricks and Śarvilaka begins to show his art 'which, when men of the town see it tomorrow, will fill them with wonder'. He wants to bore holes of different designs so that the people of the neighbourhood next day may condemn his crime, but praise his skill.

Now Śarvilaka bows down to the god Kumāra-Kārttikeya, to the sage Kanakaśakti, incarnation of the god, to Bhāskaranandin and to his preceptor Yogācārya. From the last-named the thief is said to have received a magic ointment. He believes that, if his body is anointed with it, the policemen would not see him nor any weapon could make a wound in his body. Śarvilaka now discovers that he has not brought with him his measuring rope, but is glad to discover that his sacred thread may be a substitute. He quotes a verse enumerating the benefits a Brāhmaṇa like himself may derive from the sacred thread : "With this he measures out a passage for his activity in the wall. With this he can unloosen the fastenings of ornaments. When the door is securely locked, this can open it; and it serves as a tourniquet when he is bitten by insects or snakes." This quotation from a manual on theft explains the uses of the measuring rope to the thieves.

After finishing the opening, Śarvilaka notices that a light is burning inside the room. He shows his dummy in and, as there is no reaction from the inmates, thinks that there is none inside. Then he bows again to the god Kārttikeya and enters the room. It is now found that two persons (Cārudatta and his friend Maitreya) are sleeping in the room. Śarvilaka wants to open the door as a defensive measure; but, the house being very old, the door squeaks. He then sprinkles some water on the door and opens it without noise. Next he goes near the sleeping men and makes frightening gestures to know if they are really asleep or are feigning. In this connection Śarvilaka quotes (probably from a work on theft) a verse saying, "The breathing of this man is free from all fear and quite easy; apparently he is in the midst of a dream. His eyes are completely closed. There is no strained effect and no movement inside. The body lies at ease, all joints being relaxed, and is extended beyond the measure of the bed; and further, if it had been feigned sleep, he would not have tolerated a lamp in front of him."

To know whether there is any wealth hidden underneath the ground, Śarvilaka now scatters some magic seeds. It was believed that the seeds, falling on a place beneath the surface of which there was hidden wealth, would grow bigger in size. But as the seeds scattered by Śarvilaka do not become bigger anywhere in the room, he concludes that there is no hidden wealth. In the meantime Maitreya talks in his sleep and Śarvilaka thinks, "Can it be that he knows that I have entered and is he laughing at me in the full confidence of his poverty ? Shall I kill him then, or has he a light brain that makes him talk in his sleep ?" Then he notices that there are some ornaments tied in a threadbare bath-towel in Maitreya's hand. Śarvilaka wants to take the ornaments and, as the lamp is burning, he sets the fire-moth (*āgneya-kīṭa*, named by him Bhadrapīṭha), which he is carrying, on the lamp. Soon the moth released by Śarvilaka gains the lamp, hovers over it in various circles and extinguishes it with the breeze of its wings. The thief then makes his fingers warm by putting them in his arm-pit, stealthily takes the ornaments and goes out.

III

Crimes against property were investigated very energetically as early as the Vedic age. In the *Ṛgveda* (VI.45.1), there is reference to an act of stealing cattle as well as to a class of spies forming a part of the ancient Indian police system. These spies, experienced in tracking the marks of feet and hoofs, were also known to the writers of the Smṛtis.[1] When cattle and other properties were lost, the spies were to trace the track upto its starting point. The inhabitants, headmen and proprietors of the village or meadow in question had to make the required compensation excepting when they could prove that the track

1 Jolly, *op. cit.*, p. 270.

went further out of that place. The possession of stolen property or a foot-mark was regarded as sure proof of guilt.[1]

Yājñvalkya (II. 266-68) and Nārada (Pariśiṣṭa, 9-12) indicate the various ways in which thieves may be detected and caught by the police officers; but Kauṭilya's treatment (IV. 6) of the subject is more elaborate. According to this authority, when measures taken by the spies under the guise of prophets, etc., failed, the police had to take steps as were suggested by suspicious movements of particular persons of the locality concerned. The list of persons of suspicious character included the following catergories : (1) persons whose family subsists on slender means of inheritance, (2) who have little or no comfort, (3) who frequently change their residence, caste and the names not only of themselves but also of their family, (4) who conceal their own avocation and calls, (5) who have betaken themselves to such luxurious mode of life as eating flesh and condiments, drinking liquor, and using scents, garlands, fine dress and jewels, (6) who have been squandering away their money, (7) who constantly move with profligate women, gamblers or vintners, (8) who frequently leave their residence, (9) whose commercial transaction, journey or destination is difficult to understand, (10) who travel alone in such solitary places as forests and mountainous tracts, (11) who hold secret meetings in lonely places near to or far from their residence, (12) who hurry on to get their fresh wounds or boils cured, (13) who always hide themselves in the interior of their house, (14) who are excessively attached to women, (15) who are always inquisitive to gather information as to the women and property of others, (16) who

1 *Ibid.*, 272; Nārada, XIV. 22ff., Pari. 16-18; Yājñavalkya, II. 271f. According to Kauṭilya, the thief had to restore the property stolen or its price; but, if the thief could not be traced, the officers and wardens of the country had to pay the price of the stolen articles. If the thief's footsteps were not traced as going out of the village, the property stolen in it had to be made good by the headman of the village. If the theft took place in a pasture-land or forest and the thief was not found out, the owner of it was made to pay. When the theft was committed on a road, the police officers were compelled to pay. Sometimes a whole village was made to pay compensation when the theft was committed outside the residential quarters, but the footsteps of the thief were not traced as going out of the village. When a theft took place one *krośa* from a village, the surrounding five or ten villages could be made to pay the compensation. According to Viṣṇu (VI. 367, etc.), the king is personally liable to make good the loss if the thieves cannot be caught.

associate themselves with men of condemnable learning and activity, (17) who loiter in the dark behind walls or under shades, (18) who purchase rare or suspicious articles in suspicious times and places, (19) who are known for their inimical dealings, (20) whose caste and avocation are very low, (21) who keep false appearances or put on different caste signs, (22) who change their ancestral customs under false excuses, (23) whose notoriety is already marked, (24) who, though in charge of villages, are terribly afraid of appearing before the prime minister and conceal themselves or go elsewhere, (25) who pant in fear while sitting alone, (26) who show undue agitation or palpitation of heart, (27) whose face is pale and dry while the voice is indistinct and stammering, (28) who always move in company with armed men, and (29) who keep threatening appearance. According to Kauṭilya, these and similar other persons may be suspected to be murderers or robbers or offenders guilty of misappropriation of treasure-troves or deposits or to be any other kind of knaves subsisting by foul means secretly employed.

Information regarding lost or stolen articles had to be given by the police to persons who trade in similar articles. Traders who concealed such articles after receiving information were condemned as abettors. But if they were unaware of the loss of the articles, they could be acquitted after restoring them. No person was allowed to mortgage or purchase an old or second-hand article without giving information to the Superintendent of Commerce or of the Police. On receiving information regarding the mortgage or sale of such an article, the Superintendent asked the informant as to how the person came by it. The latter might plead that the article in question was borrowed or hired or purchased or was a pledge or a sealed deposit or one obtained for sale or as a present. If he could prove his case with the help of referees or witnesses, he was let off.[1]

To determine whether a theft was committed by internal or external agencies, the following circumstances were carefully considered : (1) entrance and exit not effected through the doors, (2) breaking the door by means of special contrivances, (3) breaking the window or pulling off the roof in houses containing upstairs, (4) breaking the wall, (5) tunnelling, (6) contri-

1 Kauṭilya's *Arthaśāstra*, trans. Shamasastry, pp. 242-43.

vances as are necessary to carry off secretly hoarded treasure, information about which could be gathered only from internal sources, and (7) other accessory circumstances of wear and tear cognisable in the interior of the house. A blending of the two kinds of circumstances was thought to indicate the association of both internal and external agencies.[1]

Kauṭilya quotes another list of suspects in regard to theft believed to be the work of internal agencies : (1) a person of miserable appearance, associated with rogues or thieves. and possessed of instruments necessary for theft, (2) a woman who is born of a poor family or has placed her affections elsewhere, (3) servants of similar condemnable character, (4) a person suffering from too much sleep or sleeplessness, (5) one who shows signs of fatigue or whose face is pale and dry, with voice stammering and indistinct, and who may be watching the movements of others or bewailing too much, (6) a person whose body bears the signs of scaling heights, (7) one whose body appears to have been scratched or wounded with dress torn off, (8) a person whose legs and hands bear the signs of rubbing and scratching, (9) a person whose hair and nails are full of dirt or are freshly broken, (10)one who has just bathed and daubed his body with sandal, (11) a person who has smeared his body with oil or has just washed his hands and legs, (12) one whose footprints can be identified with those found near the house, (13) one parts of whose garlands, sandal-marks or dress can be identified with those in or near the house, and (14) a person, the smell of whose sweat or drink can be ascertained from his garments thrown out in or near the house. According to Kauṭilya, the Superintendent of the City Police tried to detect internal thieves inside fortified towns, while officers called *Pradeṣṭṛ* (Police Commissioner), with their retinue of *Gopas* (Superintendents of Rural Police) and *Sthānikas* (Officers in charge of police outposts) took steps to find out external thieves.[2]

Torture was allowed to elicit confession;[3] but care was

1 *Ibid.*, p. 244.

2 *Ibid.*, pp. 244-45.

3 Kauṭilya (IV. 8) says, "Those whose guilt is believed to be true shall be subjected to torture, but not women who are carrying or have not passed a month after delivery. Torture of women shall be half of the prescribed standard. Or women with no exception may be subjected to cross-

taken to find out whether a person was really guilty, before inflicting punishment on him. Kauṭilya says, "Guilt against a suspected person shall be established by the production of such evidences as the instruments made use of by the accused, his accomplices or abettors, the stolen article and any middlemen involved in selling or purchasing the stolen article. The validity of the above evidence shall also be tested with reference to both the scene of the theft and the circumstances connected with the possession and distribution of the stolen article. When there are no such evidences and when the accused is wailing much, he shall be regarded as innocent. For owing to one's accidental presence on the scene of theft or to one's accidental resemblance to the real thief in respect of his appearance, his dress or his weapons or possession of articles similar to those stolen or owing to one's presence near the stolen articles, as in the case of Māṇḍavya who, under the fear of torture, admitted himself to be the thief, one, though innocent, is often seized as a thief. Hence punishment shall be meted out only when the charge is quite established against the accused."[1]

The same authority further says, "Persons, who charge an innocent man with theft or conceal a thief, shall themselves be liable to the punishment for theft. When a person accused of theft proves in his defence the complainant's enmity or hatred towards himself, he shall be acquitted. Any person who keeps an innocent man in confinement shall pay a fine between 48 and 96 silver coins."[2] But when a person was seized on suspicion, he could not be acquitted on mere denial of the offence, but had to prove his innocence by evidence or ordeal.[3]

IV

There is an interesting story in the *Harivaṁśa*, *Viṣṇu Purāṇa* and some other later works,[4] which show that some of the

examination." He gives a list of persons who could not be subjected to torture. Cf. Shamasastry, *op. cit.*, p. 249; cf. p. 248.

1 *Ibid.*, p. 248.

2 *Loc. cit.*

3 Yājñavalkya, II. 269; Kane, *op. cit.*, p. 521.

4 *Harivaṁśa*, I. 38; *Viṣṇu Purāṇa*, IV. 13; *Brahma Purāṇa*, XVI; *Liṅga Purāṇa*, LXIX; *Skanda Purāṇa*, Prabhāsa-khaṇḍa, Prabhāsa, CCXXXIX; *Bhāgavata Purāṇa*, X. 56-57.

modern detective methods were often employed in ancient India to ascertain the truth.

Kṛṣṇa-Vāsudeva was the President of the Yādava republic. A chief named Satrājit, belonging to the Sātvata clan which was a branch of the Yadu or Yādava tribe, was the celebrated owner of an exceptionally valuable gem called Syāmantaka. Kṛṣṇa expressed his desire to possess that gem; but Satrājit was unwilling to part with his invaluable possession. Sometime later, Satrājit gave the gem to his younger brother Prasena who fixed it in his necklace. One day Prasena went out on a hunt and was heard of no more. Satrājit and his friends firmly believed that it was Kṛṣṇa who kidnapped and killed Prasena for the gem. Since Kṛṣṇa was previously willing to possess the gem, people were generally inclined to believe the rumour that he stole the gem after having killed Prasena.

As Kṛṣṇa knew nothing about the fate of Prasena and the jewel, he was greatly mortified at the calumny spread against him. He therefore resolved to solve the mystery. He entered the forest by the way believed to have been taken by Prasena while going out ahunting and began to follow Prasena's track. Soon he reached a place where he noticed the dead body of Prasena and that of a lion. Unfortunately, the gem could not be traced even after a thorough search of Prasena's dead body. But people who now found Prasena's mauled body by the side of that of a lion were satisfied that Kṛṣṇa had nothing to do with the death of Prasena or the theft of the gem. But Kṛṣṇa himself was not completely satisfied before the recovery of the lost gem. He went on tracing footprints from that place to another part of the forest and reached the house of an aboriginal chief named Jāmbavat.

At that place, Kṛṣṇa noticed that, at a little distance, a child was crying and his nurse was trying to soothe him with a gem. She was saying, "Do not cry my darling. You have now got the Syāmantaka gem which Jāmbavat secured after slaughtering a lion that had killed Prasena." The mystery was solved. Kṛṣṇa tried to snatch the gem away. But the nurse raised an alarm and Jāmbavat appeared on the scene. There ensued then a fight between Kṛṣṇa and Jāmbavat in which the latter was ultimately defeated. Jāmbavat gave his daughter Jāmbavatī in marriage to Kṛṣṇa who now received the gem as a present from his new father-in-law.

Kṛṣṇa then went to Satrājit, told him the whole story and gave him his gem. Satrājit was fully convinced about Kṛṣṇa's innocence in regard both to the murder of his brother and to the theft of the jewel. He gave his daughter Satyabhāmā in marriage to Kṛṣṇa and presented the gem to his new son-in-law.

The story quoted above is no doubt one of the earliest detective tales in the literature of the world.

There are many instances of the policemen handling a case of theft in early Indian literature. One typical illustration is thus supplied by the *Abhijñānaśakuntala*[1] by Kālidāsa who flourished in the fourth-fifth century A.D.

Duṣyanta, the Paurava king of Hastināpura, married Śakuntalā at the hermitage of the sage Kaṇva and, when he was returning to his capital, left his signet ring with his wife. A few months later, on her way to Hastināpura, Śakuntalā lost the ring. It was believed that it slipped from her finger as she was doing obeisance to the waters of the Śacītīrtha at Śakrāvatāra not far away from her husband's capital. Some time later, a fisherman went to sell a ring at a merchant's counter at Hastināpura. As soon as the merchant noticed the king's name engraved on the ring, he informed the police as he was required to do by ancient Indian law. Kālidāsa's remarkable treatment of the police handling the above case clearly brings out the nature of police investigation in ancient India including certain unwelcome features of it. The scene runs as follows.

Then enter Superintendent of the City Police and behind him two Policemen leading a fettered man.

Policemen—(*striking the man*) Ah. You thief, answer where thou intercepted this royal ring, the ring shining with big gems and having the royal name engraved on it.

Man—(*in fright*) Please respected sirs, I did not do such an act as theft.

1 See S. Ray's ed., Calcutta, 1933, pp. 531 ff.

First Policeman—Was it then a gift bestowed by the king taking thee for a good Brāhmaṇa ?

Man—Now listen. I am a fisherman living at Śakrāvatāra.

Second Policeman—Did we ask about your caste, you thief?

Superintendent—(*to the Second Policeman*) Sūcaka, let him tell all in order. Do not interrupt him in the middle.

Policemen—As the lord commands. (*To the man*) Go on.

Man—With nets, hooks and other means of catching fish, I achieve the maintenance of my family.

Superintendent—(*laughing*) A pure livelihood indeed !

Man—Say not so, master. The despised occupation which is indeed born with one is surely not to be discarded. The practiser of Vedic rites, though tender with pity, has to be heartless in the act of killing animals.

Superintendent—Then? What then ?

Man—One day I cut up a Rohita fish to pieces. As soon as I looked into the inside of its belly, I saw this ring glittering with bright gems. Afterwards showing it for sale, I was arrested by your honoured selves. Kill me or cut me up, this is the true story of its acquisition.

Superintendent—(*to the First Policeman*) Jānuka, the fellow, smelling of raw meat, is surely a Godhā-eating fish-catcher. The acquisition of the ring by him has to be investigated. We will go to the king's residence.

Policemen—As your lordship pleases. (*To the man*) Proceed, you knot-cutter. (*All move towards the city-gate.*)

Superintendent—(*to the Second Policeman*) Sūcaka, here at the city-gate you two wait for me until I come out after having reported to the lord exactly as this ring has come to us and having obtained orders from him.

Policemen—Let your honour enter to receive the lord's favours. *Exit Superintendent.*

Second Policeman—(*after waiting for some time*) Jānuka, his honour is indeed delaying.

First Policeman—Well, kings are to be approached at opportunities.

Second Policeman—(*pointing to the Fisherman*) My hands quiver to tie the garland for his death.

Man—It does not become your honour to slay one without reason.

First Policeman—(*espying*) Here our master, having obtained royal orders, appears facing this way with a letter in his hand. (*To the Fisherman*) Thou wilt become an offering to the vultures or wilt see the jaws of a dog.

Superintendent—(*entering, to the Second Policeman*) Sūcaka, let the fisherman be released. The story of the acquisition of the ring is indeed consistent.

Second Policeman—As your honour directs. This fellow has come back after having entered the abode of death. (*Releases the man.*)

Man—(*bowing to the Superintendent*) Please master, how shall I get my livelihood today?

Superintendent—Here, a gift commensurate with the value of the ring is also caused to be given by the lord. (*Gives money to the man.*)

Man—(*accepting with a bow*) Master, I have been favoured.

Second Policeman—Such indeed is the favour that, taken down from the stake, you are seated on the neck of the state elephant.

First Policeman—Master, the gift shows that the ring with its priceless gems must have been very much acceptable to the lord.

Superintendent—I guess it is not the invaluable gems in it that have been acceptable to the lord; some person dear to the lord was reminded by its sight. Though naturally self-possessed, he remained for a moment with tearful eyes.

Second Policeman—Service indeed has been rendered by master.

First Policeman—Well, say that for the sake of this fish-killer! (*Eyes the man with envy.*)

Man—(*to the Superintendent*) Master, let half of this money be the price of flowers for you.

First Policeman—This much is proper.

Superintendent—Fisherman, you are noble and have become a dear friend to me. Our friendship is expected to have liquor for witness. So let us go to a wine-seller's shop.

According to a passage of Buddhaghoṣa's *Sumaṅgalavilāsinī* commentary on the *Mahāparinibbānasuttanta*,[1] a person

1 PTS ed., Vol. II, p. 519; *IHQ*, Vol. XX, p. 339.

brought under arrest for theft was arraigned by the *Vṛji-rājas* before the *Viniścaya-mahāmātras*; if the latter, on enquiry, found the man to be innocent, they discharged him; if otherwise, they sent him up to the *Vyavahārikas*. In case the *Vyavahārikas* found him guilty, they made the accused over to the *Sūtradhāras*. Under similar circumstances, the *Sūtradhāras* handed him over to the *Aṣṭakulakas*, the *Aṣṭakulakas* to the *Senāpati*, the *Senāpati* to the *Uparāja*, and the *Uparāja* to the *Rājan*. The *Rājan* punished the accused, if he was found guilty, in accordance with the *praveṇi-pustaka* or Book of Precedents. In the territory of the Vṛji confederacy of North Bihar, therefore, there was little chance of injustice to a thief; but the evidence is merely theoretical.

A general rule about the punishment of the patent thieves or cheats was that it was to be proportionate to the lightness or gravity of the crime and not the wealth of the accused.[1] The goldsmith was regarded as the worst of all cheats and, when he was found committing fraud, cutting off of his limbs bit by bit was prescribed.[2] Judges giving wrong decisions for bribe and those who betrayed the trust imposed in them were banished.[3]

According to Nārada (Pariśiṣṭa, 22-24), for thefts of articles of small value, the fine was five times their price; but Manu (VIII. 326-29) prescribes only twice the price of the things. It is laid down that the fine for theft is higher in the case of the higher castes.[4] If the Śūdra thief is fined eight times the value of the stolen article, the Vaiśya, Kṣatriya and Brāhmaṇa thieves were fined 16, 32 and 64 times respectively as each was deemed to know better owing to his higher status and culture. Death sentence is prescribed for kidnapping men and women of good family and for stealing costly jewels.[5] Vyāsa prescribes death by burning on a red-hot iron-bed for kidnapping women and mutilation of hands and feet for kidnapping men. Yājñavalkya (II. 273) provides impalement for persons stealing horses and elephants, while Manu (IX.280)

1. Cf. Vyāsa quoted by Kane, *op. cit.*, p. 521.
2. Manu, IX. 292.
3. Kane, *loc. cit.*
4. Cf. Manu (VIII. 337-38) and others quoted by Kane, *op., cit.*, p. 522.
5. See Kane, *op., cit.*, pp. 521-22.

prescribes death for them as well as for people breaking the royal store-house and armoury and the inner shrine of a temple. A house-breaker was impaled after having his hands cut off. For the cut-purse the punishment was the cutting off of his thumb and index finger for the first offence, the cutting off of his hand and foot for the offence committed for a second time and death for the crime committed again. The thief had not only to undergo punishment, but was also liable to make good the loss of property to the person robbed.[1]

According to Manu (VIII. 380), a Brāhmaṇa offender was not to be killed, but banished from the country allowing him to take with him all his wealth. But this was not supported by the school of Gautama as it entails reduction of people in the country. Kātyāyana says that the thief who is a learned Brāhmaṇa should be branded and deprived of his property; but if he is neither learned nor rich, he should be kept in jail with fetters on his feet and should be fed with meagre food and made to labour hard for the king till his death. Persons who helped thieves in any way were liable to be punished exactly as the thieves themselves.[2]

In the Dharmaśāstras, often penances and punishments are prescribed for offenders at the same time. In many cases, the king was asked to decree a punishment and, at the same time, the sin had to be atoned for by a suitable *prāyaścitta*. Often, specially in small cases, a *prāyaścitta* alone was regarded as sufficient. There was also a theory that criminals receiving punishment from the king were purged of sin.[3] We hear of a very old custom, according to which the thief, who goes to the king with a club, confesses his crime and asks the king to strike him down to the ground, is purified, whether the king acts according to this or grants him forgiveness, though, in the latter case, the sin of theft is transferred to the king.[4]

In certain cases, a person appropriating the things of others without permission was not punished. Members of the three higher classes were allowed by some authorities to take grass, fuel-sticks, flowers and plants for feeding cows and wor-

1. See *ibid.*, p. 522.
2. *Ibid.*, pp. 522-23.
3. Jolly, *op. cit.*, pp. 263-64.
4. *Ibid.*, p. 271.

shipping fire as well as fruits of trees that were not enclosed. But only small quantities had to be taken and, when there was really no necessity for the action, the person was liable to have his hands cut off. When a person fasted for three days for want of food, he was allowed by some Smṛti works to steal one day's food; but a person of a lower caste was asked in such cases not to trouble one belonging to a higher caste. Vyāsa says that a person in distress for food may steal food first from one of a lower caste, then from one of the same caste and ultimately from one of a higher caste. A traveller whose food ran short was allowed to steal two sugarcane stalks, two radishes, two cucumbers or melons, five mangoes or pomegranates and a handful of dates and of such corn as rice, wheat, gram, etc.[1]

VI

According to the PTS *Pāli-English Dictionary*, the word *aṭavī* means 'a forest', 'an inhabitant of the forests' or 'a wild tribe'. Reference is made to the expression *aṭavīcorā* (robbers of the forest) in the commentary of *Jātaka*, Vol. VI, No. 55, and *aṭavī-rakkhika* (interpreted as 'guardian of the forest') occurring in *Jātaka*, Vol. II, No. 335. Mention is also made of the expression *aṭavī-saṁkopa* used in some manuscripts of the *Aṅguttaranikāya*[2] in the sense of 'inroad of savage tribes'.

The *aṭavī-rakṣika* was, however, really 'a forest-guard' and not 'a guardian of the forest'. In the *Khurappa Jātaka*,[3] they are described as living in a village near a forest and as taking the responsibility of helping travellers and caravans in passing through the forest without being robbed by the dacoits inside it. The story relates as to how a merchant of Vārāṇasī paid one thousand coins to an *aṭavī-rakṣika* who saved him from the attack of a gang of 500 armed robbers in the forest. The *Vedabbha Jātaka*,[4] speaks of a forest through which passed the road between the Vārāṇasī and Cedi countries and wherein at least two gangs of 500 dacoits each made the lives and property of the travellers utterly unsafe. Of course, 500 in these

1. See Kane, *op. cit.*, pp. 523 ff.
2. Cf. Vol. I, p. 178. See *Mahābhārata*, XII. 59.48: *caurair=āṭavikaiś=c=ograiḥ pararāṣṭrasya pīḍanam.*
3. Fausboell, *Jātaka*, Vol. II, No. 265.
4. *Ibid.*, Vol. I, No. 48.

cases is a conventional number. In any case, these forest-robbers were either the forest-folk or outsiders who made the forest the field of their nefarious activities. Other haunts of the dacoits were the waters and deserts, though we are not concerned with them for the present. Piracy on Indian waters is well attested by both Indian and foreign writers, while the depredations of the Hurs in the deserts of Sind and Baluchistan persist even today.

There is some evidence to show that often the forest-folk were habitually criminal and lived on robbery. The *Sattigumma Jātaka*[1] speaks of a *cora-grāma* (robbers' village) on the slope of a hill in the woods of the Pañcāla country. A well-known tale in the *Pañcatantra* (Section I) relates to the Foolish Friend and the Sensible Enemy. According to the second of the two stories, a group of five travellers was passing through a forest-village of the aboriginal Kirātas who attacked them for the purpose of robbing them of their wealth as they used to do in the case of rich people passing by that road. Arthur W. Ryder's translation of the *Pañcatantra* (p. 201) describes the village as a 'Bhil village nestling in a rugged bit of jungle'. The story makes it clear that the forest folk of the said village were habitual dacoits. The well-known story of Jīmūtavāhana in the *Kathāsaritsāgara* (Taraṅga XXII) mentions a gang of robbers who were foresters and one of whom was the Śabara chief Pulindaka. Among other stories offering similar evidence in the said work, mention may be made of Taraṅga XXXVII speaking of a village of robbers in a forest, who earned their living by docoity. For such accounts of wild robber tribes like the Bhilla, Kirāta, Śabara and Pulinda, the students may be referred to M. Bloomfield's excellent article entitled 'On Organised Brigandage in Hindu Fiction' appearing in the *American Journal of Philology*, Vol. XLVII, pp. 205ff. It may be noted that Al-Bīrūnī regarded the Kirātas as mountaineers and the Pulindas as hunters of the plains, who were robbers.[2]

That roads passing through forests were not safe in early and medieval India for travellers, especially pilgrims and traders, is clear from numerous other stories and accounts.

1. *Ibid.*, Vol. IV, No. 503.
2. Sachau, *Alberuni's India*, Vol. I, p. 262.

According to Beal's '*Life of Hiuen Tsiang* by Shaman Hui-li', the Chinese pilgrim Hiuen-tsang, who visited India in the second quarter of the seventh century, encountered a gang of 50 bandits in a great forest of *palāśa* trees near the town of Sākala, modern Sialkot in the Punjab. The pilgrim and his companions were deprived of their clothes and other belongings and were pursued by the robbers with drawn swords. A Brāhmaṇa peasant who happened to appear on the scene with 80 armed followers, succeeded in dispersing the robbers and saving the lives of the victims.[1] The armed followers of the peasant appear to have been no other than the forest-guards mentioned in the Jātaka literature referred to above.

We also know that criminal activities of the same type persisted till quite recent times. G.F. Whitworth says that there were dacoits who were robbers by profession and brought up their children to the same occupation. They were banditti with strongholds to retire to and often committed raids on a large scale, a gang in some cases numbering several hundreds.[2]

The word *aṭavī* is used in the sense of the habitually criminal forest-folk in Rock Edict XIII of the great Maurya emperor Aśoka (c. 272-232 B.C.). In this edict, Aśoka explains the change in his internal and external policies enunciated after the horrible experience of the Kaliṅga war in which 100,000 people died in action, 150,000 were carried away captive apparently to be sold in the slave-market and many times that number died due to the famine and pestilence resulting from wars. This change of policy was indicated by the king by stating that he had renounced the approach of settling disputes by warfare altogether and was eager to win the heart of the peoples within his own empire as well as in the dominions of the neighbouring kings by love and toleration and by preaching the ideals of what he called Dharma. And in the same context he declared that 'even if a person should wrong him, the offence would be forgiven'. But Aśoka was conscious of the fact that it was not possible for the king to forgive all crimes, and that is why he added a clause to the sentence to say, 'the offence would be forgiven if it is possible to forgive

1. Cf. p. 73; also Tripathi, *History of Kanauj*, p. 146.
2. *Anglo-Indian Dictionary.*, s. v. *Dacoit.*

it'. It is indeed interesting to note that, at the same breath, Aśoka made the significant statement, "And the forest-folk (*Aṭavī*) who live in the dominions of the Beloved of the Gods (i.e. Aśoka), even them he entreats and exhorts [in regard to their duty]. It is [hereby] explained to them that, in spite of his repentance, the Beloved of the Gods possesses power [enough to punish them for their crimes] so that they should turn [from evil ways] and would not be killed [for their crimes]."[1]

The habitually criminal nature of the *Aṭavī* or forest-folk seems to be quite clear from the section of Rock Edict XIII of Aśoka cited above.

1. See Sircar, *Select Inscriptions*, 2nd ed., 1965, p. 35; *Inscriptions of Aśoka*, 2nd ed., 1967, p. 8.

CHAPTER IX

TRIAL BY ORDEAL

The prevalence of the system of trial by ordeals in ancient Indian courts is amply attested by the Smṛti literature. The subject has been dealt with in the *Mitākṣarā* on Yājñavalkya, II. 95-113, and the Sanskrit lexicon *Śabdakalpadruma* under the word *parīkṣā*. It has also been discussed by Hopkins in *Camb. Hist. Ind.*, Vol. I, pp. 282ff., by Stenzler in *ZDMG*, Vol. IX, pp. 661ff., by Schlagintweit in *Die Gotteswitheile der Inder* (1866) and by Jolly in *Recht und Sitte*, pp. 145ff. We also refer our readers to a very interesting paper "On the Trial by Ordeal among the Hindus by Ali Ibrahim Khan, Chief Magistrate of Benares, communicated by Warren Hastings Esq." in the *Asiatic Researches*, Vol. I, pp. 389-404.[1]

According to scholars like Bühler and Jolly,[2] it is possible that all the nine forms of ordeal mentioned in the later Smṛti literature existed in India from the earliest times. This suggestion evidently takes its stand on some doubtful early references and on the solitary example of a form of the *phāla-divya* in the *Chāndogya Upaniṣad*[3] and the recognition of the *daiva* (divine) proofs in the *Āpastamba Dharmasūtra*.[4] Some scholars, e.g.

1 See also *SBE*, Vol.XXV, p. cii; Kaegi in *Alter und Hirkunft des German. Gotteswitheils* (1887), B. V. Bhat in *Bhārat Itihās Saṁśodhak Maṇḍal* (3rd Vṛtta, pp. 42 ff.) and S. N. Sen in *Administrative System of the Marathas*, 2nd ed., pp. 363-68, 571-79, 653-55.

2 *Camb. Hist. Ind.*, Vol. I, p. 283; *SBE*, Vol. XXV, p. cii; *Recht und Sitte*, p. 145.

3 VI. 16. 1-2.

4 II, 11, 3; cf. 29.6. Āpastamba—"in doubtful cases, they shall give their decision after having ascertained the truth by inference, ordeal and the like means" (*SBE*, Vol. II, p. 168). Trial by ordeals is said to have been referred to in early works like the *Pañcaviṁśa Brāhmaṇa*. Geldner thought that the ordeal by red-hot axe is referred to even in the *Ṛgveda*, and Griffith discovered in another passage of it references to the fire and water ordeals. According to Weber, the *Śatapatha Brāhmaṇa* makes mention of the balance ordeal. Macdonell and Keith, however, do not agree with any of these writers. Scholars like Schlagintweit, Weber, Ludwig and Zimmer think that the fire ordeal is mentioned in the *Atharvaveda*; but Bloomfield and Whitney have disproved this theory. The system of trial by ordeals may

Hopkins, Stenzler, Schlagintweit and Kaegi, on the other hand, believe that the fire and water ordeals were first used and then came the elaborate trials by balance and other ordeals, till eventually there were nine formal ordeals.[1] The latter view seems to be more probable.

The earliest reference to trial by ordeal in India is to be found in the *Chāndogya Upaniṣad*[2] wherein it is said that a man accused of theft takes in his hand a heated axe and is proved guilty if it burns him, but is acquitted if it does not. The above Upaniṣad seems to have been composed in a country to the south of Gandhāra (modern Rawalpindi and Peshawar Districts) and in a place between the Indus and the Jamunā.[3] The reference to the axe-ordeal in it shows that this form of the *phāla-divya* was used in that country when the Upaniṣad was composed about 550 B.C.[4] There is, however, no proof to show that the ordeal was used in the different parts of India from such an early date as the sixth century B.C.

More important seems to be the recognition of the *daiva* or divine[5] form of proof by the *Āpastamba Dharmasūtra*[6] which is a book on law. It must be noted that no other early text on criminal law prescribes trial by ordeal for the person accused. According to Bühler,[7] the Sūtras of Āpastamba are to be

or may not have been referred to in the early Vedic literature; but the practice seems to have been not unknown in India even in the early Vedic period (see *Vedic Index*, Vol. I, pp. 317-18, 364-65). A full-fledged system universally used was, however, most probably unknown. A passage from the work of Bardesanes of Babylon (3rd century A.D.), quoted by Stobaeus, refers to trial by ordeal in which water was employed (Rawlinson, *India and the Western World*, p. 144).

1 *Camb. Hist. Ind.*, Vol. I, p. 283; *ZDMG*, Vol. IX, p. 661; etc.

2 *Loc. cit.*

3 See *op. cit.*, VI. 14. 1-2; VI. 10.1.

4 See *Camb. Hist. Ind.*, Vol. I, pp. 116 and 112.

5 Cf. Nārada--"Proof is said to be of two kinds, human and divine. Human proof consists of documentary and oral evidence. By divine proof is meant the ordeal by balance and other [modes of divine test]; where a transaction has taken place by day, in a village or town, or in the presence of witnesses divine test is not applicable. Divine test is applicable [where the transaction has taken place] in a solitary forest, at night, or in the interior of a house, and in cases of violence or of denial of a deposit" (*SBE*, Vol. XXXIII, pp. 30-31).

6 *Loc. cit.*

7 *SBE*, Vol. II, 2nd ed., p. xiv.

assigned to a date not later than the third century B.C., but may be placed 150 or 200 years earlier. Āpastamba's, however, is a general recognition; none of the ordeals has been defined in his Sūtras. The chief subjects discussed by him under this head are assault, adultery and theft. It is interesting to note in this connection that Kauṭilya, to whom the authorship of the celebrated *Arthaśāstra* is assigned, does not recognise the application of ordeals in connection with civil or criminal procedure. According to the Purāṇas, the *Mudrārākṣasa*, the *Mahāvaṁsa* and the *Āryamañjuśrīmūlakalpa*, Kauṭilya lived about the time of Candragupta Maurya in the 4th century B.C. He is therefore generally supposed to have been more or less of the same age as Āpastamba and to have had in his purview the administration of the Mauryas whose kingdom embraced almost the whole of India. These facts may not be sufficient to justify us in assuming that Kauṭilya is earlier than Apastamba;[1]

1 See, however, Smith, *E. Hist. Ind.*, 4th ed., p. 161: "I have pointed out that its contents describe the state of things as existing immediately before the establishment of the Maurya empire, while Mr. Shamasastry suggests that it may refer back even to the pre-Buddhistic age. The book seems to be based on much more ancient treatises now lost and a good deal of it must have been archaic in Maurya times." We do not agree with Johnston and Jolly (see *JRAS*, 1929, pp. 77 ff.) who think that Kauṭilya, Cāṇakya or Viṣṇugupta was a fictitious figure. The testimony of the Purāṇas and other works (though not contemporaneous) regarding Kauṭilya's connection with Candragupta Maurya may be disregarded only on definite negative evidence. Absence of reference to Kauṭilya in the works of Classical writers and in early works like the *Milindapañha* is not definite proof. Kauṭilya appears to have been the founder of a new school of Political Philosophy, and the *Arthaśāstra* may be the work of this school. The original work may be ascribed to Kauṭilya; but the book, in its present form, is certainly post-Christian. The reference to Cina (derived from the name of the Tsin dynasty) proves that the *Arthaśāstra* cannot be earlier than the latter half of the 3rd century B.C. The mention of Kambu, possibly the same as Kambuja or Cambodia, and of Nepāla also suggests that it is much later than the 4th century B. C. The language and structure of the text and reference to the system of dating in terms of regnal year, month, fortnight and day (II. 6) prove that the work cannot be much earlier than the 2nd century A.D. which is the time of Rudradāman's Junagadh inscription. The present *Arthaśāstra* may be placed in the 1st or 2nd century A.D. The suggestion that works like the *Arthaśāstra* present an ideal rather than the real state of society is essentially true; but the *Arthaśāstra* could hardly avoid referring to trial by ordeals, had the system been popular in the locality where Kauṭilya's school developed.

but they may suggest that the system of trial by ordeal was not much popular and was not universally used in India about the fourth century B.C. which is generally supposed to be the time of Kautilya and Apastamba. The general reference to *daiva* trial by Āpastamba possibly shows that the system of applying ordeals, known to him and used in his time and place, was not elaborate like that illustrated by later law-givers, but was rudimentary like that recognised in the *Manusmṛti*.

In view of the fact that the law-givers lived in different ages and in different parts of this vast country, we cannot expect unanimity in their views regarding trial by ordeal. It is interesting to note that the word *divya* originally meant an 'oath', that is, a form of invoking the Supreme Being to prove the truth of an allegation; but later it was generally understood to mean 'trial by ordeal', that is, a form of appealing to the direct interposition of divine power. In connection with the development of the system of trial by ordeals, it is also interesting to note that while the system is unknown to the *Arthaśāstra* of Kauṭilya, it is seen sprouted in the Codes of Āpastamba and Manu, a little developed in the works of Yājñavalkya and Nārada, and fully grown in the Code of Bṛhaspati; cf. also the *Mitākṣarā* of Vijñāneśvara. According to Kauṭilya,[1] "Self-assertion (*svayaṁvāda*) on the part of either of the litigant parties has been found faulty; examination (*anuyoga*), honesty (*ārjava*), evidence (*hetu*) and oath (*śapatha*) these alone enable a man to win his cause." It shows that the system of trial by ordeal did not fully develop and was not popular at the time and locality of the author (or authors) of the *Arthaśāstra*. This fact possibly goes to show that the *Arthaśāstra* cannot be placed—as is the view of some scholars[2] —in the 3rd century A.D., i.e., not much earlier than the time of Yājñavalkya.[3]

For an interesting paper on the date of the *Arthaśāstra* see A.N. Bose, *Ind. Cult.*, Vol. IV, pp. 435 ff.; see also Sircar, *Studies in the Yugapurāṇa and Other Texts* (in the press)

1 *Arthaśāstra*, II. 1.

2 See Raychaudhuri, *Pol. Hist. Anc. Ind.*, 2nd ed., p. 5, note.

3 Cf. *Camb. Hist. Ind.*, Vol. I, p. 383: "As the Sūtras do not notice ordeals except for a general recognition of them as 'divine' proofs on the part of the late Āpastamba, and as the later writers Yājñavalkya and Nārada describe five ordeals adding the plough-share, scales and poison, it is reasonable to conclude that Manu stands, in time as well as description, midway

The simple *śapatha* of the *Arthaśāstra* is seen developed in the *Manusmṛti* (assigned to the 1st century A.D. or 1st century B.C., but is a little later).[1] According to Manu, a Brāhmaṇa—in order to justify the truth of his statement—should be compelled to swear by a declaration of truth; a Kṣatriya by his *vāhana* (horse, elephant, etc.), a Vaiśya by his cattle, seed-corn and gold, and a Śūdra by all sins; alternatively, a Śūdra may be put to fire, drowned into water or compelled to touch separately the heads of his sons and wives and swear. In these cases, the man who is not burnt by fire or quickly drowned by water and whose sons and wives (heads of whom were touched in swearing) do not fall ill within a short time, is to be considered as true regarding his statement.[2] Manu therefore seems to have known only three forms of ordeals, the last of which, however, is not mentioned as a legal *divya* in the works of the later law-givers.[3]

In the Code of Yājñavalkya who possibly lived in Mithilā about the 4th century A.D.,[4] the system of trial by ordeals became more developed. According to this law-giver, "Balance, fire, water, poison and *kośa*—these are the ordeals used here for

between the two sets of authors and is the first to describe ordeals already known and practised." Āpastamba is assigned to the 2nd century B.C. p.(249).

1 Cf. *Camb. Hist. Ind.*, Vol. I, p. 279. Later writers on law have prescribed *śapatha* for minor and *divya* for major crimes. Cf.

deva-Brāhmaṇa-padāṁś=ca putra-dāra-śirāṁsi ca |
ete tu śapathāḥ proktā Manunā svalpa-kāraṇe ||
sāhaseṣv-abhiśāpe ca divyāni tu viśodhanam ||
(*Śabdakalpadruma*, s.v. *śapatha*)

2 See Manu, VIII. 113-15.

3 This form of ordeal seems to have been largely used in Bengal. It can be faintly traced in the altercations of rustic people of Bengal even at the present time. Swearing before five learned Brāhmaṇas is also mentioned by Al-Bīrūnī (Sachau, *op.cit.*, Vol.II, pp. 158-59). On one occasion a man is known to have taken an oath on the feet of the Marāṭhā king Sāhu Chatrapati. "Then Bhikhājī Harpāla said that the Mahārāja's feet were the Kṛṣṇa to him and that he would take an oath on his feet. Accordingly he swore that the *watan* in the aforesaid *mauja* belonged to him and that Kamthe was a *Thalvaik* (*Mirashi*) peasant. Within a day or two of this oath, Bhikhājī Gaikwad got Cholera; he had to be carried back to the village on the back of a bullock and there he died after a month in consequence of that false oath taken on his behalf." See S.N. Sen, *Administrative Ssystem of the Marathas*, 2nd ed., p. 368.

4 *Camb. Hist. Ind.*, Vol. I, p. 279.

the proof of innocence, when the accusations are heavy and when the accuser offers to hazard a mulct (in case he should fail); or one party may be tried by ordeal if he likes, the other then must risk an amercement; but the trial may take place even without any wager if the crime committed be injurious to the king...Balance for women, children, old men, the blind, the lame, Brāhmaṇas and the sick; but for the Śūdra, fire or water or seven *yavas* of poison. Unless the loss of the accuser amounts to a thousand pieces of silver, he must not be tried by the spear-head, nor by poison, nor by balance; but if the offence be against the king or if the crime is heinous, he must acquit himself by one of these trials in all cases."[1] Yājñavalkya thus appears to have known six forms of the ordeals, viz., (1) Balance, (2) Fire, (3) Water, (4) Poison, (5) Kośa and (6) Spearhead.

The existence of trial by ordeals in Indian courts in the 7th century A.D., i.e., some time after Yājñavalkya, is evidenced by the accounts left by Hiuen-tsang who travelled in India from 629 to 645 A.D. Ordeals by water, fire, weighment or poison are said to have been much esteemed as efficient instruments for the ascertainment of truth, and are described with approval by the Chinese pilgrim.[2] The six principal ordeals, viz., poison, water, image-washed water, balance, hot-coin and spear-head, are also described by the celebrated Muhammadan savant, Al-Bīrūnī, who wrote his book on India in the second quarter of the eleventh century.[3]

The fully developed form of the system of trial by ordeals can be found in the works of later writers on law, such as Bṛhaspati, Vijñāneśvara and others. According to the Code (XIX. 4) of Bṛhaspati,[4] which may be assigned to the 7th century A.D.,[5] there are nine different forms of ordeals. They are:

dhaṭo='gnir=udakañ=c=aiva viṣaṁ kośaś=ca pañcamam|
ṣaṣṭhañ=ca taṇḍulaḥ proktaṁ saptamaṁ tapta-māṣakam||
aṣṭamaṁ phālam=ity=uktaṁ navamaṁ dharmajaṁ smṛtam||[6]

1 Yājñavalkya, II. 95-99.
2 Watters, *On Yuan Chwang's Travels in India*, Vol. I, p. 172.
3 Sachau, *Alberuni's India*, Vol. II, pp. 158-60.
4 Cf. *CHI*, Vol. I, p. 283; Jolly, *Hindu Law and Custom*, trans. Ghosh, p. 311; cf. p. 82, etc.; see also Kane, *op. cit.*, Vol. II, pp. 158-60.
5 *Camb. Hist. Ind.*, Vol. I, p. 280.
6 It is interesting to note that trial by ordeals went from India to Indo-China. The *Jala-divya*, *Taptamāṣaka-divya*, *Agni-divya* and *Taṇḍula-*

I. *Dhaṭa-divya* or *Tulā-divya*, i.e. Ordeal by Balance.

The beam having been previously adjusted, the cord fixed and the scales made perfectly even, the accused person and the Brāhmaṇa judge (*Prāḍvivāka*) fast a whole day. Then, after the accused has been propitiated with *homa* and deities have been worshipped, the person is weighed. When he is taken out of the scale, the *Prāḍvivāka* prostrates before the balance, pronounces some *mantras* and having written the substance of the accuasation on a *lipi-patra*, binds it on the head of the accused. After reciting some more *mantras*, the judge puts the man again on the scale. If he weighs more than before, he is guilty;[1] if less, innocent; and if exactly the same, he is held partially guilty. In case of doubt, the accused must be weighed again; but if any part of the balance—though well fixed—breaks down, it will be considered as proving his guilt.[2]

II. *Agni-divya*, i.e., Ordeal by Fire.

In performing the fire-ordeal, an excavation nine cubits long, two spans broad and one span deep is made in the ground and filled with a fire of Pippala wood. Into this fire the accused person must walk bare-footed; if his feet are unburnt, he is innocent; otherwise guilty.[3]

III. *Jala-divya* or Ordeal by Water.

In the water-ordeal, the accused should be caused to stand in a depth of water sufficient to reach his navel; but care should be taken that no ravenous animal be in it and that it is not moved by much air.[4] A Brāhmaṇa is then directed to go

divya have been noticed in Siam even in the 17th century (P.N. Bose, *Indian Colony of Siam*, p. 119). According to the annals of the Southern Tsi dynasty (479-501 A.D.), several Indian forms of the ordeals were prevalent in Fu-nan (Cambodia). The *Tapta-māṣaka-divya*, e.g., is described as follows: "In cases of dispute, golden rings and eggs are thrown into boiling water and they have to be taken out by the culprit who will be unharmed if innocent (B.R. Chatterjee, *Ind. Infl. Camb.*, p. 24).

1 Al-Birūnī says (*op.cit.*, p. 159), "In case he has spoken the truth, he now weighs more than the first time." We are not definite whether this is wrong or is based upon a local practice. Hiuen-tsang correctly says, "The accused is weighed against a stone; and if the latter is lighter, the charge is false; if otherwise, it is true."

2 *Śabdakalpadruma*, s.v. *tulā*.

3 *As. Res.*, Vol. I, p. 390.

4 The water ordeal is referred to by the Classical author Stobaeus (Rawlinson, *India and the Western World*, p. 144).

into the water with a staff in his hand, and a soldier shoots three arrows on dry ground from a cane bow. A man is then despatched to bring the arrows that has been shot farthest, and, after he has taken it up, another man is also ordered to run from the edge of the water. At this moment, the person accused is ordered to grasp the foot or the staff of the Brāhmaṇa who stands by him in the water, and immediately to dive into it. He must remain under water till the two men who were sent to fetch the arrows return. If he raises his body or head above the surface of the water before the arrows are brought back, his guilt is proved.[1] The water ordeal is mentioned in the *Padmāvatyavadāna* of the *Bodhisattvāvadānakalpalatā*.[2]

IV. *Viṣa-divya* or Ordeal by Poison.

The poison-ordeal was performed in two different ways:—

(a) After the *homa* is performed, and the accused person is bathed, 2½ *ratis* or 7 *yavas* of *viṣanāga* (a poisonous root) or *śaṅkhyā*[3] (i.e., white arsenic) are mixed with 6 *māṣas* or 64 *ratis* of clarified butter which the accused should take from the hands of a Brāhmaṇa. If the poison is visibly effective, the man is condemned; if not, absolved.

(b) A hooded snake, called *nāga*, is thrown into an earthen pot, into which is also dropped a ring, seal or coin. The accused person is then ordered to take it out with his hand. If the serpent does not bite him, he is proved innocent; otherwise, he is pronounced guilty.[4]

Hiuen-tsang seems to refer to a third variety of this ordeal when he says, "The poison ordeal requires that the right hind leg of a ram be cut off, and according to the portion assigned to the accused to eat, poisons are put into the leg, and if the

1 *Ibid.*, pp. 390-91. Trial by ordeal existed also in ancient Babylonia as is evidenced by the Code of Hammurabi who ruled from *circa* 2123 to 2080 B. C. (see Hall, *Ancient History of the Near East*, 7th ed., p. 211). The Code, which seems to have been based on ancient Sumerian laws, takes cognisance of a form of the water ordeal. It was used when a man was accused of sorcery and a woman of adultery without sufficient evidence. In both cases, the accused were to leap into the river, and their innocence was established if they came out alive (see *Camb. Anc. Hist.*, Vol. I, p. xiv).

2 Cf. S.N. Sen, *op. cit.*, p. 573.

3 Hindī *saṅkhiyā*; Bengali *śeṅko-viṣ*. According to Al-Bīrūnī (*op. cit.*, p. 159), the poison which the accused person was invited to drink was called *brahmana*. It may be a mistransliteration of or mistake for *viṣa-nāga*.

4 *As. Res.*, Vol. I, p. 391.

man is innocent, he survives; and if not, the poison takes effect."[1]

V. *Kośa-divya* or Ordeal by 'Image-washed' Water.

The *Kośa-divya* is performed in the following way. The accused person is made to drink three draughts of water into which images of the Sun-god, the Devī and other deities have been washed for the purpose. If the man has any sickness or indisposition within 14 days after taking the draughts, his crime is considered to be proved.[2] Al-Bīrūnī[3] says that the accused is taken to the temple of the most venerated idol of the town or realm and that the priests pour water over the idol and give it to the accused to drink. The accused, according to him, vomits blood in case he is guilty.

VI. *Taṇḍula-divya* or Ordeal by Rice.[4]

The rice ordeal is generally applied to persons suspected of theft. Some dry rice is weighed with the Śālagrāma or some *mantras* are recited over it, and the suspected persons are severally asked to chew a quantity of it. As soon as it is done, they are ordered to throw it on some leaves of the Pippala tree or on some *bhurja-patra* (bark of a tree from Nepal or Kasmir). The man from whose mouth rice comes dry or stained with blood, is pronounced guilty and the rest innocent.[5]

VII. *Taptamāṣaka-divya* or Ordeal by the Hot Māṣaka Coin.

In performing this ordeal, the appointed ground is cleared and rubbed with cowdung. The next day at sunrise, after worship of Gaṇeśa and other deities is done, the *Prāḍvivāka*, having recited some *mantras*, places a round pan of gold, silver, copper, iron or clay, with a diameter of 12 inches and depth of 3 inches, and throws into it one seer or 80 sicca weight of clarified butter or oil of sesamum.[6] After this, a *māṣaka* coin is

1 Watters, *loc. cit.*

2 *Ibid.*, p. 391.

3 *Op. cit.*, p. 159.

4 Cf. *cāl-paḍā* of rural Bengal.

5 *Ibid.*, pp. 391-92. For two cases of the Taṇḍula-divya, the first in connection with payment of money and the second with reference to a boundary question, see Rice, *Mysore and Coorg from Inscriptions*, p. 177.

6 Twenty *palas* of ghee and oil, according to Pitāmaha. The Arab merchant Suleiman (c. 851 A.D.) refers to the prevalence of this ordeal in the Deccan. He also speaks of the *phāla-divya* which is noticed by Ibn

thrown into the pan, or alternatively a ring of gold or silver or iron is cleaned and cast into the oil which some Brāhmaṇas proceed to heat. When the thing in the pan is very hot, they throw a fresh leaf of Pippala or Bilva into it; if the leaf is burnt, the thing is taken to be sufficiently hot. Then after reciting a *mantra*, the *Prāḍvivāka* orders the accused person to take the coin or ring out of the pan. If he can do this without his fingers being burnt or blistered, he is considered not-guilty; otherwise guilty.[1]

VIII. *Phāla-divya* or Ordeal by Spear-head.

In performing the *phāla-divya*, the Brāhmaṇas, after due worship of Gaṇeśa, draw nine circles on the ground, with cowdung, at intervals of 12 inches, each of the circles being 12 inches in diameter except the ninth which may be smaller or bigger than the rest. Then the *homa* is performed, gods are worshipped and some *mantras* are recited. The accused person then performs ablutions and, wearing wet clothes and facing towards the east, stands in the first circle with his hands on his girdle. After this, the *Prāḍvivāka* and the Brāhmaṇas order him to rub some unhusked rice between his palms which they carefully inspect. It any scar of a former wound, mole or any other mark appears on his palms, they stain it with a dye, so that it may be distinguished from any new mark after trial. The accused is then ordered to hold both his hands open and close

Rusta (c. 903 A.D.). See S.M. Husayn Nainar, *Arab Geographers' Knowledge of Southern India*, pp. 109-11. The Tellicherry Factory Diary (6th May, 1728) refers to a dispute between the East India Co. and certain people that had to be settled by trial by the oil ordeal. Cf. Nainar, *loc. cit.*; Logan, *Malabar Manual*, Vol. I, p. 173. This form of the ordeal is also known to have been performed before the idol of the Suchindram temple in Travancore (Kerala) some 250 years ago (*Hindu Heritage*, 1941, p. 175).

1 *As. Res.*, Vol. I, p. 392; see also Pitāmaha quoted in the *Mitākṣarā* on Yājñavalkya, II. 113, and *Alberuni's India*, Vol. II, pp. 159-60. For cases of this ordeal in records of 1580 and 1677 A.D., see S.N. Sen, *loc. cit.* Even in the 12th century A.D., the real trial in England was by the ordeal of water, failing to get through which the accused was condemned. The English water ordeal was, however, more akin to the *taptamāṣaka-divya* of the ancient Indian Penal Code. "The accused had to dip his hand into boiling water and take out a stone from the bottom of the vessel. The hand was then tied up for a time (usually, seven days), and if, when the bandages were taken off, it was found to be healed, the man was held innocent and acquitted" (Warner and Marten, *Groundwork of British History*, p. 79).

together. Having, then, put into his hands seven leaves of the trembling tree or Pippala, seven of the *śamī* or *jend*, seven blades of the *darbha* grass, a little barley moistened with curd and a few flowers, they tie the leaves on the hands with seven threads of raw cotton. Some *mantras* are then recited by the Brāhmaṇas who next write a statement of the case and the point in issue on a palmyra leaf together with the appointed *mantra*, and tie the leaf on the head of the accused person. Then they heat an iron-ball or a spear-head, weighing about five pounds, and throw it into water: they heat it again, and again cool it in the same way. The third time they heat the iron till it is red-hot. Next, the Brāhmaṇas, after reciting the *mantras*, take the red-hot iron with tongs and place it in the hands of the accused who is standing in the first circle. He must then gradually step from circle to circle, his feet being constantly in one of them. After reaching the eighth circle, he must throw the iron in the ninth to burn some grass which must be left there for that purpose. He is thereafter ordered to rub some unhusked rice between both his palms; if, on examination, any mark of burning appears on either of the palms, he is considered guilty; if no such marks appear, his innocence is proved.[1]

IX. *Dharmaja-* or *Dharmādharma-divya*, i.e., Ordeal by [the Images of] Dharma and Adharma.

In performing the image-ordeal (or Dharmādharma ordeal), two processes may be followed.

(a) An image named Dharma is made of silver, and another called Adharma of clay or iron.[2] Both of these images are thrown into a big earthen jar. If the accused can bring the image of Dharma out of the jar after thrusting his hand into it, he is considered innocent; but if he brings out the image of Adharma, he is condemned.

(b) An image is drawn on a piece of white cloth and another on a piece of black cloth. The first is called Dharma

1 *As. Res.*, Vol. I, p. 392. For a case of grasping a red-hot iron in a record of 1309 A.D., in the presence of the god Hoysaleśvara, see S.N. Sen, *loc. cit.* See also *Alberuni's India*, Vol. II, p. 160. The *phāla-divya* was popular according to Ibn Rusta 'in the cities of the *Mahrāj* (i.e. the Śailendra king of Zāvaj or Java) and also in the city of Hind called Fanṣūr'. Cf. Nainar, *op. cit.*, p.110.

2 Lead or iron, according to Pitāmaha.

and the second Adharma.[1] These are severally rolled up in cowdung[2] and thrown into a large jar, without being overseen by the accused. The accused is then ordered to bring out one of those rolls. If he brings out the figure on white cloth, he is acquitted; if that on the black cloth, convicted.[3]

Certain months and days are specified for the different species of ordeals. There are also other injunctions in the Smṛti literature; but the law-givers are not unanimous on these points. It is not necessary to notice these in detail. We simply quote[4] a passage from 'Alī Ibrāhīm Khān,[5] wherein we find the tradition based on Vijñāneśvara's *Mitākṣarā* and followed in the Varanasi region about the end of the eighteenth century.

"Agrahāyana, Pauṣa, Māgha, Phālguna, Śrāvaṇa and Bhādra for that of fire; Āśvina, Kārttika, Jyeṣṭhạ and Āṣāḍha for that by water; Pauṣa, Māgha and Phālguna for that by poison; and regularly there should be no water ordeal on the Aṣṭamī or eighth and Caturdaśī or fourteenth day of the new or full moon, in the intercalary month, in the month of Bhādra, on Śanaiścara or Saturday, and on Maṅgala or Tuesday; but whenever a Magistrate decides that there shall be an ordeal, the regular appointment of months and days need not be regarded.

"The *Mitākṣarā* contains also the following distinctions. In cases of theft or fraud to the amount of a hundred gold Mohurs, the trial by poison is proper; if eighty Mohurs be stolen, the suspected person may be tried by fire; if forty, by the balance; if from thirty to ten, by the image-water; if two only, by rice."

As has been already noticed, differences in the views of different law-givers appear to us to be due to differences in their time and place. A few instances will possibly explain the point clearly.

(a) One of the most glaring instances of such difference may be seen in the views of Bṛhaspati on the eighth form of the

1 According to Pitāmaha, "A Dharma in white and an Adharma in black are to be drawn on either *bhurja* or cloth."

2 Cowdung or clay, according to Pitāmaha.

3 *As Res.*, Vol. 1, p. 392; see also Pitāmaha quoted in the *Mitākṣarā* on Yājñavalkya, II. 113.

4 We use our method of transliteration.

5 *Op. cit.*, p. 393.

nine *divyas*, namely, the *phāla-divya*. According to Bṛhaspati, "A piece of iron, eight *aṅgulis* in length, four *aṅgulis* in breadth and weighing twelve *palas*, is called a *phāla*; when the *phāla* is red-hot (*agni-varṇa*), the thief (here, stealer of a cow) must once lave it with the tongue; if [the tongue] is not burnt, he is held innocent; if otherwise, convicted." The passage *gocaurasya pradātavyaṁ tapta-phāl-āvalehanam = iti smṛtir = iti Maithilāḥ*[1] (*Śabdakalpadruma*, s.v. *phālam*) possibly goes to show that this form of the *phāla-divya* was popular in North Bihar and that Bṛhaspati's code was composed not very far from the Mithilā region. This form of the ordeal seems to have been unknown in South India.[2] The licking form of the *phāla-divya* is mentioned by Hiuen-tsang[3] who, however, describes it as a fire-ordeal.

(b) A local variety of the third ordeal, namely *jala-divya*, has been thus noticed by 'Alī Ibrāhīm Khān : "In the villages near Benares, it is the practice for the person, who is to be tried by this kind of ordeal, to stand in water up to his navel, and then holding the foot of a Brāhmaṇa, to dive under it as long as a man can walk fifty paces very gently. If, before the man has walked thus far, the accused rise above the water, he is condemned; if not, acquitted."[4]

Al-Bīrūnī possibly refers to a slightly different custom when he says,[5] "They bring the man to a deep and rapidly flowing river, or to a deep well with much water...Then five men take him and throw him into water. If he has spoken the truth, he will not drown and die."

According to Hiuen-tsang,[6] the accused was put in one sack and a stone in another; then the two sacks were connected and thrown into a deep stream; if the sack containing the stone floated and the other sank, the man's guilt was proved.

A different form of the *jala-divya* was prevalent in the Marāṭhā country. "The parties and the Pāṇḍhara were sent

1 *Śabdakalpadruma*, s.v. *phālam*.

2 Difference in the practice of the *phāla-divya* is also evidenced by the *Chāndogya Upaniṣad* wherein the thing to be heated is said to have been a *paraśu*, i.e., axe.

3 Watters, *loc. cit.*

4 *Op. cit.*, p. 393.

5 *Op. cit.*, p. 159.

6 Watters, *op. cit.*, p. 172.

to a sacred river like the Kṛṣṇā, or better, to a *saṅgama* of special sanctity like the Kṛṣṇā-Veṇā *saṅgama*. There, at an auspicious moment, the Pāṇḍhara stood on the bank after their bath in the sacred stream, the defendant and the plaintiff still remaining standing in the river. Either the Paṭel or some other trustworthy man there present was then ordered to draw the rightful party from the water and pass a conscientious verdict."[1]

(c) Another glaring instance is in connection with the question whether ordeals should be applied to women. According to Nārada, whose code seems to have been composed in Nepal about the 5th century A. D.,[2] women cannot be tried by ordeals (*strīnāñ=ca na bhaved=divyam*). But another law-giver, Śūlapāṇi, says that this prohibition refers to *divyas* other than the *tulā-divya*, and we have already seen that Yājñavalkya prescribes trial by the balance ordeal for women. There is also a view that in connection with a quarrel between a man and a woman, the latter should undergo ordeals.[3]

The application of ordeals to women appears to be supported by the Rāmāyaṇic story of Sītā undergoing the fire-ordeal in order to prove that her chastity was not violated by Rāvaṇa during her confinement in Laṅkā, and also by certain epigraphic references. Some records[4] say that Candalādevī (Candrike or Candrikādevī), wife of Lakṣmīdeva I, the Raṭṭa king of Saundatti, 'attained victory over a number of serpents in an earthen water-jar'; the allusion here is certainly to the queen having undergone trial by the poison-ordeal.[5]

It is known from some old Bengali works that, in Bengal also, the purity of wives was sometimes examined by ordeals. Thus, Khullanā, heroine of Kavikankaṇa Mukundarāma's *Caṇḍī-kāvya* (about Śaka 1499 = 1577 A.D.) is reported to have undergone successfully four ordeals, the first three of which are in reality the water, poison and spear-head ordeals.[6] It is also stated that Khullanā was put into a *jatu-gṛha* made specially

1 Sen, *op. cit.*, p. 365. *Pāṇḍhara*=the entire village community.
2 *Camb. Hist. Ind.*, Vol. I, p. 280.
3 *Śabdakalpadruma*, s.v. *parīkṣā*.
4 E.g., *Ind. Ant.*, Vol. XIX, p. 248.
5 *Bomb. Gaz.*, Vol. I, Part ii, p. 556 and note 5.
6 See D.C. Sen, *Vaṅgabhāṣā-o-Sāhitya*, 4th ed., p. 371.

for the purpose of testing her chastity, and then it was set fire to. This form of the fire-ordeal is, however, unknown to the Smṛti literature. But the description of the *Caṇḍīkāvya* seems to be more or less conventional. It is therefore not certain whether these ordeals were actually prevalent in Bengal in the second half of the sixteenth century A.D. Behulā (Sanskrit *Vipulā*), the famous heroine of the *Manasāmaṅgala* story, is also said to have proved her purity by undergoing, with success, several of the ordeals.[1]

From the above references we see that the prevalence of the system of trial by ordeals is not only proved by the Smṛti literature, but can also be proved from references to the practice in inscriptions and other writings.[2] Here we quote three instances of trial by ordeal, one from an inscription and two from the paper of 'Alī Ibrāhīm Khān who claims to have been an eye-witness of the trials.

I. In the Kaliyuga year 4289 (1188 A.D.) and the 15th year of the Goa Kadamba king Vīra-Jayakeśideva III, 'on Sunday, the eighth day of the bright fortnight of Āṣāḍha in presence of the fortunate Prime Minister, Īśvarārya Daṇḍanāyaka, Śivaśakti, the *ācārya* (priest) of the god Śrī-Kalleśvaradeva of the well called Attibāvi at Kittūr, and Kalyānaśakti, the *ācārya* of the original local deity of that place (Mūlasthānadeva), opened a subject of dispute, the former asserting that a plot of ground in that place, called Ālakolaṇakeyi, had from of old belonged to Kalleśvaradeva, while the latter claimed it for the original local deity (Mūlasthānadeva)'.

"The agreement that they both of their own free will entered into at the presence of the same Īśvara Daṇḍanāyaka was this: Śivasakti said, 'Whereas this plot of ground [called] Ālakolaṇakeyi belonged of old to Kalleśvaradeva, Devarāśi, the father of Kalyāṇaśakti, unauthorisedly brought it under cultivation under the Caṇḍe State and had a grant written in his own favour; and I am now prepared to undergo the *phāladivya* in support of my statement that it had belonged from ancient times to Kalleśvaradea.' [On the other hand], the

1 *Pravāsī*, Kārttika, B.S., 1333 p. 67.

2 For inscriptional references, we refer our readers to *Ep. Ind.*, Vol. XIII, p. 294; Vol. XV, p. 394; and *Bomb. Gaz.*, Vol. I, Part ii, p. 556 and note 5; p. 571 and note 3.

argument of Kalyāṇaśakti under oath with the sacred symbols on his head was, if the Caṇḍe Saṁsthāna gave this plot of ground [called] Ālakolaṇakeyi to my father Devarāśi and to myself on behalf of the original local deity (Mūlasthānadeva), it has not been unauthorisedly brought under cultivation.'

"Īśvara Daṇḍanāyaka then said, 'Go both of you before the assemblage of the bankers of the village of Degāve, which has been granted in perpetuity to Brāhmaṇas; and on their assenting to this, on Sunday, the seventh day of the dark fortnight of Āṣāḍha in the same year, in the presence of all the bankers of the *agrahāra* village of Degāve and in front of the temple of Mallikārjunadeva of that place, Śivaśakti, undergoing the ordeal of *phāla-divya*, made oath that the piece of land [called] Ālakolaṇakeyi belonged of old to the god Kalleśvara of Attibāvi; while Kalyāṇaśakti, taking the sacred symbols on his head, declared that it was the property of the original local deity (Mūlasthānadeva). After this, on Monday, the eighth day of the same dark fortnight, all the bankers of the *agrahāra* village of Degāve having convened themselves in the assembly-hall and having examined the hand of Śivaśakti, decided that he had won his cause, and that Kalyāṇaśakti who had taken the sacred symbols on his head had lost it, and that the plot of ground called Ālakolaṇakeyi belongs to the god Kalleśvara of Attibāvi, and gave a certificate of success to Śivaśakti."[1]

II. "In the year of the Messiah 1783, a man was tried by the hot-ball (*phāla-divya*) at Benares in the presence of me, 'Alī Ibrāhīm Khān, on the following occasion. A man had accused one Śaṅkara of larceny, who pleaded that he was not guilty; as the theft could not be proved by legal evidence, the trial by the fire-ordeal was tendered to the appellee and accepted by him. This well-wisher of mankind advised the learned Magistrates and Pandits to prevent the decision of a question by a mode not comformable to the practice of the Company's Government, and recommended an oath by the water of the Ganges and the leaves of the *tulasī* in a little vessel of brass (copper?) or by the book *Harivaṁśa*, or by the stone Śālagrāma, or by the hallowed ponds or basins, all which oaths are used in Benares. When the parties obstinately refused to try the

1 *JBBRAS*, Vol. IX, pp. 307-09. **For 'bankers' read 'Elders'.**

issue by any one of the modes recommended and insisted on a trial by the hot-ball, the Magistrates and Pandits of the court were ordered to gratify their wishes and, setting aside those forms of trial in which there could be only a distant fear of death or loss of property as the just punishment of perjury by the sure yet slow judgment of heaven, to perform the ceremony of ordeal agreeably to the Dharmaśāstra: but it was not till after mature deliberation for four months that a regular mandate was issued for trial by the red-hot ball; and this was at length granted for four reasons: first, because there was no other way of condemning or absolving the person accused; secondly, because both parties were Hindus and this mode of trial was specially appointed in the Dharmaśāstra by the ancient law-givers; thirdly, because this ordeal was practised in the dominions of the Hindu Rājās;[1] and fourthly, because it might be useful to inquire how it was possible for the heat of fire to be resisted and for the hand that held it to avoid being burned. An order was accordingly sent to the Pandits of the courts and of Benares to this effect : 'Since the parties accusing and accused are both Hindus and will not consent to any trial but that by the hot-ball, let the ordeal desired be duly performed in the manner prescribed by the *Mitākṣarā* or Commentary on Yājñavalkya.

"When preparations were made for the trial, this well-wisher to mankind, attended by all the learned professors, by the officers of the court, the *sipāhīs* of Captain Hogan's battalion and many inhabitants of Benares, went to the place prepared, and endeavoured to dissuade the appellor from requiring the accused to be tried by fire, adding, 'If his hand be not burned, you shall certainly be imprisoned.' The accuser,

1 A case of the same ordeal (described as *agni-divya* according to the system of Nārada) has been quoted by S.N. Sen (*op. cit.*, pp. 577-78) from a Marāṭhī document. "On Wednesday, my hands were bandaged. The next day, the aforesaid Pandit sat...on the bank of the Godāvarī, opened the bandage of my hands in the presence of the god and had them rubbed with rice...The signs on the two hands were all marked, and one iron-ball, 50 *palas* or 168 *tolās* and 2 *māṣas*, was duly weighed and thrice heated in fire. They bound a *bhāgya-patra* on my forehead, placed seven *aśvattha* leaves on my hands and bound them with thread. Then they placed the ball on my head and ordered me to walk over seven circles and drop the ball in the eighth ...dropped the ball on some grains which had been kept in the appointed place and the grains took fire...," etc. The accused person in this case came out successful through the ordeal.

not deterred by this menace, persisted in demanding the trial. The ceremony, therefore, was thus conducted before me, 'Alī Ibrāhīm Khān.

"The Pandits of the court and the city, having worshipped the god of knowledge and presented their oblation of clarified butter to the fire, formed nine circles of cowdung on the ground; and, having bathed the appellee in the Ganges, brought him with his clothes wet; when, to remove all suspicion of deceit, they washed his hands with pure water: then, having written a statement of the case and the words of the *mantra* on a palmyra leaf, they tied it on his head; and into his hands, which they opened and joined together, seven leaves of Pippala, seven of *jend*, seven blades of the *darbha* grass, a few flowers and some barley moistened with curd, which they fastened with raw white cotton. After this, they made the iron-ball red-hot and, taking it up with tongs, placed it in his hands. He walked with it, step by step, the space of three gaz and a half through each of the seven intermediate rings, and threw the ball into the ninth where it burned the grass that had been left in it. He next, to prove his veracity, rubbed some rice in the husk between his hands, which were afterwards examined and were so far from being burned that not even a blister was raised on either of them. Since it is the nature of fire to burn, the officers of the court and the people of Benares, nearly five hundred of whom attended the ceremony, were astonished at the event; and this well-wisher to mankind was perfectly amazed. It occurred to his weak apprehension that probably the fresh leaves and other things which, as it has been mentioned, were placed in the hands of the accused, had prevented their being burned; besides that, the time was but short between his taking the ball and throwing it down; yet it is positively declared in the Dharmaśāstra and in the written opinion of the most respectable Pandits that the hand of a man who speaks truth cannot be burned: and 'Alī Ibrāhīm Khān certainly saw with his own eyes, as many others also saw with theirs, that the hands of the appellee in this case were unhurt by the fire. He was consequently discharged. But that men might in future be deterred from demanding the trial by ordeal, the appellor was committed for a week. After all, if such a trial could be seen once or twice by several intelligent men acquainted with natural philosophy, they might be able to assign the true reason why a man's hand may be burned in some cases and not in others".[1]

III. "A Brāhmaṇa named Ṛṣīśvara-bhaṭṭa accused one Rāmadayāla, a linen-painter, of having stolen his goods. Rāmadayāla pleaded not guilty; and, after much altercation, consented to be tried, as it had been proposed, by the vessel of oil (*taptamāṣaka-divya*). This well-wisher to mankind advised the Pandits of the court to prevent, if possible, that mode of trial; but since the parties insisted on it, an ordeal of hot oil, according to the Śāstra, was awarded for the same reasons which prevailed in regard to the trial by the ball. The Pandits who assisted in the ceremony were Bhīṣma-bhaṭṭa, Nānā-pāṭhaka, Maṇirāma-bhaṭṭa, Śiva, Anantarāma-bhaṭṭa, Kṛpārāma, Viṣṇuhari, Kṛṣṇacandra, Rāmendra, Govindarāma, Harikṛṣṇa-bhaṭṭa and Kālidāsa; the three last were Pandits of the court. When Gaṇeśa had been worshipped and the *homa* presented according to the Śāstra, they sent for this well-wisher to mankind who, attended by the two Dāroghās of the Dīvānī and Faujdārī

1. *As. Res.*, Vol. I, pp. 395-98. In connection with the above remark, it may be interesting to note what Edwin Edser writes about 'the Spheroidal State'.

"Expt. 52.........................

"Expt. 53..................The above experiments illustrate what is called the Spheroidal State of water. A laundress generally tests the temperature of her iron by observing whether it is sufficient to cause a drop of saliva to assume the Spheroidal State. Jugglers were formerly in the habit of plunging their hands into molten lead, their immunity from burning depending on the moisture on their hands assuming the Spheroidal State. Blacksmiths will often lick a bar of red-hot iron. In early times a common form of ordeal was to walk on red-hot ploughshares. Many who came through this ordeal triumphantly must have ascribed to supernatural intervention an occurrence which was strictly in accordance with natural law.

"Water is not the only substance which can assume the Spheroidal State. All liquids will do so if placed on a metal surface that is sufficiently hot. If a mixture of solid carbolic acid and ether is poured into a red-hot platinum crucible, it will assume the Spheroidal State. If mercury is poured on to the mixture, it will be frozen though the platinum dish remains red-hot."—See *Heat for Advanced Students* (Macmillan & Co., 1928), pp. 195-96. For another instance of the *phāla-divya*, see B.V. Bhat, *op. cit.*, p. 44.

courts, the Kotvāl of the town, the officers of the court and most of the inhabitants of Benares, went to the place of trial, where he laboured to dissuade Rāmadayāla and his father from submitting to the ordeal; and apprised them that, if the hands of the accused should be burned, he would be compelled to pay the value of the goods stolen, and his character would be disgraced in every company. Rāmadayāla would not desist; he thrust his hand into the vessel and was burned.[1] The opinion of the Pandits was then taken, and they were unanimous that by the burning of his hand, his guilt was established and he was bound to pay Ṛṣīśvara Bhaṭṭa the price of what he had stolen; but if the sum exceeded five hundred *ashrafīs*, his hand must be cut off by an express law of the Śāstra; and a mulct also must be imposed on him according to his circumstances.

"The Chief Magistrate, therefore, caused Rāmadayāla to pay Ṛṣīśvara seven hundred rupees in return for the goods which had been stolen; but as amercements in such cases are usual at the courts of judicature at Benares, the mulct was remitted, and the prisoner was discharged.

"The record of this conviction was transmitted to Calcutta in the year of the Messiah 1783; and in the month of April, 1784, the Governor-General, Imād-ud-daulah Jelādat Jang Bahādur,[2] having seen the preceding account of trials by ordeals, put many questions concerning the meaning of Sanskrit words in the cases here reported, to which he received respectful answers...."[3]

The judgment of a case of the *taptamāṣaka* ordeal (described as *agni-divya*) has been quoted by S. N. Sen.[4]—"You were then sent with Rājasrī Āpājī Hanumant Subhedār and Bālājī Dādājī and Baghojī Rāut, officers from the Huzur and the District, to Pāli for the performance of an *agni-divya*. The *got* of that place assembled in the temple and they lighted a fire and heated ghee and oil mixed in customary proportion. You bathed and after a declaration of your right, took two pieces

1. The boldness and persistence possibly show that poor Rāmadayāla was actually innocent.

2. The same as Warren Hastings, Governors of Bengal, 1772-74, Governor-General, 1774-85.

3. *As. Res.*, Vol. I, pp. 399-400.

4. *Op. cit.*, pp. 366-67. *Got*=members of a caste taken collectivity.

of metal from the heated liquid in the presence of all. Then your hand was bandaged and sealed. The next day the aforesaid parties were brought to the Huzur by the Karkun of the District Officer. On the third day, in the presence of the *Majalasi*, the bandage was taken off and the seals broken. On your hand were found only the marks that formerly existed there. Nothing more, nothing less. You passed the ordeal successfully."

Trial by ordeal is no doubt opposed to the principles of Islām; but the Muslim administration in India failed to shake off its influence completely. Sulṭān Jalāl-uddīn Khaljī (1288-96 A.D.) of Delhi preferred the fire ordeal in one case and Ferishta mentions it in the following words: "The king caused both Siddy Mowla and Kazy Julalood-Deen Kashany to be apprehended, and brought before him for examination. They persisted in their innocence, and as no other witness appeared against them, the accusation was rendered doubtful. The king, therefore, caused a fire to be prepared in the plain of Bahadurpoor, in order that they might be submitted to the fiery ordeal to purge themselves of their guilt; and having left the city to see the ceremony, he ordered a circle to be railed off round the pile. Siddy Mowla and the other accused were then brought, in order that they might walk through the flames to prove their innocence. Having said their prayers, they were just about to plunge into the fire, when the king stopped them, and turning to his ministers, asked, if it was lawful to try Mussulmans by the fiery ordeal. They unanimously declared that it was the nature of fire to consume, paying no respect to the righteous more than to the wicked; and they also pronounced the practice to be heathenish, and contrary to the Mahomedan law, as well as to reason."[1] It is said that, in the administration of justice, "Akbar encouraged the use of trial by ordeal in the Hindu fashion."[2] Speaking about the Muslim state of Sind, Ali Sher Kani, the author of *Tuhfatul Kirām*, says, "An ordeal, still practised among the most ignorant, is that of taking a red-hot spade. Green leaves of a tree are tied on to the hand of the suspected person with raw thread, and an iron spade, heated

1. Briggs, *Ferishta*, Vol. I, p. 299.
2. *Manucci*, ed. Irvine, Vol. III, p. 131.

to redness, being then placed on his palm, he must carry it for several paces quickly and it has often been seen that neither the thread nor the leaves have been in the slightest degree affected by the heat of the red-hot iron, although when cast to the ground it scorched it like the sand in the oven of a parcher of grain."[1] While James Forbes says that trial by ordeal was allowed under Muhammadan Governments,[2] Marāṭhā records show that it was quite common in the Southern Muhammadan kingdoms.[3]

1. V.A. Smith, *Akbar the Great Mogul*, p. 345.
2. Elliot and Dowson, *History of India as told by its own Historians*, Vol. I, pp. 329-30.
3. *Oriental Memoirs*, Vol. II, pp. 389-99.

CHAPTER X

SOME MEASURES OF LAND

I

In the age of the Guptas, the popular units of the measurements of area in Bengal are known to have been the Kulyavāpa, Droṇavāpa and Āḍhavāpa. According to the Paharpur copper-plate inscription of the Gupta year 159 (479 A.D.), 4 Āḍhavāpas made 1 Droṇavāpa, and 8 Droṇavāpas made 1 Kulyavāpa.[1] Since the introduction, in the medieval period, of the unit of measurement called Bighā (usually 80 square cubits), this one with its subdivisions has gradually ousted the older units and denominations from many parts of Bengal. But the Kulavāy (ancient *Kulyavāpa*), Doṇ (ancient *Droṇavāpa*) and Āḍha (ancient *Āḍhavāpa*) are still locally known in the eastern Districts of Bengal, now comprised in the State of Bangladesh. It is, however, unfortunate that all the three denominations are not prevalent in the same locality, that the old relation of 1 Kulyavāpa = 8 Droṇavāpas = 32 Āḍhavāpas is totally forgotten, and that the Doṇ (Droṇavāpa), which only is found in several places, is different in area in different localities. The Kulavāy which is known from the Sylhet region is equal to 14 Bighās, while the Āḍhā prevalent in the Mymensingh, Sindha, Darji Bazu, Raydam, Susang, Hussenshahi, Nasir Ujial, Khaliajuri and Baukhanda Parganas of the Mymensingh-Tangail region is equal to about 4½ Bighās. The Doṇ is more widely distributed. In the Chittagong District, it is equal to about 21 Bighās; but in the Noakhali region it is equal to about 100 Bighās in Sandvip[2] and to about 144 Bighās in the Shaistanagar Pargana. As pointed out long ago by Hunter in *A Statistical Account of Bengal*, this difference in the measurement of the same unit is due to the fact that the length of the measuring rod and also of the cubit is different in different localities. Usually a measuring rod was

1. Sircar, *Select Inscriptions*, p. 347, note 5.
2. Sandvip is now in the Chittagong District.

14 cubits in length and a cubit 18 inches long. In Sandvip, however, the length of the cubit was $20\frac{3}{4}$ inches, while, in the Shaistanagar Pargana, that of the measuring rod was no less than 22 cubits. Nowadays, 1 Cubit=18 inches and 1 *nala* (measuring rod)=16 cubits, as standardized by the Government, have ousted the earlier lengths noticed by Hunter, and 1 Doṇ is now taken, according to the Government standard, to be equal to 76 Bighās in the Noakhali District. In the Rangpur District, where the ancient unit is lost, but the name still survives, the Bighā is known by the name Doṇ. In the Hazradi, Kasipur, Nawabad, Barikandi, Joar Hussenpur, Kurikhai, Julandar, Balarampur and Idghar Paraganas of the Mymensingh region, the Doṇ is equal to about 17 Bighās; but in the Nikli, Juanshahi and Latifpur Parganas, it is equal to about 51 Bighās. Hunter does not refer to the Doṇ prevalent in other localities, e.g., in the Tipperah District. It will be seen from the above accounts that the actual area respectively indicated by the Kulyavāpa, Droṇavāpa and Āḍhavāpa in the Gupta age has little to do with that represented by the modern Kulavāy, Doṇ and Āḍhā, as they do not conform to the old relation of 1 Kulyavāpa=8 Droṇavāpas=32 Āḍhavāpas and as the Doṇ is now known to signify quite different areas in different localities. Apparently the area of all of them has changed in course of time, especially owing to the difference in the length of the cubit and the measuring rod in different localities. Attention in this connection may be drawn to the early practice of using a rod 4 cubits long for ordinary measurement, but that of the length of 8 cubits for measuring Brahmadeya lands.[1] But how can we have an idea about the original area of the Kulyavāpa, Droṇavāpa and Āḍhavāpa ?

The words Kulyavāpa, Droṇavāpa and Āḍhavapa indicate the area of land that was required to sow seed-grains of the weight respectively of one *kulya*, *droṇa* and *āḍhaka*.[2] Pargiter who tried to determine the area of a Kulyavāpa as known from the Faridpur plates[2] rightly pointed out that the staple food of Bengal is rice and the most important grain is paddy and

1. Sircar, *The Successors of the Sātavāhanas in the Lower Deccan*, p. 186, note; p. 330, note.
2. *Amarakoṣa*, Vaiśya-varga, verse 10.
3. *Ind. Ant.*, Vol. XXXIX, pp. 195 ff.

that according to the *Raghuvaṁśa* (IV. 36-37) the usual practice especially in West Bengal was to plant in the cultivated land the seedlings taken out from another field where the paddy-seeds had been originally sown. This is the system followed in rice cultivation in many parts of Bengal even today. Pargiter therefore suggested that the Kulyavāpa indicated that area of land which was required to plant the seedlings of paddy-seeds one *kulya* in weight. Unfortunately, the learned scholar did not know the actual weight of a *kulya* of grain. He had moreover to explain the passage *aṣṭaka-navaka-nalen=āpaviñchya* used in the Faridpur plates in connection with the measurement of a Kulyavāpa. He suggested that 1 Kulyavāpa of land was 9 *nalas* in length and 8 *nalas* in breadth and further conjectured the length of the *nala* or measuring rod to have been 16 cubits and that of a cubit 19 inches. Accordingly, the area of a Kulyavāpa in Pargiter's calculation was a little above one acre ($3\frac{1}{40}$ Bighās), though the suggestion is apparently conjectural. We have now to explain another expression *ṣaṭka-naḍair=apaviñchya* used in connection with the measurement of the Kulyavāpa in the Paharpur copper-plate inscription,[1] which would thus indicate an area only 6 × 6 *nalas*. It will be seen that an *aṣṭaka-navaka-nala* Kulyavāpa would be much larger than a *ṣaṭka-nala* Kuylavāpa.

According to the Faridpur plates, the price of one Kulyavāpa of land was 4 *dīnāras* (gold coins) which, according to the Baigram copper-plate inscription,[2] were equal to 64 *rūpakas* (silver coins). Now the purchasing power of a Gupta Rupee was apparently much higher than that of our Rupee. From an analysis of the '*Ain-i-Akbarī*, Moreland[3] has shown that a Rupee of Akbar's time (1556-1605 A.D.) was equal to no less than six Indo-British Rupees even in 1912, i.e., in a period prior to the First World War. The economic condition of Eastern India of the Gupta age as noticed by Fa-hien who, in his dealings with the people of this region, never saw any coin but used only cowries, possibly suggests that the purchasing power of a Gupta Rupee was much higher than that of an Akbarī Rupee. It thus seems probable that 64 Gupta Rupees

1. Sircar, *Select Inscriptions*, Vol. I, pp. 346 ff.
2. *Ibid.*, p. 343, note.
3. *India at the Death of Akbar*, p. 52.

were equal to no less than 640 Rupees of 1912 even in a quite moderate estimate. It should also be remembered that the price of cultivable land depends much on that of its produce. When one Rupee was the proper price of eight maunds of rice (as is traditionally known to have been the case during Shāista Khān's rule in Bengal in the 17th century), the price of land was undoubtedly much lower than it was in 1912. Many parts of the Faridpur District are thinly populated and settlers may even now get land in those localities on quite easy terms. The inscriptions, again, speak of a fixed concession price of Government land (mostly fallow land) for the creation of rent-free holdings for religious purposes. It is therefore highly improbable that 64 Rupees would be the proper price of one acre or $3\frac{1}{40}$ Bighās of land in the Gupta age. That the Kulyavāpa indicated a much larger area can be demonstrated also by another evidence.

According to a persistent tradition followed by the Bengali authorities on Smṛti, such as Kullūka-bhaṭṭa (15th century), Raghunandana (16th century) and Pañcānana Tarkaratna, 8 *muṣṭis* or handfuls = 1 *kuñci*; 8 *kuñcis* or 64 handfuls = 1 *puṣkala*; 4 *puṣkalas* or 256 handfuls = 1 *āḍhaka*; 4 *āḍhakas* or 1034 handfuls = 1 *droṇa*. That this refers to the measuring of paddy is perfectly clear from the fact that the verse in question is quoted by Kullūka to explain the expression *dhānya-droṇa* in Manu, VII. 126. According to Pañcānana Tarkaratna, who translated the *Manusaṁhitā* into Bengali, and the Bengali compilers of the *Śabdakalpadruma*, 1 *āḍhaka* = 16 or 20 Bengal seers, and 1 *droṇa* = 1 maund 14 seers or 2 maunds. According to the lexicographer Medinīkara, 8 *droṇas* (8192 handfuls) = 1 *kulya*. A *kulya* of paddy seeds would thus be equal to 12 maunds 32 seers or 16 maunds. These are the traditional weights of the *kulya*, *droṇa* and *āḍhaka* as recognised by the Bengali authors, especially writers on Smṛti who apparently relied on the authority handed down from old through a succession of preceptors. The traditional weight can moreover be tested by a measurement of 8192 handful of paddy for a *kulya*. It should be noticed further that the scheme of 1 *kulya* = 8 *droṇas* = 32 *āḍhakas* perfectly tallies with the other scheme of 1 Kulyavāpa = 8 Droṇavāpas = 32 Āḍhavāpas. It is therefore clear that one Kulyavāpa of land required seedlings of 12 maunds 32 seers or 16 maunds of paddy.

Both the systems of planting seedlings and of sowing seeds are prevalent in Bengal, the first in some parts and the second in others. In some localities, e.g., the Faridpur District, both the practices are followed. A cultivator of the Kotalipara region of the Faridpur District informed me that one maund of paddy seeds is required for 3 Bighās for sowing, while seedling of the same weight of paddy require 10 Bighās for planting. Seedlings of one *kulya* (12 maunds 32 seers or 16 maunds) of paddy would thus require 128 Bighās or 160 Bighās of land for plantation. A Kulyavāpa was therefore originally equal to 128 to 160 Bighās, a Droṇavāpa to 16 to 20 Bighās, and an Āḍhavāpa to 4 to 5 Bighās. Even if we believe that the original calculation was based on the system of sowing seeds and not of transplanting seedlings, the position would be : 1 Kulyavāpa = 38 to 48 Bighās; 1 Droṇavāpa = 4½ to 6 Bighās; 1 Āḍhavāpa = 1⅛ to 1½ Bighās. But this seems to have been hardly the case.

II

The Belwa copper-plate inscription[1] of king Vigrahapāla III (*c.* 1050-76 A. D.) of Bengal and Bihar contains the following passage (lines 27-29) giving details about the land granted by the charter : *śrī-Puṇḍravarddhana-bhuktau Phāṇita-vīthī-viṣay-āntaḥpāti-Puṇḍarikā-maṇḍala-saṁbaddha-adhunā-hala-kulit-ārddha-Lovanikāmaḥ ṛju-khaṇḍīkṛta sārddha-udamāna-tray-ottara-sa-pād-āḍhavāpa-tray-ādhika-droṇ-dvay-opeta- kulya-pramāṇ-āṁśa-varjjita-svasambaddh-āvicchinna-tal-opeta-ekādaś-odamān-ādhika- sārddha-sapta-droṇ-opeta-kulya-traya-pramāṇ-āṁśe*, etc. The language as usual is not free from grammatical errors; but the meaning is clear. Thus the land granted by the charter in question formed parts (*arddha*) of the recently cultivated (*adhunā-hala-kulita*) locality called Lovaṇikāma situated in the Puṇḍarikā-maṇḍala within the Phāṇitavīthī-viṣaya of the Puṇḍravardhana-bhukti. Phāṇita was originally the name of a *vīthī* (sub-division); but later it came to form a *viṣaya* (district) called Phāṇitavīthī.[2]

1. *Ep. Ind.*, Vol. XIX, pp. 9 ff.

2. Cf. Kudūra, Kudūr-āhāra, Kudūrāhāra-viṣaya and Kheṭaka, Kheṭak-āhāra, Kheṭakāhāra-viṣaya in *Suc. Sat.*, p. 42.

The locality in question was divided into two parts (*ṛju-khaṇḍīkṛta*), one of which measuring 1 Kulya 2 Droṇas 3¼ Āḍha-vāpas and 3½ Udamānas was left out, while the second part measuring 3 Kulyas 7½ Dronas and 11 Udamānas was made the subject of the grant. In this connection, attention may be drawn to the Amgachhi plate of the same Pāla king, finally edited by R.D. Banerji in the *Epigraphia Indica*, Vol. XV, pp. 293-301. The passage dealing with the measurement of the gift land in this record (lines 25-26) actually reads : *adhunā-hala-kulita-kākinī-tray-ādhik-odamāna-dvay-opeta-sapād-āḍhavāp- ottaraḥ droṇa-dvaya-sameta-ṣaṭ-kulya-pramāṇa*, although Banerji failed to read it correctly. The land granted by this charter thus measured 6 Kulyas 2 Droṇas 1¼ Āḍhavāpas 2 Udamānas and 3 Kākinīs.

We have seen above how 4 Āḍhavāpas (Āḍhakas or Āḍhāvāpas) made 1 Droṇavāpa (i.e., Droṇa) and 8 Droṇa-vāpas or Droṇas made 1 Kulyavāpa (i.e., Kulya) and how originally a Kulyavāpa, a Droṇavāpa and an Āḍhavāpa measured roughly about 128 to 160 Bighās (3$\frac{1}{10}$ Bighās making 1 acre), about 16 to 20 Bighās and about 4 to 5 Bighās respectively. It was also shown how each one of these three denominations gradually came to indicate different areas in different parts of the country. It may also be pointed out that, even in ancient Bengal, sometimes Droṇa (Droṇavāpa) and Āḍhavāpa were each regarded as the standard land-measure like the Kulya (Kulyavāpa) in the above records of Vigrahapāla III and in numerous other inscriptions. The Govindapur plate[1] of Lakṣmaṇasena (1179-1206 A.D.) gives the measurement of the land granted as *saptadaśa-unmān-ādhika-ṣaṣṭi-bhū-droṇ-ātmaka*, i.e., 60 Droṇas and 17 Unmānas. It will be seen that 60 Droṇas would make 7 Kulyas and 4 Droṇas, i. e. 7½ Kulyas. The Tarpandighi plate[2] of the same king speaks of *pañc-onmān-ādhika-viṁśaty-uttar-āḍhavāpa-śat-aik-ātmaka*, i.e., 120 Āḍhavāpas and 5 Unmānas. Now 120 Āḍhavāpas were actually equal to 30 Droṇas (Dropṇavāpas), or 3 Kulyas (Kulyavāpas) and 6 Droṇas (Droṇavāpas). It is interesting to note that even the Unmāna, which is mentioned in these records as a sub-

1. Majumdar, *Ins. Beng.*, Vol. III, p. 96.
2. *Ibid.*, p. 102.

division of the Āḍhavāpa, is referred to as the standard land-measure in the Vaṅgīya Sāhitya Parisad plate[1] of Viśvarūpa-sena. In line 59 of this record[2] the word *unmāna* has been used as a synonym of *udāna* which is mentioned in numerous pasaages of the inscription as the standard land measure. Apparently the same Unmāna = Udāna is mentioned in the Amgachhi and Belwa plates, referred to above, as Udamāna.

The relation of Udamāna = Unmāna = Udāna and of its subdivision, the Kākinī, with the Āḍhavāpa is difficult to determine. The word Kākinī seems to be the same as Kānī which is a land-measure even now prevalent in many parts of Bengal, although the area indicated by the Kānī is not the same in different places. According to Hunter's *Statistical Account of Bengal*,[3] a Kānī is a little above an acre in the Dacca and Mymensing Districts. It is regarded as $\frac{1}{16}$ of a Doṇ (Droṇa) in the Mymensingh District. In the Faridpur District, 30 Kānīs are regarded as equal to a Pākhī (3622 square cubits) of land. This would make the Kānī about 120 square cubits. In Sandvip, 4 Kaḍās are regarded as equal to 1 Gaṇḍā, 20 Gaṇḍās make 1 Kānī and 16 Kānīs make 1 Doṇ or Droṇa.[4] This scheme would suggest that the ancient Kākinī (modern Kānī) was $\frac{1}{16}$ of Droṇa or Droṇavāpa. None of these indications is, however, supported by the inscriptions. The Anulia plate[5] speaks of *sakākinīka-saptatriṁśad-unmān-ādkik-āḍhavāp-ānvita-nava-droṇ-ottara-bhū-pāṭak-aik-ātmaka*, i. e. 1 Pāṭaka 9 Droṇas 1 Āḍhavāpa 37 Unmānas and 1 Kākinī. In passing, it may be pointed out that, according to the Gunaighar plate,[6] a Pāṭaka was equal to 40 Droṇavāpas (i.e., 5 Kulyavāpas). Thus here a land-measure much bigger than the Kulyavāpa and Droṇavāpa is found in use.[7] Another land-measure bigger than the

1. *Ibid.*, pp. 143-48.
2. *Ibid.*, p. 179, note 8.
3. Vol. V, pp. 95, 448.
4. Cf. *Sel. Ins.*, p. 332.
5. Majumdar, *op. cit.*, p. 87.
6. *Sel. Ins.*, p. 332.
7. The Saktipur plate (*Ep. Ind.*, Vol. XXI, pp. 216 ff.) of Laksmanasena, however, uses the word *pāṭaka* both in the sense of the land measure and in that of the part of a village. It speaks of the six *pāṭakas* called Rāghavahaṭṭa, Varāhakoṇā, Vāllihitā, Nimā, Vijahārapura and Dāmaravaḍā as the *ṣaṭpāṭaka*. The said six *pāṭakas* are mentioned in two groups : (1) Rāghavahaṭṭa-pāṭaka together with the Varāhakoṇā, Vāllihitā and Nimā *pāṭakas* (all the

Kulyavāpa and Droṇavāpa was the Khārī or Khārikā which is known from records like the Madhainagar plate[1] of Lakṣmaṇasena. This is no doubt the same as the Khārikā° or Kharīvāpa of the *Amarakoṣa.*[2] As 16 *droṇas* are known to have made one *khārī*, the Khārīvāpa was apparently equal to 16 Droṇas or Droṇavāpas, i.e., 2 Kulyas or Kulyavāpas. Whatever that may be, the Anulia plate cited above shows that an Āḍhavāpa was equal to more than 37 Unmānas (Udamānas or Udānas) and since the Kākinī was a subdivision of the Unmāna, a much higher number of the former would have been regarded as equal to an Āḍhavāpa. That the number of Unmānas in an Āḍhavāpa was even bigger than that suggested by the above inscription is actually known from another record. The Naihati (Sitahati) plate[3] of Ballālasena (*c.* 1159-79 A. D.), father of Lakṣmaṇasena, speaks of *kāka-tray-ādhika-catvāriṁśad-unmīna-sameta-āḍhaka-nava-droṇ-ottara-sapta-bhū-pātakātmaka*, i. e., 7 Pāṭakas 9 Droṇas 1 Āḍhaka (Āḍhavāpa) 40 Unmānas and 3 Kākas. Whether Kāka mentioned here is the same as Kākinī of the other records or whether the former was a subdivision of the latter cannot be determined; but it is known from the above inscription that more than 40 Unmānas made one Āḍhavāpa.

The lost Sundarban plate[4] of Lakṣmaṇasena has a passage which seems to read : *dvādaś-āṅgul-ādhika-hastena dvātriṁśad-dhasta-parimit-onmānen=odhastaya* (?) *sārddha-kākinī-dvay-ādhika-trayoviṁśaty-unmān-ottara-āḍhavāpa-sametaḥ bhū-droṇa-tray-ātmakaḥ*. The measurement of the land is thus given as 7 Droṇas 1 Āḍhavāpa 23 Unmānas and 2½ Kākinīs. In the *Dacca University*

three together measuring 2 Pāṭakas and 4 Droṇas with the granted portion of Vāllihitā being separately mentioned as consisting of 4 Droṇas), measuring 36 Droṇas and yielding an income of 250 coins, and (2) Vijahārapura-pāṭaka, together with the Dāmaravaḍā-paṭaka, measuring 53 Droṇas and yielding an income of 250 coins. The two groups are said to have measured 89 Droṇas with the exception of land under the enjoyment of gods and Brāhmaṇas and yielded an income of 500 coins. It seems that much of the land of Varāhakoṇā, Vāllihitā and Nimā was excluded.

1. Majumdar, *op. cit.*, p. 112.
2. Vaiśya-varga, verse 10.
3. Majumdar, *op. cit.*, p. 74.
4. *Ibid.*, p. 171.

History of Bengal,[1] the passages *dvādaś-āṅgul-ādhika-hastena* and *dvātriṁśad-dhasta-parimit*[2]*-onmānena* have been taken to indicate a cubit of 12 *aṅgulas* or digits and an *unmāna* of 32 cubits respectively. But the first passage seems to refer to the cubit of 36 *aṅgulas* or 27 inches, and the second to the *nala* or measuring rod of 32 cubits of the above length.[3] Hunter also refers to the measuring rod of 22 cubits of 34 inches each prevalent in the Naldi Pargana of the Faridpur District.[4] It is difficult to take the Unmāna, as in the work cited above, in the sense of a linear (?) measure of 32 cubits. We may, however, take Unmāna of the second of the two passages quoted from the Sundarban plate in the sense of the land-measure of that name. In that case, we have possibly to regard its area to have been theoretically 32×32 cubits = 704 square cubits corresponding to about $\frac{1}{9}$ of a Bighā, although actually, in the present case, it was 2304 square cubits, as the cubit is said specially to have been 36 *aṅgulas* in length instead of the usual 24 *aṅgulas*. This is not quite irreconcilable with the details gathered from inscriptions. Since, as we have said above, the Āḍhavāpa was originally equal to about 5 Bighās and since the Unmāna may have been about $\frac{1}{9}$ of a Bighā, it is possible to suggest that 45 Unmānas made one Āḍhavāpa. But it is impossible to be sure on this point in the present state of our knowledge. Moreover, the passages *sārddha-udamāna-tray-ottara-sapād-āḍhavāpa-traya* ($3\frac{1}{4}$ Āḍhavāpas and $3\frac{1}{2}$ Udamānas) and *udamāna-dvay-opeta-sapād-āḍhavāpa* ($1\frac{1}{4}$ Āḍhavāpas and 2 Udamānas) in the records of Vigrahapāla III appear to suggest that the number of Udamānas in an Āḍhavāpa was easily divisible by 4 and was therefore an even number like 44, 48, 52, 56 or 60.

A passage in the unsatisfactorily preserved Bhowal or India Office plate[5] of Lakṣmaṇasena seems to read : *kāk-on-āṣṭaviṁśati-gaṇḍ-ādhika-āḍh-aik-opeta-droṇ-aik-ānvita*, etc. The reading of *gaṇḍa* in the passage is not beyond doubt; but it is difficult to suggest anything more probable. Thus Gaṇḍa, instead of the Udamāna = Unmāna = Udāna, appears to be mentioned

1. Vol. I, p. 653, note 1.
2. Cf. Hunter's reference to the cubit of $20\frac{3}{4}$ inches as prevalent in Sandvip as referred to above.
3. Cf. measuring rod of 56 cubits mentioned in the Anulia plate.
4. Hunter, *op. cit.*, Vol. V, pp. 322 ff.
5. *Ep. Ind.*, Vol. XXVI. p. 9, text line 41. For Gaṇḍaka (Gaṇḍā) in a medieval inscription, see *JAIH*, Vol. II, p. 74.

in this record as a subdivision of Āḍha, no doubt the same as Āḍhaka or Āḍhavāpa. It may be suggested that the Kāka is the same as the Kākinī and the Gaṇḍa is no other than the Udamāna = Unmāna = Udāna. But it is more probale that both Gaṇḍa and Kāka were smaller than the Kākinī. The second suggestion seems to be supported by the relation between the Gaṇḍā and the Kānī (i.e., Kākinī) as known in many parts of Bengal at the present time. The word Kāka is now used in Bengal to indicate a denomination which is $\frac{1}{4}$ of a Kaḍā (i.e., cowrie) and $\frac{1}{16}$ of a Gaṇḍā.

III

In the Nagarī (Cuttack District, Orissa) copper-plate inscription[1] of the Gaṅga king Anaṅgabhīma III (1211-39 A.D.), the area of 18 Vāṭis of land seems to be referred to as a Gocarman. The land measure called Vāṭi, which is equal to 20 Māṇas, is regarded now as 20 acres.[2] If it was approximately of the same area in the Gaṅga age, a Gocarman was then probably equal to about $18 \times 20 = 360$ acres. Unfortunately, the ancient authorities are not at all unanimous on this point.

Originally Gocarman may have indicated that area of land which could be covered by the hides of cows slaughtered in a sacrifice and which was granted to the priests as sacrificial fees. But, as indicated above, the expression is differently interpreted by later authorities. According to Nīlakaṇṭha's commentary on the *Mahābhārata*,[3] it was a piece of land large enough to be encompassed by straps of leather from a single cow's hide. The *Parāśarasaṁhitā*[4] and *Bṛhaspatisaṁhitā*[5] appear to suggest that the Gocarman was an area of land where one thousand cows could freely graze in the company of a hundred

1. *Ep. Ind.*, Vol. XXVIII, pp. 235 ff.

2. See Sircar, *Ind. Ep. Gloss.*, s. v. *Vāṭi* and *Māṇa*.

3. Vaṅgavāsī ed., I.30.23: *vadhrī eka-tantukā carma-rajjū...ekena go-carmaṇā kṛtayā rajjvā ākrānta-bhūr=go-carma-mātrā.*

4. Calcutta ed., XII. 43: *gavāṁ śataṁ s-aika-vṛṣaṁ yatra tiṣṭhaty=a-yantritam| tat=kṣetraṁ daśa-guṇitaṁ Gocarma parikīrttitam||*

5. Vaṅgavāsī ed., verse 9: *sa-vṛṣaṁ go-sahasraṁ tu yatra tiṣṭhaty=a-tandritam| bāla-vatsa-prasūtānāṁ tad=Gocarma iti=smṛtam||*

bulls. According to the *Viṣṇusaṁhitā*,[1] the area of land, sufficient to maintain a person for a whole year with its produce, was called a Gocarman.

There is a more specific indication of the area of the Gocarman in the Saṁhitās of Śātātapa[2] and Bṛhaspati,[3] according to which it was ten times a Nivartana which was the area of 300×300 square cubits (about 4¾ acres). Unfortunately, according to a variant reading[4] of Bṛhaspati's text referred to above, the Nivartana, regarded as one-tenth of the Gocarman, was the area of 210×210 square cubits (about 2¼ acres). Bhāskarācārya's *Līlāvatī*[5] speaks of the Nivartana as 200×200 square cubits in area (about 2 acres). Elsewhere[6] we have pointed out that the Nivartana is 240×240 square cubits (about 3 acres) according to the *Kauṭilīya Arthaśāstra* (II.20), but only 120×120 square cubits (about ¾ acre) according to its commentator. All these differences were mainly due to the varying length of the cubit and the measuring rod, of which there were no recognised standards.[7] But the very basis of the measurement of the Gocarman was, in many parts of the country, apparently vague and uncertain. Since 18 Vāṭis of land is quite a large area, the Gocarman, mentioned in the Nagarī

1. Vaṅgavāsī ed., V. 179: *eko='śnīyād=yad—utpannaṁ naraḥ saṁvatsaraṁ phalam/ go-carma-mātrā sā kṣauṇī stokā vā yadi vā bahu//*

2. Vaṅgavāsī ed. (*Ūnaviṁśatisaṁhitāḥ*) : *daśa-hastena daṇḍena triṁśad-daṇḍaṁ Nivartanam/ daśa tāny=eva Gocarma dattvā svarge mahīyate//*

3. *Loc. cit.*, verse 8: *daśa-hastena daṇḍena triṁśad-daṇḍā Nivartanam/ daśa tāny=eva vistāro Gocarm=aitan=mahāphalam//*

4. Cf. Vijñāneśvara's commentary on the *Yāiñavalkyasmṛti*, I. 210: *sapta-hastena daṇḍena triṁśad-daṇḍair=nivartanam.* See also *Śabdakalpadrumapariśiṣṭa*, p. 160. The *Prāṇatoṣaṇī Tantra*, Vasumatī ed., p. 106, ascribes the verse to the *Svarodaya-ṭīkākāra.*

5. Calcutta ed., I. 6:....................*tathā karāṇāṁ daśake-a Vaṁśaḥ/ Nivartanaṁ viṁśati-Vaṁśa-saṁkhyaiḥ kṣetraṁ caturbhiś=ca bhujair=nibaddham//* Srinivasachar (*Corpus of Inscriptions in the Telengana Districts*, pp. 204-07) cites the *Śukranītisāra*, according to which Nivartana is 28 Daṇḍas, one Daṇḍa being 4 or 5 Karas (Hastas), and quotes Vasiṣṭha who says *daśa-hastena Vaṁśena daśa-Vaṁśāḥ samantataḥ.* M.S. Sarma (*Hist. Chedi. King.*, pp. 366-67) cites Hemādri's *Caturvargacintāmaṇi* to show that Nivartana is 20 Daṇḍas=200 Hastas, i.e. 40,000 Hastas square.

6. *The Successors of the Sātavāhanas*, p. 330, note.

7. See above, pp. 143-44; *Bhāratakaumudī*, Part II, pp. 943-48.

inscription as an equivalent to that area, seems to be that recognised by such authorities as Parāśara referred to above. It may be pointed out that Bṛhaspati, who supports Parāśara in one passage, is actually mentioned in the said record in this connection.[1]

1. A land measure called Pravartavāpa is mentioned as asubdivision of Kulyavāpa in one of the Faridpur plates (*Sel. Ins.*, p. 356, text line 15; *IHQ*, Vol. XXXIII, p. 225). *Pravarta* is probably the same as the measure of capacity called *pravarti* or *pravartikā* (Sircar, *Ind. Ep. Gloss.*, s.v.). The Mainamati plate (No. 1) of Laḍahacandra mentions a plot of land measuring 8 Pāṭakas $4\frac{3}{4}$ Droṇas 5 Yaṣṭis 3 Kākas 2 Bindus (Sircar, *Epigraphic Discoveries in East Pakistan*, p. 47).

CHAPTER XI

BHOGA AND ALLIED TERRITORIAL EXPRESSIONS

I

A stone pillar bearing an inscription was discovered at Bhumara in the former Nagaudh State in Bundelkhand by Cunningham who noticed the epigraph in his *Arch. Surv. Ind. Rep.*, Vol. IX, 1879, p. 16, No. 9, with a translation and an illustration (Plate IV, No. 9). It was edited by Fleet in *Corp. Ins. Ind.*, Vol. III, p. 111. The text runs as follows:

Svasti Mahādeva-pād-ānuddhyāta-mahārāja-Hasti-rājye Āmblode mahārāja-Sarvvanātha-bhoge Indanā-naptrā Vasu-grāmika-puttra-Śivadāsena vala-yaṣṭiḥ ucchritaḥ Mahā-Māghe saṁvatsare Kārttika-māsa-divasa 18//

As regards the reading of the text, it may be pointed out that the name at the end of line 4 is clearly *Indanā* and not *Indana* while the numerical figure at the end of line 9 is 8 and not 9. The name Śarvanātha is spelt generally as 'Sarvvanātha' in the records of the king in question.

The date of the record is quoted in the concluding passage as the 18th day of the month of Kārttika in the Mahā-Māgha year of Jupiter's twelve-year cycle. This year has been variously taken as corresponding to the Gupta year 165 (484 A.D.), 189 (508 A.D.) and 201 (520 A.D.).[1] The object of the inscription is to record the setting up of what is called a *valayaṣṭi* (no doubt the stone pillar bearing the inscription) on the date referred to above in Mahārāja-Śarvanatha-bhoga in Āmbloda in Mahārāja-Hasti-rājya by Śivadāsa who was the son of the *grāmika* Vasu and the grandson of Indanā. The word *grāmika* seems to have been used here in the sense of 'the headman of a village'.

Cunningham took the word *yaṣṭi* in the inscription to mean 'a sacrificial pillar'. But at the same time he observed, "I suppose the pillar may have been set up as a boundary-

1. See Bhandarkar's List, No. 1661.

mark between the territories of the two Rājās (i.e. Hastin and Śarvanātha)." Fleet believed that the expression *vala-yaṣṭi* is a mistake for *valaya-yaṣṭi* which he understood in the sense of 'a boundary-staff or pillar'. His translation of the principal sentence of the record in lines 1-7 runs as follows : "In [the boundary of] the kingdom of the *Mahārāja* Hastin who meditates on the feet of [the god] Mahādeva; at [the village of] Āmbloda; [and] in [the boundary of] the *bhoga* of the *Mahārāja* Śarvanātha,—[this] boundary-pillar has been set up." Like Cunningham, Fleet also suggests that the object of the inscription is to 'record the erection, at Āmbloda, of a boundary-pillar between the territories of the two *Mahārājas*'.

The two kings mentioned in the inscription are Hastin of the Parivrājaka family and Śarvanātha of Uccakalpa. Besides the present record, the Parivrājaka king Hastin is known from his charters issued in the Gupta years 156 (475 A.D.), 163 (482 A.D.), 170 (489 A.D.) and 191 (510 A.D.) while the known dates of his son and successor Saṁkṣobha are the Gupta years 199 (518 A.D.) and 209 (528 A.D.).[1] Similarly, the known dates of the Uccakalpa king Śarvanātha are the Gupta years 191 (510 A.D.), 193 (512 A.D.), 197 (516 A.D.) and 214 (533 A.D.) and those of his father and predecessor Jayanātha are the Gupta years 174 (493 A.D.) and 177 (496 A.D.).[2] Roughly speaking therefore Hastin was the contemporary of the father of Śarvanātha who was the contemporary of Hastin's son. Some scholars wrongly refer the dates in the Uccakalpa records to the Kalacuri era of 248 A.D. instead of the Gupta era of 319 A.D.[3] This is improbable in view of the fact that there is hardly any possibility of the spread of the Kalacuri era in the Uccakalpa area in the age in question. On the other hand, the prevalence of the Gupta era in the same area during the age of the Uccakalpa kings is indicated by the Parivrājaka inscriptions.[4]

The suggestion that the Bhumara pillar bearing the inscription under study was set up for demarcating the boundary

1. Bhandarkar's List, p. 399; *Ep. Ind.*, Vol. XXVIII, pp. 264 ff.
2. Cf. Bhandarkar's List, p. 404.
3. *Loc. cit.*; also Nos. 1194-98, 1200, 1702.
4. For an inscription of the Imperial Guptas in the same area, cf. *Ep. Ind.*, Vol. XXXIII, pp. 306 ff.

between the kingdoms of the two kings Hastin and Śarvanātha is highly improbable in view of the following facts. In the first place, as will be seen below, the expression *bala-yaṣṭi* is found in a similar context in another inscription of the same age and area, and this clearly shows that there is no justification for correcting *vala-yaṣṭi* to *valaya-yaṣṭi*. It is clear from the record referred to that the intended reading for *vala-yaṣṭi* in the Bhumara inscription is *bala-yaṣṭi*. We know that the records of the Parivrājaka king Hastin as well as others of the age and area in question often use *v* for *b* even though they employ *b* correctly or wrongly in some cases.[1] Secondly, even if the emendation is regarded as justifiable, *valaya-yaṣṭi* would scarcely mean 'a boundary-pillar' since the word *valaya* does not really mean 'a boundary'. Thirdly, it is difficult to believe that an ordinary villager without any authority would think of taking upon himself the responsibility of fixing the boundary between the dominions of two neighbouring kings. Fourthly, the language of the record shows that the locality where the pillar was set up lay in both Hastin's dominions and Śarvanatha's *bhoga*, and this hardly suits a line of demarcation between the kingdoms of the two rulers. Fifthly, Fleet's interpretations of the passages *Mahārāja-Hasti-rājye* and *Mahārāja-Śarvanātha-bhoge* respectively as 'in the boundary of the kingdom of *Mahārāja* Hastin' and 'in the boundary of the *bhoga* of *Mahārāja* Śarvanātha' are no doubt arbitrary, while the suggestion that they refer to the boundary between two kingdoms is quite unconvincing since it is unintelligible why Hastin's kingdom should be called a *rājya* and Śarvanātha's dominions a *bhoga*. Sixthly, the word *bhoga* does not really mean 'a kingdom'. Seventhly, the language of the epigraph suggests that Mahārāja-Śarvanātha-bhoga lay within the dominions of Hastin.

The expression *Mahārāja-Hasti-rājya* in such a context would normally mean 'during the reign of *Mahārāja* Hastin', even though the meaning 'in the kingdom of *Mahārāja* Hastin' may not be quite improbable in a particular case. But whether the word *rājya* in our record is taken to mean 'sovereignty' or 'kingdom', the sentence in question makes it clear, as already suggested above, that what has been called Mahā-

1. Cf. *Corp. Ins. Ind.*, Vol. III, pp. 106 ff.

rāja-Śarvanātha-bhoga lay within the dominions of Hastin whose reign (less probably, kingdom) is specifically mentioned in relation to the setting up of the pillar bearing the inscription. What can be the meaning of the word *bhoga* in such a context?

Fleet says, "*Bhoga*, lit. 'enjoyment, possession, government', is a technical terriotorial term, probably of much the same purport as the *bhukti* of other inscriptions." It is true that, like *bhukti*, 'a province', the word *bhoga* is often used to indicate a district of a kingdom. In many copper-plate grants, the gift village is stated to have been situated in a particular territorial unit styled *bhoga*. Mention may be made, e.g., of Kumārivaḍao near Bṛhannārikā in the Gorajjā-bhoga within the Bharukaccha-viṣaya in the Sarsavani plates (lines 19-20)[1] of Kalacuri Buddharāja; Koṇiyānāṁ near Bhaṭaürikā in the Vaṭanagara-bhoga in the Vadner plates (line 19)[2] of the same king; Vīra-grāma in the Sāṭimāla-bhoga in the Paḻayaṭṭhāna-viṣaya in the Jejuri plates (lines 25-27)[3] of the Cālukya king Vinayāditya; Jijjika-grāma attached to Voṅkhāra-bhoga in the Jirjingi plates (line 11)[4] of the Eastern Gaṅga king Indravarman; Vaṇikā-grāma in the Āvaraka-bhoga within the Hūṇa-maṇḍala in the Gaonri plates (B, lines 7-8)[5] of the Paramāra king Vākpati Muñja; Kailāsapura-grāma belonging to the Taraḍaṁśaka-bhoga in the Mallar plates (lines 5-6)[6] of the Pāṇḍuvaṁśī king Mahā-Śivagupta Bālārjuna, etc. It will be seen from some of these instances from inscriptions found in different parts of the country that *bhoga* was a smaller territorial unit than a district called *viṣaya* or *maṇḍala*. It is also interesting to note that the same territorial unit is called Eḍevoḻal-bhoga in the Sorab plates of Cālukya Vinayāditva, but Eḍevoḻal-viṣaya in the Harihar plates of the same king.[7] But, if the word *bhoga* in the Bhumara inscription is supposed to be used in the sense of a territorial unit like a district or its subdivision, we can hardly escape the conclusion that Mahārāja-Śarva-

1. *Ep. Ind.*, Vol. VI, p. 298.
2. *Ibid.*, Vol. XII, p. 34.
3. *Ibid.*, Vol. XIX, p. 64.
4. *Ibid.*, Vol. XXIII, p. 64, note 9.
5. *Ibid.*, p. 108.
6. *Ibid.*, p. 120.
7. *Ibid.*, Vol. IX, p. 16.

nātha-bhoga was a small district of the kingdom of Hastin, even though its name was associated with that of *Mahārāja* Śarvanātha, apparently the contemporary Uccakalpa king of that name. This does not appear to support the suggestion that the pillar in question was set up in order to demarcate the boundary between the kingdoms of Hastin and Śarvanātha.

Monier-Williams' *Sanskrit-English Dictionary* recognises the word *bhoga* in the senses of 'possession, property, wealth, revenue', besides others. Wilson's *Glossary of Judical and Revenue Terms* mentions two kinds of *bhoga* or possession, viz. *sa-vādha* (with obstruction) and *nir-vādha* (unobstructed, undisputed). He also recognises the following expressions containing the same word: (1) *bhoga-lābha*, usufruct in lieu of interest; (2) *bhogottara*, a grant of revenue for the enjoyment of a person or deity; and (3) *bhoga-bandhaka*, a kind of mortgage in which the articles mortgaged may be converted to use and the profits are to be appropriated by the mortgagee in lieu of interest. We have also inscriptions speaking of a *vīthī* (i.e. a shop or stall in a market) as *bhog-ādhīnā tiṣṭhati* and *bhog-ādhīnā gṛhītā* with reference to its lying in the possession or being brought under the possession of an individual.[1] From the sense of 'possession', the word *bhoga* came to be used in the sense of 'the property under one's possession'. The word is used in this sense, e.g., in the Vaṅgīya Sāhitya Pariṣad plate[2] of Viśvarūpasena. The use of *bhoga* (and also of *bhukti*) in the sense of a territorial unit seems to be due to a further expansion of this meaning of the word.

Inscriptions often mention the expressions *bhogika* and *bhoga-pati*. Since *bhoga-pati* is sometimes mentioned in association with *nṛ-pati* (i.e. king) and *viṣaya-pati* (i.e. governor of a district),[3] it may be understood in the sense of 'an officer in charge of a territorial unit called *bhoga*', although the meaning 'one in the possession of a *bhoga*, i.e. landed property or *jāgīr*' is also not impossible in such cases. But the word *bhogika*

1. *Ibid.*, Vol. XXX, pp. 212-13.

2. N.G. Majumdar, *Ins. Beng.*, Vol. III, p. 146, text line 42; *JAS*, Letters, Vol. XX, p. 203.

3. *Ep. Ind.*, Vol. IV, p. 242, text line 44; Vol. VI, p. 141, note; p. 300; Vol. XII, p. 34; Vol. XXIII, p. 159, text line 4; Vol. XXVII, p. 40.

seems to be often used in the sense of a *jāgīrdār*.[1] Thus the donee of the Srungavarapukota plates (line 9-10)[2] of Anantavarman is called *Acaṇṭapura-bhogika* Mātṛśarman. It appears that Mātṛśarman was the *jāgīrdār* of the village of Acaṇṭapura and not the governor or resident of the Acaṇṭapura-bhoga.

We have also other instances of the word *bhoga* being affixed to a personal name in a compound exactly as in Mahārāja-Śarvanātha-bhoga in the Bhumara inscription. A stone inscription,[3] from Kosam (?), now preserved in the Allahabad Museum, reads as follows:

Mahāsāmantādhipati-śrī-Śrīdhara-bhoge duṣṭasāhānī[4]*-Bhīmena kīrttan*[5]*=eyaṁ kārāpitā*[6] // *bhaṭṭāraka-Lāhaḍena*[7] *Saṁvat* 1133 //

Mahāsāmantādhipati Śrīdhara's *bhoga* mentioned in this record, which is no doubt similar to *Mahārāja* Śarvanātha's *bhoga* known from the Bhumara pillar inscription, appears to indicate the *jāgīr* or fief in the possession of Śrīdhara and not the district governed by him. Since it is impossible to believe that *Mahārāja* Śarvanātha was the governor of a territorial unit in the kingdom of Hastin, the sense of 'a *jāgīr*' is certainly more suitable to the word *bhoga* in the context of the Bhumara inscription. It may be argued that a district originally named after Śarvanātha was later included in Hastin's kingdom. This is improbable in view of the fact that Śarvanātha was a later contemporary of Hastin.

As regards Mahārāja-Śarvanātha-bhoga lying in or com-

1. The word *bhojaka* is often used in the same sense. Cf. *Suc. Sāt.*, pp. 64f., etc.

2. *Ep. Ind.*, Vol. XXIII, p. 60.

3. This is No. 519 of 1957-58, Appendix B. See *ASI, AR*, 1935-36, p. 95.

4. For *sāhānī*, cf. *Ep. Ind.*, Vol. XXXII, pp. 141-42. The designation *Duṣṭasāhānī* seems to be the same as *Dauḥsādhanika*, *Duḥsādhyasādhanika* or *Dauḥsādhyasādhanika* mentioned in many records (cf. Majumdar, *Inscriptions of Bengal*, Vol. III, p. 185).

5. The word *kīrttanā* is the same as *kīrtana* or *kīrti* often used to indicate an image, a temple, a grant, etc., calculated to render famous the name of the person responsible for it. Cf. *Ep. Ind.*, Vol. XXVIII, p. 185.

6. Read *kāritā*.

7. The intended reading may be *Lāhaḍasya* since the object of the inscription seems to be to record the construction of a shrine for a deity named Lāhaḍa or Lāhoḍeśvara apparently after a person of that name.

prising Āmbloda within Hastin's dominions, there is nothing improbable, in our opinion, in *Mahārāja* Śarvanātha enjoying a *jāgīr* within his neighbour's kingdom. This possibility is suggested by the well-known story of the locality called Kāśi-grāma or Kāśi-nigama which lay within the dominions of the king of Kosala, but was for a considerable period of time in the possession of the king of Magadha.[1] The said locality yielding a revenue of one lakh coins was given by Mahākosala, king of Kosala, to his daughter Kosaladevī for her bath and perfume money when she married king Bimbisāra of Magadha and, as a result, became a part of the Magadha kingdom. After Bimbisāra's death, Prasenajit, son and successor of Mahākosala, withdrew the gift from Ajātaśatru, son and successor of Bimbisāra. This led to a protracted war between Magadha and Kosala. Ultimately Prasenajit gave his daughter Vajrā in marriage to Ajātaśatru and the locality was given back as part of her dowry. It is not impossible that the village or territorial unit called Āmbloda lay in or comprised a *bhoga* under the enjoyment or possession of *Mahārāja* Śarvanātha even though the area formed a part of the dominions of *Mahārāja* Hastin, just as Kāśi-grāma or Kāśi-nigama in the kingdom of Kosala was in the possession of the king of Magadha when Mahākosala and Prasenajit were on the throne of the Kosala country, although it is difficult to say whether matrimonial relations existed between Hastin and Śarvanātha.

We have now to determine the purpose behind the setting up of the stone pillar at Bhumara since it does not appear to be the demarcation of the boundary between the kingdoms of Hastin and Śarvanātha. Inscribed and uninscribed pillars of stone, found in different parts of India, are innumerable. They were raised for various purposes in all the ages of Indian history. Amongst the inscribed pillars, the earliest belong to the days of the Maurya emperor Aśoka (c. 272-232 B.C.).[2] These are called *stambha* or *śilā-stambha* in the epigraphs they bear. There are some pillars which may be classified as *dhvaja-stambha*[3] (often standing before a temple and bearing inscrip-

1. See Malalasekera, *Dictionary of Pali Proper Names*, s.v. *Kāsigāma*, *Kāsinigama*, *Kosaladevī*, *Ajātasattu* and *Pasenadi*.
2. See *Corp. Ins. Ind.*, Vol. I, pp. xvff.
3. Cf., e.g., the Eran pillar inscription of the Gupta year 165 (*ibid.*, Vol. III, pp. 88ff.).

tions in some cases), *jaya-stambha*[1] (often bearing the eulogy of a conqueror) and *kīrti-stambha*[2] (often bearing the eulogy of a person who performed a pious deed calculated to make him famous). Certain memorial pillars known as hero stones[3] (often with inscriptions recording the deaths of warriors while fighting against enemies) and *satī* stones[4] (often bearing inscriptions which record the deaths of widows burning themselves in fire) are found in large numbers in the southern and western regions of India, though they are also well known from other parts of the country. Besides these, we have also other kinds of inscribed pillars bearing small inscriptions as the one on the Bhumara pillar. Some of these are votive pillars set up in religious establishments by pious men, especially pilgrims, for acquiring religious merit. They are generally referred to as *stambha* in Sanskrit in the records incised on them. Instances of such votive pillars are numerous in the inscriptions discovered in the ruins of old Buddhist Stūpas like those at Barhut, Sanchi and Nagarjunikonda.[5] There is another class of memorial pillars similar to the hero and *satī* stones. The erection of such pillars in honour of one's dead relatives is referred to in early records like the Suivihar inscription,[6] dated in the 11th regnal year of the Kuṣāṇa emperor Kaṇiṣka I, and the Andhau inscriptions[7] of the year 52 apparently referable to the Śaka

1. The Eran and Mandasor pillars bearing the inscriptions respectively of Samudragupta and Yaśodharman fall in this category. Cf. *Select Inscriptions*, pp. 260ff., 393ff. A *jaya-stambha* could sometimes be also regarded as a *kīrti-stambha*.

2. The Talagunda pillar bearing a *praśasti* of the Kadamba king Kākusthavarman, who excavated a tank near a Śiva temple, belongs to this class. Cf. *ibid.*, pp. 450ff.

3. See, e.g., *Ep. Ind.*, Vol. XXXI, pp. 323 ff.

4. See, e.g., Hiralal's List, p. 46 (No. 78), p. 53 (No. 95), etc. In many cases, the inscriptions on the pillar record both the death of a hero and the self-immolation of his widow. Cf. e.g., the Eran inscription of the Gupta year 191 (510 A.D.) in the same work, p. 49 (No. 83).

5. See Barua and Sinha, *Barhut Inscriptions*; *Ep. Ind.*, Vol. II, pp. 87ff.; Vol. XX, pp. 1ff., etc. Cf. *JRASB*, Letters, Vol. XV, 1949, pp. 6-8.

6. *Select Inscriptions*, pp. 35-36. For sacrificial pillars called *yūpa*, see, e. g., *ibid.*, pp. 92-93.

7. *Ibid.*, pp. 167-68. A memorial pillar bearing the representation of a dead person is called a *chāyā-stambha* in the Nagarjunikonda inscriptions (cf. *Ep. Ind.*, Vol. XXXV, p. 25) and elseedhere.

era and corresponding to 130 A.D. Such pillars are generally mentioned in the inscriptions incised on them as *yaṣṭi*. The use of the word *yaṣṭi* in the expression *bala-yaṣṭi* occurring in our inscription may suggest that the Bhumara pillar was a memorial raised in honour of a dead relative of Śivadāsa. This relative was possibly his grandfather or grandmother Indanā, although it is not clearly stated in the inscription.[1]

It is interesting in this connection to note that another stone pillar inscription of the middle of the fifth century A.D., discovered in the Bhumara region of Central India, refers to the setting up of a *bala-yaṣṭi* in the following words: *sva-puṇy-āpyāyan-ārthaṁ yaśah-kīrtti-pravardhamāna-gottra-śailikā bala-yaṣṭiḥ pratiṣṭhāpitā Varga-grāmikeṇa.*[2] This was a memorial pillar apparently raised in honour of several dead relations of a *grāmika* (headman of a village) named Varga and that is why the *bala-yaṣṭi* appears to be described as a *gottra-śailikā*, 'a family stone'. There is absolutly no indication in the inscription that it could have been a boundary-pillar of any kind.

The meaning of the expression *bala-yaṣṭi* is not clear. The *Medinīkoṣa* recognises the word *bala* in the adjectival sense of *bala-yukta*, 'strong, stout', and this is suitable in the present context. *Bala-yaṣṭi* may thus indicate a strong or stout (i.e., everlasting) pillar. Even if *bala* is taken in its ordinary sense of 'strength', *bala-yaṣṭi* would offer the same meaning in a compound expression. It is difficult to say whether such memorial pillars were popularly and conventionally known to have been 'Balarāma's *yaṣṭi* or stick' just as Aśoka's Delhi-Siwalik pillar is called 'Bhīmasena's *lāṭ* or *lāṭh* (derived from *yaṣṭi* or *laṣṭi* and meaning 'a pillar').

In this connection, reference may be made to a late pillar inscription[3] from the former Rewa State, now preserved in the Allahabad Museum. It reads as follows:

Saṁvat 1417 *samaye*/ *Jeṣṭa*[4]*-vadi* 13 *Vuddhe*[5] *Mahārājādhirāja-*

1. We have other pillar inscriptions without indication as regards the object of setting up the pillars in question, especially when they were raised in a religious establishment. See *JRASB*, Letters, Vol. XV, pp. 5ff.

2. Cf. *ibid.*, p. 6; *Ep. Ind.*, Vol. XXXIII, pp. 306ff.

3. This is No. 528 of 1957-58, Appendix B. See *ASI,AR*, 1935-36, p. 96.

4. Read *Jyeṣṭha*.

5. Read *Budhe*.

śrī-Ballāladeva-rājye / ato[1] *Nāyakapālaḥ tasya vaṁśe su-putra-Mahārāja-nāmā pratyutpannaḥ / tad-abhāgyāt=parmeśvara-vaikulyāt=satībhyāṁ saha para-lok-āntaritaḥ / tad-arthaṁ gātram=akārṣīt / ā camdra-bhānū yāvat=tāvat=tiṣṭhatv=idam / Bhamīṇa Somaka / tathā Colo Sahadeva*[2] */ kṛtaṁ gātraṁ //*

This inscription refers to a memorial pillar raised by some persons in the memory of a dead man named Mahārāja whose two wives appear to have committed *Satī*, on Wednesday, Jyeṣṭha-vadi 13, Vikrama 1417 (May 13, 1360 A.D.), during the *rājya* or reign of *Mahārājādhirāja* Ballāladeva, as a *gātra*. The word *gātra* (occurring twice in the record in lines 5 and 7) in the sense of 'a pillar' is unintelligible. It, however, appears to be a mistake or modification of the word *gotra* which may be a contraction of what is called *gotra-śailikā* in the Rewa inscription of the Gupta period, to which reference has been made above. The pillar in question may be regarded as 'a family stone' since it was raised in memory of three persons (i.e. the husband and his two wives) of a particular family. It is interesting to note that the use of *gotra-śailikā* and *gātra* in the sense of a memorial pillar has so far been found only in the said records of the Rewa region.

II

It is well known that among words indicating territorial and administrative units, we often come across *bhoga*, *bhukti*, *viṣaya*, *āhāra* and *bhāga* in the epigraphic records of the early and medieval Indian rulers. We have seen above how Monier-Williams' *Sanskrit-English Dictionary* recognises *bhoga* in the senses of 'possession, property, wealth, revenue', besides others, while Wilson's *Glossary of Judicial and Revenue Terms* mentions two kinds of *bhoga* or possession as 'with obstruction' and 'unobstructed or undisputed' and also recognises the following expressions of which *bhoga* forms a part—(1) *bhoga-lābha* (usufruct in lieu of interest), (2) *bhogottara* (grant of revenue for the enjoyment of a person or deity), and (3) *bhoga-bandhaka* (mortgage in which the mortgaged articles may be converted to use and the profits are to be appropriated by the mortgagee in lieu of interest).

1. A word like *āsīt* would suit the context.
2. Better read *Bhamīna-Somaka-Cola-Sahadevābhyām*.

We have also noted that there are epigraphic records speaking of a stall in a market as lying in the possession (*bhoga*) or being brought under the possession of an individual.[1] From the sense of 'possession', the word *bhoga* came to be used in the sense of 'the property under one's possession'. Thus the Vaṅgīya Sāhitya Pariṣad plate of Viśvarūpasena mentions *Devahāra-devabhoga*, meaning that the locality called Devahāra was a *deva-bhoga* or god's property, i.e. the property of a temple.[2] In expressions like *Mahārāja-Śarvanātha-bhoga* and *Mahāsāmantādhipati-śrī-Śrīdhara-bhoga*, the word *bhoga* means a *jāgīr* or the territory in the possession of an individual[3] as also we have indicated above. The development of the sense of a territorial or administrative unit out of the above meaning of the word is easy to understand especialy in view of the fact that early Indian rulers generally allotted *jāgīrs* not only to the queens, princes and princesses for their personal expenditure and to scholars, etc., for their maintenance, but also to high officers in lieu of salary.[4]

In many copper-plate grants, as we have seen, the gift village is often stated to have been situated in a territorial or administrative unit styled *bhoga* which was a group of villages or a small district within a kingdom; e.g. Vaṭanagara-bhoga, Sāṭimāla-bhoga, Voṅkhāra-bhoga, Āvaraka-bhoga, Taraḍaṁśaka-bhoga, etc.[5] It is of course difficult to say whether the localities called Vaṭanagara, Sāṭimāla, Voṅkhāra, Āvaraka and Taraḍaṁśaka had themselves been *jāgīrs* allotted to individuals in an earlier period or the word *bhoga* was suffixed to the geographical names in the modified and stereotyped geographical sense. But, if the course of modification in the meaning of

1. *Ep. Ind.*, Vol. XXX, pp. 212-13.

2. N. G. Majumdar, *Ins. Beng.*, Vol. III, p. 146, text line 42; *JAS*, Letters, Vol. XX, p. 203. The expression *Kaivarta-bhoga* (fisherman's holding) occurs in an edict of Aśoka (*Select Inscriptions*, p. 62). The same thing is called *Kaivarta-vṛtti* in the Belwa plate of Vigrahapāla III (*Ep. Ind.*, Vol. XXX, pp. 9ff.). In South Indian inscriptions, *bhoga* and *mānya* are used to indicate tax-free land set apart for the enjoymnt of a person for the performance of specified services. Cf. T. N. Subramanian, *South Indian Temple Insciptions*, Vol. III, Glossary, s.v.

3. *Ep. Ind.*, Vol. XXXIII, pp. 167, 170.

4. Cf. Watters, *On Yuan Chwang's Travels in India*, Vol. I, p. 177.

5. *Ep. Ind.*, Vol. XXXIII, p. 169; cf. above, p. 158.

bhoga (primarily 'enjoyment or possession', secondarily 'property enjoyed or possessed', and lastly 'a small territorial or administrative unit') is remembered, all the four words become at once intelligible.

Bhukti offers no difficulty at all, since both *bhoga* and *bhukti* are derived from the same root (*bhuj* meaning 'to eat, to enjoy, to possess') and bear the same sense, one resulting from the addition of the grammatical suffix *ghañ* and the other from that of *ktin*. Thus, like *bhoga*, *bhukti* means primarily 'enjoyment or possession' and finally 'a province or a small district of a kingdom'. In Eastern India, the word *bhukti* indicated a bigger territorial or administrative unit which included several districts,[1] though elsewhere (especially in South India) it was a smaller unit like the *bhoga*.[2]

The word *viṣaya* primarily means 'the sphere of influence or activity' according to Monier-Williams' *Sanskrit-English Dictionary*. The meanings 'dominion, kingdom, territory, district, country, abode' (for *viṣayaḥ* in the singular) and 'lands, possessions' (for *viṣayāḥ* in the plural) plainly developed out of the above primary sense. The expression *koṭṭa-viṣaya* (a district around a fortress, a fort being the headquarters of a district) occurs in an edict of Aśoka.[3]

The word *āhāra*, derived from the root *ā-hṛ*, 'to fetch, give, take, get', etc., means 'taking food, food, livelihood'. From this, the secondary meaning of the word was 'property, etc., given for the maintenance of a person' (i.e. a *jāgīr*), and finally it came to mean 'a district or a group of villages'. In the sense of 'a district', *āhāra* is used in Indian epigraphs from the days of the Mauryas.[4] Although derived from the same root, the word *āharaṇī* known from West Indian epigraphs,[5] is the feminine form of *āharaṇa* (gathering) and probably refers to the collection of revenue either for the king or for the maintenance of the *jāgīrdār*.

Another word, used in inscriptions in the sense of a territory, district or sub-division, is *bhāga*. Thus the early medieval

1. *History of Bengal*, Dacca University, Vol. I, 1943, pp. 24ff.
2. T. V. Mahalingam, *South Indian Polity*, p. 308.
3. *Select Inscriptions*, p. 76.
4. *Ibid.*, p. 51.
5. See *ibid.*, p. 404, text line 3.

records of Bengal sometimes mention Vikramapura in Vaṅga as a *bhāga* comprising a large number of villages.[1] But the real meaning of *bhāga* is 'a part, share, allotment, inheritance'. The geographical sense therefore seems to have developed not only because considerable areas were often allotted to high officers as *jāgīrs*, but also because even high offices were usually held by people hereditarily. Śāba Vīrasena of the Kautsa-gotra claims to have inherited the post of a minister of Candragupta II (376-414 A.D.) from his ancestors.[2]

1. N.G. Majumdar, *op. cit.*, p. 125, text line 47; p. 137, text line 42.
2. *Select Inscriptions*, p. 272, text line 3. There are numerous other instances of the kind.

CHAPTER XII

PANGA AND SOME OTHER LEVIES

I

The earliest reference to the word *paṅga* is found in the Hitnahebbagilu plates[1] of the Kadamba *Dharmamahārāja śrī-vijaya-śiva*-Mṛgeśavarman (c. 470-90 A.D.) of Vaijayantī. In this case, a village was granted in favour of a Brāhmaṇa with a number of privileges, one of which is indicated by the expression *parihṛta-paṅg-otkoṭa* (lines 17-18). In a similar context, the expression *sarva-paṅga-parihṛta* is used as an epithet of the gift village in the Goa plates[2] of Cālukya Satyāśraya Dhruvarāja Indravarman, dated Śaka 532 (610 A.D.). The passage *Vaṁśavāṭake... udaka-pūrvvakaṁ sarvva-paṅga-parihṛto datto* occurs in lines 11-12 of the Kapoli (Belgaum District) plates[3] of king Aśaṅkitavarman of the Bhoja family, who seems to have flourished in the sixth or seventh century A.D. The same word occurs in the form *pāṅga* in the following passage in lines 26-27 of a copper-plate grant[4] (dated Śaka 1028 = 1107 A.D.) of Kadamba Tribhuvanamalla: *śatāt = krītvā dadau sarvam = etat = pāṅg-ādi-varjitam.* In a similar passage in line 42 of the Panjim plates[5] (Śaka 981 = 1059 A.D.) of Kadamba Jayakeśin I, which would appear to be a *kara-śāsana*, it is stated that the donee was to pay *pāṅga* at a fixed rate every year for the village that was granted to him by the king.

The word *paṅga* = *pāṅga* has not been properly interpreted. B.L. Rice while translating the Hitnahebbagilu plates admitted his inability to interpret the expression *paṅg-otkoṭa.*[6] K.T. Telang while editing the Goa plates of Satyāśraya Dhruvarāja

1. *Ep. Carn.*, Vol. IV, p. 136, Hunsur No. 18, and Plates.
2. *JBBRAS*, Vol. X, pp.348ff. and Plates; *Ep. Ind.*, Vol. VI, p.13, note 3. Cf. also *sarva-paṅga-parihṛta-parihāram* in line 7 of the Bandora plates (*ibid.*, Vol. XXXIII, p. 295).
3. *Ep. Ind.*, Vol. XXXI, pp. 234ff.
4. *Ibid.*, Vol. XXX, pp. 77ff.
5. Cf. *QJMS*, Vol. XLV, p. 66.
6. *Ep. Carn.*, Vol. IV, trans., p. 85. We also failed to explain the expression while discussing the inscription in the *Successors of the Sātavāhanas*, p. 266.

Indravarman read *sarva-paṅgu-parihṛta* and translated the expression as 'free from all lame people', although Kielhorn later pointed out that the correct reading is *paṅga* and not *paṅgu*.[1]

P.B. Desai offered several suggestions on the interpretation of this word. In a note published in the *Quarterly Journal of the Mythic Society*, he explained *pāṅga* as 'form' or 'shape' and interpreted the passage *Bhairavāḥ pāṅge Gadyāṇakāḥ* occurring in the Panjim plates as 'Gadyāṇakas (i.e. coins of that name) of the Bhairava type', although an alternative suggestion offered was that *pāṅge* may be a mistake for *poṅge* derived from *pon* meaning 'gold'.[2] But later he gave up the above interpretations of the word and offered the following suggestion : "The expression is not found in Sanskrit or Prakrit. It may, however, be connected with the Kannaḍa *paṅgu* meaning 'obligation' or 'indebtedness'. This suggestion is supported by the context which shows that the ground for the collection of *pāṅga* or fee was obligation. The word has passed into the Marāṭhī language and is used in expressions like *pāṅga pheḍṇeṁ* (to discharge the debt)."[3]

The word *paṅga=pāṅga* as found in the inscriptions referred to above is no doubt the same as Telugu *paṅgamu* recognised in Brown's *Telugu-English Dictionary* in the sense of 'a tax in the shape of one-fourth of the produce collected in olden times by the government on lands in the possession of gods and Brāhmaṇas' (*deva-Brāhmaṇa-vṛttula mida pūrvapu sarkāruvāru tīsikone caturth-āṁśam=ayina kappamu*). It may be connected with Tamil *paṅgu* and Malayalam *paṅka* recognised in Wilson's Glossary in the sense of 'a share'. R. Narasimha Rao drew my attention to the use of the word in a large number of Telugu inscriptions of the medieval period.

Inscription No. 588 in the *South Indian Inscriptions*, Vol. VI, dated Śaka 1189 (1267 A.D.), contains the passage *āya-suṁkkamu paṅgga lĕkuṁḍān=istimi*, "we have made this grant with the exemption of *āya-śulka* and *paṅga*". No. 257 of Vol. X of the same work, dated Śaka 1133 (1211 A.D.) has similarly

1. *JBBRAS*, *op. cit.*, pp. 365-66; *Ep. Ind.*, Vol. VI, p. 13, note 3.
2. *QJMS*, *loc. cit.*
3. *Ep. Ind.*, Vol. XXX, p. 75; cf. also *ibid.*, Vol. XXXI, p. 236, note 2.

i vṛttiki paṅgāmu lēdu, "there is no *paṅgā* in respect of this gift land". No. 405 (Śaka 1187 = 1265 A.D.), No. 422 (Śaka-1191 = 1269 A.D.), Nos. 449 and 450 (Śaka 1202 = 1280 A.D.), No. 488 (Śaka 1221 = 1299 A.D.), No. 492 (Śaka 1225 = 1303 A.D.), No. 499 (Śaka 1233 = 1311 A.D.), No. 520 (Śaka 1238 = 1316 A.D.), No. 527 (Śaka 1241 = 1319 A.D.), No. 539 (of the time of Kākatīya Rudra) and No. 540 (of the time of Kākatīya Pratāparudra) of the same volume have the following passages respectively: (1) *dunnuvārikīṁ baṁggamu lēdu* (the cultivators of this land are exempted from *paṅga*), (2) *evaru dunninānu paṁga-tappu paṁga-suṁkamu pannu kānika darišanamu e-mēralavārūnu ēmīṁ gona-lēdu* (*paṅga-tappu*, *paṅga-śulka*, *pannu*, *kānika* and *darśana* are not levied from the cultivators anywhere), (3) *paṁgamu sarvvamānyamu* (a free holding which is *paṅga*, i.e. free from *paṅga*), (4) *paṁga* (not *paṁggu* as in the printed text) *kānika mannana ā-camdr-ārkkamugānu* (we have permanently exempted it from *paṅga* and *kānika*), (5) *i cēniki paṁga-tappu-suṁkamu aḍigina-vaṟu* (*vāru*) *paṁca-mahāpātakānaṁ baḍuduru* (the collectors of *paṁga-tappu-śulka* will be committing the five great sins), (6) *paṁgamu lēkuṁḍānuṁ sarvva-mānyamugānu mānitimi* (no *paṅga* will be levied by us on the free-holding), (7) *ellanāṇṭikini upakṣiti paṁgamu puṭṭi māḍalu kānika darišanamu maṁnimstimi* (we exempt from *upakṣiti*, *paṁga*, *puṭṭi*, *māḍalu*, *kānika* and *darśana* for ever), (8) *paṁga-sarvva-mānyamu... iciri* (made the grant of a free-holding as *paṅga*, i.e., exempted from *paṁga*), (9) *paṁga-mānyamu* (a free-holding which is *paṅga*, i.e. free from *paṅga*), (10) *paṁgamu veṭṭina paḍupāpālaṁ baḍu-vāru* (the collectors of *paṅga* from the cultivators of this land will be committing all sins), and (11) *paṅga-mānyamugā viḍice* (made the free-holding *paṅga*, i.e. free from *paṅga*). The passage *paṁggamu lēdu* (exempted from *paṁga*) also occurs in Inscription No. 7 from Ongole in the *Inscriptions of the Nellere District*, Vol. II.

In these records *paṅga* or *pāṅga*, besides *paṅga-tappu* and *paṅga-śulka*, or *paṁga-tappu-śulka* in a single compound, is in some cases mentioned along with other levies called *āya-śulka*, *pannu*, *kānika*, *darśana*, *upakṣiti*, *puṭṭi* and *māḍalu*. In some cases, the word *paṅga* has been taken as an adjective in the sense of 'free from *paṅga*'. The distinction between *paṅga-tappu* and *paṅga-śulka* is not clear. While *paṅga-śulka* may be the same as *paṅga* explained above, *paṅga-tappu* may indicate interest or fine on arrears of *paṅga.*

Of the seven other items mentioned in the records quoted above, *darśana* is the same as Persian *nazrāna,* originally a gift or present from an inferior to a superior, a holy man or a prince. Both *āya* and *śulka* mean 'toll, tax, customs,' etc., and the compound *āya-śulka* may have been used in the records in the sense of 'customs duties'. Wilson's Glossary recognises *pannu* as a Tamil word meaning 'tax, tribute, custom, rent'. It is also recognised in Brown's *Telugu-English Dictionary* in the sense of 'a tax, rent, duties'. *Kānika* seems to be the same as Kannaḍa *kāṇike-kāṇe* or *kāṇike-kappa* recognised by Wilson in the sense of 'a present from an inferior to a superior, a subscription, a donation'. Brown recognises Telugu *kānika* or *kānuka* in the same sense. *Puṭṭi* reminds us of Telugu *puṭṭi-dōsillu* recognised by Wilson in the sense of 'a fee of two handfuls from each *puṭṭi* of grain paid to the village servants'. *Māḍalu* similarly reminds us of what Wilson says under *māḍa*: "a half pagoda; whence it is applied to a rate of rent or payment of 50 per cent." The real meaning of *upakṣiti* is doubtful; but it may be a tax on inferior land or a levy to meet the royal *upakṣaya* (loss in some undertaking).[1]

The Hitnahebbagilu plates of Kadamba Mṛgeśvarman uses the expression *parihṛta-paṅg-otkoṭa* (exempted from *paṅga* and *utkoṭa*), in which *utkoṭa* is another allied fiscal term like *paṅga.* The Sanskritic form *utkoṭa* is not found in the lexicons; but its Prakrit form *ukkoḍa,* as used in the Jain *Vyavahārasūtra,* has been recognised by H.T. Seth in his *Pāiasaddamahaṇṇavo* in the sense of 'things to be offered to the *rājakula* (the king, royal officers and members of the royal family)' and 'presents made to the king and others'. The same lexicon recognised *ukkoḍā,* which appears to be a feminine form of the same word, as found in works like the *Deśīnāmamālā, Praśnavyākaraṇasūtra* and *Vipākaśruta,* in the allied sense of 'bribe'.

While the form *pāṅga* may be a word derived from *paṅga* in the same sense, *paṅgā* may be a wrong spelling of *paṅga.* The expression *sarva-paṅga-parihṛta* (exempted from all the *paṅgas*) used in some cases would suggest that *paṅga* often indi-

1. See Sircar, *Indian Epigraphical Glossary,* p. 351.

cated a levy in general and that there were various kinds of it. The use of expressions like *paṅga-śulka* and *paṅga-tappu* (cf. also *paṅga-tappu-śulka*) in the same context along with other taxes seems to suggest that *paṅga* was sometimes also used to indicate a particular group of levies.

II

The Anjaneri copper-plate inscription of Bhogaśakti and Tejovarman, published in the *Epigraphia Indica*, Vol. XXV, pp. 225ff., contains the following passage in lines 32ff.—

Samagiri-vāstavyānāṁ vaṇijāṁ candr-ārkka-kālikaṁ śulkam = ādeyaṁ samasta-rajye n = āsti / aparaṁ ca aputra-dhanaṁ n = āsti / umbara-bhedaḥ rāja-puruṣāṇām = āvāsakɔ jemakaś = ca n = āsti /

The passage has been translated as follows:

"The merchants residing in Samagiri [pattana] shall, for ever, be exempt from the payment of customs duties throughout the kingdom; their property shall not escheat to the State in the absence of a male heir; nor [shall they pay registration fee] owing to partition of joint property; and they shall not have to provide accommodation and provisions to the State officials."

As regards *umbara-bheda*, which was forbidden for the royal officers along with *āvāsaka* and *jemaka*, it was interpreted as 'the partition of joint property' and the editor of the inscription says, "Rao Bahadur K.N. Dikshit informs me that *umbara* (derived from Sanskrit *udumbara*) wood is still used for the door sill in Maharashtra and that therefore the sense is partition of the joint family property." This view is, however, clearly wrong since the passage apparently prohibits the royal officers to do what is called *umbara-bheda*.

Umbara is no doubt the same as *unmara* of the charter of Viṣṇuṣeṇa,[1] in which the injunction *umbara-bhedaḥ rājapuruṣāṇāṁ...n = āsti* of the Anjaneri plates appears as *unmara-bhedo na karaṇīyo rājapuruṣeṇa*. The word *umbara* = *unmara* is the same as Pāli *ummāra*, Prakrit *ummara* and Gujarātī *umbro* or *umro*, all meaning 'a threshold'. The reference is apparently to the door of a

1. *Ep. Ind.*, Vol. XXX, p. 170. See also below.

house. The royal officers were therefore prohibited to break open the door of a merchant's house for confiscation of any movable property or for arresting a person. The *Viṣṇusmṛti* (V. 116) prescribes a fine of 100 Paṇas for the *samudra-gṛha-bhedaka* (i.e. one who breaks open the sealed or closed door of a house) while the *Kauṭilīya Arthaśāstra* (III. 20) speak of 48 Paṇas as the fine for the same offence. But the royal officers were apparently not barred if the entrance into a house was necessary in connection with the discharge of their duty. The prohibition in both the Anjaneri plates and Viṣṇuṣeṇa's record constitutes a privilege granted in favour of certain merchants.

The passage *rājapuruṣāṇām=āvāsako jemakaś=ca n=āsti* is to be compared to such privileges as *rājasevakānāṁ vasatidaṇḍa-prayāṇadaṇḍau na staḥ* (i.e. 'there should be no levy either for the stay of the king's servants at the village or for their passage through it'),[1] *a-paramparā-balīvarda-grahaṇa* (i.e. 'no bullocks should have to be supplied in succession by the villagers when the king's officials would have to pass through their village'),[2] *a-kūra-collaka-vināśi-khaṭv-āvāsa* (i.e. 'the villagers should not have to supply to the touring officials of the king such articles as boiled or unboiled rice, pot, fuel and cot and also accommodation')[3], etc., found in numerous other copper-plate grants.

It is well-known that the villagers were required to provide for the food, accommodation and conveyance to the royal officials who visited their villages for the purpose of collecting the king's grain-share or taxes. The Anjaneri plates use the expression *āvāsaka*, which is no doubt the same as *vasati-daṇḍa* and *āvāsa* mentioned in the other records, apparently with reference to the villagers' obligation to provide for accommodation to the royal officials on tour. As indicated above, this was one of the three principal obligations of the villagers, the other two being the provision for food and conveyance for the officials. *Jemaka*, mentioned along with *āvāsaka* in the Anjaneri plates, thus means either of these two.

Jemaka also occurs in some other records, e. g., in the passage *sarva-ditya-viṣṭi-jemaka-kara-bhara-parihīna* used as an

1. *Ind. Ant.*, Vol. XIV, p. 318.
2. Sircar, *The Successors of the Sātavāhanas*, pp. 186-87.
3. *Loc. cit.*

epithet of the gift village in the Nagardhan plates[1] of Svāmikarāja. The passage no doubt means, 'exempted from the burden of all *ditya*, forced labour (*viṣṭi*), *jemaka* and taxes'. But V.V. Mirashi, while translating the above inscription, takes *jemaka-kara* as a compound expression and says, "*jemaka-kara* was a cess levied on villagers for providing boarding to royal officers camping in the village."[2] It seems, however, that *kara* meaning 'taxes in general' should have to be understood here separately from *jemaka* which was not a cess collected periodically, but refers to the obligation of the villagers for offering certain facilities to the royal officials when the latter happened to visit their villages or camped therein in connection with their official business.

The word *jemaka* no doubt means the obligation of the villagers to provide for the food of the royal officers on tour since it is apparently the same as Marāṭhī *jevā* explained in Wilson's *Glossary of Judicial and Revenue Terms*, s.v. *jewā* as 'a feed, a meal, subsistence which the villagers were bound to provide for the subordinate servants or peons when sent to receive the collections'.

Molesworth's *Marāṭhī-English Dictionary* derives it from *jevṇeṁ* = Sanskrit *jamana*, from *jam*, 'to eat,' through Hindi *jīvnā*, and likewise explains it as 'a dinner or supper, a meal, a feed, board [as of a Peon biletted]'.

In this connection, a few words may be said about *ditya* mentioned in the Nagardan plates along with the obligation to supply free labour (*viṣṭi*) and free food (*jemaka*) and to pay *kara* (taxes). It occurs in some other records, e.g., in the passage *sa-ditya-dāna-karaṇa* occurring as an epithet of the gift land in the Mota-Machiala plates of Dhruvasena I, dated 525 A.D.[3] *Ditya* seems to be a modification of Sanskrit *datti* (an offering, a gift) or a re-Sanskritized form of Prakrit *dijja* = Sanskrit *deya* (a gift), in the sense of presents to be made on such occasions as the birth of a prince.

In the passage quoted above from the Mota-Machiala plates, *dāna* means cess, tolls or customs duties as indicated by

1. *Ep. Ind.*, Vol. XXVIII, p. 9, text lines 19-20.
2. *Ibid.*, p. 11, note 4.
3. *Ibid.*, Vol. XXXI, p. 301, text line 14.

the *Lekhapaddhati* in passages like *dānadāya-dānibhog-ādikam*, *dāna-volāpan-ādi-viṣaya*, etc.,[1] while *karaṇa* seems to be a levy for paying the *Karaṇas* who were the tax-collectors. Wilson's Glossary explains *Karaṇa* as 'a scribe or writer, a clerk, and, in some places, a collector of revenue, a tax-gatherer' and refers to Tamil *Karṇika-mirāsi* and Kannaḍa *Karaṇika-vartana* or *Karnikvartan* respectively as 'the hereditary fees or perquisites of the village accountant', and a 'a cess levied originally for the support of the district accountant'.[1]

1. At p. 170 above, the word *paṅga* has been interpreted in a few cases as 'free from *paṅga*' (Nos. 3, 8 and 11). The real meaning may be that, in these cases, all the taxes were exempted but not the cess called *paṅga* which was usually levied from rent-free holdings according to Brown's Dictionary. See also the Panjim plates, cited at p. 168 above, which reeord such a gift of land.

Chapter XIII

CHARTER OF VIṢṆUṢEṆA

I

The charter of Viṣṇuṣeṇa, apparently found somewhere in the Gujarat region and belonging to the sixth century A. D., is of considerable palaeographical and lexical interest. In it, the symbol for 'five' exactly resembles the *akṣara nā* while that for 'ten' looks somewhat like *ndā*, and, in writing 'one-half' and 'one-fourth,' a symbol exactly resembling the *akṣara vi* has been employed before those for 'ten' and 'five' respectively. Thus the symbol indicating 'one-half' looks somewhat like *vindā* and that indicating 'one-fourth' exactly like *vinā*. Whether these are developed and modified forms of the symbols originally used in writing 'one-half' and 'one-fourth' cannot be satisfactorily determined and the occurrence of the symbols for 'five' and 'ten' respectively for 'one-fourth' and 'one-half' is also not very easy to explain. It should, however, be pointed out that *vi* may be taken to stand for the word *viṁśati* meaning 'twenty'. In that case, it can be suggested that *vi*-5 means '5 in relation to 20', i. e. $\frac{5}{20}=\frac{1}{4}$, and *vi*-10 indicates '10 in relation to 20', i.e. $\frac{10}{20}=\frac{1}{2}$. In this system $\frac{3}{4}$ may have been expressed with *vi* placed before the two symbols jointly indicating 15. It is clear, however, that all fractions could not be written with the help of 20 alone. But whether a fraction like $\frac{1}{8}$ was expressed as '5 in relation to 40' is more than what we can say in the present state of our knowledge.

The language of the inscription is Sanskrit. But the record abounds in words which are not to be traced in the standard Sanskrit lexicons and are in many cases extremely difficult to interpret. As will be seen from our discussion below, some of these words are of Prakrit origin and may be explained with the help of the vocabularies of some forms of Prakrit speech. A number of obscure and technical words, which could not be traced to any other work, have been conjecturally explained.

The document is dated on the 5th day of the bright half of Śrāvaṇa in the year 649 and the endorsement it bears on the 7th day of the dark half of Kārttika in the year 357. Both the dates are expressed in symbols instead of numerical figures of the decimal notation. We have to note that the year 357 refers to a date later than that indicated by the year 649 as, it will be clear from our discussion below, the endorsement must be some years later than the document itself. Now, considering the palaeography of the document, the year 649 can only be referred to the Vikrama era and taken as corresponding to 592 A.D. This is also supported by the fact that the later date, year 357, which, considering the palaeography of the endorsement, can only be referred to the Traikūṭaka-Kalacuri-Cedi era or the Gupta-Valabhī era, corresponds either to 605 A.D. or to 676 A.D. This no doubt precludes the possibility of referring the year 649 to the Śaka era and taking it to correspond to 727 A.D. which would be later than 605 or 676 A.D. That the use of the Vikrama era was not unknown in the Kathiawar (Gujarat) region, to which our record seems to belong, is suggested by the Dhiniki plates of Jāikadeva, dated Vikrama 794 (737 A.D.),[1] found from Okhamandal (Jamnagar District, Gujarat). The Vikrama Saṁvat seems to have penetrated into that region from Rajasthan where we notice its use in records dating from the third century A.D.[2] The use of the Vikrama era in the present inscription may possibly be explained by the suggestion that the merchants, in whose favour the document was issued, were accustomed to its use. It seems reasonable to think that the Jains, mostly a mercantile community, were greatly responsible for the development of the Vikrama and Śālivāhana-Śaka sagas as well as for the spread of both the Vikrama and Śaka eras.[3]

The document records an order, issued from the *vāsaka* (residence) at Lohāṭā, by a ruler named Viṣṇuṣeṇa (called Viṣṇubhaṭa in the endorsement) who is endowed with the subordinate titles *Mahākartākṛtika*, *Mahādaṇḍanāyaka*, *Mahāpratīhāra*, *Mahāsāmanta* and *Mahārāja*. The real meaning of

1. Bhandarkar, *op. cit.*, No. 17.
2. *Ibid.*, Nos. 1ff.
3. Cf. *The Age of Imperial Unity* (*Hist. Cult. Ind. Peop.*, Vol. II), p. 114; *IHQ*, Vol. XXIX, p. 296.

Kārtākṛtika is unknown; but it may have indicated a royal agent[1] or a judge of a superior court or an officer, like the present day Legal Remembrancer, inviting the king's attention to what was done or left undone. *Daṇḍanāyaka* was either a leader of the army or the chief of the police with power of judging criminal offences.[2] *Mahāpratīhāra*, literally 'the great door-keeper', was the king's chamberlain who may have also been the chief of the palace-guards and the royal bodyguards.[3] It is interesting to note that precisely the same five feudatory titles, the *pañca-mahāśabda*,[4] are also known to have been used by Dhruvasena I (Gupta-Valabhī years 206-26=525-45 A.D.) of the Maitraka dynasty of Valabhī,[5] although to whom exactly he owed allegiance is difficult to determine in the absence of further light on the subject.

The order of *Mahāsāmanta-Mahārāja* Viṣṇuṣeṇa was addressed to his subordinates and officials such as the *Rājan*, *Rājaputra*, *Rājasthānīya*, *Āyuktaka*, *Viniyuktaka*, *Śaulkika*, *Coroddharaṇika*, *Vailabdhika*, *Drāṅgika*, *Cāṭa* and *Bhaṭa*, to other officials executing the ruler's orders as well as to the *Dhruvādhikaraṇa*. *Rājan* and *Rājaputra* apparently refer to subordinate rulers and their sons put in charge of administrative units. *Rājasthānīya* means a feudatory or viceroy.[6] *Āyuktaka* possibly means a magistrate appointed by the king and *Viniyuktaka* (the same as *tad-āyuktaka*, *tan-niyutaka* or *tad-viniyuktaka*) an officer of a similar category appointed by the viceroy.[7] *Śaulkika* is of course a customs officer and *Coroddharaṇika* a prefect of the police. *Vailabdhika* may have been the custodian of recovered stolen property as the *yukta* (officer) of the *Manusmṛti* (VIII. 34), although the *Rājataraṅgiṇī* (VII. 161-63) uses the word *vilabdhi* probably in the sense of an assignment. The *Drāṅgika* must have been the officer in charge of a *draṅga* which is explained as 'a town'

1. *Sel. Ins.*, Vol. I, p. 360, note 9.
2. *Ibid.*, p. 260, note 1.
3. *Ibid.*, p. 33, note 9.
4. Cf. *Rājataraṅgiṇī*, IV. 140-43 and 680; *IHQ*, Vol. XXIII, p. 226. In the South Indian records, *pañca-mahāśabda* seems to refer to the privilege to enjoy the sounds of five kinds of musical instruments (*Corp. Ins. Ind.*, Vol. III, p. 276, note).
5. Cf. Bhandarkar, *op. cit.*, Nos. 1304-05.
6. *Sel. Ins.*, p. 391, note 5.
7. *Ibid.*, p. 360, note 7; p. 351, note 1; p. 284, note 3.

in the lexicons and used in the sense of 'a town or village' in Jain literature, but is known to have the sense of 'a watch-station' in the *Rājataraṅgiṇī* (VIII. 2010).[1] *Cāṭa* and *Bhaṭa* are often taken to mean regular and irregular soldiers respectively, although the *Bhaṭas* appear to have been policemen, watchmen or peons, and *Cāṭa* the leader of a group of them. Instead of *Cāṭa*, some inscriptions use the word *Chātra*, often explained as 'an umbrella-bearer'.[2] It is interesting to note that the word *chātra* has actually been used in the sense of 'a court peon' in line 12 of Viṣṇuṣeṇa's charter. In the former Chamba State, the *Cāḍ* (*Cāṭa*) was the ruler of a Pargana.[3]

Viṣṇuṣeṇa's order was addressed not only to the subordinates and officials, but also to the *dhruv-ādhikaraṇa*, i.e. the office of the *dhruva*. The expressions *dhruvādhikaraṇa*, *dhruvasthān-ādhikaraṇa* and *Dhruv-ādhikaraṇika* are peculiar to the records of the Maitrakas of Valabhī. *Dhruva* has been explained as being still used in Saurashtra and Kutch to denote 'a person who superintends, on behalf of the Rājā, the collection of the royal share from lands', and Dhruva is still a surname among the Gujarati people.[4] Viṣṇuṣeṇa has the interesting epithet *paramabhaṭṭāraka-śrī-bāva-pād-ānudhyāta*, i.e. meditating on (or, favoured by)[5] the feet of the illustrious *bāva* who was a paramount ruler. This reminds us of the fact that, in several Maitraka records, *Paramabhaṭṭāraka-Mahārājādhirāja-Parameśvara Śīlāditya* III (Gupta-Valabhī years 343-65 = 662-84 A.D.) is represented as *paramabhaṭṭāraka-mahārājādhirāja-parameśvara-śrī-bāva-pād-ānudhyāta*, while his son Śīlāditya IV is endowed with the same epithet with the only substitution of the word *bappa* (i.e. 'father') for *bāva*. Fleet explained *bāva* as indicating an uncle or a relation of the father's generation.[6]

In connection with the possible relation of the issuer of our record with the Maitrakas, reference should also be made

1. Cf. Stein, *Kalhaṇa's Rājataraṅgiṇī*, trans., Vol. II, pp. 291f.
2. Cf. *Sel. Ins.*, p. 414, note 5.
3. Sircar, *Ind. Ep. Gloss.*, p. 64.
4. Cf. *Sel. Ins.*, p. 404, note 1; *Corp. Ins. Ind.*, Vol. III, p. 190, note; H. D. Sankalia, *Archaeology of Gujarat*, p. 200 and note. The word *dhruva* may refer to the fixed shares of different crops collected for the king.
5. Cf. *Sel. Ins.*, p. 454, note 3.
6. *Corp. Ins. Ind.*, Vol. III, p. 186, note.

to his name, viz. Viṣṇuṣeṇa or Viṣṇubhaṭa. We know that the names of the Maitraka kings ended usually with the word *sena*, but sometimes also with the word *bhaṭa*.[1] What is, however, more interesting is that, as in the case of Viṣṇuṣeṇa-Viṣṇubhaṭa, sometimes a Maitraka ruler is found to have borne a name ending with both *sena* and *bhaṭa*. We know that Maitraka Dhruvasena II Bālāditya (Gupta-Valabhī years 310-21 = 629-40 A.D.), who was the son-in-law of king Harṣa of Kanauj, has been mentioned in the *Si-yu-ki* of Hieun-tsang by the name Dhrubhaṭa or Dhruvabhaṭa.[2]

We have seen that *Mahāsāmanta-Mahārāja* Viṣṇuṣeṇa (Viṣṇubhaṭa) claimed some relation with his overlord or predecessor described as *paramabhaṭṭāraka-śrī-bāva*. The date of the document, 592 A.D., as well as its possible place of issue somewhere in the Gujarat-Kathiawar region would suggest that this overlord was probably the Kalacuri king Śaṅkaragaṇa whose Abhona plates are dated in the Kalacuri year 347 (595 A.D.).[3] This seems to be supported further by other facts. The Sarasavni plates of Kalacuri Buddharāja, son of Śaṅkaragaṇa, dated in the year 361 (609 A.D.),[4] were issued from Ānandapura, which is the modern Anand[5] in the Kaira District in Gujarat. Dadda I of the Gurjara house of Nāndīpurī (Nandor in the old Rajpipla State) and Broach is described as *Gurjara-nṛpati-vaṁśa-mahodadhau Śrī-saha-jammā Kṛṣṇa-hṛday-āhit-āspadaḥ kaustubha-maṇir=iva*[6] with a probable allusion to his allegiance to Kalacuri Kṛṣṇa, father of Śaṅkaragaṇa. The Kalacuris certainly extended their power over the northern Maratha country and Malwa[7] and probably also over some adjoining regions. King Kṛṣṇa's coins, styled *Kṛṣṇarāja-rūpaka* in the Anjaneri inscription of Pṛthivīcandra Bhogaśakti, dated

1. Cf. names like Dharasena (I-IV), Dhruvasena (I-III) and those like Dhrūbhaṭa and Derabhaṭa (Bhandarkar, *op. cit.*, p. 394). The name-ending *bhaṭa* also occurs in the contemporary ruling family of the Gurjaras of Nāndīpurī.

2. Cf. Watters, *On Yuan Chwang's Travels in India*, Vol. II, pp. 246-47.

3. Bhandarkar, *op. cit.*, No. 1206.

4. *Ibid.*, No. 1208.

5. *Ep. Ind.*, Vol. VI, p. 297.

6. Cf., e.g., *Ind. Ant.*, Vol. XIII, pp. 82, 88.

7. They granted lands in the Nasik region and issued charters from Ujjayinī and Vaidiśa (Vidiśā). Cf. Bhandarkar, *loc. cit.*, Nos. 1206-08.

709 A. D., are not only found in the Nasik District, but also in the islands of Bombay and Salsette.[1] The above facts no doubt suggest that the Kalacuris very probably succeeded in extending their power over the Gujarat-Kathiawar region or at least over wide regions of that area and that, from the middle of the sixth century A.D., all rulers of that region, bearing subordinate titles, owed allegiance to the Kalacuris. It may further be noted that the date of our inscription falls in the period between the rule of the Maitraka king Dharasena II (Gupta-Valabhī years 252-70=571-89 A.D.) and that of Śīlāditya I Dharmāditya (Gupta-Valabhī years 286-90=605-09 A.D.). Thus if Viṣṇuṣeṇa (Viṣṇubhaṭa) actually belonged to the Maitraka dynasty, his rule may be accommodated between 589 and 605 A.D., although it has to be admitted that the introductory part of the epigraph under study does not follow that of the Maitraka records. But if Lohāṭā, and not Valabhī, was his headquarters, it is possible to suggest that he was ruling side by side with the Maitraka king or kings of Valabhī, even though he belonged to the same family or a branch of it. Lohāṭā is, however, mentioned as Lohāṭaka-grāma in the endorsement and may have been merely a village in the dominions of Viṣṇuṣeṇa.

The inscription says that Viṣṇuṣeṇa had been approached by the community of merchants, apparently of Lohāṭā as suggested by the endorsement, with the request of being favoured with the ruler's *ācāra-sthiti-pātra*[2] which they might utilise in protecting and favouring their own people (*loka-saṁgrah-ānugrah-ārtham*) and that the merchants were actually favoured with the ruler's *sthiti-pātra* used in the protection and settlement of the people of his dominions (*janapadasya....parirakṣaṇa-sanniveśanāya*). This *sthiti-pātra* or *ācāra-sthiti-pātra* is elsewhere also called *anugraha-sthiti-pātra*, *sthiti-vyavasthā* and *sthiti-pātra-vyavasthā* and is actually a long list of regulations which look like prevalent customary laws without much modification. At the end, king Viṣṇuṣeṇa (Viṣṇubhaṭa) further says that, in addition to the *ācāras* quoted, he also approved of other *ācāras* that were handed down from ancient times. He ends

1. *Ep. Ind.*, Vol. XXV, p. 229.
2. The word *pātra* has been used in the sense of *patra*.

with the request that his *anugraha-sthiti-pātra* should be approved and followed by the future rulers of the country. The executor (*Dūtaka*) of the document was Bhaḍḍaka who was an officer of the department of war and peace (*sandhivigrah-ādhikaraṇ-ādhikṛta*). The main document ends with the date and the representation of Viṣṇuṣeṇa's signature.

This is followed by an endorsement according to which *Sāmanta* Avanti issued an order from Darpapura to his own officials informing them that he had given his assent to the *sthiti-vyavasthā* granted by the illustrious Viṣṇubhaṭa (Viṣṇu-ṣeṇa) to the community of merchants residing at Lohāṭaka-grāma (apparently the same as Lohāṭā, from where Viṣṇuṣeṇa's document had been issued) and that persons conducting their respective trades and following the above *sthiti-pātra-vyavasthā* should not be disturbed in any way. The endorsement ends with the second date referred to above. Whether *Sāmanta* Avanti was a subordinate of *Mahāsāmanta-Mahārāja* Viṣṇuṣeṇa (Viṣṇubhaṭa) or whether the Lohāṭā area came to form a part of the district ruled by Avanti at a later date cannot be satisfactorily determined. It is not improbable that Avanti was a Gurjara who dated his document in the Kalacuri era. If this suggestion may be accepted, the endorsement is to be regarded as dated in 605 A.D., only about 13 years after the original document.

The said list of regulations or customary laws, which is full of obscure and technical words, is very valuable not only to a lexicographer, but also to all students of ancient Indian history. We know of an *ācāra-vyavathā* embodied in the Lakshmeshwar Kannaḍa inscription[1] (*circa* 725 A.D.) of *Yuvarāja* Vikramāditya II of the Cālukya house of Badami; but that record is small and damaged and is not of any help in the elucidation of the text of the *ācāras* quoted in the inscription under discussion. Some of the *ācāras* are mentioned in the Anjaneri plates[2] of Bhogaśakti and Tejovarman. A

1. *Ibid.*, Vol. XIV, pp. 190-91.

2. *Ibid.*, Vol. XXV, p. 237—*Samagiri-vāstavyānāṁ vaṇijāṁ candr-ārka-kālikaṁ śulkam=ādeyaṁ samasta-rājye n=āsti/aparaṁ ca aputra-dhanaṁ n=āsti/ umbara-bhedaḥ rājapuruṣāṇām=āvāsako jemakaś=ca n=āsti/ kumārīsāhase rūpakā-ṇām=aṣṭ-ottara-śatam/ saṁgrahaṇe dvātriṁśad-rūpakāḥ/karṇa-troḍanikāyāṁ ṣodaśa*

record[1] of Śaka 973 (1050 A.D.) from Sudi, Dharwar District, registers the *śāsana-maryāde* granted to eight Seṭṭis and eighty householders of the village whose shops and households were granted immunity from all imposts including the fixed land-rent for two *srāhes* (years) after which they would have to pay the usual dues (*sarv-āya*).

II

We quote below the text of the seventy-two *ācāras* and make an attempt to explain them one by one.[2]

1. *Āputrakaṁ na grāhyam. Āputraka* means 'the property belonging to a person who died without leaving a son'.[3] This seems to say that such property should not be confiscated by royal officials diregarding the claim of any legal heir other than the son.

2. *Ummara-bhedo na karaṇīyo rāja-puruṣeṇa.* This is probably connected with No. 1 above. The royal officials are asked not to break open or violate the *ummara*, the meaning of which is unknown. It may be related to the word *udumbara* (Pali *uṁmāra*; Prakrit *ummara*; Gujarati *umbro*, *umro*, 'threshold'). The reference may be to the threshold or door of a house. Viṣṇu (V. 116) prescribes a fine of 100 *paṇas* for a *sa-mudra-gṛha-bhedaka* (one who breaks open the sealed door of a house); but Kauṭilya speaks of 48 *paṇas* as the fine for the same offence (*Arthaśāstra*, III. 20).

rūpakāḥ| śiraḥ-sphoṭane catvāri rūpakāḥ| bhārikāyāṁ vaṇik-putrasy=āṣṭ-ottara-śataṁ rūpakāṇām| naṅge gṛhītasya yac=c=āṣṭau ṣoḍaśa vā nagara-mahallakā vicārya vadante tad=eva pramāṇam |

1. *Ibid.*, Vol. XV, pp. 77ff. The rules regarding the Seṭṭis were not applicable to the country, nor those of the country to the Seṭṭis. The guilt of the father should not affect the son, nor that of the son, his father. If a shop-keeper would strike a thief, robber, burglar, enemy or an evil-minded person in the verandah near the screen of the shop, there should be no guilt and no fine; but if he would strike them elsewhere, he should be fined 6 gold *gadyāṇas*.

2. The list reminds us of Kātyāyana's view quoted in Devaṇṇa-bhaṭṭa's *Smṛticandrikā*, Vol. III, Part I, p. 58 : *deśasy=ānumaten=aiva vyavasthā yā nirūpitā | likhitā tu sadā dhāryā mudritā rāja-mudrayā || śāstra-vad=yatnato rakṣyā tāṁ nirikṣya vinirṇayet* || It seems to recognise *rāja-śāsana* among the sources of law.

3. *Ep. Ind.*, Vol. XXVIII, p. 291 and note 13.

3. *Udbhāvaka-vyavahāro na grāhyah.* The word *vyavahāra* here may be taken in the sense of 'a law-suit'; but the real meaning of *udbhāvaka* is uncertain. It may, however, refer to a case carelessly put before the court (cf. *udbhāvana*, 'neglect') or to one based on fabrication or false allegation.

4. *Śaṅkayā grahaṇaṁ n=āsti.* This is apparently related to No. 3 above. The royal officials should not go in for the apprehension of persons or for taking up a case against one or for seizing one's things through mere suspicion (*śaṅkā*) of a crime.

5. *Puruṣ-āparadhe strī na grāhyā.* This means to say that the wife should not be apprehended for her husband's guilt.

6. *Kṣem-āgni-samutthāne chalo na grāhyaḥ.* The word *chala* ordinarily means 'a pretext'. But, in the Smṛti literature, it is used in the sense of 'careless declaration', while *bhūta* means 'a solemn statement of truth'.[1] The word occurs in Nos. 7, 9 and 31 below. Although the technical meaning seems to be preferable, the ordinary meaning of the word may be applied to all the cases, especially to No. 31. *Kṣem-āgni* seems to mean 'sacred fire' such as is kindled on the occasion of marriage, etc. If we follow the technical sense of *chala*, the *ācāra* may mean that no half-hazard allegation should be entertained against one's neighbour for the burning of one's house when, according to the accused, the conflagration resulted from the sacred fire kindled in his house. But, if the ordinary meaning of the word is preferred, this may refer to a case involving the burning of a neighbour's house, in which the plea that the conflagration was due to the sacred fire kindled in the house of the accused would not be acceptable. In Marāṭhī. *chala* means 'harrassment, or persecution,' and it may be taken to indicate in the present context to signify 'prosecution'.

7. *Svayaṁ hrasite karṇṇe chalo na grāhyaḥ.* This means either that (1) there was no pretext for a man who was himself responsible for cutting a bit from a neighbour's ear, or that (2) no careless accusation was acceptable from a man in regard to the cutting of a bit from his own ears. Cf. *karṇṇa-troṭana*

1. Cf. *Yājñavalkyasmṛti*, N. S. Press ed., p. 130 : *chalaṁ nirasya bhūtena vyavahārān=nayen=nṛpaḥ*, wherein the *Mitākṣarā* explains *chala* as *pramād-ābhihita* and *bhūta* as *tattv-ārtha-saṁyukta*.

in No. 37 below. If *hrasita* may here be taken in the sense of 'sounded', the reference may also be to a case in which the details of a dispute had previously reached the ears of the judge who was thus in a position to detect the fabricated element in the statement put to him without investigation.

8. *Arthi-pratyarthinā vinā vyavahāro na grāhyaḥ.* A law-suit could be taken up for disposal only when the complainant and the defendant were both present and never in the absence of either of the parties.

9. *Āpaṇe āsanasthasya chalo na grāhyaḥ.* This means either that (1) the pretext of being engaged in work at the shop should not justify the absence of a party to a law-suit from the court (cf. No. 8 above), or that (2) no careless statement of accusation was acceptable from a person who had been, at the time of occurrence, busy in selling things in a shop or market (cf. No. 21 below).

10. *Go-śakaṭaṁ na grāhyam.* This seems to be related to No. 11 below.

11. *Sāmant-āmātya-dūtānām=anyeṣāṁ c=ābhyupāgame śaya-nīy-āsana-siddhānnaṁ na dāpayet.* When a subordinate chief, an officer or an envoy of the king came to a village, the inhabitants thereof should not be compelled to supply beds or couches, seats and boiled rice. Some of these things, however, are known to have been usually supplied by the villagers, and the kings are found to have exempted gift villages from these obligations. Cf. such *parihāras* or exemptions as *a-kūra-collaka-vināśi-khaṭvā-saṁvāsa* and *a-paramparā-balīvarda-grahaṇa* explained in *The Successors of the Sātavāhanas*, pp. 187ff. It may be pointed out that inscriptions speak of supplying bullocks to the touring officials by the inhabitants of different villages in succession, but not of supplying carts (cf. No. 10 above). The reference to boiled rice (*siddh-ānna*) in particular may suggest that unboiled rice had to be supplied. But the expression *siddh-ānna* also reminds us of *sidhā*, 'uncooked victuals', in Hindi, Bengali, etc.

12. *Sarva-śreṇīnām=ek-āpaṇako na deyaḥ.* Members of different guilds should not be allowed to flock to the same market. The idea seems to be that different mercantile guilds should occupy different markets or at least different quarters of the same market. Otherwise, there might be disturbance.

13. *Sarva-śreṇibhiḥ khovā-dānaṁ na dātavyam.* All the guilds should not be compelled to pay *khovā*, the meaning of which is unknown. It may be the same thing as the *aṭṭapati-bhāga* or 'the share of the lord of the market', mentioned as a tax in the *Rājataraṅgiṇī* (V. 164).

14. *Rājakule='dhikaraṇasya ca rāj-ārgghikā deyā; anyeṣām=adeyā.* Periodical offerings to be made to the king should be brought to the palace or to the particular office engaged in collecting them, but not to anybody else. *Rāj-ārgghikā* may be the same as *rāja-pradeya* of the *Manusmṛti* (VII. 119).[1] The word also occurs in No. 45 below.

15. *Vārikasya haste nyāsako na sthāpanīyaḥ.* This is probably related to No. 14 above. The offerings meant for the king were not to be deposited with (or, no deposits should be entrusted to) the *Vārika.* The word (cf. No. 72 below) seems to indicate a class of officials, three of which are mentioned in the record (cf. Nos. 27, 28, 31, 47). It may be compared with Gujarati *Vāredār* or tax-gatherer. The *Bṛhaspatismṛti*[2] mentions *Vārika* along with the *cāturvaidya, vaṇik, sarva-grāmīṇa, mahattara* and others, while the *Rājataraṅgiṇī* (VI. 345) speaks of the *Kaṭaka-vārika.* The meaning is, however, not clear. The word may be connected with *vāra*, probably meaning 'the member of a committee' and occurring in such expressions as *vāra-goṣṭhī, pañca-vārī* and *vāra-pramukha* found in inscriptions.[3] But the official designation *Śānti-vārika*, occurring in the inscriptions of the Candra kings of Bengal, has been explained as 'probably a priest in charge of propitiatory ceremonies',[4] while Monier-Williams recognises the word *Nāga-vārika* in his Sanskrit Dictionary and explains it as 'an elephant-driver or keeper' and 'the chief person in a court or assembly'.

16. *Para-viṣayāt=kāraṇ-ābhyāgato vaṇijakah para-reṣe na grāhyaḥ.* The word *reṣa* means 'injury'; but its significance in

1. According to Manu, however, 'the headman of the village should get all of what is daily payable by the villagers to the king in the shape of food, drink, fuel and other things'. Cf. *Successors of the Sātavāhanas*, p. 187.

2. Cf. *Bṛhaspatismṛti*, GOS ed., p. 159: *rājā kṣetraṁ dattvā cāturvaidya-vaṇig-vārika-sarvagrāmīṇa-mahattara-svāmipuruṣ-ādhiṣṭhitaṁ paricchindyāt.*

3. Cf. *Ep. Ind.*, Vol. V, p. 138, note.

4. N.G. Majumdar, *Inscriptions of Bengal*, Vol. III, pp. 8, 166.

the present context is unknown. The meaning of the *ācāra* may be that a merchant belonging to another district or kingdom should not be accepted as a witness in a criminal case involving persons of a locality where he happened to be present on account of some reason or other.

17. *Āvedanakena vinā utkṛṣṭī na grāhyā.* This seems to be related to No. 16 above; but the meaning of *utkṛṣṭī* is unknown. *Āvedanaka* may indicate 'a formal complaint in court' and *utkṛṣṭī* may be the same as Pāli *ukkuṭṭhī* and Sanskrit *utkruṣṭī* or *utkrośa*, meaning 'wailing'. A proper complaint, and not mere wailing, was acceptable to court.

18. *Vākpāruṣya-daṇḍapāruṣyayoḥ sākṣitve sārī na grāhyā.* The *sārikā* bird could not be allowed to be a witness in cases of defamation and assault.

19. *Ḍheṅku-kaḍḍhaka-nīla-ḍumphakāś=ca viṣṭiṁ na kāra-yitavyāḥ.* The *Ḍumphaka* of a *nīla-kuṭī*, liable to pay a certain tax, is also referred to in No. 48 below; but who are actually exempted from forced labour (*viṣṭi*) in the present case cannot be determined. The words *ḍheṅku*, *kaḍḍhaka* and *ḍumphaka* are unknown. *Ḍhenku* may de compared with Hindi *ḍheṅki* or *dheṅkulī* meaning a machine for extracting juice, while *kaḍḍhaka* seems to be a Prakrit form of Sanskrit *karṣaka*. *Ḍumphaka* may be the same as Sanskrit *dṛmphaka* meaning 'one who presses'. The *Nīla-ḍumphaka* possibly manufactured blue dye from the indigo plant. If *ḍheṅku* is the same as Gujarati *ḍhīkvo*, Hindi *ḍheṅklī* or *ḍheṅkul*, in the sense of the contrivance (based on the principle of lever) for drawing water from a well, the drawers of water for the irrigation of fields may be the persons indicated by *Ḍheṅku-kaḍḍhaka*.

20. *Prapāpūraka-gopālāḥ rāja-graheṇa na grāhyāḥ. Prapā-pūraka* is a person entrusted with *prapā-pūraṇa*, i.e. 'filling the cisterns with water in a place for watering cattle or supplying water to travellers'. Such persons as well as the milkmen were not to be apprehended or recruited for free labour on the king's behalf.[1]

21. *Gṛh-āpaṇa-sthitānāṁ mudrā-patraka-dūtakaiḥ sāhasa-varjjam=āhvānaṁ na karaṇīyam.* Persons engaged in work at

1. Cf. *Bṛhaspatismṛti*, p. 26 : *gavāṁ pracāre gopālāḥ sasy-ārambhe kṛṣīvalāḥ* in the section on *āhvāna* (summons) and in the list of the *n=āsedhyāḥ*.

home or at their shops should not be summoned to court by means of a seal-ring or a letter or by a messenger unless they were involved in a criminal case.[1]

22. *Pareṇ=ārth-ābhiyuktānāṁ vāda-pratisamāsane yajña-sattra-vivāh-ādiṣu āhvānaṁ na kārayet.* Persons engaged in such works as a sacrifice or a marriage ceremony should not be summoned to court to refute the charges brought against them. *Artha* may refer to an *artha-mūla* or civil (and not a *hiṁsā-mūla* or criminal) suit.[2] Or, there may be reference here to two different sets of persons who should not be summoned, viz., (1) one engaged in *yajña*, etc.,[3] and (2) one already involved in another case.[4] A word like *niratānām* seems to be understood after °*ādiṣu.*

23. *Ṛṇ-ādān-ābhilekhita-vyavahāre a-kāṣṭha-loha-baddhena kṛta-pratibhuvā guptir=upāsyā.* In connection with a written complaint about the realisation of borrowed money, the debtor, when he was not under wooden or metal handcuffs because of security having been furnished for him by somebody, should enjoy the protection of the court. This seems to say that in the case of a debtor, for whom security had been furnished, neither handcuffs nor guards at court were necessary. When no *pratibhū* was furnished, the court had to arrange for the person's watch and the cost of it had to be borne by the parties.[5] The word *ādāna* frequently occurs in the latter part of the document; see Nos. 25, 48-51, 55-57, 59, 66 and 69.

24. *Varṣāsu sva-viṣayāt bīj-ārtham=āgataka-karṣakāḥ svāminā na grāhyāḥ.* Cultivators coming out of their areas for sowing seeds during the rainy sesson were not to be apprehended or engaged by the king or landlord in free labour.[6] See below, No. 52.

1. Cf. *ibid.*, p. 24 : *mudrāṁ dadyāt tathā patraṁ puruṣaṁ vā visarjayet.* See also P.V. Kane, *Kātyāyanasāroddhāra*, verse 88.

2. Vide *Kātyāyanasāroddhāra*, verse 108.

3. Cf. *Bṛhaspatismṛti*, p. 22 : *sattr-odvāh-odyato*, etc., in the list of the *n=āsedhyāḥ.*

4. Cf. *Yājñavalkyasmṛti*, N.S. Press ed., p. 125 : *abhiyuktaṁ ca n=ānyena.*

5. Cf. *ibid.*, p. 126, quotation from Kātyāyana: *atha cet pratibhūr=n=āsti kārya-yogyas=tu vādinaḥ | sa rakṣito dinasy=ānte dadyād=bhṛtyāya vetanam ||*

6. Cf. *Kauṭilīya Arthaśāstra*, III. 11 : *a-grāhyāḥ karma-kāleṣu karṣakā*

25. *Āṣāḍha-māsi Pauṣe ca draṣṭavyaṁ māna-pautavam; ādāne rūpakaḥ sa-pādaḥ saha dhārmikeṇa.* The *māna-pautava*,[1] which had to be examined in the months of Āṣāḍha and Pauṣa, seems to have been a store-house where grains were measured and stored. Possibly there were two kinds of store-houses, one working on a small fee and the other working free of charges; but there was no reduction of the tax for the latter. *Ādāna* no doubt refers to the collection of tax and *dhārmika* may point to an extraordinary case somehow associated with religious merits or, as suggested by No. 65 below, with the permission or grace of the authorities. It is also possible to think that *dhārmika* was a cess payable [in the name of a religions function] in addition to the usual tax (but cf. No. 43). This term is frequently mentioned in the latter part of the document; see Nos. 27, 29-30, 32-33, 43, 45, 49, 51, 53-56, 58, 60-61, 65-67 and 69.

26. *A-saṁvādya vyavaharataḥ śulk-ādikaṁ ca dhāny-ādi praveśayato niṣkāśayato vā śulkam=aṣṭa-guṇaṁ dāpyaḥ.* It seems to be related to No. 25 above. If a store-house collected fees and stored and disposed of grains without informing the royal officials, it had to pay eight times the usual tax, i.e. ten silver coins. This may also refer to the bringing and taking out of goods without official checkup in regard to matters of *śulka*, etc., as per the rules laid down.[2]

27. *Peṭavika-vārikeṇa pañca-rātrake pañca-rātrake kartavyam=arggha-nivedanam; anivedayato vinaye*[3] *rūpakāḥ ṣaḍ=dhārmike pādaḥ.* *Peṭavika-vārika* appears to be a particular class of *Vārika* or official, that was responsible for the delivery of the *rāj-ārgghikā* received from the subjects once in five days. The word *peṭavika* is possibly associated with Marāṭhī *peṭhā* (sub-division of a Taluk) or *peṭh* (a trading town or an emporium). The fine for non-delivery was six silver coins; but, in the case of *dhārmika*, i.e. when there was any reasonable excuse, the fine

rāja-puruṣāś=ca. See also *Bṛhaspatismṛti*, pp. 22, 26, and *Kātyāyanasāroddhāra*, verse 109.

1. For *pautava* (measures), *tulā-māna-pautava* and *pautav-āpacāra* (fraud in regard to measures), see *Kauṭilīya Arthaśāstra*, IV. 2 (cf. pp. 103-05 of the Mysore ed.).

2. See *Kauṭilīya Arthaśāstra*, II. 23 (cf. Mysore ed., p. 112) on *niṣkrama* and *praveśa*.

3. In similar contexts, the author uses both *vinaye* and *vinayaḥ* (cf. No. 30 below).

was only one-fourth silver coin. Vinaya[1] means 'fine'. It is also possible that the *ācāra* refers to the rule that, every five days, the official should fix prices (*arggha*) of commodities and inform the higher authorities about the prices so fixed.[2]

28. *Uttarakulika-vārikaiḥ māna-bhāṇḍa-meya-gate bahir=na gantavyam. Uttarakulika*, like *Peṭavika*, apparently meant another class of *Vārika* or official. The *Uttarakulikas* appear to have been associated with the law-court. In cases of dispute in regard to the measurement, the measuring pot or the thing measured, such officers were possibly not allowed to go out of the court to be influenced by one party or the other.

29. *Uttarakulika-varikāṇām=eva karaṇa-sannidhau Chātreṇa trir=āghuṣitānāṁ nirupasthānād=vinaye rūpaka-dvayaṁ sa-pādaṁ saha dhārmikeṇa. Karaṇa* apparently means *adhikaraṇa*, 'a law-court', and *Chātra* seems to indicate a peon or a constable. *Karaṇa* as a contraction of *adhikaraṇa* is found in the Midnapur plates of Śaśāṅka,[3] while the word *chātra* is used in the above sense in several inscriptions.[4] It seems that there was no excuse for the absence of the *Vārikas* of the *Uttarakulika* class when thrice summoned to court by a court peon. The fine for the offence was two and one-fourth silver coins even if there was any good reason for absence.

30. *Vyavahār-ābhilekhitaka-karaṇa-sevakasy=ā-madhyāhnād=ūrdhvaṁ nirupasthitasya vinayo rūpakāḥ ṣaṭ=sa-pādās=saha dhārmikeṇa.* If the clerks[5] who had to write down the statements of cases in the law-court were absent from the court after midday, they were liable to a fine of six and one-fourth silver coins together with the *dhārmika*.

31. *Ā-madhyāhnād-ūrdhvam=Uttarakulika-vārikāṇāṁ chalo n=āsti.* No pretext of the *Uttarakulika-vārikas*, absent from the court after midday, was to be accepted. For *chala*, see

1. Cf. Nārada quoted in the *Yājñavalkyasmṛti*, p. 126. For the word *vinaya*, cf. Nos. 29-30, 33-34 and 37-38.

2. Cf. *Manusmṛti*, VIII. 402 : *pañca-rātre pañca-rātre pakṣe pakṣe='thavā gate / kurvīta c=aiṣāṁ pratyakṣam=argha-saṁsthāpanaṁ nṛpaḥ.* See also *Yājñavalkyasmṛti*, p. 270.

3. Vide *Pravāsī* (Bengali), Śrāvaṇa, B.S. 1350, pp. 291ff.; *JRASB*, Letters, Vol XI, 1945, pp. 8-9.

4. Cf. *Select Inscriptions*, p. 414 and note 5.

5. Cf. *adhikaraṇa-lekhaka*, 'an official recorder', in the *Rājataraṅgiṇī*, VI. 38.

Nos. 6, 7 and 9 above. The ordinary meaning of the word seems to suit the present context better.

32. *Arggha-vañcane rūpaka-trayaṁ sa-pādaṁ saha dhārmikeṇa.* This may refer to the *Peṭavika-vārikas* (cf. No. 27 above). In cases of fraud in regard to the delivery of *rāj-ārgghikā*, the officers concerned were liable to a fine of three and one-fourth silver coins and the fine could not be reduced even when there was a reasonable excuse. *Arggha-vañcana* may, however, also refer to the flouting of the prices fixed by the authorities (cf. No. 27 above).

33. *Mudr-āpacāre vinaye rūpakāḥ ṣaṭ=sa-pādāḥ saha dhārmmikeṇa. Mudr-āpacāra* is the crime of using counterfeit coins (or, the misuse of official seals), the fine for which was six and one-fourth silver coins and no execuse for reduction of the fine was allowed.[1]

34. *Sthāvara-vyavahāre sāmantaiḥ avasitasya vinayo rūpaka-śatam-aṣṭ=ottaraṁ* 108. *Sāmanta* possibly means a subordinate ruler (cf. No.11 above). The meaning of the *ācāra* may be that a subordinate ruler was liable to pay a fine of 108 silver coins if he disposed of a case involving landed property without informing his overlord (cf. No. 35 below). If the word *sāmanta* may be taken in the sense of men from neighbouring villages who had to settle boundary disputes,[2] the meaning of the *ācāra* may possibly be that the defeated party in a boundary dispute had to pay a fine of 108 silver coins. But the fine seems to be rather heavy for a case like this.

35. *Saṁvadane rūpakāḥ catuṣpañcāśat.* Taking *sāmanta* in the sense of a subordinate ruler (cf. No. 34 above), this seems to mean that the fine was only 54 silver coins (i.e. half the amount prescribed in No. 34 above), if information had been later given to the overlord about the case. In case the alternative interpretation of the word *sāmanta* is preferred, the *ācāra* may refer to the party that had itself invited arbitration in a boundary dispute, but was defeated.

36. *Jayike bhāṣā; phālāvane ca rūpaka-trayaṁ sa-pādam.*

1. Vide *Yājñavalkyasmṛti*, p. 268 (verse 240) : *tulā-śāsana-mānānāṁ kūṭakṛn=nāṇakasya ca / ebhiś=ca vyavaharttā yaḥ sa dāpyo damam=uttamam //* Cf. also quotation from Kātyāyana : *pramāṇena tu kūṭena mudrayā v=āpi kūṭayā / kāryan=tu sādhayed=yo vai sa dāpyo daṇḍam=uttamam //*

2. See *Yājñavalkyasmṛti*, II.152.

This is probably connected with Nos. 34-35 above. This *ācāra* is difficult to explain. But it may mean that the winning party (*jayika*) in a boundary dispute was to be granted a written declaration (*bhāṣā*) in its favour although it had to pay 3 $\frac{1}{4}$ silver coins for the protection of his ploughed field (*phāl-āvana*) from the encroachment of the defeated party in this dispute. We may also take *cā* as a combination of *ca* and *ā*. In that case, *ā-rūpaka-trayaṁ sa-pādam* would mean 'any amount upto 3$\frac{1}{4}$ silver coins'.

37. *Ullambane karṇṇa-troṭane ca vinayo rūpakāḥ saptaviṁśatiḥ.* The word *ullambana* is recognised in the lexicons in the sense of 'leaping over someone'; but the *Kauṭilīya Arthaśāstra* (IV. 8), uses it to indicate 'hanging' which seems applicable to the present case, although the punishment appears to be rather mild. *Karṇa-troṭana*, i.e. 'cutting off of a bit from some one's ear', seems to be also referred to in No. 17 above. For these offences, the fine was 27 silver coins.

38. *Vākpāruṣya-daṇḍapāruṣyayoḥ vinaye rūpakāḥ ṣaṭ=sa-pādāḥ.* The fine for the offence of defamation and assault (or, rough behaviour) was six and one-fourth silver coins.

39. *Kṣata-darśane rūpakāḥ aṣṭacatvāriṁśat.* In the case of *daṇḍa-pāruṣya* involving visible injury or infliction of wounds, the fine was 48 silver coins.[1]

40. *Gavāṁ tauṇḍike viṁśopakāḥ pañca.* Five *viṁśopakas* were equal to one-fourth of a silver coin, a *viṁśopaka* being $\frac{1}{20}$ of the standard silver money.[2] The meaning of *tauṇḍika* is 'biting of crops with the mouth'.[3] The offence involving *tauṇḍika* by cows caused a fine of five *viṁśopakas*.

41. *Mahiṣyās=tad-dviguṇam.* But the offence involving *tauṇḍika* by a she-buffalo was ten *viṁśopakas*, i.e. one-half silver coin. Yājñavalkya prescribes four *māṣas* for the offence indicated in No. 40 and eight *māṣas* for that in No. 41. Nārada, however, speaks of one *māṣa* and two *māṣas* respectively. The

1. Cf. *Viṣṇusmṛti*, V. 66-67: *śonitena vinā duḥkham=utpādayitā dvātriṁśat-paṇān; saha śonitena catuḥṣaṣṭim.*

2. It is to be noted that, in No. 57 discussed below, five *viṁśopakas* have been separately indicated by the symbols for $\frac{1}{4}$. This shows that five *viṁśopakas* were equal to $\frac{1}{4}$ silver coin. Cf. D. R. Bhandarkar, *Carmichael Lectures*, 1921, p. 210; Sircar, *Stud. Ind. Coins*, pp. 299ff.

3. Cf. *Yājñavalkyasmṛti*, II. 159 (see also Nārada quoted in the *Mitākṣarā*); *Nāradasmṛti*, XI. 31; *Viṣṇusmṛti*, V. 139 and 142.

same authority regards *māṣa* as one-twentieth of the *paṇa* which is explained by Vijñāneśvara as the well-known copper coin of that name. Viṣṇu supports Yājñavalkya.

42. *Madya-bhājanasy=āvalokye rūpakāḥ pañca. Avalokya*, derived from *avaloka*, seems to indicate 'detection'. If one was found out with a vessel full of wine distilled illegally, his fine was five silver coins.

43. *Prathama-bhājane dhārmike adhikaraṇasya rūpaka-dvayaṁ s-ārdham rū* 2½. But, when it was the first offence and no bad motive could be substantiated, the fine to be paid to the court was only 2½ silver coins.

44. *Anāpṛcchya sandhayato dvitīye='hani tad-dviguṇaṁ dāpyaḥ.* The first two words appear to mean *adhikaraṇam=anāpṛcchya rājapuruṣaiḥ sandhayataḥ.* This seems to say that, if a man, let off for the first offence, was caught with a vessel full of wine for the second time, his fine was double the amount prescribed in No. 43.

45. *Surā-karaṇasy=āvalokye rūpaka-trayam; dhārmike rūpakaḥ sa-pādaḥ; rāj-ārghikayā madya-cāturtha-dvayam* 2. If one was caught while distilling liquor, his fine was three silver coins. But the fine was only 1¼ silver coins if no bad motive could be substantiated, although two *cāturthas* (one *cāturtha* possibly being ¼ of the standard measure of liquid substances; cf. Nos. 47 and 70 below) of wine had to be paid as *rāj-ārghikā* (cf. No. 14 above).

46. *Kāṁsya-dosy-āyudhānām Āṣāḍhī-paurṇṇamāsī-bharolaka-nirodhena grahaṇaka-praviṣṭaṁ bhavati; grahaṇakeṣu daṇḍako n=ānusaraṇīyaḥ.* This is apparently related to the distillation of wine which is the subject of No. 45 above and No. 47 below; but the *ācāra* is extremely difficult to explain. The word *āyudha* may be taken in its old sense of 'a vessel'; but *dosya* is unknown although it may be a metal like *kāṁsya* or bell-metal. It seems that the *bharolaka* (distillery ?) was closed on the full-moon day of Āṣāḍha and the vessels (connected with the distillation of wine ?) were put into the *grahaṇaka* (custody?); the *daṇḍaka* (rule about the supply of the royal share of wine ?) was not to be followed when the distilling vessels were in the *grahaṇaka*. Alternatively, it may be suggested that *kāṁsya*= bronze utensils; *dosya*=clothes; *āyudha*=arms; *bharolaka*= store-house. If the king's share of these articles was not deli-

vered by the producers by the full moon day of Āṣāḍha (which was, according to Kauṭilya, the last day of the financial year),[1] then to such objects the law of mortgage (*grahaṇaka*) was applied and they were subject to the payment of interest at the mortgage rate, but no fine (*daṇḍaka*); or, such objects were confiscated and no fine was levied.

47. *Rājakīya-gañje Kalvapāla-vārikeṇa cāturtha-śoṭī-hastena meyaṁ muktvā n=ānyat=kiṁchit=karaṇīyam.* The word *gañja* is used in the *Rājataraṅgiṇī* (IV. 589; VII. 125-26) in the sense of 'a treasury' or 'a fund', but may be taken here to signify 'a store-house' as in the lexicons. The *Vārika* of the *Kalvapāla* community was apparently in charge of a store-house of wine. The word *Kalvapāla* is no doubt the same as *Kalyapāla* or *Kalyāpāla* found in the lexicons in the sense of 'a spirit-distiller'.[2] It is also found in the form *Kalpāla* in Viśvarūpa's commentary on the *Yājñavalkyasmṛti* (Vyavahāra, verse 50) and is the same as Prakrit *Kallāla* and Hindi and Gujarati *Kalāl*. *Śoṭī* seems to mean a pot for measuring liquids like wine.[3] While measuring wine in *cāturthas* or quarter-measures at the royal store-house with the measuring pot in hand, the *Vārika* or officer of the *Kalvapāla* community was possibly not allowed to divert his attention to some other work. The word *cāturtha* is also found in No. 45 above and No. 70 below.

48. *Nīla-kuṭy-ādānaṁ Ḍumphakena deyaṁ rūpaka-trayaṁ rū* 3. *Nīla-kuṭī* may mean an indigo factory and *Ḍumphaka* (cf. No. 19 above) its owner or supervisor. The *Ḍumphaka* had to pay the tax of three silver coins for a *nīla-kuṭī.*

49. *Ikṣu-vāṭ-ādānaṁ rūpakāḥ dvātriṁśat rū* 32; *dhārmike rūpaka-dvayaṁ sa-pādam.* The tax for a sugar-cane plantation was 32 silver coins; but it was only $2\frac{1}{4}$ silver coins if the field belonged to a religious establishment. The word *vāṭa* may have indicated a particular area of land.

50. *Alla-vāṭasy=āto='rdh-ādānam.* The tax for an *alla-vāṭa* was half the amount prescribed in No. 49 above. *Alla* is the Prakrit form of Sanskrit *ārdraka*, 'ginger', and *alla-vāṭa*

1. *Arthaśāstra*, II. 7.
2. Cf. *Rājataraṅgiṇī*, IV. 467.
3. Cf. *soṭu*, *sauṭu*, *soṇṭige*, etc., meaning a specific liquid measure in some early Kannaḍa inscriptions, and *savaṭu* in modern Kannaḍa in the sense of 'a ladle'.

may possibly mean 'a ginger plantation'. It shoud, however, be noticed that the word *ārdraka* itself occurs in No. 60 below. The word *alla* in Pali means 'moist' and *alla-vāṭa* may probably indicate 'low land'. But *ikṣu-vāṭa* in No. 50 seems to suggest that *alla* was a produce like *ikṣu*.

51. *Yantra-kuṭy-ādānaṁ rūpaka-trayaṁ ru* 3; *dhārmike rūpakaḥ sa-pādaḥ*. *Yantra-kuṭī* may indicate an oil-mill or manufactory, for which the tax to be paid was three silver coins, although the tax was only 1$\frac{1}{4}$ silver coins if the productions were meant for a religious cause.

52. *Varṣa-paryuṣitā vaṇijaḥ prāveśyaṁ śulk-ātiyātrikaṁ na dāpanīyāḥ*; *nairgamikaṁ deyam*. Merchants staying abroad for a year were not to pay any entrance fee while returning to their native place; but they had to pay the exit tax when they went out again on business. *Atiyātrika* is no doubt connected with *atiyātrā* used in the *Divyāvadāna*[1] in the sense of 'fare for crossing the boundary'. The *ācāra* may also refer to merchants coming and staying in the kingdom for a year, or for the rainy season (cf. No. 24) when business was in abeyance.

53. *Bhāṇḍa-bhṛta-vahitrasya śulk-ātiyātrike rūpakāḥ dvādaśa rū* 12; *dhārmike rūpakaḥ sa-pādaḥ rū* 1$\frac{1}{4}$. For a boat (or carriage)[2] full of vessels probably of metal, the crossing fare was 12 silver coins; but if the vessels were meant for any religious purpose, the tax was only 1$\frac{1}{4}$ silver coins.[3] It is difficult to determine whether *bhāṇḍa* may here be taken in a general sense of manufactured articles or merchandise. Nos. 53-59 may refer to the customs duties on loads of goods carried in various ways.

54. *Mahiṣ-oṣṭra-bharakasya rūpakāḥ pañca sa-pādāḥ saha dhārmikeṇa*. For a boat full of buffaloes and camels, the tax was 5$\frac{1}{4}$ silver coins and there was no reduction even if they were meant for some religious cause. *Bharaka* seems to mean the same thing as *bhṛta-vahitra*. If *bharaka* may be taken in the sense of a load carried on the back of an animal, Nos. 54-56, 59 and 60 may not refer to a boat. The second interpretation seems to be more suitable in the case of Nos. 54-56; cf. No. 62.

1. Ed. Cowell and Neil, p. 92, line 27.
2. Cf. the Anjaneri plates, lines 35-36—*sārtha-vahitreṣu praveśe nirgame ca pratyekaṁ rūpakaḥ devasya yātr-otsave dātavyaḥ* (*Ep. Ind.*, Vol. XXV, p. 232).
3. Cf. the rates of customs duty for ferry crossing in the *Manusmṛti*, VIII. 403ff., and *Yājñavalkyasmṛti*, p. 274, with commentary thereon.

55. *Balīvard-ādānaṁ rūpaka-dvayaṁ s-ārdhaṁ rū* 2½; *dhārmike pādaḥ* ¼ The tax for a boat full of bulls was 2 silver coins; but, if they were meant for a religious cause, the tax was only ¼ silver coin. See No. 54 above.

56. *Gardabha-bharak-ādāne rūpakaḥ sa-pādaḥ rū* 1¼ *saha dhārmikeṇa*. The tax for a boat full of asses was 1¼ silver coins and there was no reduction even if they were meant for a religious cause. Cf. Nos. 53-54 above and 61 below.

57. *Ato='rdhena poṭṭalikā=saṁkacitak-ādānam; avalambakasya viṁśopakāḥ pañca* ¼. The tax for bundles suspended from loops probably in shops was half of 1¼ silver coins and for the hanger of such loops the tax was five *viṁśopakas* or ¼ silver coin. The word *saṁkācitaka* is no doubt related to *kācita* used in the lexicons as an adjective; but, in No. 68 below, it has been used as a noun possibly in the sense of 'a loop' (*kāca*). The same may also be the meaning in the present case. If *avalambaka* refers to the carrying of bundles of goods by a person, *saṁkācitaka* may refer to a mechanical means of carrying loads.

58. *Pala-śatasya viṁśopaka-dvayaṁ saha dhārmikeṇa*. A bundle weighing 100 *palas* was taxed at two *viṁśopakas*.

59. *Yath-opari-likhita-bhāṇḍ-ādānāt dhānyasy=ārdh-ādānam*. This seems to be related to No. 53 above. A boat or wagon full of paddy (or grains in general) was taxed at half the amount prescribed for a boat or wagon full of vessels.

60. *Ārdraka-lakaṭāyāḥ śulk-ātiyātrike rūpakaḥ sa-pādaḥ saha dhārmikeṇa rū* 1¼. The crossing fare for a boat full of dried ginger sticks (*lakaṭā*) was 1¼ silver coins and there was no reduction even if the things were meant for a religious purpose. *Lakaṭā* may also be the same as Hindi *lakḍī*. In that case *ārdraka-lakaṭā* would mean 'undried fire-wood'.

61. *Vaṁśa-bhṛta-vahitrasya rūpakāḥ ṣaṭ saha dhārmikeṇa*. The tax for a boat full of bomboos was 6¼ silver coins and there was no reduction even if the material was meant for a religious purpose. Cf. Nos. 53-54 and 56 above.

62. *Skandha-vāhyaṁ dhānyaṁ śulkaṁ na pradāpayet*. There was no tax for paddy (or grains in general) to be carried by a person on his shoulder.[1]

1. Cf. *Nāradasmṛti* (ed. Jolly, p. 134) : *skandha-vāhyaṁ ca yad=dravyaṁ na tad=yuktaṁ (c=chulkaṁ) pradāpayet*.

63. *Kanikkā-kustumbarī-rājikā-prabhṛtīnāṁ vaṇikā-grahaṇe setikā grāhyā.* *Kanikkā* is the Prakrit form of *kaṇikā* meaning 'cummin seed'. *Rājikā* is black mustard, while *kustubmarī* is the coriander seed. *Vaṇikā* is the same as Prakrit *vanniā* meaning 'sample', while *setikā*[1] is the same as Prakrit *seiā* or *seigā* indicating a measure equal to two *prasṛtis*. The word *prasṛti* means the palm of the hand stretched out and hollowed and also a handful of things regarded as equivalent to two *palas* in weight. It seems therefore that only two handfuls of cummin seed, black mustard and coriander seed could be taken as sample by royal officials.

64. *Vivāha-yajñ-otsava-sīmantonnayaneṣu ca śulkaṁ na pradāpayet.* Ceremonies such as marriage were not to be taxed.[2]

65. *Vara-yātrāyāṁ śulk-ātiyātrike rūpakāḥ dvādaśa; paṭṭaka-dhārmike rūpakaḥ sa-pādaḥ rū* $1\frac{1}{4}$. If the procession of a bridegroom had to cross the boundary of the kingdom or district to reach the house of the bride, it had to pay the crossing fare of 12 silver coins; but, if it was legalised by means of a *paṭṭaka* or passport, the fare was only $1\frac{1}{4}$ silver coins. If *vara-yātrā* is taken in the sense of a public procession, *paṭṭaka-dhārmika* may refer to an authorised religious procession.

66. *Madya-vahanakasy=ādāne rūpakāḥ pañca rū* 5; *dhārmike rūpakaḥ sa-pādaḥ rū* $1\frac{1}{4}$. If a vehicle or boat full of wine had to cross the border, it was taxed at five silver coins, although the tax was reduced to $1\frac{1}{4}$ silver coins if the wine was meant for a religious purpose.

67. *Khalla-bharakasya rūpakaḥ sa-pādaḥ saha dhārmikeṇa rū* $1\frac{1}{4}$. The tax for a *khalla* (literally 'leather'; cf. Bengali-Hindi-Gujarati *khāl*) measure was only $1\frac{1}{4}$ silver coins even if the material was required for a religious purpose. *Khalla* seems to mean here a leather vessel for carrying a liquid like wine which is mentioned in No. 66.

68. *Kelāyāḥ saṁkācitakasya ca ato='rdh-ādānam.* For a loop (cf. No 57 above) holding *kelā*, the tax was half of $1\frac{1}{4}$ silver coins prescribed in No. 67 above. The meaning of *kelā* is uncertain, although *kelā* in Hindi stands for Sanskrit *kadalī*.

1. Cf. *Ep. Ind.*, Vol. XXV, p. 235 and note 3.
2. Cf. the receipts of the office called *gṛha-kṛtya* in the *Rājataraṅgiṇī*, V. 157; VII. 42.

Can *kelā* in our record stand for a Prakrit form midway between *kīlā* and *khelā* for Sanskrit *krīḍā* in the sense of *krīḍanaka*? It may also mean a vessel for carrying wine, which was smaller than *khalla*.

69. *Pāda-ghaṭasya viṁśopakāḥ pañca saha dhārmikeṇa*. The tax for a *pāda-ghaṭa* was five *viṁśopakas*, i.e. $\frac{1}{4}$ silver coin, and it was not reduced even when the thing was meant for a religious cause. The word *pāda-ghaṭa* possibly indicates a jar holding a quarter measure of wine.

70. *Kaṭu-madye sīdhu-cāturtha-trayam* 3. Three *cāturthas* or quarter measures (cf. Nos. 45 and 47 above) of the liquor called *sīdhu* were regarded as the tax for very strong liquors.

71. *Chimpaka-Kolika-Paḍakārāṇāṁ yath-ānurūpa-karmaṇaḥ janapada-mūlyād=rājakule='rdh-ādānam*. The *Chimpakas*, *Kolikas* and *Padakāras*, who appear to have been followers of particular professions, possibly had to pay as tax half the money that would be the price of the things produced by them according to the rate prevalent in the land. *Kolika* may be the same as Sanskrit *Kaulika* or a weaver and *Padakāra* may possibly be a shoe-maker. *Chimpaka* is Prakrit *Chimpaya* (Gujarati *Chipo*) meaning 'a dyer of clothes'. If *Padakāra* is the same as Hindi *Paukār*, he was a retailer hawking his goods on foot.

72. *Lohakāra-rathakāra-nāpita-kumbhakāra-prabhṛtīnāṁ Vārikeṇa viṣṭiḥ karaṇīyā*. The blacksmiths, carpenters, barbers, potters and others could be recruited for forced labour under the supervision of the *Vārika* or officer.

Chapter XIV

TWO GRANTS OF VIŚVARŪPASENA

I

A copper-plate grant had been discovered in 1925 in the neighbourhood of Dacca, which is now the capital of Bangladesh, and later found its place in the Museum of the Vaṅgīya Sāhitya Pariṣad, Calcutta. The inscription was first edited by H. P. Sastri in *Ind. Hist. Quart.*, Vol. II, 1926, pp. 77-86, and then by N. G. Majumdar in his *Inscriptions of Bengal*, Vol. III, pp. 140-48, 177-80. J. C. Ghosh published a short note on the record in *Ind. Hist. Quart.*, Vol. IV, 1928, pp. 637ff. A large number of errors crept into Sastri's transcript of the inscription, which was not accompanied by any translation of the text. Sastri failed to interpret the record properly. Majumdar succeeded very considerably in improving upon Sastri's transcript and also offered an English translation of the whole epigraph. But his reading of the difficult grant portion of the charter seems to suffer from some errors while a number of passages in this part either were left uninterpreted in his translation or were, in our opinion, misunderstood by him.

It may be pointed out at the outset that there is a serious error in the reading of verse 15 (lines 23-25) of the introductory part of this record in the transcripts of both Sastri and Majumdar. Sastri reads the stanza as follows:

Yāṁ nirmmāya pavitra-pāṇir = abhavad = Vedhāḥ satīnāṁ śikhā-ratnaṁ yā kim = api sva-rūpa-caritair = viśvaṁ yay = ālaṅkṛtam |
Lakṣmīr = bhūr = api vāñchitāni vidadhe yasyāḥ sapatnyor = dvayaṁ śrīmat-Taṭṭaṇadevy = amuṣya mahiṣī s = ābhūt = tri-varg-ocitā ||

Majumdar reads the fourth foot of the stanza as : *śrīmat-Tyaṣṭanadevy = a ...... vargg-ocitā*. His *vargg-ocitā* is no doubt correct; but what has been read as *sapatnyor = dvayaṁ* by both Sastri and Majumdar seems really to be *sapat(n*)y[or] = dvaya(ṁ*)* or *sapatyī(tnī)-dvaya(ṁ*)*. More important is, however, the name of king Viśvarūpasena's mother, which has been read by Sastri as *Taṭṭaṇadevī* and Majumdar as *Tyaṣṭanadevī*. In our opinion, both these readings are wrong, although the third letter in the name is certainly *ṇa*. The *akṣara* after *śrīma* looks quite clearly like *tṛ* followed by an *ā*-matra. This *ṛ*-like sign must have been taken by Sastri to be a subscript *ṭ*. But in that case, he should have properly read the *akṣara* as *tṭa* (and not *ṭṭa*), although the conjunct *tṭ* is an impossibility as admitted by Sastri himself. As to Majumdar's reading of the *akṣara* as *ttya*, it should be observed that the *ṛ*-like and *ā*-like signs may be together taken to stand for a subscript *y*. But the reading of the *akṣara* in that case would be *tya* and not *ttya*, there being no trace at all of the reduplication of *t*. The *akṣara* certainly looks like *tya* and, therefore, it appears that the name of the queen-mother began with the letter *a* and was preceded in the passage in question by the expression *śrīmatī*. The *akṣara* following *tya* has been read by Sastri as *ṭṭa* and by Majumdar as *ṣṭa*. There are numerous instances of the occurrence of *ṭṭa* and *ṣṭa* in the inscription; cf. eight cases of *ṭṭa* in lines 38, 41, 50, 52, 55 and 60, and four cases of *ṣṭa* in lines 26, 45, 52 and 65. But the *akṣara* in question has no resemblance whatsoever with *ṭṭa* or *ṣṭa* as found elsewhere in the record. The most reasonable reading of the second *akṣara* in the queen-mother's name, which is apparently a conjunct, seems to be *hva*, as its superscript looks like *h* and subscript like *v*. Thus the name of the mother of king Viśvarūpasena, as quoted in the inscription under review, seems to be *Ahvaṇadevī*. The reading *Alhaṇadevī* (a well-known female name), suggested by N. P. Chakravarti in *Ep. Ind.*, Vol. XXVI, p. 9, note 4, is near the truth. It may be pointed out in this connection that the same stanza occurs in a slightly different form in the Madanpāḍā and Idilpur plates. In both the cases, however, the queen-mother's name was incised later on an erasure suggesting that originally a different name had been engraved in the space. The same is also the case with the name of the issuer of these charters.

The grant portion of the Sāhitya Pariṣad plate runs from line 35 to line 68. Of these, lines 35-38 speak of king Viśvarūpasena as the son of king Lakṣmaṇasena and the grandson of king Ballālasena while lines 38-41 mention a number of the king's subordinates, dependants, .officers and others, to whom the royal order regarding the grant recorded in the charter was addressed. The details of the grant are quoted in the king's order that follows in lines 41-68. We shall take up this part section by section for the sake of convenience. The languge of this part of the record is Sanskrit; but it is greatly influenced by the local dialect. We have the use of Prakritic words like *laggāvayitvā* (Bengali *lāgāiyā*, 'having planted'), etc. The rules of Sanskrit grammar, especially those regarding *Sandhi*, have been often ignored. But the most interesting feature of the said part of the inscription is the use of a number of contractions; e.g., *u* for *udāna* or more properly *udānāni*. We have made no attempt to emend the text when the meaning is clear.

1. (a) Lines 41-44 : *Viditam=astu bhavatāṁ yathā Pauṇḍravarddhana-bhukty-antaḥpāti-Vaṅge Nāvye Rāmasiddhi-pāṭake Varāhakuṇḍa-dakṣiṇa-paścime pūrvve Devahāra-devabhoga-sīmā dakṣiṇe Vaṅgālavaḍā-bhūḥ sīmā paścime nadī sīmā uttare tathā nadī sīmā evaṁ catuḥ-sīm-āvacchinna-vāstu-bhūmy-udāna* $34\frac{3}{4}$ /

(b) Lines 43-45 : (1) *tathā Devahāra-pūrvve ṭī* 4 *vyā-bhū-u* $4\frac{1}{2}$ *vāstu-u-p[r]ati-hi* $1\frac{3}{8}$ / *tathā nāla-bhū-u* $26\frac{3}{4}$ / (2) *Devahāra-uttare nāla-bhū-u* 2 *nāla-u-prati-hi* $1\frac{1}{8}$/ (3) *evaṁ sa-vāstu-bhū-udāna* $67\frac{3}{4}$ *grāma-patyā sāṁ-hi* 80 $\frac{5}{16}$ /

(c) Lines 45-47 : *tath=aitad-grāme vāra-Nāko-Lokta-Gāñik-ādīnāṁ nūtana-baraja-catuṣṭaya-sameta (tā) Vāra-Śremano-Udayi-Apara-Loktakānāṁ baraja-traya-saṁvalita-(bhūḥ*) sāṁ-hi* 19 $\frac{11}{16}$ / *militvā kā* 2 *khaṁ* 7 *dvābhyāṁ trayodaś-ābdīya-Uttarāyaṇa-mahāsaṁkramaṇa-sambandhena samutsarggita-bhū-saṁ-sāṁ-hi* 100 /

Subsection (a) mentions the first plot of the gift land measuring $34\frac{3}{4}$ *Udānas*. In writing fractions in the record, each quarter ($\frac{1}{4}$) is indicated by a vertical *daṇḍa* while each quarter of a quarter ($\frac{1}{16}$) by a slanting *daṇḍa*. In the case occurring in the above subsection, three quarters are indicated by three vertical *daṇḍas*. The exact area of an *Udāna* is unknown; but we have given a rough idea of this land measure elsewhere.[3] The subsection speaks of a plot of homestead (*vāstu*) land situated to the south-west of Varāha's *kuṇḍa* (i. e. the tank belonging to the temple of the god Varāha or the

1. See Majumdar, *op. cit.*, pp. 118, 139.
2. See below.
3. About $\frac{1}{9}$ Bighā; cf. Sircar, *Ind. Ep.*, p. 418.

Boar incarnation of Viṣṇu)[1] in the village called Rāmasiddhi-pāṭaka. This village is stated to have been lying in the Nāvya (literally, 'navigable') Division of Vaṅga forming a part of the Pauṇḍravardhana *bhukti* (Province). The plot of land referred to was bounded in the east by the *deva-bhoga* at Devahāra, i.e. land belonging to a god (possibly Varāha mentioned above) worshipped at a locality called Devahāra apparently in the village of Rāmasiddhi-pāṭaka. Its southern boundary was a piece of land forming part of an area called Vaṅgālavaḍā while in the west and north it was bounded by a river.

Subsection (b) speaks of three other plots of the gift land situated near the plot mentioned in subsection (a) and also quotes the total area of the four plots of land together with its annual revenue income. Several contractions have been used in this subsection. Of these, *ṭī* in extract (1) seems to stand for *ṭīkara* meaning 'a mound'.[2] This abbreviation occurs many times in the Mehār plate.[3] *Vyā-bhū-u* stands apparently for *vyāmiśra-bhūmy-udāna* (better *udānāni*), in which *vyāmiśra-bhūmi* no doubt means 'mixed land', i.e. land containing some of the *vāstu* (homestead) category and some of the *nāla* (arable, in which sense the word *nāl* is still used in Bengali) class, although some other types of land may also have been included in it (cf. *khila* or waste land mentioned in line 60). In the same extract *nāla-bhū-u* similarly means *nāla-bhūmy-udāna*. But more interesting is the passage *vāstu-u-prati-hi* $1\frac{3}{8}$, in which *hi* certainly stands for *hiraṇya* in the sense of 'coin, money or cash'. The passage thus stands for *vāstu-bhūmy-udāna-prati*[4]*-hiraṇya* $1\frac{3}{8}$, which means to say that the annual revenue income was at the rate of $1\frac{3}{8}$ of the standard coin per *Udāna* of homestead land. In line 59 of the inscription, the standard coin is mentioned as *Cūrṇī* which is known to have been another name of the well-known Purāṇa.[5] The meaning of the contraction *hi* is clearly suggested by the passage *etan-mūlyaṁ hi* 40 in lines 50-51, which no doubt means : 'the price of this is in coins 40

1. Cf. Sanskrit and Bengali lexicons, s.v. *kuṇḍa*.
2. Cf. Hindi *ṭīkar*, *ṭīkrā*, Bengali *ṭikar*, *ṭikrā*; Oriya *ṭikara*, etc., in the lexicons of these languages and also *ṭikarī* and *ṭikaribasti* in Wilson's Glossary.
3. *Ep. Ind.*, Vol. XXVII, pp. 182-91.
4. Expressions like *udāna-prati*, 'per *Udāna*', are common in Bengali.
5. See *ibid.*, Vol. XXIX, p. 45 and note 3.

only'. Similarly, in extract (2), *nāla-bhū-u* and *nāla-u-prati-hi* stand respectively for *nāla-bhūmy-udāna* and *nāla-bhūmy-udāna-prati-hiraṇya*. The rates of the annual revenue income per *Udāna* of homestead and arable land in these two cases have been specially mentioned because they were lower than the usual rates. The expression *grāma-patyā* used in extract (3) seems to stand for *grāma-jana-patitvāt* possibly suggesting that the revenue income came from the tenants who were inhabitants of the village of Rāmasiddhi-pāṭaka in question (cf. *nānā-patyā* below). In this extract, the contraction *sāṁ* has been used to indicate *sāṁvatsarika* (i.e., annual). Thus *sāṁ-hi* stands for *sāṁvatsarika-hiraṇya*, i.e. annual revenue income in the standard coin called Cūrṇī or Purāṇa.

Therefore the three plots of land mentioned in subsection (b) were : (1) four mounds of mixed land lying to the east of Devahāra and measuring $4\frac{1}{4}$ *Udānas*, of which the *vāstu* portion fetched annually revenue income at the rate of $1\frac{3}{8}$ *Purāṇas* per *Udāna*, (2) $26\frac{3}{4}$ *Udānas* of arable land lying in the same place; and (3) 2 *Udānas* of arable land lying to the north of Devahāra and fetching annually revenue income at the rate of $1\frac{1}{8}$ *Purāṇas* per *Udāna*. Extract (3) says that all the plots of land [at Rāmasiddhi-pāṭaka], a part of which was homestead land (*sa-vāstu*), together measured $67\frac{3}{4}$ *Udānas*, of which the annual revenue income was 80 $\frac{5}{16}$ *Purāṇas*. Elsewhere this grant is stated to have been made in the month of Pauṣa during the thirteenth regnal year of Viśvarūpasena.

In subsection (c) the word *vāra* (cf. also frequent use of the word below) has been used before a group of personal names. The word means 'collection' in Sanskrit lexicons and, in the present case, it apparently means to say that a group of *barajas* or betel-vine plantations was held jointly by the persons mentioned. The words *sameta* and *saṁvalita* have been used in the sense of *saṁyukta* or *sambaddha* meaning 'attached to', with which the word *bhūmi* is to be understood. *Milivalitā* is Sanskrit *militā* or *sammilitā*. *Kā* stands for *Kāṇḍa* or a cluster, and *khaṁ* for *khaṁḍa* or a piece. The contraction *saṁ* stands for a word like *sambaddha*, *sambandhena*, etc., i.e., for *saṁkrānta* in its Bengali sense.

Thus subsection (b) says that in the same village (i.e. Rāmasiddhi-pāṭaka) four new betel-vine plantations in the joint possession of Nāko, Lokta, Gāñika and others and three other [old] betel-vine plantations in the joint possession of Śremano, Udayi, Apara and Loktaka,[1] in all seven units in two lots, fetching an annual revenue income of 19 $\frac{11}{16}$ *Purāṇas*, were also granted. The income of these, viz. 19 $\frac{11}{16}$ *Purāṇas*, added to that of the land mentioned in subsection (a), viz. 80 $\frac{5}{16}$ *Purāṇas*, is stated to make up the annual revenue income of 100 *Purāṇas* attaching to the grant made on the occasion of the Uttarāyaṇa-saṅkrānti [in the month of Pauṣa] during the year 13 (i. e. the thirteenth regnal year of king Viśvarūpasena).

II. Lines 47-48 : *tathā Nāvye Vinayatilaka-grāme pūrvve samudra-sīmā dakṣiṇe P[r]anullī-bhūḥ sīmā paścime jaṅghāla-sīmā uttare śāsana-sīmā evaṁ catuḥ-sīm-āvacchinna-savāstu-bhū-udāna* 25 *nānā-patyā sāṁ-hi* 60 /

This section speaks of another plot of land including some homestead land and measuring 25 *Udānas*. The annual revenue income accruing to it was 60 *Purāṇas*. The expression *nānā-patyā* used in this connection possibly means *nānā-grāma-jana-patitvāt* suggesting that the tenants holding the plot of land in question were inhabitants of different villages of the neighbourhood. The plot was situated at Vinayatilakagrāma in the Nāvya Division of Vaṅga referred to above and was bounded in the east by the sea (possibly indicating one of the wide mouths of a river falling in the Bay of Bengal), in the south by a piece of land belonging to Pranullī (either a locality or a person), in the west by a *jaṅghāla* (an embankment) and in the north by a *śāsana*. The word *śāsana* here means a piece of land enjoyed rent-free by virtue of a *śāsana* or royal charter (cf. line 57 of the inscription). If Rāmasiddhi-pāṭaka and Vinayatilaka-grāma (both in the Nāvya Division) were neighbouring villages, *śāsana* in the present case may refer to a plot of land, of which the grant is recorded in section I of the present charter.

II. Lines 48-51 : *tathā Madhukṣīrak-āvṛttau Navasaṁ-*

1. He may be the same as Lokta mentioned above. Apara-Loktaka may also mean 'a second Loktaka', i.e. other than his namesake mentioned earlier.

graha-caturake Ajikulā-pāṭake yathā-prasiddha-sva-sīm-āvacchinna[1] *Śauvasā-Kirito-Maito-Ucchok-ādīnāṁ anen = aiv=Āvallika-paṁ-Halāyudhena. krīta-paṭṭolī-saṁ-savāstu-bhūmy- udāna* 165 *nānā-patyā ucchannatvāt sāṁ-hi* 100 / *tath=aitad=vāstu- bhūmau kalana-saṁ-sā(ṁ*)-guvāka-śata* 30 *etan-mūlyaṁ hi* 40 / *dvā sāṁ-hi* 140 /

Of the abbreviations used in this section, *paṁ* stands for *Paṁḍita* and *dvā* for *dvābhyām* (i. e. of, by or from the two referred to above). Line 64 of the inscription shows that the *Āvallika Paṇḍita* Halāyudha was the donee of the present charter. The meaning of the expression *Āvallika* is uncertain; but Halāyudha may have been the resident of a locality called Avalla or Āvalla. This section speaks of a big piece of land measuring 165 *Udānas*; but its annual revenue income was only 100 *Purāṇas*. This unusually low amount of revenue seems to be explained by the expression *ucchannatvāt* possibly suggesting that many of the tenants, who were residents of different villages of the neighbourhood (cf. *nānā-patyā* explained above), were dead. It is stated that this plot of land was attached to (*saṁ=sambaddha*) the *paṭṭolī* (here meaning 'land purchased by a *paṭṭolī* or deed of purchase') that had been bought by Halāyudha (the donee of the present charter) from Śauvasā, Kirito, Maito, Ucchoka and others. The absence of the word *vāra* in this connection suggests that these persons held different portions of the land severally. This piece of land, the boundaries of which were fixed and well known, was situated in a village called Ajikulā-pāṭaka in the Navasaṁgraha *caturaka* (a small administrative unit) within the Madhukṣīraka *āvṛtti* (a slightly bigger administrative unit). The fact that the land was purchased by the donee shows that the king (the donor of the present charter) merely made it revenue-free. It should be noticed that, while *śāsana* means a rent-free holding, the holder of a *paṭṭolī* had to pay rent for his holding.

Along with the above plot of land was also granted a *kalana* (cf. line 59 of the inscription), apparently meaning a betelnut plantation, situated on the *vāstu* portion of it. The produce (cf. *saṁ=sambaddha*) of this plantation was stated to be 30 hundred (i.e. three thousand) betelnuts per annum, the price of which was calculated to be an annual income of

1. Correctly we should have °*āvacchinnāni...bhūmy-udānāni*.

40 *Purāṇas* (i.e. at the rate of 75 arecanuts per *Purāṇa*.[1] It has to be noticed that the rent-paying holders of the land, from whom Halāyudha purchased it, did not own the betelnut plantation, the possession of which was a monopoly of the kings, *jāgīrdārs* and privileged tenants (cf. line 60 of the inscription). When the king made the plot rent-free in favour of Halāyudha, the right of ownership of the plantation had to be automatically made over to the donee.

The annual income of the plot of land, viz. 100 *Purāṇas*, added to the income from the price of betelnuts annually produced by the plantation on it, viz. 40 *Purāṇas*, made up the income of 140 *Purāṇas* per year.

IV. Lines 51-52 : *tathā Vikramapura-bhāge Lāuhaṇḍā-caturake Deulahastyāṁ nadī-pūrvva-paścime rāja-hitā*[1] *sa eva vāra-Āranto-Kāmya-Piṇṭhanāg-ādīnāṁ anen=aiva krīta-paṭṭolī-saṁ-savāstu-bhūmy-udāna* 25 *sāṁ-hi* 50 /

This section speaks of another piece of land situated to the east and west of a river in the village of Deulahastī within the Lāuhaṇḍā-caturaka forming a part of the Vikramapura *bhāga* (Division). The expression *rāja-hitā* (literally, 'the income of which is enjoyed by the king'), used in relation to the land, suggests that the plot formed a part of the king's Khās Mahāl although it was held jointly by the tenants Āranto, Kāmya, Piṇṭhanāga and others, from whom Halāyudha secured it as a *paṭṭolī* by purchase. A portion of the plot was of the homestead category. It was 25 *Udānas* in area and fetched an annual income of 50 *Purāṇas*.

V. Lines 52-53 : *tribhiḥ mātṛ-caraṇānāma*(*nāṁ*) *dṛṣṭe naḥ soma-grāse samutsarggita-bhū-sambandhena guvāka-mūlya-sameta-sāṁ-hi* 250 /

This section sums up the total income of the three gifts mentioned in sections II-IV and says that the annual income of the land granted, including the price of the annual yield of arecanuts, comes up to 250 *Purāṇas* per annum. We have

1. Since the price is abnormally high, the meaning intended by the passage may be that the plantation contained 3000 arecaunt palms, the produce of which was calculated to fetch annually 40 *purāṇas* as price.

2. Apparently the author had in his mind *rāja-hitā sā eva......bhūmiḥ*; but the expression he uses below is *bhūmy-udāna*. Correctly, therefore, we should have *rāja-hitāni tāni eva......bhūmy-udānāni*.

seen that the annual income of the grants made in the villages of Vinayatilaka-grāma, Ajikulā-pāṭaka and Deulahastī was respectively 60, 140 and 50 *Purāṇas*, i.e. in all 250 *Purāṇas*. It is stated that these three gifts were made on the occasion of the observation of a lunar eclipse by the king's mother.

VI. Lines 53-54 : *tath=aitad-grāme vāra-Brahmo-Amṛtokayoḥ anen = aiva krīta-paṭṭolī-saṁ varṣa-vṛddhau kumāra-Sūryyasena-pradatta-nāla-bhū-u* 7 *guvāka-vāstu-bhū-u* 3 / *dvā savā-bhū-u* 10 *sāṁ-hi* 25 /

Mention is made here of one other plot of land situated at the same village (i.e. Deulahastī). It was attached to the *paṭṭolī* purchased by Halāyudha from the joint holders Brahmo and Amṛtoka. One part of it consisted of seven *Udānas* of arable land and the other of three *Udānas* of homestead land containing a betelnut plantation. These two parts made up in all ten *Udānas* of land containing some of the *vāstu* category (*dvā savā-bhū-u=dvābhyāṁ savāstu-bhūmy-udānāni*) and fetched an annual income of 25 *Purāṇas*. This grant was made by Prince Sūryasena (very probably a son of Viśvarūpasena) on the occasion of his birthday anniversary and the king merely ratified the creation of the rent-free holding. The land owned by the donee by purchase now became rent-free and the donee acquired the additional right to enjoy the betelnut plantation on it. This plot of land apparently formed part of a *jāgīr* under Prince Sūryasena. It seems that the holder of *jāgīrs* could grant a piece of land out of it, although the action required the king's approval.

VII. Lines 54-56 : *tathā tath=aitad-grāme vāra-Kano-Amṛtokayoḥ anen=aiva krīta-paṭṭolī-saṁ-sāndhivigrahika-Nāñisiṁha-pradata* (*tta*)-*nāla-bhū-u* 3 *guvāka-vāstu-bhū-u* 4/*dvā savāstu-bhū-u* 7 *sāṁ-hi* 50 /

The expression *tathā* seems to be unnecessarily duplicated at the beginning. In the same village of Deulahastī was granted another piece of land consisting of a *nāla* and a *vāstu* section. The arable part measured three *Udānas* and the homestead part, which contained a betelnut plantation on it, was four *Udānas* in area. The two sections of the plot, containing some land of the homestead category, together measured seven *Udānas*, of which the annual income was 50 *Purāṇas*.

The land was originally under the joint possession of

Kano and Amṛtoka (the same person as mentioned in section VI), from whom Halāyudha purchased it as a *paṭṭolī*. It apparently formed part of a *jāgīr* in the possession of Nāñīsiṁha who was the *Mahāsāndhivigrahika* (minister for war and peace probably of king Viśvarūpasena). The king no doubt ratified the minister's gift of the land as a rent-free holding.

VIII. Lines 56-57 : *tathā Phandra-dvīpe Urā-caturake Jayajāhaḍā-pūrvve Ghāgharakāṭṭī-pāṭake rājapaṁ-Mahesa (śva)-rasya anen = aiv = Āvallika-paṁ-Halāyudhena krīta-śāsana-saṁ-savāstu-bhū-udāna* 12¾ *sāṁ-hi* 50 /

This section refers to a plot of land situated in the village called Ghāgharakāṭṭī-pāṭaka lying to the east of Jayajāhaḍā in the Urā-caturaka of Phandra-dvīpa. It was attached to the *śāsana* (i.e. land granted rent-free by a charter) which was purchased by Halāyudha from the *Rājapaṁ* (i.e. *Rāja-paṇḍita*) Maheśvara. The area of the land was 12¾ *Udānas* and its annual revenue income 50 *Purāṇas*. In this case, the king merely allowed Halāyudha the rent-free enjoyment of the land by recognizing its alienation by Maheśvara. It appears that a revenue-free holding lost its special character on alienation and that its new owner had to pay the annual rent-fixed for it unless the king again made it revenue-free.

IX. Lines 57-58 : *tathā Phandra-dvīpe Pātilādivīke kumāra-śrī-Puruṣottamasena-bhujyamān-āya-saṁ anen = aiva caturddaś-ābdīya-utthānadvādaśyāṁ samutsarggita-bhū-sambandhena datta-savā-stu-bhūmy-udāna* 24 *sāṁ-hi* 50 /

This section speaks of a piece of land situated in the village of Pātilādivīka in Phandra-dvīpa. It was attached to the *āya* meaning 'income' or 'property' and referring apparently to a *jāgīr* enjoyed by Prince Puruṣottamasena (possibly another son of Viśvarūpasena) and was granted by the Prince in favour of Halāyudha on the occasion of the Utthāna-dvādaśī [in the month of Kārttika] during the year 14 (i.e. in the fourteenth regnal year of king Viśvarūpasena). The king merely ratified the grant of the plot of land as a revenue-free holding. A portion of this plot was of the *vāstu* category. It measured 24 *Udānas* and its annual revenue income was 50 *Purāṇas*.

X. Lines 58-61 : (a) *militvā sārddha-ṣaṭtriṁśad-unmān-ādhika-śatatray-odān-ātmaka-kalanaguvākamūlya-varajāya-sameta-sāṁ-cūrṇṇī-pañcasatika-bhūmiḥ*

(b) *sa-jala-sthalā sa-jhāṭa-viṭapā sa-gartt-oṣarā sa-khila-nālā sa-guvāka-nārikelā a-caṭṭa-bhaṭṭa-praveśā ā-candr-ārka-kṣiti-sama-kālaṁ yāvat*

(c) *davakula-puṣkariṇy-ādikaṁ kārayitvā guvāka-nārikel-ādikaṁ laggāvayitvā putra-pautr-ādi-santati-krameṇa svacchand-opa-bhogen=opabhoktuṁ....*

The sentence is incomplete. Subsection (a) says that altogether the area of the various plots of land enumerated above came up to 300 *Udānas* and 36½ *Unmānas*. As the total of the number of *Udānas* enumerated separately in Sections I-IX actually comes up to 336½ *Udānas*, the word *Unmāna* mentioned here has to be taken as a synonym of *Udāna*. Subsection (b) says that the plots were granted together with land and water, bushes and branches, pits and barren tracts and waste and arable land and without the right of entrance for the *Caṭṭa-Bhaṭṭas* (*Cāṭas* and *Bhaṭas* of the earlier records, possibly meaning Pāiks and Barkandāzes). It is also said that the grant was meant to last as long as the sun, the moon and the earth would endure. Subsection (c) says that the donee and his descendants, such as sons, grandsons and others were allowed to enjoy the lands at their pleasure by causing on them the erection of temples, excavation of tanks, plantation of betel-nut, coconut and other trees, and similar other works which were ordinarily not allowed to rent-paying tenants.

XI. Lines 61-64 : *Vātsya-sagotrasya Aurva-Cyavana-Bhārgava-Yā (Jā)madagnya-Āpnuvat-pañcapravarasya Yajurved-āntargata-Kāṇva-śākh-aikadeś-ādhyāyino Lakṣmīdharadevaśarmmaṇaḥ prapautrāya tathā Devadharadevaśarmmaṇaḥ pautrāya tathā Adhyayadevaśarmmaṇaḥ putrāya Vātsya-sagotrāya Aurva-Cyavana-Bhārgava-Yā (Jā)madagnya-Āpnuvat-pañcapravarāya Yajurved-āntargata-Kāṇvaśakh-aikadeś-ādhyāyine Āvallika-paṁ-śrī-Halāyudhadevaśarmmaṇe Brāhmaṇāya....*

The sentence is still incomplete. This section mentions the donee of the charter under study. He was *Paṇḍita* Halāyudhadevaśarman (probably a resident of Avalla or Āvalla), who belonged to the Vātsya-gotra and the five *pravaras*, viz. Aurva, Cyavana, Bhārgava, Jāmadagnya and Āpnuvat, and was a student of a part of the Kāṇva branch of the Yajurveda. The donee was the son of Adhyayadevaśarman, grandson of Devadharadevaśarman and great-grandson of Lakṣmīdhara-devaśarman.

XII. Lines 64-68 : (a) *Nāvye mahā-uttarāyaṇa-mahā-saṁkramaṇe svaya[ṁ-datta]-saṁ-sā (ṁ*)-bhū-hi* 100 /

(b) *Nāvya-Madhukṣīraka-Vaṅga-bhāgeṣu mātṛcaraṇānāma-(nāṁ) dṛṣṭe naḥ soma-grāse datta-saṁ-sā (ṁ*)-bhū-hi* 250 /

(c) *Vikramapura-bhāge varṣa-vṛddhau kumāra-śrī-Sūryya-sena-pradatta-saṁ-sā(ṁ*)-bhū-hi* 25 /

(d) *tathā hi sāndhi-Nāñīsiṁha-datta-saṁ-sā (ṁ*)-bhū-hi* 25 /

(e) *Phandra-dvīpe Urā-caturake krīta-śāsana-saṁ-sāṁ-bhū-hi* 50 /

(f) *tathā Pātilādivīke kumāra-Puruṣottamena datta-saṁ-sā-(ṁ*)-bhū-hi* 50 /

(g) *militvā śrīmat-Sadāśiva-mudrayā mudrayitvā bhūcchidra-nyāyena tāmraśāsanīkṛtya pradatto='smābhiḥ yatra baraja-guvāk-āya-sameta-tāmraśāsana-saṁ-bhū-hi* 500 //

The sentence is concluded in this section. Sub-sections (a)-(f) refer again to the gift lands in different areas and mention the amounts of annual revenue allotted to them : (1) 100 *Purāṇas* per annum attaching to the gift land in Nāvya granted by the king himself on the occasion of the Uttarāyaṇa-saṅkrānti in his thirteenth regnal year (see section I) ; (2) 250 *Purāṇas* per annum attaching to the gift land in the Nāvya-Madhukṣīraka-Vaṅga area granted on the occasion of the observation of a lunar eclipse by the king's mother (see sections II-V); (3) 25 *Purāṇas* per annum attaching to the gift land in the Vikramapura Division granted by Prince Sūryasena on the occasion of his birthday anniversary (see section VI); (4) 25 *Purāṇas* per annum attaching to the gift land in the same area granted by the *Sāndhi* (i.e. *Sāndhivigrahika*) Nāñīsiṁha (see section VII); (5) 50 *Purāṇas* per annum attaching to the gift land in the Urā-caturaka in Phandra-dvīpa, which had been purchased by the donee as a *śāsana* or rent-free holding (see section VIII); and (6) 50 *Purāṇas* per annum attaching to the gift land at Pātilādivīka granted by Prince Puruṣottamasena (see section IX). Subsection (g) says that the plots of land were collectively granted as one lot by making it a *tāmra-śāsana* (i.e. a rent-free holding) according to the principle of *bhūmicchidra* (i.e. rent-free enjoyment of a piece of land by one who brings it under cultivation for the first time) and by endowing it with a stamp of the Śadāśiva seal (i.e. the royal seal of the Senas of Bengal). It is also stated that the income arising out of the *tāmra-śāsana*, including the income of the betel-vine plantations and betelnuts, come up to 500 *Purāṇas* per annum. Subsection (h) requests the officials, etc., whom the king addressed (cf. lines 39-41 of the inscription), to approve of the grant made by him.

II

In the year 1892, N. N. Vasu secured a copper-plate grant discovered in the village of Madanpāḍā (near Piñjāḍī) in the Kotalipada Pargana of the Faridpur District now in Bangladesh. He edited the inscription with Plates in the *Journal of the Asiatic Society of Bengal*, Vol. XLV, 1896, Part I, pp. 6-15. The copper plate was subsequently acquired by the Asiatic Society of Bengal, although later it could no longer be traced in the Society's collection. Unfortunately, Vasu's transcript of the grant portion of the charter is full of lacunae and errors while the facsimile of the inscription published by him is not a faithful reproduction of the original. Owing to this difficulty, N. G. Majumdar, while re-editing the record in his *Inscriptions of Bengal*, Vol. III, 1929, pp. 133-39, failed in improving considerably upon Vasu's treatment. He observed, 'This portion of the text being extremely corrupt and full of scribal mistakes, it is difficult to say what is actually intended.'[1] As will be seen below, these remarks are unjustifiable. The text of the grant portion of the charter is fairly free from scribal errors while the meaning of it is quite clear.

Sometime ago, the inscription was purchased for the Dacca Museum, and we had an opportunity of examining the original record and its estampages in 1952. The scrutiny helped us in detecting the errors in the published text, and the interpretation of the grant portion of the epigraph became quite clear to us. But, before entering into that subject, it is necessary to refer to an exceptionally interesting feature of the grant. This is the fact that a large number of passages on the plate, especially in the grant portion of the charter on its reverse side, have been engraved on erasures. They raise certain problems which require careful consideration.

It is well known that the Madanpāḍā and Vaṅgīya

1. *Op. cit.*, p. 138, note 4.

Sāhitya Pariṣad plates[1] of Viśvarūpasena and the Idilpur plate[2] assigned to Keśavasena, supposed to be the younger brother and successor of Viśvarūpasena, have practically the same set of introductory stanzas. This introductory part deals with the Sena kings : (1) Vijayasena, his son (2) Ballālasena, his son (3) Lakṣmaṇasena, and his son (4) either Viśvarūpasena or Keśavasena who was the reigning monarch. More than half of the stanzas describe the reigning king and his father Lakṣmaṇasena. In this section in verse, three stanzas are very interesting. The first and second of them describe Lakṣmaṇasena while the third introduces the issuer of the charters. They are quoted below.

(1) *pūrvaṁ janma-śateṣu bhūmi-patinā saṁtyajya mukti-grahaṁ*
nūnaṁ tena sut-ārthinā Suradhunī-tīre Haraḥ prīṇitaḥ |
etasmāt katham=anyathā ripu-vadhū-vaidhavya-baddha-vrato
vikhyāta-kṣitipāla-maulir=abhavac=chrī-Viśvarūpo nṛpaḥ ||

This is verse 10 of the Madanpāḍā and Idilpur plates and verse 11 of the Sāhitya Pariṣad plate. N. G. Majumdar translated the stanza as follows : 'In hundreds of previous births, that king (i.e. Lakṣmaṇasena), leaving aside all care for liberation, surely propitiated Śiva, on the bank of the Ganges, being desirous of having a son. Otherwise, how could be born to him the head of the princes, the illustrious king Viśvarūpa who was determined to cause the widowhood of his enemies' wives ?' He takes the word *etasmāt* in the sense of 'from this [king, i.e. Lakṣmaṇasena]'. It may also mean 'owing to this [reason, i.e. the propitiation of Śiva referred to in the first half of the stanza]', although the implication of the verse as a whole remains the same.

(2) *yāṁ nirmmāya pavitra-pāṇir=abhavad=Vedāḥ satīnāṁ śikhā-*
ratnaṁ yā kim=api sva-rūpa-caritair=viśvaṁ yay=ālaṅkṛtam |
Lakṣmīr=bhūr=api vāñchitāni vidadhe yasyāḥ sapa[*tnyor*= (or *tnī*-)] *dvayaṁ*
śrīmaty=Ahvaṇadevy=amuṣya mahiṣī s=ābhūt=tri-var-ggocitā ||

This is the reading of verse 15 of the Sāhitya Pariṣad plate of Viśvarūpasena. But in the published transcripts of the

1. Majumdar, *op. cit.*, pp. 140-48, 177-78, with Plates.
2. *Ibid.*, pp. 118-31; see *JASB*, Vol. VII, 1838, pp. 43-51 and Plates.

Madanpāḍā (verse 13) and Idilpur (verse 14) plates we have, in the place of the passage *dvayaṁ śrīmaty = Ahvaṇadevy= amuṣya*, respectively the passages *mahārājñī śrī-Tāḍā* (or *ndrā*)-*devi tad=asya* and *maharājñī śrī-Cāndrādevī svasya*.[1] It is clear that the passage quoted from the transcripts of the Madanpāḍā and Idilpur plates violate the metre horribly and can hardly be attributed to the original author of the stanzas. What is, however, more interesting is that, on the Madanpāḍā plate, the *akṣaras* read as *Tāḍā* (or *ndrā*)*devi* are incised on an ensure showing plainly that originally a different name, no doubt agreeable to the metre and in three *akṣaras* only, had been engraved in the space. This is also suggested by the expression *tad=asya* following the name in the Madanpāḍā plate, in which the word *tad* means 'therefore', the whole stanza implying that, owing to the enumerated qualities of the queen, she became to her husband as agreeable as the three *vargas*, viz. *Dharma, Artha* and *Kāma*. The female name that had been originally engraved in the space in question and was later erased for the incision of a different name in four *akṣaras* (a fifth *akṣara* could have been merged in the preceding *śrī* in *Sandhi*) was thus written in three syllables, the first and second of which were short and the third long (e.g., Varadā, or Indumatī with the initial syllable merged in *śrī*).

There is reason to believe that, on the Idilpur plate also, the name of the queen, that had been originally engraved, was later erased and substituted by a different name.

(3) *etābhyāṁ Śaśiśekhara-Girijābhyām = iva babhūva Śaktidharaḥ* |
śrī-Viśvarūpasenaḥ pratibhaṭa-bhūpāla-mukuṭa-maṇiḥ ||

This is the clear reading of verse 16 of the Sāhitya Pariṣad plate, which speaks of the birth of Viśvarūpasena from king Lakṣmaṇasena and queen Ahvaṇadevī mentioned in the immediately preceding verse quoted above. But, in the place of *śrī-Viśvarūpasenaḥ*, the transcripts of the Madanpāḍā and Idilpur plates have respectively *śrī-Viśvarūpasenadevaḥ* and *śrī-Keśava-senadevaḥ*. It is interesting to note that, on the Madanpāḍā plate, the *akṣaras Viśvarūpa* have been engraved on an erasure

1. The actual reading of the last two *akṣaras* seems to be *muṣya* suggesting *devy=amuṣya* as in the Sāhitya Pariṣad plate.

clearly indicating that originally a name in two *akṣaras* only was incised in the space. A superscript *r* on the second of these two *akṣaras* of the original royal name still remains undisturbed. Equally interesting is the fact that exactly these two features are also characteristic of the incision of the *akṣaras* *Viśvarūpa* in the royal name again occurring in the grant portion (line 38) of the plate. The erased name in two *akṣaras* must have read something like *Sūryya*, *Darppa*, *Sarvva*, *Parvva*, etc.

Owing to the compression of four *akṣaras* in the space only for two and to the presence of the superscript *r* above the second of the two *akṣaras* originally incised, the *akṣaras* Viśvarupa on the Madanpāḍā plate look like *viśvarrā* in line 22 (verse 14 quoted above) and *viśvarra* in line 38 in the grant portion. It is admitted that the *akṣaras Keśava*, read in the corresponding places in lines 24 (verse 15 quoted above) and 43 of the Idilpur plate, are similarly engraved on erasures. In Prinsep's retouched fascimile, the vowel-mark in the first *akṣara* of the name looks like *i*. The fact that the *akṣaras* looking like *viśvarrā* on the Madanpāḍā plate may be quite easily confused with the familiar name Keśava leads us to feel that it is the name *Viśvarūpa*, compressed in the space for two *akṣaras* on the Idilpur plate, that was wrongly read by Prinsep's Pandit in 1838 as *Keśava*.[1] The transcript of the Idilpur plate contains numerous obvious errors. Considering the large number of mistakes committed by N. N. Vasu in 1896[2] and H. P. Sastri in 1926[3] in transcribing respectively the Madanpāḍā and Sāhitya Pariṣad plates and especially those noticed in the transcripts prepared by Prinsep's Pandits of such epigraphic records as the Tezpur plates[4] of Vanamālavarman, we are sure about the possibility. We are therefore entirely in agreement with those

1. This was the view of F. Kielhorn, N.N. Vasu and H.P. Sastri. See Kielhorn's List of Inscriptions (North India), No. 649, and Bhandarkar's List, No. 1693. The last letter of the name looks more like *pa* than *va* in Prinsep's facsimile. What has been read as *keśava* looks actually like *kiśvapa*.

2. *JASB*, Vol. XLV, Part I, pp. 6ff.

3. *Ind. Hist. Quart.*, Vol. II, pp. 77ff.

4. *JASB*, Vol. IX, 1840, pp. 766ff.: cf. *Kāmarūpaśāsanāvali*, pp. 58ff.; see also *Ep. Ind.*, Vol. XXIX, pp. 145ff.

who already expressed this suspicion upon an examination of the Madanpāḍā plate, attributed the Idilpur plate to Viśvarūpasena and referred the rule of Keśavasena to the imagination of one of Prinsep's Pandits. Indeed anyone having an opportunity to examine the Madanpāḍā plate or its faithful reproduction is sure to entertain this view.

We have seen that the name of the Sena king who originally issued the Madanpāḍā plate and probably also the Idilpur plate was something like *Sūryyasena*, *Darppasena*, etc. When the three stanzas quoted above are read together in the context of the Madanpāḍā and Idilpur plates, they give the idea that the issuer of these charters was a son of Viśvarūpasena. This is supported remarkably by the grant portion of the Madanpāḍā plate, in which, as will be shown below, the names of Ballālasena, his son Lakṣmaṇasena, his son Viśvarūpasena and his son (**sena) have been erased and substituted respectively by those of Vijayasena, his son Ballālasena, his son Lakṣmaṇasena and his son Viśvarūpasena. It is again very interesting in this connection to note that lines 54 and 66 of the Sāhitya Pariṣad plate of Viśvarūpasena actually speak of a *Kumāra* or Prince named Sūryyasena who was very probably a son of Viśvarūpasena. Under the circumstances, the name of the original issuer of the Madanpāḍā plate and most probably also of the Idilpur plate may be almost confidently restored as *Sūryyasena*. The mention of Viśvarūpasena as king in his son's records and the substitution of the name of the son by that of the father in the 14th regnal year of the latter (*vide infra*) show that Sūryyasena ruled for some time between the begining and end of the reign of Viśvarūpasena. The actual circumstances of the case cannot be determined; but it seems that Viśvarūpasena was temporarily incapacitated by being captured by some enemy or being attacked by some disease like insanity from which his recovery was not expected. Sūryyasena was then raised to the throne; but he restored the crown to his father as soon as the latter returned or recovered. The passage *bṛhan-nṛpati-caraṇaiḥ* in line 49 of the Idilpur plate seems to refer to Viśvarūpasena who was still living during Sūryasena's reign. It may be noticed that Sūryyasena mentions his father respectfully and is himself mentioned in a later record of his father. He does not appear to have been a rebel against

Viśvarūpasena.[1] Sūrya adapted for his charters the draft of his father's records, in which he put his own name in the place of his father's and his mother's name in that of his grandmother's. This he could very easily do as in his father's records the name of Viśvarūpa occurs once earlier in the description of Lakṣmaṇasena although this adaptation led Sūrya to use in his father's description a few stanzas which describe his grandfather in his father's Vaṅgīya Sāhitya Pariṣad plate.[2]

The name of king Sūryasena's mother cannot be restored with confidence. It is unrecognizable under the re-engraved name of his grandmother. The two *akṣaras* (following *śrī*) of this re-engraved name of Viśvarūpasena's mother are extremely doubtful; this is because the *akṣaras* originally incised were not completely erased and the new *akṣaras* were engraved on the traces of the old ones. We suspect that the reading intended is *śry-Ahvaṇadevi tasya* (*śry-Ahvaṇa-devy=amuṣya* in the Idilpur plate) in conformity not only with the metre but also with the information supplied by the Vaṅgīya Sāhitya Pariṣad plate. The word *devi* for *devī* is not correct, although it is often adopted by versifiers for the metre's sake (e.g. in verse 8 of the Kuretha plate of Malayavarman).[3] The adoption of the rather unorthodox spelling for metrical necessity shows, however, that the officers responsible for the erasure were fully conscious of the requirements of the metre. The fact, as will be shown below, that entire lines of the inscription have been erased and re-engraved on the reverse of the plate also suggests that, instead of writing *Tāḍā* (or *ndrā*)*devī* which goes against the metre (and also against the information of the Vaṅgīya Sāhitya Pariṣad plate), they would have erased some more *akṣaras*, originally engraved, and reincised a suitable passage.

The grant portion of the Madanpāḍā plate runs from line 31 to line 60. We shall take up this part section by section. The language of the record is Sanskrit which is, however, influenced by the local dialect. We have not corrected the passages which violate the rules of Sanskrit grammar especially in regard to *Sandhi*.

1. Of course the possibility of the father being temporarily overthrown by the son is not precluded entirely.

2. The title *Vṛṣabhāṅkaśaṅkara* for *Vṛṣabhaśaṅkara* (cf. p. 218) and the double introduction of the king now appear to us to suggest that the Sāhitya Pariṣad plate of Viśvarūpa may have actually adopted Sūrya's draft.

3. *Ep. Ind.*, Vol. XXX, pp. 144 ff.

1. Lines 31-38:

(a) *iha khalu Phaṣphagrāma-parisara-samāvāsita-śrīmaj-jayaskandhāvārāt*

(b) *samastasva(su)prasasty-upeta-Arirājavri (vṛ)ṣabhaśaṅkara-Gauḍeśvara-śrīma[d*]-Vijayasenadeva-pād-ānudhyāta-*

(c) *samastasupraśastyupeta-Arirājaniḥśaṅkaśaṅkara-Gauḍeśvara-śrīmav-Va (d-Ba)llālasenadeva-pādānudhyāta-*

(d) *samastasva (su)praśastyupeta-aśvapati-gajapati-narapati-rāja-tray-ādhipati-Senakulakamalavikāsabhāskara-Somavaṁśapradīpa-pratipannakarṇṇa-satyavratagāṅgeya-śaraṇāgatavajrapañjara-parameśvara-paramabhaṭṭāraka-paramasaura-mahārājādhirāja-Arirājamadana-śaṅkara-Gauḍeśvara-śrīma (l*)-Lakṣma[ṇa]senadeva-pād-ānudhyāta-*

(e) *aśvapati-gajapati-narapati-rājatray-ādhipati-Senakulakamalavikāsabhāskara-Somavaṁśapradīpa-pratipannakarṇṇa-satyavrata-gāṅgeya-śaraṇāgatavajrapañjara-parameśvara-paramabhaṭṭāraka- paramasaura-mahārājādhirāja-Arirājavri (vṛ)ṣabha (bhā)ṅkaśaṁkara- Gauḍeśvara-śrīmat-Viśvarū (pa*)senadeva-pādā vijayinaḥ* ।

This section speaks of the reigning king and his three ancestors and also of the locality whence the charter was issued. Subsection (a) shows that the grant was issued from a locality called Phasphagrāma. I do not think that the name can be read as *Phalgugrāma*. In subsection (b) which mentions the great-grandfather of the reigning king, the *akṣaras vri (vṛ)ṣabha* in *Arirāja-vṛṣabha-śaṅkara* bear clear traces of being re-engraved on an erasure offering space for three *akṣaras*. It can be clearly seen that the first of the three erased *akṣaras* was *niḥ*, its *visarga* sign and *i-mātrā* being still visible.[1] It is almost certain therefore that the passage originally engraved was *Arirāja-niḥśaṅka-śaṅkara* which was the title of Ballālasena. Similarly, the *akṣaras Vijaya* after *śrīma* seem to have been written on a space where *d-Vallāla* had been originally incised, although the traces of the original letters are not quite clear in this case, apparently because the old *akṣaras* were here more successfully erased. Sub-section (c) mentions the grandfather of the reigning monarch. In this subsection, exactly as in subsection (b) discussed above, *niḥśaṅka* in *Arirāja-niḥśaṅka-śaṅkara* and what is intended to read *d-Vallāla* are very clearly re-engraved on erasures. It appears that what was originally *lla* was erased

1. The original *n* was changed into *v* merely by retouching its loop.

and substituted by what is intended to read *dva*. This suggests that the original reading of the passages concerned was *Arirāja-madana-śaṅkara* and *śrīmal-Lakṣmaṇasena*. In the second of the two passages, *Arirāja-madana-śaṅkara* and *śrīmal-Lakṣamaṇasena* in subsection (d), *l-Lakṣamaṇa* is obviously incised on an erasure offering space for no less than four *akṣaras*. Moreover, an *i-mātrā* of the first of the erased *akṣaras* is still traceable. We are confident that the four *akṣaras*, after erasing which *l-Lakṣmaṇa* was engraved, read *d-Viśvarūpa*[1] in the original writing. It should be remembered that the only known Sena king having a name in four syllables was Viśvarūpasena. Moreover, Lakṣmaṇasena is here described as *parama-saura*, although he was really a Vaiṣṇava. This anomaly is quite clearly explained by the fact that the official responsible for writing *l-Lakṣmaṇa* after erasing the name of Viśvarūpa, who was really a *parama-saura* as known from his Sāhitya Pariṣad plate, forgot to change *saura* into *vaiṣṇava*. As no other member of the Sena family before Viśvarūpasena was a Saura, it must have been his name that was erased. Consequently, in *Arirāja-madana-śaṅkara*, the *akṣaras madana* must have been engraved on an erasure. Unfortunately, the traces of the erased *akṣaras* are not clear in this case. Another point to be noticed is that here *madana* does not cover a space required for more than three *akṣaras*, although, according to the Sāhitya Pariṣad plate, Viśvarūpasena's *biruda* was *Arirāja-vṛṣabha* (*bhā*)*ṅka-śaṅkara* and in that case the *akṣaras* erased to make place for *madana* would be four, viz. *vṛṣabhāṅka*. It, however, appears to us that the original writing had *Arirāja-vṛṣabha-śaṅkara* (cf. the *biruda* of Vijayasena, great-grandfather of Viśvarūpasena) and not *Arirāja-vṛṣabhāṅka-śaṅkara*. Thus *madana* seems to have been incised after having erased *vṛṣabha*. In subsection (e), the *akṣaras vri* (*vṛ*)*ṣabha* in what is intended to read *Arirāja-vṛṣabhāṅka-śaṅkara* are engraved on an erasure. But the three *akṣaras* have been incised in a space for two letters only. The facts that *ṅka* after the erasure belongs to the original writing and that the *i-mātrā* of the first of the two erased *akṣaras* is still visible suggest that *Arirāja-niḥśaṅka-śaṅkara* was originally engraved. We have already discussed how the four *akṣaras Viśvarūpa* have been written on

1. The letter *pa* underneath *ṇa* can be clearly traced.

an erasure offering a space for only two *akṣaras* and how these two erased *akṣaras* may have read *Sūryya.* Attention has to be drawn to the expression *śrīmat* prefixed to the name. In *Sandhi,* the word suits the name *Sūryya,* but not the name *Viśvarūpa.*[1] The person responsible for the substitution of the former name by the latter did not change *t* into *d-Vi* through oversight, although this would have provided him with some space which he badly required. It seems that Viśvarūpa was an *Arirāja-vṛṣabha-śaṅkara* (or °*bhāṅka*°)[2] like his great-grandfather Vijayasena, while Sūryasena assumed the title *Arirāja-niḥśaṅka-śaṅkara* in imitation of his own great-grandfather Ballālasena. It has to be noted in this connection that Prinsep's facsimile of the Idilpur plate, although it is retouched, still bears traces of re-engraving on erasures in this section exactly as the Madanpāḍā plate. In *Arirāja-asahya-śaṅkara* (epithet of the so-called Keśavasena), as read in the Idilpur plate, *asahya* is a wrong reading for *vṛṣabha* written on an erasure of letters that appear to have read *niḥśaṅka.* The first consonant still looks more like *n* than *v.*

II. Lines 38-41 : *samupāgat-āśeṣa-rājanyaka....Viṣayapaty-ādīn=anyāṁś=ca sakala-rājapād-opajīvino='dhyakṣapravarān caṭṭa-bhaṭṭa-jātīyān Brāhmaṇān Brāhmaṇ-ottarāṁś=ca mānayanti bodha-yanti samādiśanti ca / viditam=astu bhavatāṁ....*

This section refers to the subordinates, dependants and officials of the king as well as others whom the king addressed in announcing the grant recorded in the charter.

III. Lines 41-43 : *yathā Pauṇḍravarddhana-bhukty-antaḥ-pāti-Vaṅge Vikramapura-bhāge pūrve Aṭhayāgagrāma-jaṅghāla-bhūḥ sīmā dakṣiṇe Vārayīpaḍāgrāma-bhūḥ sīmā paścime Uñcokāṭṭigrāma-bhūḥ sīmā uttare Vīrakāṭṭī-jaṅghāla-sīmā itthaṁ catuḥsīm-āvacchin-naḥ(nna)....*

This section shows that the gift land was situated in a village in the Vikramapura Division of Vaṅga which formed a part of the *bhukti* or Province of Pauṇḍravarddhana. The boundaries of this village are also stated. It was bounded in the east by an embankment and a piece of land belonging to

1. Cf. the other royal names in this section joined in *Sandhi* with the preceding *śrīmat.*

2. *Vṛṣabhaṅka* may be a mistake for *vṛṣabha.* See also above, p. 216, note 2; cf. p. 218.

the village called Aṭhayāgagrāma, in the south by a piece of land belonging to Vārayīpaḍāgrāma (literally 'a village consisting of a habitation of the Bārayīs or betelvine-growers'), in the west by a piece of land belonging to Uñcokāṭṭīgrāma and in the north by the embankment belonging to the village of Vīrakāṭṭī. In this section, a few letters in the name of the village standing in the eastern boundary of the gift land may have been engraved on an erasure. But this is of little importance.

IV. Lines 43-46 : *Piñjokāṣṭhīgrāma-ma[dh]yāt Kandarpa-śaṅkar-āśramīya-Padātiśāpāmārka-sāṁ-vā (dvā) triṁśat- purāṇ- ottara-cūrṇṇī-śat-aika* 132 *bahiḥ* 500 *tathā Kandarppaśaṅkar-āṁśa-bhūmau Nāraṇḍapagrāme svakīya-pālya-svaṁ sā (ṁ*)-hi* [1]27 *dvābhyāṁ sapta[v]iṁśati-purāṇ- ādhika-sāṁ- cūrṇṇ[ī] -ṣaṭśatik-otpattika-Piñjo-kāṣṭhīgrāmaḥ sa-jala-sthalaḥ sa-jhāṭa-viṭapaḥ s-oṣaraḥ sa-guvāka-nārikelas = tṛṇa-yūti-paryyanta uparilikhita-catuḥsi (sī) m-āvacchinnaḥ Piñjothīyagrāmo = 'yaṁ. . . .*

With the exception only of the last three *akṣaras* (*viz. grāmo = 'yaṁ*), this entire section in engraved on erasure. Clear traces of the erased *akṣaras* are still visible under many of the *akṣaras* in this section. The passages in lines 43-45 (from the beginning of this section down to *nārikelas = tṛṇa-yū*) are written in *akṣaras* which are smaller in shape and pressed against each other. This was done for the fear that all the *akṣaras* might not find space enough to be accommodated in the blank created by the erasure. But when the work of re-engraving had reached the beginning of line 46, it was found that the remainder of the *akṣaras* were not sufficient to fill up the remaining space created by the erasure. The *akṣaras* in *ti-paryyantaḥ...Piñjoṭhīya* were therefore incised in a bigger size and with more space between any two of them than even in the original part of the writing.

This section shows that the gift land was situated in the village of Piñjokāṣṭhī or °kāṭṭī or °ṭhīya (°kāṭhīya ?) (modern Piñjāḍī), the boundaries of which are enumerated in section III. A portion of the village yielding an annual (*sāṁ = sāṁvat-sarika*) income of 132 *Purāṇas* or *Cūrṇīs* was excluded (cf. *bahiḥ* = Bengali *baï*) and only the remainder yielding 500 *Purāṇas* or *Cūrṇīs* per annum was made the subject of the grant. The smaller part of the village, yielding 132 *Purāṇas* per year, was known as Padātiśāpāmārka and belonged to the *āśrama* of

Kandarpaśaṅkara, apparently the name of a saintly person or a deity. It may have been a deity named after Lakṣmaṇasena whose *biruda* was *Madanaśaṅkara*, the same as *Kandarpaśaṅkara*. It appears that, in the original grant of Sūryasena, the whole village of Piñjokāṣṭhī, otherwise called Piñjokāṭṭī or °(kā*) ṭhīya, was granted in favour of the donee of the charter and sometime later, when it was brought to the notice of the authorities that a part of the village really belonged to the Kandarpaśaṅkara *āśrama*, the necessity of changing the language of the document was felt. The donee's loss of 132 *Purāṇas* or *Cūrṇīs* per year was sought to be compensated by an additional gift of a piece of land yielding 127 *Purāṇas* or *Cūrṇīs* annually (cf. *sāṁ-hi = sāṁvatsarika-hiraṇya*). This piece of land was situated in the village of Nāraṇḍapagrāma belonging to the share of the said *āśrama* of Kandarpaśaṅkara; but it was the property of a dependant of the king, i.e. it formed part of a *jāgīr* enjoyed by one of the king's dependants. Thus the donee received two pieces of land, one at Piñjokāṣṭhī (°kāṭṭī or °kāṭhīya) and another at Nāraṇḍapa, together yielding an annual revenue income of 627 *Purāṇas* or *Cūrṇīs*. That the two plots of the gift land situated in two different villages were still collectively referred to as *Piñjo (kā*) ṭhīyagrāmo = 'yam* seems to be due to the influence of the original document in which, as suggested above, the whole of this village was granted. The officers probably did not feel any necessity of changing the language of this part of the record because only a small portion of the neighbouring village of Nāraṇḍapa was now added to the donee's share which mainly consisted of the major portion of Piñjokāṣṭhī.

V. Lines 46-53 : *Śivapurāṇ-okta-bhūmidāna-phalaprāpti-kāmanayā......śrī-Viśvarūpadevaśarmmaṇe Brāhmaṇāya vidhivad = utsṛjya Sadāśiva-mudrayā mudrayitvā bhūcchidra-nyāyena caturdaśay-ābdīya-Bhādra-dinā tāmraśāsanīkṛtya pradatto = 'smābhiḥ / yatra catuḥ-sīm-āvacchinna-sāṁ-śāsanabhū-hi* 627 / *tad = bhavadbhiḥ sarv-vair = ev = ānumantavyaṁ bhāvibhir = api nṛpatibhir = apaharaṇe narakapāta-bhayāt pālane dharmma-gauravāt pālanīyam /*

In this section the intended reading for *dinā* may be *dina* 8, while *sāṁ-śāsanabhū-hi* stands for *sāṁvatsarika-śāsana-bhūmi-hiraṇya*, i.e. the annual revenue income of the gift land in coins or cash. But what is more interesting is that, in *caturddaśay-ābdīya*, *caturddaśa* is incised on an erasure offering space only for two *akṣaras*. The *i-mātrā* of the first of these two *akṣaras* originally engraved and the *ī-mātrā* of the second of them are still traceable. There can hardly be any doubt that the original reading here was *dvitīy-ābdīya*. Thus Sūryasena's grant was made in the second year of his reign while the corrections in the document, as will be seen below again, were effected in the fourteenth regnal year of Viśvarūpasena. The second date could not have come very long after the first.

This section says that the gift land in question was granted as a *tāmraśāsana* (i.e. rent-free holding), according to the principle of *bhū-cchidra*, to the Brāhmaṇa Viśvarūpadevaśarman. It has to be noticed that the Brāhmaṇa Īśvaradevaśarman,[1] donee of the Idilpur plate, was a brother of this Viśvarūpadevaśarman. The grant is stated to have been endowed with an impression of the Sadāśiva seal which was the royal seal of the Sena kings. The section concludes with the mention of the total revenue income of the gift land, viz. 627 *Purāṇas* or *Cūrṇīs* per annum, and the king's entreaty for the protection of the grant.

VI. Lines 53-58 : *bhavanti c=ātra dharmm-ānuśaṁsinaḥ ślokāḥ* //

......*para-kīrttayo vilopyāḥ* //

This section quotes some of the ordinary imprecatory and benedictory stanzas.

VII. Lines 58-60 :
saciva-śata-mauli-lālita-pad-āmbujasy = ānuśāsane dūtaḥ / *śrī-Kopiviṣṇur = abhavad = Gauḍa-mahāsāndhivigrahikaḥ* // *śrīman-mahāsā-karaṇa-ni* // *śrī-mahā-mahattaka-karaṇa-ni* // *śrīmat-karaṇa-ni* // *saṁ* 14 *Āśvina-dine* 1 //

The date *Saṁ* 14 *Āśvina-dine* 1 has not been engraved on an erasure. Possibly the space, on which it is incised, was blank in the original charter. This section says that Kopiviṣṇu, the *Mahāsāndhivigrahika* (minister for peace and war) of Gauḍa, was the *dūta* or executor of this grant of the king. *Śrīman-mahāsā-karaṇa-ni* stands for *śrīman-mahāsāndhivigrahika-karaṇa-*

1. Prinsep's facsimile shows that the name was re-engraved on an erasure offering space for a slightly bigger name than Īśvara. The name erased may have been that of Viśvarūpadevaśarman. The change of donee possibly necessitated the modifications in the record carried out at a later date.

nibaddha. The word *nibaddha* here apparently means 'registered or passed or endorsed'. The occurrence of the word *dṛṣṭam* in the same context on some of the Early Pallava and Vākāṭaka charters may suggest that *ni* stands for *nirīkṣitam*.[1] The document was thus recognized first by a clerk of the *Mahāsāndhivigrahika*, then by a clerk of the *Mahāmathattaka* and finally by a clerk of the *Śrīmat*, i.e. the king himself.

1. Cf., however, *nibaddha* in records like the Barah plate of Bhoja (*Ep.Ind.*, Vol. XIX, p.18). Recently it has been suggested that *ni* stands for the sixth case-ending (*Proc. IHC*, 1950, p. 107). This is quite impossible in view of the fact that *ni* stands singly in many cases in the copper-plate grants of the Pālas such as the Bangadh and Belwa plates of Mahīpāla I, the Amgachi and Belwa plates of Vigrahapāla III (cf. *Ep. Ind.*, Vol. XXIX, pp. 2, 9, etc.), not to speak of the unconvincing nature of the association of an early Central Asian linguistic trait with a medieval East Indian record without any connecting link.

CHAPTER XV

CHARTER OF DĀMODARA

The Mehar copper-plate inscription was edited jointly by B.M. Barua and P.B. Chakravarti.[1] Unfortunately, the treatment of the record by the said scholars is not quite satisfactory since both the transcript and translation of the inscription, as published by them, contain many errors in our opinion. The grant portion of the record in lines 17-32 has suffered the most at the hands of the editors.

Although we are chiefly concerned here with lines 17-32 of the Mehar plate detailing the grant recorded in the inscription, the nature of the editor's treatment of the introductory verses may be illustrated by an examination of their reading and interpretation of at least one of the stanzas in this part of the epigraph.

Verse 7 of the inscription has been read and translated as follows :

Devendrasya yath=aiva Mātalir=abhūt Kṛṣṇasya yantā varaḥ
khyāto Dāruka-va(ba)ndhula(r=a)sya nṛpater=Vārṣṇeya-līlādharaḥ |
tat-tulyo='bhavad=asya vāraṇa-ghaṭā-satpātra-mukhyaḥ kṛtī
śrī-Gaṅgādharadeva eṣa samare Prāgjyotiṣendr-opamaḥ ||

"Just as Mātali was to Indra, [just as] Dāruka was the well-known charioteer and friend of Kṛṣṇa, so to this king was the illustrious Gaṅgādharadeva, the foremost among the honest courtiers, resourceful like the scion of the Vṛṣṇi family (i.e., Kṛṣṇa). His elephant column was like his (i.e., of the king). He equalled in battle [even] the lord of Prāgjyotiṣa (i.e., Bhagadatta)."

A minor defect in the treatment of the verse may be mentioned at the outset. This is the indication of its metre as *Sragdharā*, although actually it is *Śārdūlavikrīḍita*. What is, however, more important is that the above translation of the stanza exhibits a number of blemishes, some of which show

1. *Ep. Ind.*, Vol. XXVII, pp. 182-91.

that the learned interpreters have failed to grasp the real implication of the verse. In the first place, the words *vara* in the first and *kṛtī* in the third foot of the stanza have been left out in the translation. Secondly, the expression *Dāruka-bandhu* in the emended passage *Dāruka-bandhur=asya* in the second foot does not appear to be quite happy. Moreover, the emendation involves the unnecessary and unpoetic duplication of the word *asya* which actually occurs in the following (i.e., the third) foot. Thirdly, it is difficult to believe with the editors of the record that a poet worth the name would have compared a person at the same time with both Kṛṣṇa (Vārṣṇeya) and Kṛṣṇa's charioteer Dāruka. Fourthly, although the text of the stanza rightly gives *vāraṇa-ghaṭā- sat-pātra-mukhya* (i.e., the chief of the worthy officers in charge of the elephant columns) as a single compound expression, in the translation, *satpātra-mukhya*, interpreted as 'the foremost among the honest courtiers', has been wrongly separated from the compound. Fifthly, the passage *tat-tulyo='bhavad=asya vāraṇa-ghaṭā*, in which *vāraṇa-ghaṭā* has been wrongly separated from the said compound, has been quite unjustifiably interpreted as "His (i.e., Gaṅgādharadeva's) elephant column was like his (i.e., the king's)." This is clearly against the rules of Sanskrit grammar as the expression *tat-tulyaḥ* in the masculine cannot possibly qualify *vāraṇa-ghaṭā* in the feminine. Moreover, it is impossible to believe with the editors that a poet of any merit would have clumsily introduced the elephant force of a courtier (as the word *pātra* has been taken to mean) in the king's description to indicate its equality with the elephant corps of the royal army. Is it possible that a courtier was allowed to enjoy an elephant force as strong as the king's ? What is then the point in the former's comparison with the charioteers Mātali and Dāruka ?

It seems to us that the intended reading of what has been read as *Dāruka-vandhulasya* is not *Daruka-bandhur=asya*, but *Darukavan=Nalasya*.[1] It should be noted that Vārṣṇeya was

1. As regards the reading *ndhu*, it may be pointed out that there is usually little difference in the Gauḍīya alphabet among *ndh*, *nv* and *nu* and that sometimes the same sign was used to indicate *nn* as well. For this form of *nn*, cf. *unnayan* in line 15 and *avacchinna* in line 31 of the Sobharampur plate of Dāmodara (*Ep. Ind.*, Vol. XXX, pp. 184 ff.).

the celebrated charioteer of the famous king Nala of the Niṣadhas just as Mātali and Dārkua were the charioteers respectively of Indra and Kṛṣṇa. Our *anvaya* of the stanza would thus run as follows : *yathā Mātaliḥ Devendrasya khyātaḥ varaḥ yantā abhūt tat-tulyaḥ eva Kṛṣṇasya Dārukavat Nalasya Vārṣṇeya-līlā-dharaḥ samare Prāgjyotiṣendr-opamaḥ asya nṛpateḥ vāraṇaghaṭā-satpātra-mukhyaḥ eṣa kṛtī śrī - Gaṅgādharadevaḥ* [*asya khyātaḥ varaḥ yantā*] *abhavat*. We are inclined to translate the verse in the following words : "Just as Mātali was the famous [and] excellent charioteeer (*yantā*) of the lord of the gods, exactly like him this illustrious Gaṅgādharadeva, who is competent, who is like Kṛṣṇa's [*yantā*] Dāruka, who resembles Nala's [*yantā*] Vārṣṇeya, who is an equal to the lord of Prāgjyotiṣa in battle [and] who is the chief of the worthy officers in charge of the elephant columns of the king, was his famous [and] excellent rider (*yantā*)."

It may further be pointed out that the learned interpreters of the verse have absolutely nothing to say why the poet has introduced the leader of the elephant force of king Dāmodara in a charter purporting to record a grant of land made by the king in favour of certain Brāhmaṇas. It, however, seems to us that the nature of the verse quoted above is similar to that of the two concluding stanzas of the Bangaon plate[1] of Vigrahapāla III. In the Bangaon copper-plate inscription, a grant of land, actually made by a royal officer named Ghaṇṭīśa out of his own *jāgīr*, is represented as a gift of the Pāla king because, according to the legal procedure of those days, the king had to ratify the creation of a rent-free holding by any of his fief-holders. The Vaṅgīya Sāhitya Pariṣad (Calcutta) plate of Viśvarūpasena likewise refers to the ratification by the Sena king of similar grants of revenue-free land made by Prince Sūryasena, Prince Puruṣottamasena and the minister (*Sāndhi-vigrahika*) Nāññisiṁha out of their respective *jāgīrs*.[2] In the Mehar inscription, the real donor of the grant, therefore, seems to have been the royal officer Gaṅgādharadeva, the village of Mehāra in which the gift land was situated probably lying in

1. *Ibid.*, Vol. XXIX, pp. 48 ff.
2. See *JAS*, Letters, Vol. XX, pp. 209 ff.; above, pp. 207-08, 210.

his own *jāgīr*. Unless Gaṅgādhara was intimately associated with the charter in this way, it is impossible to explain his introduction in the document.[1] It seems also that on previous occasions the village of Mehāra formed part of the *jāgīrs* of two other officers, viz., *Mahāsāndhivigrahika* Munidāsa and *Mahākṣapaṭalika* Dalaeva, who had created two rent-free holdings in the village with the king's sanction. These two grants are referred to in our record in lines 29-31 without any specification of the amounts of rent allotted to them to show that the king and the new owner of the *jāgīr* (i.e., Gaṅgādharadeva) recognised the rent-free nature of the holdings in question. It is of course difficult to say whether these free-holdings were created during the reign of Dāmodara or one of his predecessors.

Before taking up the grant portion of the Mehar copper-plate inscription for scrutiny, a word may also be said in regard to the reading of the fractions employed in this section of the record in enumerating the area of different pieces of the gift land given in the land measure called *Droṇa* or *Droṇavāpa* and the amount of its income given in the coin called *Purāṇa*. As in other medieval records of Eastern India such as the Vaṅgīya Sāhitya Pariṣad plate[2] of Viśvarūpasena, $\frac{1}{4}$ is indicated by a vertical *daṇḍa* and $\frac{1}{16}$ by a *daṇḍa* slanting from upper right towards lower left. That is to say, one vertical *daṇḍa* $=\frac{1}{4}$, two vertical *daṇḍas* $=\frac{2}{4}$ $(\frac{1}{2})$, and three vertical *daṇḍas* $=\frac{3}{4}$, while one slanting *daṇḍa* $=\frac{1}{16}$, two slanting *daṇḍas* $=\frac{2}{16}$ $(\frac{1}{8})$ and three slanting *daṇḍas* $=\frac{3}{16}$. In line 19, the area of the plot of land granted to the Brāhmaṇa Śāṅkoka is given in a peculiar symbol which has been read by the learned editors as the numeral 7. But it has been overlooked that the total area of all the twenty-three pieces of gift land is quoted in line 32 as $2\frac{11}{16}$ *Droṇas*+2 *Dronas*, i.e., altogether $4\frac{11}{16}$ *Droṇas* only. This shows beyond doubt that the area of any one piece of the gift land cannot be 7 *Droṇas*. Moreover, what has been read as 7 has no resemblance with that figure as found in epi-

1. It appears that the donor of the grant mentioned in verses 8 and 12 as *Dviradapati* and *Gajapati* is Gaṅgādhara, the leader of the elephant force, and not the king.

2. N.G. Majumdar, *Inscriptions of Bengal*, Vol. III, pp. 140 ff.

graphic records and manuscripts. On the other hand, it resembles very closely the modern Bengali form of $\frac{2}{16}$ ($\frac{1}{8}$). Another point deserving notice is that, although the editors have noted in their transcript (lines 20, 21,23,25, 26 and 29) seven cases of a cross being used after the slanting *daṇḍa* indicating $\frac{1}{16}$, in the enumeration of the area of a piece of the gift land, this has been altogether ignored in their interpretation of the inscription. What has, moreover, been read as a cross in line 26 is actually a cross with a dot on its left and another on its right. The real value of the cross and the cross flanked by dots cannot be determined in the present state of our knowledge; but it may be tentatively suggested that the former indicates $\frac{1}{64}$ and the latter $\frac{2}{64}$ ($\frac{1}{32}$).[1] It will be seen below that these readings appear to be supported by the total area of the gift land quoted in line 32 of the record.

Let us now quote the text of the grant portion of the Mehar inscription in lines 17-32.

uparilikhita-grāme Sāvarṇṇya[2]*-sagotra-paṁ-śrī-Kāpaḍīkasya pañcaviṁśati-purāṇ-otpattika-gṛha-vāṭik-ādi-ṭī* 3 *vyā-bhū*[3] $\frac{2}{4}$ ($\frac{1}{2}$) *sāṁ-hi* 25/ *tathā Brā-śrī-Śāṅkokasya pañca-purāṇ-otpatti* (*ka**)-*ca-ṭī* 1 *vyā*[4]*-bhū* $\frac{2}{16}$[5] ($\frac{1}{8}$) *sāṁ-hi* 5/ *tathā Brā-śrī-Sudokasya ca-ṭī* 1 *vyā-bhū* $\frac{3}{16}$ *sāṁ-hi* 8/ *tathā Brā-*(*śrī**)*-Kālemīkasya*[6] *ṭī* 1 *vyā*[4]*-bhū* $\frac{2}{16}$($\frac{1}{8}$) *sāṁ-hi* 4/ *Brā-*(*śrī**)*-Tārāpateḥ ca-ṭī* 1 *vyā*[4]*-bhū* $\frac{2}{16}+\frac{1}{64}$ ($\frac{9}{64}$) *sāṁ-hi* $4\frac{2}{4}$ ($4\frac{1}{2}$)[7] / *Bharadvāja-sagotra-paṁ-śrī-Pāṇḍokasva*[8] *gṛ-ṭī* 1 *vyā*[4]*-bhū* $\frac{3}{16}+\frac{1}{64}$ ($\frac{13}{64}$) *sāṁ-hi*

1. If such was the case, it may be conjectured that, according to this system, $\frac{3}{64}$ was written by a cross having four dots at the four sides—left, right, upper and lower.

2. The editors read *Sāva*(*r*)*ṇnya* apparently because they took the clear sign of superscript *r* to stand for a top *mātrā*, although, in the Gauḍīya alphabet, the letter *ṇ* is written without top *mātrā*.

3. The editors read 2 *byā-bhū*.

4. The editors read *byā*.

5. The editors read 7. The symbol, however, stands midway between the form of $\frac{1}{8}$ written with two slanting *daṇḍas* and its modification now used in Bengal.

6. The editors' transcript has *Kālemikasya*.

7. This has been omitted in the editors' transcript; but in their translation it is given as '$\frac{3}{16}$' *purāṇas* (sic)'.

8. The editors' transcript has *Paṇḍokasya*.

10 $\frac{2}{16}$ (10 $\frac{1}{8}$) / *tathā Brā-śrī-Deukasya*[1] *gṛha-ṭī* 1 *vyā*[2]*-bhū* $\frac{2}{16}+\frac{1}{64}$ ($\frac{9}{64}$) *sāṁ-hi* 4/ *tathā Brā-śrī-Sudoksya gṛha-ṭī* 1 *vyā*[2]*-bhū* $\frac{1}{4}$ *sāṁ-hi* 8 $\frac{7}{16}$ / *Kāṇṭāmaṇīya*[3] *Brā-śrī-Keśavasya gṛ-ṭī* 1 *vyā*[2]*-bhū* $\frac{2}{16}$ ($\frac{1}{8}$) *sāṁ-hi* 4 $\frac{14}{16}$ ($4\frac{7}{8}$) / *tath=āsya mu-ṭī* 1 *vyā*[2]*-bhū* $\frac{1}{16}+\frac{1}{64}$($\frac{5}{64}$)*sāṁ-hi* $\frac{9}{16}$/ 1 *tathā Brā-śrī-Brahmokasya gṛ-ṭī* 1 *vyā*[2]*-bhū* $\frac{3}{16}$ *sāṁ-hi* 2/ *eda-(vaṁ) tath=āsya mu-ṭī* 1 *vyā*[2]*-bhū* $\frac{2}{16}$ ($\frac{1}{8}$) *sāṁ-hi* [1 $\frac{1}{4}$] / [*ta*]-*th=āsya nā-bhū* $\frac{1}{2}$[5] *sāṁ-hi* 2/ *tathā sya* (*ca*) *Brā-śrī-Sirokasya gṛha-ṭī* 1 *vyā*[2]*-bhū* $\frac{2}{16}+\frac{1}{64}$($\frac{9}{64}$) *sāṁ-hi* $5\frac{3}{4}$ / *Pūrvagrāmīya-Brā-śrī-Dharaṇikasva Guṇombh-ārddha-ca-ṭī* 1 *vvā*[2]*-bhū* $\frac{1}{16}+\frac{2}{64}$ ($\frac{3}{32}$) *sāṁ-hi* $2\frac{2}{4}$ ($2\frac{1}{2}$) /*Sidhalagrāmīya-paṁ-śrī-Pāukasya*[6] *ca-ṭī* 1 *vyā*[2]*-bhū* $\frac{1}{4}$ *sāṁ-hi* 4/ *Ātreya-*(*sa**)*gotra- Brā-śrī-Śāṅkokasya nā-bhū* $\frac{1}{4}$ *sāṁ-hi* $1\frac{1}{4}$/ *Diṇḍisāyīya-Brā-śrī-Prajāpateḥ gṛha-vāṭyāṁ bhū* $\frac{1}{16}$ *sāṁ-hi* $3\frac{1}{4}$/ *gṛhi-paṁ-śrī-Nāthokasya nā-bhū* $\frac{5}{16}$ *sāṁ-hi* $1\frac{1}{4}$ *Brā-śrī-Jalokasya*[7] *grā-hi* 1 $\frac{2}{16}$ ($1\frac{1}{4}$)/ *Brā-śrī-Viśvarūpasya gṛ-ṭī* 1[8] *vyā*[2]*-bhū* $\frac{2}{16}+\frac{1}{64}$($\frac{9}{64}$) *sāṁ-hi* $3\frac{6}{16}$ ($3\frac{3}{8}$) / *Brā-śrī-Mādhokasya ci*[9]*-khi-mu-ṭī* 1[10] *vyā*[2]*-bhū* $\frac{1}{4}$ /*Keśarakoṇīya-Brā-śrī=Śrīpateḥ mahāsāndhivigrahika-śrī-Munidāsa-kārita-śāsana-ca-ṭī* 1 *vyā*[2]*-bhū* $\frac{3}{16}$ / *Brā-śrī-Śrīvatsasya mahākṣapaṭalika-śrī-Dalaeva-kārita-śāsana-gṛ-ca-ṭī* 1 *vyā*[2]*-bhū* $\frac{5}{16}$ / *evaṁ śāsanika-Brāhmaṇa*[11] 20 *vā-ṭī* 16 *bhū-dro* $2\frac{1}{16}$[12] *nāla-bhū-dro* 2 *sāṁ-hi* 100////

1. The editors read *Deḍakasya*. But note the resemblance of the initial *u* in this word with the same letter in *uparilikhita* in line 17 and its difference form *ḍ* in *Kāpaḍika* in the same line.
2. The editors read *byā*.
3. The editors read *Kāṇyāmalīya*.
4. The amount and the *akṣara ta* are broken away; but, adding the other amounts and comparing the result with the total given in line 32, the lost amount can be confidently restored. The editors say, "As the total of the yearly income from different lands falls short by 1 *purāṇa* from the total given in line 32, we may take the income of Brahmoka's land as 1 *purāṇa* yearly." This is due to a mistake in their calculation.
5. The editors' transcript has $\frac{1}{8}$ at this place.
6. The editors read *Pā*(*ṁ*)*ḍukasya* and observe, "The name does not seem to be Pāūka." The initial *u* employed here closely resembles the same *akṣara* as found in *uparilikhita* in line 17. Cf. *Kāmarūpaśāsanāvalī*, p. 161, note 3.
7. The editors read *Jano*(*lo*)*kasya*. But compare *l* in this word with the same letter in *līlā* in line 12.
8. The editors read 2.
9. The editors read *bi*.
10. The editors read 3.
11. For °*hmaṇāḥ*.
12. The editors' transcript has here $2\frac{5}{8}$.

Of the many contractions used in the section of the inscription quoted above, *paṁ* and *Brā* no doubt stand respectively for *paṇḍita* and *Brāhmaṇa*. Similarly, *bhū-dro* apparently stands for *bhūmi-Droṇa* or *bhūmi-Droṇavāpa* (i.e., a *Droṇa* or *Droṇavāpa* of land) and *nā-bhū* for *nāla-bhūmi* (i.e., cultivated land). The other abbreviations used in the inscription besides these are : (1) *sāṁ-hi*, (2) *grā-hi*, (3) *vyā-bhū*, (4) *ṭī* and (5) the composite contractions, of which *ṭī* is a component, such as *gṛ-ṭī* or *gṛha-ṭī*, *ca-ṭī*, *mu-ṭī*, *gṛ-ca-ṭī*, *ci-khi-mu-ṭī*, and *vā-ṭī*.

As regards the meaning of *sāṁ-hi*, the editors of the Mehar inscription observe, "N.G. Majumdar (*Inscriptions of Bengal*, Vol. III, p. 146, f.n. 3) explains *sāṁ* in the sense of *sākalyena*, 'in all,' while on page 125, f.n. 2, he rightly suggests that *sāṁ-hi* stands for *śāśvatam*. In the Edilpur (Idilpur) copper plate of Keśavasena (sic), *sā* or *sāṁ* stands for *sā* (*śā*)-*śvatan* = *dāy-otpattika* (*m*), *hi* being oviously *sahiḥ* (Madanapāḍā copper plate of Viśvarūpasena, line 44)." It should, however, be noticed that the suggestion regarding *sāṁ-hi* = *śāśvatam* has been wrongly attributed to N.G. Majundar who never said anything like that. Again, what was read in the Madanpāḍā plate as *sahiḥ*, which gives little sense, is undoubtedly *bahiḥ* (Bengali *baī*, 'excluding').[1] Moreover, how can the meaningless *sahiḥ* clarify the implication of *sāṁ-hi* and how can the latter stand for *śāśvataṁ* in which neither *sāṁ* nor *hi* occurs ? As we have shown above,[2] *sāṁ* and *hi*, together forming the composite contraction *sāṁ-hi*, stand respectively for the words *sāṁvatsarika* (i.e., annual) and *hiraṇya* (i.e., coin or cash). Thus *sāṁ-hi* = *sāṁvatsarika-hiraṇya* indicates the annual revenue income of a piece of land in cash. This contraction is invariably followed by the number of *Purāṇas* constituting the annual revenue income.

Similarly *hi* in *grā-hi* also stands for *hiraṇya*, and *grā* is a contraction for the word *grāhya*, 'to be realised'. This contraction occurs only in line 28 which says that the *gṛhi-paṇḍita* Nāthoka received a plot of *nā-bhū* or arable land which was $\frac{5}{16}$ *Droṇa* in area and fetched the annual revenue income

1. See above, p. 220.
2. Above, p. 203.

of $1\frac{1}{4}$ *Purāṇas*. Of this amount, however, $1\frac{1}{8}$ *Purāṇas* were realisable by the Brāhmaṇa Jaloka, so that the land was made rent-free in respect only of the donor's share in the income constituting $\frac{1}{8}$ *Purāṇa* only.

In regard to the contraction *vyā-bhū*, the editors say, "Its meaning has so far been missed. The Sāhitya Pariṣat plate clearly attests that it stands only for *catuḥ-sīm-āvacchinna-vāstu-bhūmi*, i.e., *vyāvṛtta-vāstu-bhūmi*, 'demarcated homestead land or residential site'. In it *vyā-bhū* is aptly distnguished from *nāla-bhū* precisely as in our plate." This interpretation of the contraction *vyā-bhū* is, however, clearly wrong. In the first place, if *vyā* means merely 'demarcated', how can it go only with 'homestead land' and never with 'arable land'? It is impossible to believe that the boundaries of a plot of *nāla-bhūmi* were never demarcated. The editors themselves have quoted the passage *catuḥ-sīm-āvacchinna-vāstu-nāla-bhūmi* from an epigraphic record. Secondly, although *vyā-bhū* and *nā-bhū* have been clearly distinguished, there is definite evidence to prove that the category of land styled *vyā-bhū* often included some land of the class called *nā-bhū* or *nāla-bhūmi*, 'cultivated land'. This is shown by the fact that, though our inscription specifically mentions only three plots of *nā-bhū* respectively measuring $\frac{1}{2}$ *Droṇa* (line 24), $\frac{1}{4}$ *Droṇa* (line 27) and $\frac{5}{16}$ *Droṇa* (line 28), i.e., in all only $1\frac{1}{16}$ *Droṇas*, the total area of the gift land of this category as quoted in line 32 is 2 *Droṇas*. There is thus no doubt that $\frac{15}{16}$ *Droṇa* of *nā-bhū* was included in the *vyā-bhū* plots specified in the record. As we have elsewhere[1] suggested, *vyā-bhū* probably stands for *vyāmiśra-bhūmi*, 'mixed land', consisting of land of various types such as *vāstu* (homestead land), *nāla* (arable land), *khila* (fallow land), etc.

The editors have suggested that the contraction *ṭī* stands for *vāṭī* or *caṭī*, while *gṛ-ṭī* or *gṛha-ṭī* and *mu-ṭī* have been supposed to stand respectively for *gṛha-vāṭī* and *mukhya-vāṭī* or *mukhya-caṭī*. But what they understood by *caṭī* is not clear. In Sanskrit, the word *vāṭī* or *vāṭīkā* means 'a house-site', a

1 Above, p. 202.

garden', etc.; but there is no such word as *caṭī*. It has to be noticed that the abbreviations of words like *vāṭī* and *caṭī* are expected to be *vā* and *ca* respectively and not *ṭī* for both of them. The contraction *mu-ṭī*, moreover, cannot stand for *mukhya-vāṭī* meaning 'a prominent or principal house-site or garden', not only because the word *mukhya* would in that case be quite meaningless, but also because an analysis of the specified revenue income of the different plots of land as quoted in the inscription shows that the rent of a *Droṇa* of *gṛ-ṭī* and *ca-ṭī* was very considerably higher than that of a *Droṇa* of *mu-ṭī*. In line 29, the editors have read *bi*(sic *ci*)-*khi-mu-ṭī* 3 (sic 1) *byā* (sic. *vyā*)-*bhū* $\frac{1}{4}$ and translated the passage as "one main house with low and fallow land—demarcated homestead land $\frac{4}{18}$ (*droṇa*)." It has been suggested that *bi-khi-mu-ṭī* stands for *bila-khila-mukhya-vāṭī*. Unfortunately, the interesting point that this particular plot of land had no rent allotted to it has been overlooked. This fact undoubtedly suggests that *ci-khi* stands for *cira-khila* referring to a piece of land that was never brought under cultivation or any other profitable use and therefore fetched no revenue income at all. Similarly, that *ṭī* does not stand for *vāṭī* is quite clear from the passage *gṛha-vāṭik-ādi-ṭī* 3 *vyā-bhū* $\frac{1}{2}$ *sāṁ-hi* 25 occurring in line 18 of the inscription. The passage apparently means, "*ṭī* of house-site, garden, etc. 3 in number; mixed land—$\frac{1}{2}$ *Droṇa* in area; annual revenue income in cash—25 *Purāṇas*". It is also interesting to note that *ṭī* occurs only in connection with *vyā-bhū* and never with *nā-bhū*. We have elsewhere[1] suggested that *ṭī* may stand for the word *ṭikkara* or *ṭīkar* recognised in Hindi, Bengali and Oriya lexicons in the sense of 'a mound'.

The real meaning of *ca* in *ca-ṭī* and *mu* in *mu-ṭī* is very difficult to determine. An analysis of the specified revenue income allotted to the various plots of land would suggest the following averages : (1) 37 $\frac{2}{3}$ *Purāṇas* for a *Droṇa* of *gṛ-ti* or *gṛha-ṭī* land; (2) 30 $\frac{2}{17}$ *Purāṇas* for a *Droṇa* of *ca-ṭī* land; (3) 4 *Purāṇas* for a *Droṇa* of *mu-ṭī* land; and (4) 4$\frac{4}{17}$ *Purāṇas* for a *Droṇa* of *nāla* or arable land. This shows that *gṛ-ṭī* was the most profitable kind of homestead land while *ca-ṭī* was a

1. Above, p. 202.

slightly less profitable type of the same kind of land. That these two kinds were almost equal in value is further suggested by the following indications. In line 31, a plot of land is characterised as *gṛ-ca-ṭī*, i.e., as mixed *gṛ-ṭī* and *ca-ṭī*. It will be seen that our record specifies 21 *ṭīs* of the three classes, viz., *gṛ-ṭī*, *ca-ṭī* and *mu-ṭī*, in the body of the charter, but that, in the total quoted in line 32, it speaks only of *vā-ṭī* 16. In the contraction *vā-ṭī*, *vā* apparently stands for *vāstu* meaning 'homestead land'.[1] It seems that the unprofitable plots characterised as *mu-ṭī* were not regarded as proper *vāstu* land and were left out in the calculation of the total. But in the details of the grant, we have specific mention only of 3 *mu-ṭīs*. We are therefore short of 2 *mu-ṭīs*. Can it be suggested that the passage *gṛha-vāṭik-ādi-ṭī* 3 in line 18 included 1 *ṭī* of the *vāstu*=*gṛha-vāṭikā* category and 2 of the *mu-ṭī* class ? Can it further be conjectured that *gṛ-ṭī* indicated a mound containing houses and gardens, *ca-ṭī* a mound containing plantations only and *mu-ṭī* a mound without houses and gardens and covered with grass or jungle ?[2] But all three appear to have contained, possibly on the borders, small patches of land of the *nāla* category if not also of any other type such as *khila*.

For easy reference we quote below the details of the grant portion of the Mehar copper-plate inscription in a table.

Number and Name of the Donee.	*Category and Area of Land.*	*Annual Revenue Income.*
1. *Paṇḍita* Kāpaḍika of the Sāvarṇṇya-gotra.	*gṛha-vāṭik-ādi-ṭī* 3; *vyā-bhū* ½ *Droṇa*.	25 *Purāṇas*.

1. The contraction *vā* for *vāstu* occurs in records including the Chittagong plate of Dāmodara himself (N.G. Majumdar, *op. cit.*, p. 181).

2. Wilson's Glossary recognises some Bengali and Hindi names of particular types of land, which begin with the syllable *ca* or *mu*, e.g., *cacar* or *cañcar* (land that has lain fallow only for a few years), *car* or *cācar* (inferior fallow land or sandy land on the banks or in the bed of river), *carāi* (pasture lands), *mus* (land along the high banks of rivers), *musavi* (an embankment), etc. But these do not appear to have anything to do with the *ca-ṭī* and *mu-ṭī* of our record. For *mu*=*muṇḍa*, *muṇḍā*, i.e. bare or barren, see now *JAIH*, Vol. II, p. 68.

2. Brāhmaṇa Śāṅkoka (of the same *gotra* ?).	*ca-ṭī* 1; *vyā-bhū* $\frac{1}{8}$ *Droṇa*	5 *Purāṇas.*
3. Brāhmaṇa Sudoka (of the same *gotra* ?).	*ca-ṭī* 1; *vyā-bhū* $\frac{3}{16}$ *Droṇa*	8 *Purāṇas.*
4. Brāhmaṇa Kālemīka (of the same *gotra* ?).	*ṭī* (*gṛ-ṭī* or *ca-ṭī*) 1; *vyā-bhū* $\frac{1}{8}$ *Droṇa.*	4 *Purāṇas.*
5. Brāhmaṇa Tārāpati (of the same *gotra* ?).	*ca-ṭī* 1; *vyā-bhū* $\frac{9}{64}$ *Droṇa*	4 $\frac{1}{2}$ *Purāṇas.*
6. *Paṇḍita* Pāṇḍoka of the Bhāradvāja-gotra.	*gṛ-ṭī* 1; *vyā-bhū* $\frac{13}{64}$ *Droṇa*	$10\frac{1}{8}$ *Purāṇas.*
7. Brāhmaṇa Deuka (of the same *gotra* ?).	*gṛha-ṭī* 1; *vyā-bhū* $\frac{9}{64}$ *Droṇa*	4 *Purāṇas.*
8. Brāhmaṇa Sudoka (of the same *gotra* ?).	*gṛha-ṭī* 1; *vyā-bhū* $\frac{1}{4}$ *Drona*	$8\frac{7}{16}$ *Purāṇas.*
9. Brāhmaṇa Keśava of Kāṇṭāmaṇi.	*gṛ-ṭī* 1; *vyā-bhū* $\frac{1}{8}$ *Droṇa*	$4\frac{7}{8}$ *Purāṇas.*
Do.	*mu-ṭī* 1; *vyā-bhū* $\frac{5}{64}$	$\frac{9}{16}$ *Purāṇa.*
10. Brāhmaṇa Brahmoka (of the same place ?).	*gṛ-ṭī* 1; *vyā-bhū* $\frac{3}{16}$ *Droṇa*	2 *Purāṇas.*
Do.	*mu-ṭī* 1; *vyā-bhū* $\frac{1}{8}$ *Droṇa*	$1\frac{1}{4}$ *Purāṇas.*
Do.	*nāla-bhūmi* $\frac{1}{2}$ *Droṇa*	2 *Purāṇas.*
11. Brāhmaṇa Siroka (of the same place ?)	*gṛha-ṭī* 1; *vyā-bhū* $\frac{9}{64}$ *Droṇa*	$5\frac{3}{4}$ *Purāṇas.*
12. Brāhmaṇa Dharaṇika of Pūrvagrāma.	*ca-ṭī* 1 (half of which was in the possession of Guṇombha); *vyā-bhū* $\frac{3}{32}$ *Droṇa.*	$2\frac{1}{2}$ *Purāṇas.*
13. *Paṇḍita* Pāuka of Sidhalagrāma.	*ca-ṭī* 1; *vyā-bhū* $\frac{1}{4}$ *Droṇa*	4 *Purāṇas.*
14. Brāhmaṇa Śāṅkoka of the Ātreya-gotra.	*nāla-bhūmi* $\frac{1}{4}$ *Droṇa*	$1\frac{1}{4}$ *Purāṇas.*
15. Brāhmaṇa Prajāpati of Diṇḍisāya	*bhū* (forming a part of his *gṛha-vāṭī*) $\frac{1}{16}$ *Droṇa.*	$3\frac{1}{4}$ *Purāṇas.*

16. *Gṛhi-Paṇḍita* Nāthoka (of the same place ?)	*nāla-bhūmi* $\frac{5}{16}$ *Droṇa.*	$1\frac{1}{4}$ *Purāṇas* (minus $1\frac{1}{8}$ *Purāṇas* to be realised by the Brāhmaṇa Jaloka, i.e., $\frac{1}{8}$ *Purāṇa* only).[1]
17. Brāhmaṇa Viśvarūpa (of the same place ?)	*gṛ-ṭī* 1 ; *vyā-bhū* $\frac{9}{64}$ *Droṇa*	$3\frac{3}{8}$ *Purāṇas.*
18. Brāhmaṇa Mādhoka (of the same place ?)	*ci-khi-mu-ṭī* 1 ; *vyā-bhū* $\frac{1}{4}$ *Droṇa.*	No rent as it was *cira-khila.*
19. Brāhmaṇa Śrīpati of Keśarakoṇa	*ca-ṭī* 1 (belonging to a *śāsana* or rent-free holding created by *Mahāsāndhivigrahika* Munidāsa); *vyā-bhū* $\frac{3}{16}$ *Droṇa.*	No rent as it belonged to a *śāsana.*
20. Brāhmaṇa Śrīvatsa (of the same place ?).	*gṛ-ca-ṭī* 1 (belonging to a *śāsana* created by *Mahākṣapaṭalika* Dalaeva); *vyā-bhū* $\frac{5}{16}$ *Droṇa.*	No rent as it belonged to a *śāsana.*
In all : donees (Brāhmaṇas)—20	*vāstu-ṭī* 16: *bhūmi-droṇa* $2\frac{11}{16}$ + *nāla-bhūmi-droṇa* 2, i. e., together $4\frac{11}{16}$ *Droṇas* of land of the different categories.	*Sāṁ-hi* 100 *Purāṇas.*

1. In the editor's translation, Jaloka has been made a donee; but this is impossible in view of no mention of a piece of land in his connection and also of the total amount of the donees' revenue income quoted in line 32. If Jaloka's amount is counted, the total will be more than 100 *Purāṇas* even without considering the amount lost in line 24.

APPENDICES

I

ANCIENT INDIAN DEMOCRATIC TRADITIONS

The word *democracy* is derived from Greek *dēmokratia* in which *demos* means 'the people' while *cracy* is from Greek *kratein* 'to rule'. It is used in the sense of a form of government or State in which the people decide their own affairs either directly or indirectly through their representatives. The earliest democracies are supposed to have been the Greek City States which were small and in which the citizens could take a part personally in the deliberations. The said kind of State is also called a republic (from Latin *respublica*, meaning 'commonwealth'), in which there is no sovereign, so that it is the opposite of a monarchy. In later times, big republics emerged in the history of some countries. Another kind of early Greek State was called *oligarchy* which means the government by a small exclusive class and is derived from Greek *oligos* meaning 'a few' and *arkhein* , 'to rule'.

It is sometimes believed that the only form of government known to early Indian political thinkers was what is usually called 'Oriental despotism'. Investigations of scholars like T.W. Rhys Davids,[1] K. P. Jayaswal,[2] D. R. Bhandarkar,[3] R.K. Mookerji,[4] R.C. Majumdar[5] and others have, however, shown that democratic rule was prevalent in India during the ancient period. Early Indian literature often mentions republican tribes, usually referred to as *gaṇa* or *saṅgha*. Some of them ruled over small City States while the territories of others were fairly big. Thus the early Buddhist works speak

1. *Buddhist India*, London, 1903.
2. 'An Introduction to Hindu Polity' in the *Modern Review*, 1913; also *Hindu Polity*, Calcutta, 1924; 2nd ed., Bangalore, 1943.
3. *Carmichael Lectures on Ancient Indian History*, 1918, Calcutta, 1919.
4. *Local Government in Ancient India*, Oxford, 1919.
5. *Corporate Life in Ancient India*, 3rd ed., Calcutta, 1969.

of such republican tribes living in the age of the Buddha (c. 566-486 B.C.) as the (1) Śākyas of Kapilavāstu, (2) Bhargas of Śiśumāra-giri, (3) Bulis of Allakappa, (4) Kālāmas of Keśaputra, (5) Koliyas of Rāmagrāma, (6-7) Mallas of Kuśīnagara and of Pāvā, (8) Mauryas of Pippalīvana, (9) Videhas of Mithilā, and (10) Licchavis and Vṛjis of Vaiśālī.[6]

Kauṭilya's *Arthaśāstra*[7] mentions two classes of *saṅgha*, the first of which was associated with the Kṣatriyas and other classes among the Kāmbojas and Surāṣṭras who adopted the professions of *vārtā* (trade, agriculture and cattle-rearing) and *śastra* (i.e. fighting). The second type of *Saṅgha* is mentioned in connection with the Licchavis, Vṛjis, Mallas, Madras, Kukuras, Kurus and Pāñcālas who enjoyed the title of *Rājan*. The first category seems to refer to guilds and the second to republican states. Several types of such institutions are sometimes mentioned side by side as *saṅgha*, *gaṇa*, *pūga* and *śreṇī*.[8] A kind of guild was called *vrāta*.[9] It may be noted that the republican Kurus and Pāñcālas have to be distinguished from the well-known Kuru and Pāñcāla monarchies. It is supposed that the Vṛji confederacy of 8 clans, flourishing about North Bihar during the Buddha's age, consisted of the

6. Raychaudhuri, *PHAI*, 1938, pp. 158 ff.; Majumdar, *CLAI*, 1969, pp. 216-17.

7. XI. 1 : *Kamboja-Surāṣṭra-Kṣatriya-śreṇy-ādayo vārtā-śastr-opajīvinaḥ Licchivika-Vṛjika-Mallaka-Kukura-Madraka Kuru-Pāñcāl-ādayo rāja-śabd-opajīvinaḥ*. The *Aitareya Brāhmaṇa* (VIII. 14-15) speaks of *vairājya* (explained by some as 'non-monarchical government') and associates it with the Uttara-Kurus and Uttara-Madras living beyond the Himavat. The belief that the *Atharvaveda* (V. 18-10) speaks of the joint rule of one thousand Vaitahavyas (Majumdar, *op. cit.*, pp. 212-13) is doubtful.

8. Majumdar, *op. cit.*, p. 23. Because we have coins like those of the Śibi-janapada, Bhandarkar regarded *janapada* as a form of republic (*op.cit.*, p. 173). In such cases, however, the word *janapada* seems to mean a State or territory.

9. *Ibid.*, pp. 214-15. Such names are sometimes theoritecally applied to different types of corporations; e.g., *naigama* of the citizens, *vrāta* of the fighting men, *pūga* of the merchants, *pāṣaṇḍa* of the ascetics, *gaṇa* of the Brāhmaṇas, *śreṇī* of the artisans, *saṅgha* of the Buddhist *arhats*, and *gulma* of the Cāṇḍālas and others. See Kātyāyana (referring to Bṛhaspatī) quoted in Vardhamāna's *Daṇḍaviveka*, G.O.S. ed., p. 31. It is not possible to justify the use of the terms exclusively in the said senses. See *Early Indian Political and Administrative Systems*, ed. Sircar, p. 8, note. See alos p. 246 and note 55 below.

Videhas, Licchavis, Vṛjis, Jñātṛkas, Ugras, Bhojas, Aikṣvākus (Ikṣvākus) and Kauravas (Kurus).[10] These Kauravas may be the republican Kurus flourishing in the Bihar region.

Very little is known about the functioning and administration of the early Indian Republican States, though Buddhist literature offers us bits of information about the Śākya and Vṛji-Licchavi administration as well as the functioning of the Buddhist *saṅgha* or church which is supposed to have been organised primarily after the Śākya constitution, the great Buddha having been essentially a member of the Śākya clan. The *Mahāvagga*[11] and *Cullavagga*[12] suggest that the Buddhist church had rules regarding—(1) the manner of moving resolutions in the assembly, (2) quorum of a meeting, (3) determination of the opinion of the assembly by votes of the majority in the case of difference of opinion, (4) voting by ballot and counting of votes, (5) reference of complicated matters to a committee which referred back the matter on which it failed to come to any decision, (6) votes by absentees, and (7) subsequent legislation on acts done by an illegally constituted assembly.[13]

The Jain *Kalpasūtra*[14] speaks of the nine Mallakis, nine Licchavis and the eighteen Gaṇarājas of Kaśī and Kosala probably meaning nine Gaṇa-rājas each of the Malla, Licchavi, Kāśī and Kosala territories or the 18 Gaṇarājas of Kāśī and Kosala, of which 9 were Mallas and 9 Licchavis. The second alternative interpretation would suggest that the Licchavis, like the Śākyas, were subordinate to the king of Kosala. But the Jātakas speak of 7707 Licchavi Rājans who formed the

10. Raychaudhuri, *op.cit.*, pp. 99 ff. The *Aṅguttaranikāya* (I. 26; III. 49; IV. 208) speaks of the Ugras' connection with Vaiśālī, the capital of the confederacy, while the Jñātṛkas lived at Kuṇḍagrāma (Kuṇḍapura) and Kollāga in the suburbs of Vaiśālī. The Videhas had their head-quarters at Mithilā; but a branch of the people may have settled near Vaiśālī.

11. IX. 3.2, 5-6.

12. IV. 2.2, 9; 14.24, 26; XI.1.4; XII.1.10.

13. Majumdar, *op.cit.*, p. 234. Food belonging to the Buddhist *saṅgha* was often distributed to the monks by tickets called *śalākā*, while the priests sometimes voted by *śalākā* in a sort of ballot.

14. Ed. Jacobi, p. 65 : *nava Mallaī nava Lecchaī Kāsī-Kosalassa aṭṭhārasa vi gaṇa-rāyāṇo.*

Supreme Assembly of the Licchavis. The number of the Licchavi Rājans is sometimes also given as 500, though both the numbers are conventional.[15]

The *Ekapaṇṇa Jātaka*[16] refers to the 7707 Licchavi Rājans who had the same number of viceroys (*uparāja*), generals and treasurers, while the *Cullakāliṅga Jātaka*[17] says that all the 7707 Licchavi Rājans had their abode at Vaiśālī and all of them were given to argumentation and disputation. The doubtful nature of these statements is obvious. It is sometimes suggested that the Licchavi Rājans were really each one the ruler of a portion of the Licchavi territory.[18] But this is not reconcilable with the statement that all of them had their abode at Vaiśālī. That their sons, the princes, also lived at the headquarters of the tribal territory is clear from the story how the Śākyas sent their princes away to the villages so that they might not meet Viḍūḍabha when the latter visited Kalpilavāstu.[19]

About the republic of the Śākyas, we know that their Rājans met at the *saṁsthāgāra* or assembly hall. But they describe their country as the *ājñā-pravṛtti-sthāna* of the Kosala king, i.e. a region meant for the introduction (*pravṛtti, pravarttana*) of the Kosala king's order. This shows that they were subordinate to the king of Kosala.

An interesting information about the Licchavi administration of justice is that a culprit when he could not be released by a judicial officer, had his case submitted to the next higher officer till it reached the Rājan (the Rājans or one of them) who could punish him in accordance with the *Praveṇīpustaka* or Book of Precedents. The officers through whose hands the case had to pass were the (1) *Viniścaya-mahāmātra*, (2) *Vyava-*

15. See *JAIH*, Vol. III, pp. 86 ff. The *Mahāvagga* states that the dominions of king Bimbisāra of Magadha embraced 80,000 townships, the overseers (*Grāmika*, literally 'village-headman') of which used to meet in a great assembly (cf. Raychaudhuri, *PHAI*, 1938, p. 167). The number of townships (villages?) may be fictitious; but the reference to the assemblage of the *Grāmikas* of the whole kingdom is interesting.

16. Vol. I, No. 149.

17. Vol. III, No. 301; cf. Majumdar, *op. cit.*, p. 220.

18. Majumdar, *op.cit.*, p. 221.

19. See the introduction to the *Bhaddasāla Jātaka* (*Jātaka*, Vol. IV, No. 465)

hārika, (3) *Sūtradhara*, (4) *Aṣṭakulaka*, (5) *Senāpati*, and (6) *Uparāja*, with the Rājan at the end of the chain.[20]

The Greek authors who wrote on the campaigns of Alexander the Great in India (327-324 B.C.) speak of a large number of republican and oligarchical tribes in the area about the present Pakistan region of the Indian sub-continent.[21] The Sabarcae, Nysaians, Cathaeans, Adraistai, Siboi (Śibi), Agalassoi, Oxydrakai (Kṣudraka), Malloi (Mālava), Abastanoi (Ambaṣṭha), Xathroi (Kṣatṛ), Ossadioi (Vasāti), Sodrai (Śūdra), etc., were some of the non-monarchical clans. About the Sabarcae, Quintus Curtius says that 'the form of their government was democratic and not regal'.[22] Their strength is indicated by the fact that their army consisted of 60,000 foot, 6,000 cavalry and 500 chariots. According to Arrian, the governing body of the Nysaians consisted of the President and 300 members of the aristocracy. Elsewhere Arrian says that the officers called Superintendent made their reports 'to the king where the people have a king and to the magistrates when the people are self-governed'.[22] But some of the statements of the Greek authors have been misunderstood by modern writers. Thus Arrian speaks of the country beyond the Vipāśā, i.e. the Nanda empire during Alexander's invasion, and says that the people there were 'living under an excellent system of internal government, for the multitude was governed by the aristocracy, who exercise their authority with justice and moderation'. This may not refer to democratic rule,[24] but to the administration of the provinces by princes of the royal blood assisted by the Mahāmātras who were members of the nobility. Then again, according to Megasthenes who lived for some years at the court of Candragupta Maurya (c.324-300 B.C.), most of the Indian cities in his time

20. See *JASB*, Vol. VII, pp. 993-94; Majumdar, *op.cit.*, pp. 224-25. It is difficult to believe that all criminal cases passed through such a long chain.

21. See Raychaudhuri, *op.cit.*, pp. 196ff.; Majumdar, *op.cit.*, pp. 235ff.

22. Arrian's *Indika*, trans. McCrindle, p. 252.

23. *Ibid.*, p. 212.

24. Cf. Majumdar, *op. cit.*, p. 237.

'adopted the democratic form of government'; the tribes like the Malticorae and Singhae were free and had no kings; and those who lived near the sea had no kings.[25] These statements appear to suggest that some old tribal republics and City States were allowed to maintain their time-honoured administrative system even after their subjugation by the Magadhan emperors, especially the Nandas and Mauryas.

The above view is supported by the fact that tribal republics and City States flourished in India down to the fourth century A.D. and that they existed even in the dominions of the Kuṣāṇas where they apparently owed allegiance to the imperial foreign power. Epigraphic and numismatic evidence refers to the republican tribes like the Ārjunāyanas, Uddehikas, Mālavas, Śibis, Rājanyas, Yaudheyas, Uttamabhadras and others who appear to have submitted to the Śakas and Kuṣāṇas, some of them having become powerful on the decline of Kuṣāṇa power.[26] Among such republican tribes which issued coins, some like the Agratyas of Agrodaka (modern Agroha in the Hissar District, Haryana) appear to have ruled each over a small City State.[27]

The Buddhist *Avadānaśataka*, assigned to the 2nd century A.D., speaks of the existence of both *rāj-ādhīna* and *gaṇ-ādhīna deśas* (i.e. territories under the king's rule and those under republican rule) in Madhyadeśa.[28] In the age of the Guptas, the Licchavis appear to have had a republican state in North

25. McCrindle, *op.cit.*, pp. 40, 143-44.

26. See Sircar in *The Age of Imperial Unity*, ed. Majumdar, pp. 159 ff.

27. Sircar, *Studies in Indian Coins*, pp. 213-14.

28. See *Avadāna* 88; also Majumdar, *op.cit.*, p. 216; cf. Winternitz, *Hist. Ind. Lit.*, Vol. II, p. 279. It is said that a few merchants of Madhyadeśa went to the Deccan and, being asked about the form of government in their country, replied—*Kecid=deśā gaṇ-ādhīnā kecid=rāj-ādhenāḥ*. As regards the existence of republican states in South India during the early period, reference may be made to Aśoka's RE II mentioning the kingdoms under the Kerala-putra and Sātiya-putra side by side with the Coḷas and Pāṇḍyas, both names used in the plural number probably suggesting that they were republican peoples.

Bihar and a monarchical one in Nepal[29]. The Allahabad pillar inscription[30] of Samudragupta (c. 335-76 A.D.) mentions such republican tribes of Central and Western India as the Mālavas, Ārjunāyanas, Yaudheyas, Madrakas, Ābhīras, Prārjunas, Sanakānīkas, Kākas and Kharaparikas. But republican rule seems to have received a setback during the reign of the Guptas, and we do not hear of such States after the Gupta age. The republican tradition was, however, maintained by certain assemblies including guilds and *pañcāyats* of various types, and it has come down to our own times.[31]

While thinking of institutions influenced by democratic ideas, we are reminded of the *sabhā* and *samiti* mentioned in the Vedic literature,[32] sometimes specifically in connection with monarchy. Of these, the first may have been an assembly of the nobles and the second a gathering of the common people, although it is difficult to be sure about their function, and both *sabhā* and *samiti* may also have been one and the same institution.

In the same context, scholars generally mention a number of cases of the election of king.[33] It has been supposed that the Junagarh inscription (150 A.D.) refers to Śaka Rudradāman I as having been elected as their lord by the people of all *varṇas* for their protection;[34] but this is wrong. The passage concerned really means that, because Rudradāman was enjoying royal fortune continuously from the time he was in his mother's womb, the people of all *varṇas* accepted him as their lord for their protection, even though he was a foreign barbarian.[35] However, there are many other cases of election of

29. Cf. *Licchavayaḥ* in the plural on the reverse of a type of Gupta coins and also the inscriptions of the Licchavis of Nepal (Sircar, *Sel. Ins.*, Vol. I, 1965, pp. 262, 378).

30 *Ibid.*, pp. 262 ff.

31. Cf. *Panchait* and allied words in Wilson's *Glossary of Judicial and Revenue Terms*, 1855.

32. Cf. Macdonell and Keith, *Vedic Index*, s.v.; Majumdar, *op.cit.*, pp. 106 ff.

33. Majumdar, *op. cit.*, pp. 92 ff.

34. *Ibid.*, p. 105.

35. Sircar, *Sel. Ins.*, Vol. I, 1965, p. 177—*ā garbhāt=prabhṛty=avihata-samudita-rājalakṣmī-dhāraṇā-guṇatas=sarva-varṇair=abhigamya rakṣaṇ-ārthaṁ patitve vṛtena.*

the king in inscriptions. The Kasakudi plates[36] say that the Pallava king Nandivarman II Pallavamalla (c. 730-96 A.D.) was elected by the subjects (*prajā*) while the Vaikuntha Perumal temple inscriptions[37] suggest that the subjects included the important officers (*mātra*), chief subjects (*mūla-prakṛti*) and the *ghaṭakayar*, elsewhere called 'feudatory chiefs, members of the mercantile guild and the *mūla-prakṛtis*' and also mentioned as *kula-malla* (literally, chiefs of clans) explained as 'chief potentates'. It seems that the election was not the result of voting by ballot. The same appears to have been the case of the Pallava king's contemporary, Gopāla (c. 750-70 A.D.), founder of the Pāla dynasty of Bengal and Bihar, and of Brahmapāla (c. 1005-15 A.D.) who founded the Pāla dynasty of Prāgjyotiṣa (Assam). In the Khalimpur plate[38] of Gopāla's son, he is stated to have been married to the royal fortune by the subjects (*prakṛti*) who were eager to do away with the prevailing anarchy (*mātsya-nyāya*). Likewise, in the records of king Ratnapāla of Assam, his father Brahmapāla is stated to have been made their king (*narapati*) by the subjects (*prakṛti*).[39]

Various kinds of assemblies, guilds and *pañcāyats* flourished in India throughout the ages. The village assemblies called *mahājana-sabhā*[40] usually consisting of Brāhmaṇas, and the mercantile guilds often called *nagara*, *sva-deśī*, *para-deśī* and *nānā-deśī*, and their working are referred to in a very large number of South Indian inscriptions. Most of the early Indian guilds were organised on the basis of caste and profession, e.g., the guild of the weavers (*kaulika-nikāya*) at Govardhana and of the wheat-grinders (*samitākara-śreṇī*) at Mathurā.[41] That the guilds were often not very big is suggested by the fact that there were at least two weavers' guilds at Govardhana, near modern Nasik.[42] Whether the guilds were discharging their

36. *SII*, Vol. III, Part II, p. 349.

37. *Ep.Ind.*, Vol. XVIII, p. 117.

38. *Ibid.*, Vol. IV, p. 248—*mātsya-nyāyam=apohitum prakṛtibhir=Lakṣmyāḥ karaṅ=grāhitaḥ.*

39. Bhattacharya, *Kāmarūpaśāsanāvalī*, p. 94— *pakṛtayo ...paricakrire narapatiṁ*. Cf. Yaśaskara's selection by the Brāhmaṇas as Kashmir's king in preference to Kamalavardhana (*Rājatar.*, V. 456ff.).

40. Cf. Majumdar, *op. cit.*, pp. 153 ff.

41. Sircar, *Sel. Ins.*, *op. cit.*, pp. 152, 165.

42. *Ibid.*, p. 165.

duty properly was looked after by the *nigama-sabhā*, usually headed by a *Śreṣṭhin.*[43] Such *nigama-sabhās* acted like a sort of *pañcāyat* board. In Bengal during the Gupta age, such boards were headed by the *Nagara-śreṣṭhin* who was aided by the representatives of the scribes, merchants, artisans and others; they acted side by side and conjointly with the administrators of a unit like *viṣaya* or *vīthī* headed by officers like the *Viṣayapati* and *Āyuktaka*, the members of the board being apparently called *viṣaya-mahattara* and *vīthī-mahattara* respectively.[44] A study of the Kalaikuri-Sultanpur and Jagadishpur plates[45] together shows how the *mahattara* of a *vīthī* lost his status probably owing to his failure in a sort of election. The board was often called *adhikaraṇa*, sometimes associated with *aṣṭakula*, e.g., *grām-āṣṭakul-ādhikaraṇa* (Dhanaidaha plate), *mahattar-ādy-aṣṭakul-ādhikaraṇa* (Damodarpur plates), etc.[46] *Aṣṭakula* is the same as *ūr-eṭṭu* of Tamil inscriptions meaning the committee of eight members of the village assembly.[47] In Tamil we have also the expression *añjaṣṭa-sabhai*, i.e. an assembly of five or eight members.[48] But the numbers are conventional and the actual number of members of the board may have been large. The early Bengal institution of the *adhikaraṇa* headed by the *Nagaraśreṣṭhin*, who was assisted by the chief scribe (*Prathama-Kāyastha*) and others, has its parallel in the unpaid magistracy of medieval Rajasthan, called Cauthiyā, which was headed by the *Nagarseṭh*, i.e. *Nagaraśreṣṭhin*, who was aided by the *Paṭel* (village headman) and *Paṭwārī* or scribe-accountant (i.e. *Kāyastha*).[49] In West and Central Indian records of the early medieval period, reference is often made to the *pañcāyat* board called *pañcakula* just as there is mention of *aṣṭakula* in East Indian

43. Cf. Sircar in *Indian Museum Bulletin*, Vol. IV, No. 2 (July, 1969), pp. 7ff.; see also below, Appendix III, pp. 259ff.

44. Cf. Sircar, *Sel. Ins.*, *op.cit.*, pp. 291, 293, 333, 337, 347, 352-53, 356, 364, 368.

45. *Ibid.*, pp. 352 ff.; *Bāṅglā Academy Patrikā*, Dacca, Caitra, B.S. 1370, pp. 36ff. See also Sircar, *Epigraphic Discoveries in East Pakistan*, pp. 8ff.

46. Sircar, *Sel. Ins.*, *op. cit.*, pp. 288, 333.

47. Sircar, *Ind. Ep. Gloss.*, s.v.

48. *Loc. cit.*

49. Sircar in *Journal of the University of Gauhati*, Vol. VI pp. 81ff.; also above, pp. 78ff. *Paṭwārī*=*Paṭṭavārika* (Chief Official).

epigraphs.[50] A Gupta record from East Malwa mentions *pañcamaṇḍalī* apparently in the sense of *pañcakula*.[51]

Several years ago, when we proposed the identification of the designation *Nagaraśreṣṭhin* of the early Bengal records with the *Nagarseṭh* of the Cauthiyā of medieval Rajasthan, we did not notice what Wilson's *Glossary* says about the similar designation *Purseṭh* or *Purseṭhī*, modified in Bengali and Oriya from Sanskrit *Puraśreṣṭhin* in which *pura* is the same as *nagara*. As regards the nineteenth century function of the *Purseṭh* or *Purseṭhī* of Eastern India, Wilson has the following note : "The headman of a town or a ward of a town; in Cuttack, the elected head or representative of the people of a village, who was admitted to engage with government for the rent of the ground on which the village was built, and was thence sometimes considered as the Zamindar, having a title to any difference between the sum he might receive from the villages and that which he paid to the government."[52] In this connection, we are also reminded of the family name *Purkāyet* or *Purakāyastha* prevalent in Bengal and its neighbourhood.[53]

We have said above how assemblies like the *mahājana-sabhā*, as well as their constitution and working are very often mentioneed in South Indian inscriptions. Such records are rare in North India where we have incriptions referring very vaguely to similar institutions. An inscription[54] of the time of the Gāhaḍavāla king Jayaccandra (1170-93 A.D.), however, shows that the functions of such assemblies were similar in North India as well. This interesting document is written in five stanzas. The first two verses say that in Saṁvat 1230, Āśvina-badi 12, i.e. the 5th September, 1173 A.D., during the reign of Jayaccandra, the Brāhmaṇas assembled at Lāhaḍapura in the Gāhaḍavāla kingdom and drafted a *sthiti* or ordinance and made a *saṁvid* or contract because they were suffering from the depredations of unsocial elements. The assembled Brāhmaṇas appear to have been members of the local *mahājana-sabhā*,

50. Sircar, *Ind. Ep. Gloss.*, s.v.
51. Sircar, *Sel. Ins.*, *op. cit.*, p. 281.
52. *Glossary of Judicial and Revenue Terms*, 1855, s.v.
53. *Prācyavidyā-taraṅgiṇī*, ed. Sircar, pp. 498, 502.
54. *Ep. Ind.*, Vol. XXXII, pp. 305 ff.

whatever may have been its designation. Verse 3 suggests that the unsocial activities of the criminals were meant to put the Brāhmaṇas to disrepute (*parivāda*). It seems that the *Mahattaras* or elders responsible for law and order in the locality were discredited by the successful operations of the marauders. The text of the *sthiti* or *saṁvid* mentioned in the second stanza comes in verses 3 ff. and says that the person who would plunder the village (Lāhaḍapura) or would be guilty of *droha* (mischief) of any other kind to the villagers, such as the seizure of the villagers' cattle (*go-mahiṣy-ādi-veṣṭana*) should be killed at once (*cakṣur-vadha*) and his whole property will be confiscated, while his abettor (*avaṣṭambha-dāyaka*) should be expelled from the village and his house in the village should be demolished. This shows that the unsocial elements were inhabitants of the same region. Besides the principal culprit and his abettor, the instigator of the crime (*vimantṛ*) should be ostracised (cf. *vārayan*) and should be treated as a dog, an ass or a Caṇḍāla. Thus, while the chief offender was killed and his whole property confiscated and his abettor was expelled from the locality, his counsellor was permitted to stay in the village though nobody was allowed to have any intercourse with him. This shows that the local assembly enjoyed some power normally expected to be exercised by the king or his administrator.

The said Gāhaḍavāla record reminds us of the statement in early Buddhist literature that a female thief should not be ordained as a nun without the sanction of the *rājan*, *saṅgha*, *gaṇa*, *pūga*, or *śreṇī*, i.e. the ruling chief or any type of tribal republic or guild that may be concerned.[55] A commentator says in explanation of the passage that the king's permission will have to be taken where the king or chief rules while the permission of the *śreṇī* will be required where the guild rules.[56]

55. Majumdar, *op. cit.*, p. 23—*rājānaṁ vā saṁghaṁ vā gaṇaṁ vā pūgaṁ vā seṇiṁ vā anapaloketvā*. Cf. p. 237 and note 9 above.

56. *Loc.cit.—rājā nāma / yattha rājā anusāsati rājā apaloketabbo/ seṇi nāma/ yattha seṇi anusāsati seṇi apaloketabbā //*

II

SOME PRINCIPLES OF RĀJA-DHARMA

It is well known that, in Chapter 100 of the Ayodhyā-kāṇḍa of the *Rāmāyaṇa*, there are many questions which Rāma put to Bharata when the latter met the former in the forest. The said questions are all related to the welfare of the king and his State. It is also well known that similar questions were put to Yudhiṣṭhira by Nārada in the *Mahābhārata*, Sabhā-parvan, Chapter 5. There are similar sections elsewhere also. Cf. *ibid.*, XV.5.

Students of the epics must have noticed that a number of stanzas in the said two chapters of the two epics are common and that some of them have not even variant readings (at least in the copies of the epics consulted by us). The stanzas appear to have been borrowed by the epics from the popular floating literature. While the verses comprising the questions are 65 in the *Rāmāyaṇa*, their number is 107 in the *Mahābhārata*, the common stanzas being as many as 33. All these stanzas refer to popular principles of *Rāja-dharma* which is part of the science called variously as *Rāja-śāstra, Rāja-nīti, Rāja-vṛtta, Rāja-tantra, Nīti-śāstra, Daṇḍa-nīti, Nīti*, etc. The 33 common verses may be regarded as some of the most popular among the principles of *Rāja-dharma.* Another interesting fact is that, in a few cases, the idea noticed in one stanza is found repeated in another verse, and the principle involved in such repetitions may be regarded as specially important; e.g., verses 1-2; see also verses 4 and 6, 15-16, 21-22, and also verse 31 compared to verses 4, 6 and 7. The said 33 stanzas are quoted and commented on in the following lines.

1. *Kaccid=arthena vā dharmaṁ dharmeṇ=ārtham=ath=āpi vā |*
   ubhau vā prīti-sāreṇa na kāmena pravādhase ||
   M. 9; *R.* 62 : v. 1. *prīti-lobhena kāmena na vivādhase.*

The stanza prescribes the king's enjoyment of the *tri-varga* in a balanced way. He should not put *artha*, in the way of *dharma*, nor *dharma* in the way of *artha*. Likewise, he should not put *kāma* in the way of either *dharma* or *artha* or the latter in the way of the former. The same idea, also noticed in other works, is continued in the following stanza.

2. *Kaccid=arthaṁ ca dharmaṁ ca kāmaṁ ca jayatāṁ vara /*
vibhajya kāle kāla-jña sadā varada sevase //
M. 10; *R.* 63 : v. 1. *sarvān* for *sadā*.

This verse also refers to the balanced enjoyment of *artha*, *dharma* and *kāma*, each of the three of which should be enjoyed in proper measure and in proper time.

The emphasis put on the same principle by its repetition is intelligible. The history of India and the world offers illustrations of kings or their States being led to ruin by an excessive attachment to any one of the above three. We know, e.g., how king Jayāpīḍa (8th-9th century A.D.) of Kashmir lost his life, how the great emperor Aśoka (c. 272-232 B.C.) caused the decline and downfall of the Maurya empire and how the Rāṣṭrakūṭa king Govinda II (c. 775-80 A.D.) lost his throne as a result of excessive enjoyment of *artha*, *dharma* and *kāma* respectively.[1]

3. *Kaccid=ātma-samā buddhyā śucayo jīvita-kṣamāḥ /*
kulīnāś=c=ānuraktāś=ca kṛtās=te vīra mantriṇaḥ //
M. 16; *R.* 15 : v. 1. *vṛddhāḥ śuddhāḥ saṁbodhana-kṣamāḥ*,
śūrāḥ śrutavantaḥ jit-endriyāḥ; *iṅgitajñāḥ* for *anuraktāḥ*.

Here we have the qualifications of the *mantrins* to be appointed by the king. They should be as intelligent as the king himself (*ātma-samā buddhyā*) and should also be honest (*śuci*, *śuddha*), capable of earning their livelihood (*jīvita-kṣama*) born in noble families (*kulīna*) and attached to their master (*anurakta*). The variant readings suggest that they should be valiant warriors (*śūra*), learned or proficient in the sacred knowledge (*śrutavantaḥ*), having control over their senses or passions (*jitendriya*) and skilled in interpreting signs (*iṅgitajña*).

1. See Stein, *Kalhaṇa's Rājataraṅgiṇī*, Vol. I, p. 95; Sircar, *Inscriptions of Aśoka*, 1967, pp. 28-29; Altekar, *The Rāṣṭrakūṭas and their Times*, 1934, p. 50

Such qualifications are often noticed in literary and epigraphic records and reference may be made to the description of Suviśākha and Parṇadatta in the Junagadh inscriptions of Rudradāman and Skandagupta respectively.[2]

4. *Vijayo mantra-mūlo hi rājñāṁ bhavati Bhārata* /
susaṁvṛto mantra-dhanair=amātyaiḥ śāstra-kovidaiḥ //
M. 17; *R*. 16: v. 1. *kaccit saṁvṛta-mantrais=te, susaṁvṛta-mantri-dhuraiḥ*; *Rāghava* for *Bhārata*.

This verse speaks of the importance of the *amātyas*, apparently the same as *mantrins* referred to in the previous stanza. If the secrecy of policies or secret plans of a king is maintained by his *amātyas* who are learned in the *śāstras*, it leads to victory. The secrecy of plans is also referred to below, No. 6.

5. *Kaccin=nidrā-vaśam n=aiṣi kaccit kāle vibudhyase* /
kaccic=c=āpara-rātreṣu cintayasy=artha-dharma-vit //
M. 18; *R*. 17 : v. l. *artham=artha-vit, artha-naipuṇyam*.

According to this stanza, the king should have control over sleep and should get up from bed at the right time. He should formulate plans regarding *artha* and *dharma* about the end of the night, i.e. very early in the morning.

6. *Kaccin=mantrayase n=aikaḥ kaccin=na bahubhiḥ saha* /
kaccit=te mantrito mantro na rāṣṭram=anudhāvati //
M. 19; *R*. 18 : v. l. *paridhāvati*.

In the verse, the king is advised not to formulate secret plans alone or discuss them with too many people, and it is suggested that such plans should not be divulged to the people (*rāṣṭra*). The secrecy of plans is also referred to above, No. 4.

7. *Kaccid=arthān viniścitya laghu-mūlān mah-odayān* /
kṣipram=ārabhase kartuṁ na vighnayasi tādṛśān //
M. 20; *R*. 19 : v. l. *artham*, etc.; *karma* for *kartuṁ*; *Rāghava* for *tādṛśān*.

2. Sircar, *Select Inscriptions*, Vol. I, 1965, pp. 180, 309-10.

In this verse, the king is advised to concentrate on plans of work which are easy to perform, but bring in important results and to begin their execution as quickly as possible and not to delay them in any way.

8. *Kaccit sahasrair=mūrkhāṇām=ekaṁ krīṇāsi paṇḍitam* /
paṇḍito hy=artha-kṛcchreṣu kuryān =niḥśreyasaṁ param //
M. 24; *R.* 22 : v. l. *icchasi* for *krīṇāsi*; *mahat* for *param*.

The king is advised here to discard one thousand unlettered people (*mūrkha*) in favour of a single learned man (*paṇḍita*) because, in difficult matters or financial troubles (*artha-kṛcchreṣu*), a learned man alone is capable of helping him in finding a way out.

9. *Kaccid=durgāṇi sarvāṇi dhana-dhāny-āyudh-odakaiḥ* /
yantraiś=ca paripūrṇāni tathā śilpi-dhanurdharaiḥ //
M. 25; *R.* 53: v. l. *pratipūrṇāni*.

The verse says that the king should keep all his fortresses supplied with enough money (*dhana*), food or provisions (*dhānya*), missiles (*āyudha*), water (*udaka*), contrivances (*yantra*), artisans (*śilpin*) and archers (*dhanurdhara*).[3]

10. *Eko='py=amātyo medhāvī śūro dānto vicakṣaṇaḥ* /
rājānaṁ rājaputraṁ vā prāpayen=mahatīṁ śriyam //
M. 26 : *R.* 24 : v. l. *dakṣo* for *dānto*.

This stanza is associated with Nos. 3 and 8 and says that even a single *amātya*, who is valiant and has self-control (*dānta*; or *dakṣa*, skilful or upright) and wisdom (*vicakṣaṇa*), is capable of bringing in great prosperity for the king or prince whom he serves.

11. *Kaccid=aṣṭādaś=ānyeṣu sva-pakṣe daśa pañca ca* /
tribhis=tribhir=a-vijñātair=vetsi tīrthāni cārakaiḥ //
M. 27; *R.* 36: v. l. *cāraṇaiḥ*.

3. For the defence of cities, see *Mahābhārata*, III. 15 or 16.

The king is advised here to employ three spies (*cāraka*, *cāraṇa*) each for getting information about the 18 *tīrthas* (the king's counsellors) on the enemy's side and 15 *tīrthas* on his own side. The spies should be unknown to each other and to the persons about whom they would gather information. The eighteen *tīrthas* in the enemy's territory are enumerated by the commentators as the following: (1) minister, (2) priest, (3) crown-prince, (4) leader of forces, (5) chief guard of the palace or city gate, (6) superintendent of the harem, (7) superintendent of jails, (8) treasurer, (9) officer delcaring royal orders in respect of work to be continued or undertaken, (10) judge (*pradeṣṭṛ*), (11) governor of a city or prefect of the city police, (12) administrator, (13) judicial officer in charge of gifts, (14) superintendent of the gambling halls (*sabh-ādhyakṣa*), (15) officer in charge of the punishment of criminals, (16) governor of the forts, (17) warden of the marches, and (18) officer in charge of forests. The fifteen *tīrthas* of the king's own realm are Nos. 4-18 of the above list.[4]

12. *Kaccid = dviṣām = aviditaḥ pratiyattaś=ca sarvadā* |
nitya-yukto ripūn sarvān vīkṣase ripusūdana ||

M. 28 : *R*. 37 : v. 1. *vyapāstān = ahitān pratiyātāṁś = ca*; *durbalān = anavajñāya vartase*; *pratipanna* for *pratiyatta*.

According to this verse, the king should be always on the alert and ready to fight with the enemy, though the latter would have to be kept in the dark about his own plans. The

4. Nīlakaṇṭha's commentary quotes the following stanzas (cf. *Pañcatantra*, III. 66 ff.):

Mantrī Purohitaś=c=aiva Yuvarājaś=Camūpatiḥ |
pañcamo Dvārapālaś=ca ṣaṣṭho='ntarveśikas=tathā ||
Kārāgār-ādhikārī ca Dravya-sañcaya-kṛt tathā |
kṛty-ākṛtyeṣu c=ārthānāṁ navamo Viniyojakaḥ ||
Pradeṣṭā Nagar-ādhyakṣaḥ Kārya-nirmāṇa-kṛt tathā |
Dharm-ādhyakṣo Sabh-ādhyakṣo Daṇḍapālas=tri-pañcamaḥ ||
ṣoḍaśo Durga-pālaś=ca tathā Rāṣṭr-ānta-pālakaḥ ||
Aṭavī-pālakas=tāni tīrthāny=aṣṭādaś=aiva tu ||
Cārān=vicārayet tīrtheṣv=ātmanaś=ca parasya ca |
pākhaṇḍ-ādīn=avijñātān=anyo='nyam=itareṣv=api ||
Mantriṇaṁ Yuvarājañ=ca hitvā teṣu Purohitam ||

variant reading suggests that the king should not neglect the strength of the defeated enemy returning to attack even if the latter looks like weak.

13. *Kaccid=vinaya-sampannaḥ kulaputro bahu-śrutaḥ* |
anasūyur=anupraṣṭā satkṛtas=te purohitaḥ ||
M. 29; *R*. 11 : v. 1. *anuddraṣṭā* for *anupraṣṭā*.

This verse refers to the qualifications of a good *purohita* whom the king should honour. The priest should be endowed with *vinaya* (discipline, moral training, or decency, modesty), born of respectable parentage, learned in the sacred lore, devoid of jealousy and eager to perform duty without question. The word *anuddraṣṭā*, which seems to be a better reading, means one who does not direct in a wrong way.

14. *Kaccid=agniṣu te yukto vidhijño matimān=ṛjuḥ* |
hutaṁ ca hoṣyamāṇañ=ca kāle vedayate sadā ||
M. 30 ; *R*. 12.

Here we have a reference to the officer (i.e. priest) placed in charge of the king's household fire. He should be an expert in rituals, intelligent and honest and should inform the king in proper time the rituals already performed and those which should have to be performed. The stanza refers to the importance the Indians attached to religious rites. See also No. 32 below.

15. *Kaccin=mukhyā mahatsv=eva madhyameṣu ca madhyamāḥ* |
jaghanyāś=ca jaghanyeṣu bhṛtyāḥ karmasu yojitāḥ ||
M. 32; *R*. 25 : v. 1. *tāta* for *karmasu*.

The stanza advises the king to engage high-class officers in important work, middle-class officers in less important work and low-class officers in unimportant work. The same idea is continued in the following stanza.

16. *Amātyān upadh-ātītān pitṛ-paitāmahāñ=śucīn* |
śreṣṭhāñ=śreṣṭheṣu kaccit=tvaṁ niyojayasi karmasu ||
M. 33 (cf. XV. 5.14); *R*. 26.

The advice to the king implied in this verse is an elaboration of the statement in No. 15 above. It says that the king should engage the best of his officers, who are honest, hereditarily engaged in royal service and passed in the tests (*upadhā*). It is difficult to say whether the reference is to the passing in only one or in several tests. The four important tests are described in Kauṭilya's *Arthaśāstra* (I. 10) as *dharm-opadhā* or religiousness-test, *arth-opadhā* or greed-test, *kām-opadhā* or lustfulness-test and *bhay-opadhā* or fear-test.

17. *Kaccin = n = ogreṇa daṇḍena bhṛśam = udvejita-prajāḥ* /
rāṣṭraṁ tav = ānuśāsanti mantriṇo Bharatarṣabha //

M. 34; *R*. 27: v. 1. *rāṣṭre tav = ānujānanti*; *udvejitāḥ* or *udvijase* for *udvejita*⁰; *Kaikeyīsuta* for *Bharatarṣabha.*

Here the king is warned against his *mantrins* who oppress the subjects by their tyranny while governing the territory. The variant reading *udvejitāḥ prajāḥ rāṣṭre tav = ānujānanti* suggests that the *mantrins* should not allow the subjects to be oppressed by the officers.

18. *Kaccit = tvāṁ n = āvajānanti yājakāḥ patitaṁ yathā* /
ugra-pratigrahītāraṁ kāmayānam = iva striyaḥ //

M. 35: *R*. 28: v. 1. *ugrā-pratigrahītāram.*

This verse warns the king of being despised by the priests (or better, by the people or officers) just as the outcast person is hated by the sacrificing priests and the violent and lustful husband by the wives. The variant *ugrā-pratigrahītāram*, which is a better reading, suggests that the husband of an *ugrā*, meaning a cruel woman of violent temper, is hated (i.e. avoided) by other women.

19. *Kaccid = dhṛṣṭaś = ca śūraś = ca matimān dhṛtimāñ = śuciḥ* /
kulīnaś = c = ānuraktaś = ca dakṣaḥ senāpatis = tava //

M. 36; *R*. 30 : v. 1. *kṛtaḥ* or *tathā* for *tava.*

Here the qualifications of the commander of the forces, suitable for being appointed by the king, are enumerated. He should be contented, valiant, intelligent, steadfast, honest, born in a good family, attached to his master, and skilful.

20. *Kaccid = balasya te mukhyāḥ sarve yuddha-viśāradāḥ* /

dṛṣṭ-āpadānā vikrāntās = tvayā satkṛtya mānitāḥ ||
M. 37; *R.* 31: v. 1. *balavantaś = ca kaccit = te, mukhāḥ sarva°, dhṛṣṭ-āvadātā* for *dṛṣṭ-āpadānā.*

The king is advised here to honour all the leaders of his forces, who are experts in fighting, have proved their worth by excellent work and are valiant. The same idea is noticed in the expression *kṛt-opadhānaṁ* (explained by Nīlakaṇṭha as *kṛta-viśeṣam*; v. 1. *kṛt-āpadānaṁ*) *balam* in the *Mahābhārata*, III. 15 (or 16). 21. The importance of the appreciation of merits of generals for their successes in order to encourage them is recognised all over the world.[5]

21. *Kaccid = balasya bhaktañ = ca vetanaṁ = ca yath-ocitam* |
samprāpta-kālaṁ dātavyaṁ dadāsi na vikarṣasi ||

M. 38; *R.* 32: v. 1. *vilambase* for *vikarṣasi*; *kāle* for *kālaṁ.*

This stanza advises the king to pay his soldiers their pay (*vetana*) and allowance (*bhakta*) at the proper time whenever they are due and not to delay in this matter. In the *Mahābhārata*, III. 15 (or 16). 21, also we are told that the army (*bala*) should be—*datta-vetana-bhaktaṁ ca datt-āyudha-patricchadam* | *kṛt-opadhānañ = ca* (v. 1. *kṛt-āpadānañ = ca*), etc. In the same context (verse 22), it is further said that, at the time of war, *na kupya-vetanī kaścin = na c = ātikrānta-vetamī* | *n = ānugraha-bhṛtaḥ kaścit*, etc., which shows that each soldier re ceived wages in

5. Cf. D.C. Boulger, *A Short History of China*, p. 50—"Among soldiers it is necessary to preserve the spirit of pre-eminence and warlike zeal by granting rewards and decorations. Genghis realised the importance of this matter, and instituted the order of *Baturu* or *Bahadur*, meaning 'warrior'. He also made his two leading generals Muhula and Porshu princes, one to sit on his right hand and the other on his left. He addressed them before the council in the following words: 'It is to you that I owe my empire. You are and have been to me as the shafts of a carriage or the arms of a man's body.' Sealsof office were also granted to all the officials, so that their autho rity might be the more evident and the more honoured."

precious metals, and there was none who did not receive any wages and was merely serving for the master's favour. The disastrous result of delayed payment of pay and allowance is indicated in the following verse. The fact that the king's soldiers received wages does not support the prevalence or popularity of the Feudal System in ancient India as is claimed by some recent writers.[6] The idea is continued in No. 22.

22. *Kāl-ātikramaṇād=dhy=ete bhakta-vetanayor=bhṛtāḥ* /
bhartuḥ kurvanti daurgatyāt so='narthaḥ sumahān smṛtaḥ //

M. 39; *R.* 33 : v.l. *°kramaṇād=ete, °kramaṇe hy=eva; bhartuḥ kupyanti duṣyanti.*

The verse, associated with the previous stanza, says that the persons, who receive from the king wages and allowances for their maintenance, suffer hardship if they are not paid in proper time and, as a result, do great harm to their master.

23. *Kaccit sarve='nuraktās=tvāṁ kulaputrāḥ pradhānataḥ* /
kaccit prāṇāṁs=tav=ārtheṣu saṁtyajanti sadā yudhi //

M. 40; *R.* 34 : v. l. *samāhitāḥ* for *sadā yudhi.*

Importance is attached in this verse to the attachment of all people, including the noble men, to the king, from the highest to the lowest, and their eagerness to offer their lives on the king's behalf.

24. *Kaccit=sv-anuṣṭhitā tāta vārtā te sādhubhir=janaiḥ* /
vārtāyāṁ saṁsthitas=tāta loko='yaṁ sukham=edhate //

M. 69; *R.* 47 : v. l. *kaccit=te dayitāḥ sarve kṛṣi-gorakṣā-jīvinaḥ; sāmprataṁ* or *saṁśritaḥ* for *saṁsthitaḥ.*

Here importance is attached to *vārtā*, i.e. agriculture, cattle-breeding and trade, being properly carried on in the king's dominions by good people, because the happiness of the subjects greatly depends thereon.

6. For the payment of *bhakta* and *vetana* to the king's servants including soldiers, in other works, see Sircar, *Landlordism and Tenancy in Ancient and Medieval India as revealed by Epigraphical Records*, p. 41; cf. pp. 34-35. See also *Arthaśāstra*, VIII. 5; Shama Shastry's trans., p. 366.

25. *Kaccit striyaḥ sāntvayasi kaccit=tāś=ca surakṣitāḥ*|
kaccin=na śraddadhāsy=āsāṁ kaccid=guhyaṁ n=ābhāṣase ||

M. 73; *R.* 49 : v. l. *tās=te na bhāṣase.*

Here we have reference to the proper treatment of the king's wives and other ladies of the harem. The king is advised to appease and protect the ladies, but not to believe in their statements and to confide any secret to them.

26. *Kaccit=jñātīn gurūn vṛddhān daivatāṁs=tāpasān=api* |
caityāṁś=ca vṛkṣān kalyāṇān Brāhmaṇāṁś=ca namasyasi ||

M. 90; *R.* 61 : v. l. *Kaccid=gurūṁś=ca vṛddhāṁś=ca tāpasān devat-āthithīn; caityāṁś=ca sarvān; devatāḥ* for *daivatān.*

This stanza advises the king to bow down to the elderly kinsmen, other elders, old men, ascetics, auspicious *caitya-vṛkṣas* (ficus religiosa or any other tree standing on a sacred spot or near the funeral sites) and the Brāhmaṇas. The suggestion here is that the king should follow strictly the Indian code of seemly behaviour towards others.

27. *Kaccid=āryo viśuddh-ātmā kṣāritaś=caura-karmaṇi* |
a-dṛṣṭaḥ śāstra-kuśalair=na lobhād=vadhyate śuciḥ ||

M. 93; *R.* 56 : v. l. *āryo='pi*; *c=āpakarmaṇā.*

It has been said here that, in case a noble man of pure heart is incarcerated on the allegation of theft or any other crime, he should not be killed out of greed for his property without being examined by people who are learned in the *śāstras.* The idea is that the dignity of justice should be maintained; cf. also the following stanza.

28. *Pṛṣṭo gṛhītas=tatkārī taj-jñair=dṛṣṭaḥ sa-kāraṇaḥ* |
kaccin=na mucyate steno dravya-lobhān=nararṣabha ||

M. 94; *R.* 57 : *gṛhītaś=c=aiva pṛṣṭaś=ca kāle*; *caura* for *stena*; *duṣṭo* for *pṛṣṭo.*

The verse, also referring to the mintenance of the dignity of justice, suggests that, when a person has been interrogated and fettered after experts regarded him as having actually committed theft, the said thief should not be released out of greed for his possessions.

29. *Vyutpanne kaccid=āḍhyasya daridrasya ca Bhārata* |
arthān=na mithyā paśyanti tav=āmātyā hṛtā janaiḥ ||

M. 95; *R*. 58 : v. l. *vyasane* or *utpannān* for *vyutpanne*; *durbalasya ca Rāghava* | *arthaṁ virāgāḥ paśyanti tav=āmātyā bahu-śrutāḥ*.

According to this stanza, also relating to justice, when there is litigation between a rich and a poor man, the facts should not be wrongly viewed by the king's judicial officers after taking bribes from interested people.

30. *Nāstikyam=anṛtaṁ krodhaṁ pramādaṁ dīrghasūtratām* |
adarśanaṁ jñānavatām=ālasyaṁ kṣipta-cittatām ||

M. 96; *R*. 65 : *pañca-vṛttitām* for *kṣipta-cittatām*.

This verse, together with the following two (Nos. 31-32), cites the 14 *rāja-doṣas* which a king should avoid. Here in the present stanza, we have the following 8 out of the 14—(1) atheism, (2) falsehood, (3) anger, (4) carelessness (*pramāda*), (5) dilatoriness (*dīrghasūtratā*), (6) lack of intercourse with wisemen, (7) laziness, and (8) absentmindedness (*kṣipta-cittatā*). The variant *pañca-vṛttitā* seems to mean 'having different attitudes' or 'following various courses of action' at the same time. It is well known that Aśoka enumerates the following among *doṣas* to be avoided by high officers—(1) jealousy (*īrṣā*), (2) anger (*āśulopa*), (3) cruelty (*naiṣṭhurya*), (4) hastiness (*tvaraṇā*), (5) want of perseverance (*anāvṛtti*), (6) laziness (*ālasya*) and (7) fatigue (*klamatha*).[7]

It will be seen that anger, laziness and dilatoriness or want of perseverance are common to both the lists.

31. *Eka-cintanam=arthānām=anarthajñaiś=ca cintanam* |
niścitānām=anārambhaṁ mantrasy=āparirakṣaṇam ||

M. 97; *R*. 66: v. l. *mantraṇam* for *cintanam*.

Four out of the 14 *rāja-doṣas*, mentioned in the present stanza, are the following: (1) determination of plans and

7. See Sircar, *Select Inscriptions*, Vol. I, 1965, pp. 41, 43; also *Inscriptions of Aśoka*, 1967, p. 63.

policies by the king alone, (2) their determination with the help of those who have no experience in such matters, (3) delay in undertaking projects on which decisions have been taken already, and (4) failure to preserve the secrecy of schemes. Some of these are alluded to separately above; cf. Nos. 4,6-7.

32. *Maṅgalasy=āprayogaṁ ca prasaṅgaṁ viṣayeṣu ca /*
kaccit=tvaṁ varjayasy=etān rāja-doṣāṁś=caturdaśa //
M. 98; *R*. 67 : *maṅgal-ādy-aprayogañ=ca pratyutthānaṁ ca sarvataḥ.*

The remaining two of the fourteen *rāja-doṣas* are enumerated in this verse as (1) neglect in the performance of auspicious rites, and (2) excessive addiction to the pleasures of the senses (fighting with the enemies on all fronts at the same time, according to the variant reading). Cf. Nos. 14 and 1-2 above.

33. *Kaccit=te saphalā vedāḥ kaccit=te saphalaṁ dhanam /*
kaccit=te saphalā dārāḥ kaccit=te saphalaṁ śrutam //
M. 99; *R*. 72: v. l. *saphalāḥ kriyāḥ* for *saphalaṁ dhanam.*

The stanza suggests that the success of the king should be particularly conspicuous in four fields: e.g. (1) his study of the Vedas should be utilised in the proper conducting of Vedic rituals, etc., (2) his wealth should be properly spent in charity, etc. (or, according to the variant reading, his deeds should be characterised by success), (3) he should have wives capable of giving birth to children, and (4) his knowledge of the various sciences should guide him to the successful conclusion of his projects.

III

NIGAMA AND ŚREṆĪ

The Damodarpur copper-plate grants generally mention, at the same time, the reigning Gupta monarch, his viceroy in the province of Puṇḍravardhana (North Bengal), and the governor of the Koṭivarṣa district (Dinajpur), who enjoyed the official rank or designation like *Kumārāmātya* (officer of the rank of a prince of the royal blood), *Āyuktaka* (administrative officer) or *Viṣayapati* (governor of a district). The extant seal of one of the documents bears the legend *Koṭivarṣ-ādhiṣṭhān-ādhikaraṇasya*, i.e. [the seal] of the *adhikaraṇa* (court and office of non-military administration) of the *adhiṣṭhāna* (city) of Koṭivarṣa (i.e. headquarters of the district of that name), when the business of the *adhiṣṭhān-ādhikaraṇa* was conducted or transacted by a body headed (cf. *puroge*) by four persons entitled (1) *Nagaraśreṣṭhin*, (2) *Sārthavāha*, (3) *Prathama-Kulika* and (4) *Prathama-Kāyastha*.[1] The Paharpur plate[2] records an order of the *Āyuktaka* (or, *Āyuktakas*) stationed at the provincial capital of Puṇḍravardhana and the *adhiṣṭhān-ādhikaraṇa* headed by the *Ārya-Nagaraśreṣṭhin*, while the Baigram plate[3] records the order of the *Kumārāmātya* stationed at Pañcanagarī and the *adhikaraṇa* of the *viṣaya* or district around the city. The Kalaikuri-Sultanpur plate contains an order of the *Āyuktaka* stationed at Pūrṇakauśikā, the headquarters of a *vīthī* (subdivision) and of the *adhikaraṇa* of the said *vīthī*. The above instances and the seal of the Damodarpur plate, referred to above, show that the board in question was usually called *adhikaraṇa*.

1. *Select Inscriptions*, 1965, pp. 291, 293, 336-37, 347-48. See also *Journ. Univ. Gauhati*, Vol. VI, 1955, pp. 81 ff. While writing earlier on the subject, we did not notice that the word *puroge* points to the number of the members of the board to have been more than four mentioned particularly in the text. Cf. also above, pp. 76ff.

2. *Sel. Ins.*, pp. 359 ff.

3. *Ibid.*, p. 356.

4. *Ibid.*, p. 352. See also the Jagadishpur plate of the Gupta year 128 (Sircar, *Epigraphic Discoveries in East Pakistan*, pp. 8ff., 61ff.).

The *Pañcāyat*-type board of administration headed by the *Nagaraśreṣṭhin* (the chief banker), *Sārthavāha* (the merchant), *Prathama-Kulika* (the chief artisan) and *Prathama-Kāyastha* (the chief of the scribes) was compared by us with the Rājasthānī institution of unpaid magistracy called the Cauthiyā, which included the *Nagarseṭh* (*Nagaraśreṣṭhin*) and his assistants like the *Paṭel* (village headman) and *Paṭwārī* (the village scribe).[5] The board being headed by the *Nagaraśreṣṭhin* and others apparently means that it was headed by the *Nagaraśreṣṭhin* who was assisted by the others. About the Cauthiyā, Tod says as follows : Besides the resident ruler of the district, who was also a judicial functionary, there was a special officer of the Government in each frontier Thānā or garrison post. He united the triple occupation of embodying the quotas, levying the transit duties and administering justice, in which he was aided at the *Cabutrā* or court, by assembling the Cauthiyās or assessors of justice. Each town and village has its Cauthiyā, the members of which were elected by their fellow citizens, and remained as long as they conducted themselves impartially in disentangling the intricacies of complaints preferred to them. They were the aids to the *Nagarseṭh* or chief magistrate, an hereditary office in every large city in Rajasthan. Of this Cauthiyā, the *Paṭel* (headman) and *Paṭwārī* (accountant) were generally members; these were the special and fixed council of each town; the general *Pañcāyats* were formed from the respectable population at large and were formerly from all classes of society. The Cabutrās or terraces of justice were always established in the Khalisa or crown demene.[6]

The administrative board headed by the *Nagaraśreṣṭhin* assisted by others, which appears to be similar to the Cauthiyā headed by the *Nagarseṭh* aided by others, seems also to resemble the *nigama* (sometimes described as headed by the *Śreṣṭhin*) or *nigama-sabhā* as mentioned in certain early inscriptions.

The damaged Nagarjunikonda inscription of the time of the Ikṣvāku king Ehuvula Śāntamūla, dated in the cyclic year Vijaya probably corresponding to 333 A.D., refers to a lady

5. See *Journ. Univ. Cau.*, *loc. cit.*

6. *Annals and Antiquities of Rajasthan*, ed. W. Crooke, Vol. I, p. 171; cf. p. 231; also Vol. II, p. 682. For the passage, see also above, pp. 78-79.

who made a *devakula* (a shrine) and a *sthala* (in the present case, probably a platform in an area surrounded by a wall) for the god Noḍagīśvarasvāmin (possibly a form of Viṣṇu), with the assistance of a few other ladies, and created an *akṣayanīvī* (permanent endowment) apparently for the maintenance of the religious establishments in question.[7] In connection with the above endowment, mention is made of the interest accruing to it month by month; and it appears from the partially deciphered writing that the sum of one hundred *dināris* (probably gold coins) was deposited in four different *śreṇīs* or guilds, 70 coins in one of them and 10 in each of the other three. The names of two out of the four guilds have been read as *pārṇika-śreṇī* (guild of the growers or sellers of betel leaves) and *āpūpika-śreṇī* (guild of the confectioners). The concluding sentences state that the embellishment (*citraṇa*), apparently of the *devakula* and *sthala*, should be done by an agency indicated by the word *ātmanā*; otherwise, it says, the *nigama* (the same as the *nigama-sabhā* mentioned elsewhere), headed by the *Śreṣṭhin*, should get it done. While editing the inscription, we suggested that the embellishment had to be done by the person responsible for the creation of the religious establishment and also that the *nigama* was probably a board like the *Pañcāyat* which we compared with the board of administrators like that formed by the *Nagaraśreṣṭhin* assisted by the *Śārthavāha*, *Prathama-Kulika*, *Prathama-Kāyastha* and others and also the Cauthiyā of medieval Rajasthan headed by the *Nagarseṭh* (*Nagaraśreṣṭhin*).[8] The first suggestion was based on the use of the word *ātmanā* in the singular. The word *ātman* is, however, used in the sense of 'self' or 'oneself' reflexively for all the three persons and in the singular number and masculine gender irrespective of the number and gender of the noun to which it refers, so that a more suitable meaning of the passage seems to us now to be that it was the four guilds that were required to do the embellishment of the *devakula* and *sthala* and that such embellishment included periodical white-washing, etc. It has to be noticed that when a permanent endowment was created for the main-

7. See *Ep. Ind.*, Vol. XXXV, p. 4.
8. *Ibid.*, p. 5.

tenance of the *devakula* and *sthala*, their *citraṇa* is not expected to have been left to a temporary agency. Moreoever, one could hardly request the *nigama* to compel oneself to do something towards the maintenance of an institution created by one's own self. If then the new interpretation is accepted, it would suggest that the *nigama* or *nigama-sabhā* had some kind of jurisdiction over the *śreṇīs* because, as we have seen, it was requested to compel the *śreṇīs* to do the embellishment if it was not done by them of their own accord.

In the Sanskrit and Pali lexicons, one of the senses of the word *nigama* is given as 'a city or township', but no meaning like 'guild'. But the words *naigama* and *nigamaputra* occurring in early inscriptions have been understood in the sense of a 'merchant'.[9] In the *Pāiasaddamahaṇṇavo*, moreover, the following senses of *nigama* have been recognised : (1) a commercial centre or town inhabited by many tradesmen (on the authority of the *Praśnavyākaraṇasūtra*, *Aupapātikasūtra* and *Ācārāṅgasūtra*) and the community of tradesmen (on the authority of the *Samavāyāṅgasūtra*). This is analogous to the following secondary meaning of the word *nagara* (primarily 'a city or town') as noticed in the early medieval inscriptions of South India : 'a guild of merchants, a mercantile town'; 'in Telugu inscriptions, a territorial assembly like the *sabhā* and *ūr*; the merchant community in general or the organisation of the merchant community of a town. In some places, the *nagara* and *ūr* carried on their functions side by side.—The word is sometimes, used to indicate occupational groups like *śāleyanagarattom*."[10]

There are certain seals which belonged to the *Śreṣṭhi-nigama* or *Kulika-nigama* or *Śreṣṭhi-Kulika-nigama* or *Śreṣṭhi-Sārthavāha-Prathama-Kulika-nigama*, and it has been suggested that *śreṇī* and *nigama* refer to guilds of two different types, the former consisting of persons belonging to one or more communities, but following the same profession, and the latter incor-

9. See Sircar, *Ind. Ep. Gloss.*, s.v. *naigama*, *nigama-putra*.

10. *Ibid.*, s.v. *nagara*. The Sendraka king Bhogaśakti is stated to have re-colonised the township of Samagiri along with four other localities and to have given it to the *nagara* headed by two *Śreṣṭhins*. See Sircar, *Landlordism and Tenancy in Ancient and Mediaeval India as revealed by Epigraphical Records*, Lucknow 1969, p. 30.

porating persons following various crafts, or merchants dealing in various commodities.[11]

The legends, however, really mean 'the *nigama* headed by a *Śreṣthin* (banker)', 'the *nigama* headed by the *Kulika* (artisan)', 'the *nigama* headed by the *Śreṣṭhin* assisted by the *Kulika*' and 'the *nigama* headed by the *Śreṣṭhin* aided by the *Sārthavāha* (trader) and the First *Kulika* (the chief artisan or the head of the *Kulika* guild)'. As indicated above, in these cases, *nigama* may be interpreted as the *nigama-sabhā* which occurs in a Nasik inscription of 120 A.D.

The Nasik inscription[12] of Śaka 42 (120 A.D.) speaks of the creation of a permanent endowment by depositing 3,000 *kārṣāpaṇas* in the *śreṇīs* or guilds functioning at Govardhana and of the deposit of (1) 2,000 *kārṣāpaṇas* (out of the 3,000 *kārṣāpaṇas*) in a weaver's guild at an interest of 1 per cent per month for providing 12 *kārṣāpaṇas* for *cīvaras* to each of the 20 monks residing in a particular cave on the Nasik hill, and (2) 1,000 *kārṣāpaṇas* in a second weavers' guild at an interest of $\frac{3}{4}$ per cent per month for the provision of light food for the said monks. The inscription further speaks of a gift of 8,000 coconut saplings at the village of Cikhalapadra in the district of Kāpūra apparently in favour of the same monks. All these grants are stated to have been declared at the *nigama-sabhā* and written on plates according to the prevailing custom.

There are some interesting points in this record. In the first place, we find that there were at least two weavers' guilds at the city of Govardhana, so that even the community of weavers at a particular locality were not combined under a single guild. Secondly, the creation of the permanent endowment and the gift of the coconut palms (albeit in a different district) in favour of some monks residing in a Nasik cave, were declared at the *nigama-sabhā*, 'the council of the town'. This appears to have been done because the *nigama-sabhā* had the power to compel the *śreṇīs* to supply the amounts for the

11. K.K. Thaplyal in *JNSI*, Vol. XXX, pp. 133 ff. (p. 150, where in line 1 '*nigama* and *śreṇi*' should be corrected to '*śreṇi* and *nigama*' according to the author).

12. See Sircar, *Sel. Ins.*, pp. 164 ff.

purchase of *cīvara* and light food for the monks if they did not supply them of their own accord.

The *nigama-sabhā*, literally 'the citizens' council' may be an administrative board of the *Pañcāyat* type. As we have seen, the board of administrators formed by the *Nagaraśreṣṭhin*, *Sārthavāha*, *Prathama-Kulika*, *Prathama-Kāyastha* and others, known from records like the Damodarpur plates of the Gupta age, was of the same type, the *Nagaraśreṣṭhin* probably being its President.

We have seen above that the governor of a district working side by side with the administrative board headed by the *Nagaraśreṣṭhin* often enjoyed the title *Kumārāmātya*. It is interesting therefore to note that there is an East Indian seal[13] bearing the double impression, viz. (1) *Śreṣṭhi-Sārthavāha-Kulika-nigama* and (2) *Kumārāmāty-ādhikaraṇa* probably pointing to a transaction involving both the office of the governor of the district and the *Pañcāyat*-type board of administration.

13. *Journ. Anc. Ind. Hist.*, Vol.II, p. 261.

IV

THE ROYAL EPITHET 'PARAMADAIVATA'

Some of the copper-plate grants of the Gupta age, discovered in Bengal, mention the Gupta emperors by name, e.g., those found at Dhanaidaha (Rajshahi District) and Damodarpur (Dinajpur District) in Northern Bengal, now in Bangladesh. In these records, the Gupta monarchs Kumāragupta I (413-55 A.D.) and Budhagupta (477-94 A.D.) are endowed with the epithets *Paramadaivata*, *Paramabhaṭṭāraka* and *Mahārājādhirāja*.[1] Of these epithets, *Paramabhaṭṭāraka* and *Mahārājādhirāja* were popularised by the Guptas as titles of paramount rulers, to which the title *Parameśvara* was soon added, and the three together are generally found as Imperial style in the records of subsequent ages belonging to wide areas of India.

The epithet *Paramadaivata* was, however, by far less popular. It is noticed in a few epigraphs found in particular areas of the country. Since the word *daivata* means both 'a god' as well as 'a devotee of a god or of the gods', there is difference of opinion among scholars as regards the real implication of the epithet. It has sometimes been taken to be a paramount title like *Paramabhaṭṭāraka* and *Mahārājādhiraja*[2] and sometimes explained either as 'a great devotee of the *devatās* (gods)'[3] or even as 'a great divinity'.[4] In the following lines, we are trying to show that *Paramadaivata* as a royal epithet really means 'a great devotee of the gods in general or of one of the great gods' and that it is neither an imperial title nor does it signify 'a great divinity'.

The Gupta emperors enjoyed the sectarian epithet *Paramabhāgavata* (a great devotee of the *Bhagavat*, i.e. Viṣṇu) from

1. See *Ep. Ind.*, Vol. XV, pp. 113 ff.; Vol. XVII, pp. 345 ff.; cf. *Select Inscriptions, op. cit.*, pp. 280 ff., 283 ff., 324ff., 328ff., 337 ff.
2. Cf. *Ep.Ind.*, Vol. XV, p. 116; Vol. XXVII, p. 136.
3. Cf. *ibid.*, Vol. XXVIII, p. 235.
4. *Ibid.*, Vol XXVII, p. 136; see Raychaudhuri, *Pol. Hist. Anc. Ind.*, 1950, p. 559.

the days of Candragupta II (376-413 A.D.). Since the Dhanaidaha and Damodarpur plates describe Kumāragupta I and Budhagupta not as *Paramabhāgavata* but as *Paramadaivata,* it is possible that, in these cases, *Paramadaivata* has been used in the sense of *Parambhāgavata* to mean 'a great devotee of the God, i.e. Viṣṇu'. But as we shall see below, there are cases in which a king is endowed with the epithet *Paramadaivata* along with a sectarian epithet like *Paramamāheśvara* (a great devotee of the god Maheśvara or Śiva). In such cases, *Paramadaivata* would mean 'a great devotee of the gods (and not of a particular god)'. The implication would then be that the rulers in question were generally devoted to all gods and particularly to one of the great gods.[5]

That the conception of the king as a god in human form was quite popular in the Gupta age is clear from the *Manusmṛti*[6] belonging to the early centuries of the Christian era. The Allahabad pillar inscription of Samudragupta (c. 335-76 A.D.) likewise describes the monarch as 'a man only in the matter of performing the usual practices of human beings, but otherwise a god dwelling on the earth'.[7] Under these circumstances, if the epithet *Paramadaivata* was an echo of the same conception, it is difficult to understand why it was not popular throughout India, but was confined to a few rulers in certain areas of the country. Moreover, we shall presently see that, in a number of cases, the ruling king represents his deceased father, and not himself, as *Paramadaivata.* If the epithet was meant to emphasise the divine nature of kingship, it is absurd that a past ruler would be called 'a god' in preference to the ruling king, even when the two are mentioned side by side.

Among the inscriptions of Eastern India, besides the

5. There are a few inscriptions of a much later date, in which a ruler is represented as a devotee of both Viṣṇu and Śiva (cf. *Ep. Ind.*, Vol. XXVIII, p. 240) or of several deities (cf. *ibid.*, Vol. XXXIII, pp. 43,126-27).

6. VII. 4-8.

7. Cf. *loka-samaya-kriy-ānuvidhāna-mātra-mānuṣasya loka-dhāmno devasya* in line 28 (*Select Inscriptions*, p. 259). Besides this, the Vaiṣṇava king Samudragupta seems to have claimed to be an incarnation of 'the Inscrutable Being that was the cause of the prosperity of the good folk and the destruction of the wicked' (*sāddhv-asādh-ūdaya-pralaya-hetu-Puruṣasy=ācintyasya* in line 25) meaning the god Viṣṇu.

copper plates from Bengal referred to above, the stone inscription of king Bhūtivarman of the Bhauma-Nāraka dynasty of Prāgjyotiṣa discovered at Barganga in the Nowgong District of Assam, follows the style of the Gupta records and endows the monarch with the epithets *Paramadaivata*, *Paramabhaṭṭāraka* and *Mahārājādhirāja*.[8] But, in the coastal regions of Andhra Pradesh and Orissa, sometimes the ruling king is described as meditating on or favoured by his *Paramadaivata* father, who was also his predecessor on the throne, without claiming the epithet for his own self. Thus the Andhavaram (Srikakulam District) and Madras Museum plates of the Māṭhara *Mahārāja* Anantaśaktivarman (6th century A.D.) describe the ruler as *Paramadaivata-bappabpaṭṭāraka-pāda-prasād-āvāpta-śarīra-rājya-vibhava* (or *°pratāpa*),[9] while, in the Soro (Balasore District) plate of 579 A.D., *Mahārāja* Śambhuyaśas is called *Paramadaivata-bappa-pād-ānudhyāta*.[10] The Dharikatura Prakrit grant of the Śālaṅkāyana *Yuvamahārāja* (crown-prince) Acaṇḍavarman (4th century A.D.) also calls himself *Parama-devata-bappa-bhaṭṭāraka-vāda-bhatta*[11] though the reference in this case is to a *de jure* king and not to a dead ruler as in the Andhavaram, Madras Museum and Soro plates.

That *Paramadaivata* was not a special title of paramount rulers is also quite clearly indicated by two inscriptions from Nepal. Thus the Tyagal Tole (Gancha Nani, Deopatan) image inscription of the year 489, referred to the reign of *Bhaṭṭāraka Mahārāja* Gaṇadeva, speaks of the installation of the deity called Śaṅkaranārāyaṇasvāmin by Svāmivārta described as *Paramadaivata-śrī-Bhaumagupta-pād-ānudhyāta*[12] while the Chowkitar (near Balambu, Thankot District) stone inscription of the year 482 states how *Bappa-pād-ānduhyāta Bhaṭṭāraka Mahārāja* Gaṇadeva issued a *sthiti-paṭṭaka* at the request of *Sarvadaṇḍanāyaka Mahāpratīhāra* Bhaumagupta.[13] There can

8. *Ep. Ind.*, Vol. XXX, p. 67.
9. *Ibid.*, Vol. XXVIII, pp. 178, 235.
10. *Ibid.*, Vol. XXIII, p. 201.
11. *Ibid.*, Vol. XXXVI, p. 5. The name Acaṇḍavarman was formerly read wrongly as 'Caṇḍavarman'.
12. R. Gnoli, *Nepalese Inscriptions in Gupta Characters*, p. 28 (No. XX).
13. *Ibid.*, p. 26 (No. XIX).

be no doubt that Bhaumagupta, mentioned as an officer of king Gaṇadeva in the second record, is identical with *Paramadaivata* Bhaumagupta of the first epigraph incised seven years later during the reign of the same Gaṇadeva. In any case, this *Paramadaivata* Bhaumagupta can by no stretch of imagination be regarded as a paramount ruler.

We have seen how the Soro plate of *Mahārāja* Śambhuyaśas represents him as *Paramadaivata-bappa-pād-ānudhyāta.* The Patiakella (Cuttack District) plate of Śivarāja, a feudatory of *Paramamāheśvara* Śambhuyaśas, however, uses the expression *Parama-devat-ādhidaivata* (correctly *Parama-daivatādhidaivata*) not in the description of the father of Śambhuyaśas, but of Śambhuyaśas himself.[14] There can be no doubt that *Parama-daivata* and *Parama-daivat-ādhidaivata* have similar implications since, of the two Soro plates of Somadatta, one calls him *Paramadaivata-śrī-Paramabhaṭṭāraka-pād-ānudhyāta* and the other *Paramadaivat-ādhidaivata-Paramabhaṭṭāraka-pād-ānudhyāta.*[15]

If the same person is called *Paramadaivata* at one place and *Parama-daivat-ādhidaivata* at another, there cannot be any basic difference in the implications of the two epithets. The second expression therefore means 'a great devotee of the gods and of the supreme god (*adhidevatā*)'.

There are a few cases in which the epithet *Paramadaivata* is found even further modified than *Parama-daivat-ādhidaivata.* Thus, in the Bamhani (Shahdol District, Madhya Pradesh) plate, *Mahārāja* Bharatabala and his father, *Mahārāja* Nāgabala, are both described as *pād-ānudhyāta* of their father and as *Paramamāheśvara*, *Paramabrahmaṇya* and *Paramaguru-de(dai)-vatādhidaivata-viśeṣa.*[16] A Sanskritist, who retains *devatā* without correcting it to *daivata* in the passage *Parama-guru-devat-ādhidaivata-viśeṣa*, in the light of the form *Parama-daivat-ādhidaivata* found in a Soro plate of Somadatta, has translated the

14. *Ep. Ind.*, Vol. IX, p. 287.

15. *Ibid.*, Vol. XXIII, p. 202. Bhānudatta, possibly the successor of Somadatta, is called *Paramadaivata-śrī-Paramabhaṭṭāraka-pād-ānudhyāta* in his Kanas (Puri District) plate (*ibid.*, Vol. XXVIII, p. 334), his other records having no such expression. In the Kanas plate of Lokavigraha-bhaṭṭāraka, the king is called *Parama-de(dai)vat-ādhidaivata* (*ibid.*, p. 331).

16. *Ibid.*, Vol. XXVII, p. 140

epithet as 'distinguished as a highly venerable personage, a deity and a supreme deity'.[17] But it is difficult to agree with this interpretation. In the first place, the epithet is clearly an elaboration of *Paramadaivata* and *Parama-daivat-ādhidaivata* found in several other records discussed above, and we have seen that, in these epithets, the kings are represented as devotees of gods and not as gods themselves. Secondly, if Bharatabala and Nāgabala are represented as 'a deity' and even 'a supreme deity', it is difficult to believe that they should, at the same breath, be called devotees not only of the god Maheśvara (Śiva), but also of the Brāhmaṇas (cf. *Paramabrahmaṇya*). Thirdly, the expression *Paramaguru* does not appear to mean 'a highly venerable personage' since it is found in the list of royal epithets in an inscription of 1281 A.D.belonging to the reign of the Yajvapāla (Jajpella) king Gopāla of Nalapura, who has been called *Paramabhaṭṭāraka, Parameśvara, Paramamāheśvara, Paramaguru* and *Paramarāja*.[13] It seems that the word *guru* has been used here as well as in the Bamhani inscription in the sense of 'a lord, head, superintendent, ruler', as in Kālidāsa's *Raghuvaṁśa*, II. 68 and V.19. How the king was the teacher of his subjects is also indicated in the same work, I.17. We are therefore inclined to translate the epithet *Paramaguru-de(dai)vat-ādhidaivata-viśeṣa* as 'a great teacher [of his subjects] and a distinguished devotee of the gods and of the supreme god'.

There are reasons why epithets like *Paramadaivata*, etc., are rarely met with in inscriptions. Firstly, most of the rulers preferred to call themselves devotees of a particular deity (*Paramabhāgavata, Paramamāheśvara,* etc.) even if they had regards for various divinities. Secondly, the idea conveyed by the epithets *Paramadaivata*, etc., was sometimes indicated by other expressions. Thus the meanings of *Paramadaivata* and *Paramabrahmaṇya* are expressed by the epithet *Atyanta-deva-brāhmaṇa-bhakta* in the Khoh plate of the Parivrājaka *Mahārāja* Saṁkṣobha, dated 529 A.D., in the description of

17. *Ibid.*, p. 136.
18. *Ibid.*, Vol. XXXI, p. 331.

the king's father *Mahārāja* Hastin.[19] It may be noted in this connection that epithets like *Atyanta-deva-brāhmaṇa-bhakta* throw welcome light on the interpretation of *Paramadaivata*, etc., since the meaning in this case can only be 'extremely devoted to the gods and Brāhmaṇas'.

19. *Select Inscriptions*, p. 375. Such synonymous expressions are also noticed in other cases. Thus queen Prabhāvatiguptā is called *Bhagavat-pād-ānudhyātā* in one record and *atyanta-Bhagavad-bhaktā* in another (*ibid.*, pp. 413 and 416).

V

THE OFFICIAL DESIGNATION 'NIHILAPATI-NIHELAPATI'

A copper-plate grant issued by *Mahāsāmanta Mahārāja* Samudrasena, who was the son and successor of Ravisena, grandson of Sañjayasena and great-grandson of Varuṇasena and probably flourished in the seventh century A.D., was discovered in the forties of the nineteenth century at the village of Nirmand near the right bank of the Satlaj river, 21 miles north-east of Plach, chief town of the Tahsil of that name in the Kullu Sub-Division of the Kangra District which was formerly in the Punjab, but now belongs to Himachal Pradesh. It was edited by Rajendralal Mitra in the *Journal of the Asiatic Society of Bengal*, Vol. XLVIII, Proceedings, pp. 212 ff., and again by J.F. Fleet in the *Corpus Inscriptionum Indicarum*, Vol. III, pp. 286 ff. (No. 80, Plate XLIV). The inscription records the ratification of the grant of the village of Sūlisagrāma made by the ruler's mother Mihiralakṣmī in favour of the Brāhmaṇa students of the Atharvaveda at the *agrahāra* of Nirmaṇḍa for the god Śiva Mihireśvara established by the said lady at the temple of Kapāleśvara apparently in the same *agrahāra*, which is stated to have previously received a land grant from *Mahārāja* Sarvavarman, probably the Maukhari king of that name (c. 565-80 A.D.). The *dūtaka* or executor of Samudrasena's grant was *Nihilapati* Kuśalaprakāśa. As regards *Nihilapati,* which is obviously the official designation of Kuśalaprakāśa, Fleet says, "I have not been able to obtain any explanation of the first component of this official title."[13]

The same designation occurs in the Sungal plate[14] of king Vidagdha of Chamba, who flourished in the fi:st half of the eleventh century A.D., in the form *Nihelapati* in the usual list of officers addressed by the king in connection with a grant of land made by him. Here *Nihelapati* is mentioned in the

13. Cf. Fleet, *op.cit.*, p. 291, note 2.
14. See Vogel, *Antiquities of Chamba State*, Part I, p. 166.

company of other officers—*Kumārāmātya-Uparika-Viṣayapati-Nihelapati-Kṣetrapa-Prāntapāla*. Because *Nihelapati* is mentioned immediately after *Viṣayapati* (the governor of a district), we wrote about it as follows in our *Indian Epigraphical Glossary*, 1966, s.v.—"official designation of uncertain import; probably, the governor of a territorial unit; also spelt *Nihilapati*."

It is true that the word *nihela* or *nihila* cannot be traced in the Sanskrit lexicons : but *ṇihela* is well known in Prakrit as a form of Sanskrit *nīla*. Under the rule *ḍāḍh-ādayo bahulam* in the *Prākṛtaprakāśa* (IV.33) of Vararuci (c. 4th-5th century A.D.), both the early commentaries, viz. the *Prākṛtamañjarī* by Kātyāyana (c. 6th-7th century A.D.) and the *Manoramā* by Bhāmaha (c. 7th-8th century A.D.) quote *nīlaṁ=ṇīhelaṁ* among the illustrations.[15] According to a *vārttika* on Pāṇini's *Aṣṭādhyāyī*,[16] the word *nīla* is used in the sense of 'dyed with indigo' while *nīlī* means the indigo plant. There is, however, evidence in epigraphic literature to show that *nīla* was also used in the sense of 'indigo'. Thus the Sanskrit charter[17] (592 A.D.) of king Viṣṇuṣeṇa, from the Gujarat region of Western India, uses the expression *nīla-ḍumphaka* in the passage *ḍheṅku-kaḍḍhaka-nīla-ḍumphakāś=ca viṣṭiṁ na kārayitavyāḥ* (line 8) and the expression *nīla-kuṭī* in another passage reading *nīla-kuṭy-ādānaṁ ḍumphakena deyaṁ rūpaka-trayaṁ rū* 3 (lines 19-20). The expression *nīla-kuṭī* has been explained as 'an indigo factory' and *ḍumphaka* has been taken to stand for Sanskrit *dṛmphaka* meaning 'one who presses' so that *nīla-ḍumphaka* would mean a manufacturer of blue dye from the indigo plant. In *ḍheṅku-kaḍḍhaka*, *ḍheṅku* has been compared to Gujarātī *ḍhikvo*, Hindī *ḍheṅklī* or *ḍheṅkul* used in the sense of a contrivance (based on the principle of lever) for drawing water from a well, while *kaḍḍhaka* has been regarded as the Prakrit form of Sanskrit *karṣaka* so that *ḍheṅku-kaḍḍhaka* would be the drawer of water for the irrigation of fields. In the first of the two sentences quoted from Viṣṇuṣena's charter, the water-drawers and indigo-pressers are exempted from free labour (*viṣṭi*) while

15. See Sircar, *A Grammar of the Prakrit Language*, p. 38; cf. p. 3.

16. IV. 22—*Lākṣārocanāṭ=ṭhak-nītyā an vaktavyaḥ.*

17. *Ep. Ind.*, Vol. XXX, pp. 163 ff. See above, Chapter XIII, pp. 76ff.

the second sentence says that the indigo-presser maintaining an indigo-factory was liable to pay a tax of three *rūpakas* (silver coins each about 20 *ratis* in weight).[18]

The quotations from Viṣṇuṣeṇa's charter of the close of the sixth century would show that often Prakrit words were adopted in Sanskrit inscriptions.[19] It is therefore not improbable that the Nirmand plates of the seventh century uses the pseudo-Sanskrit expression *nihilapati* in the sense of *nilīpati* or *nīlapati,* i.e. an officer in charge of indigo or the indigo factories.

It has been suggested that India used a far larger number of plants for extracting the blue dye than any other country of the world, so that the Aryans may have made acquaintance with indigo in India itself.[20] Indian indigo was valued in Western Asia, Egypt and the Mediterranean countries both as a dye and as a medicine.[21] The *Periplus of the Erythraean Sea* (c. 82 A.D.) refers to its export from the Lower Valley of the

18. Cf. Sircar, *Stud. Ind. Coins*, pp. 68-69, 300-01.

19. Other interesting words used in the inscription are *unmara* (Sanskrit *udumbara*, threshold), *khovā* (possibly, 'the share of the lord of the market'), *vārika* (officer; cf. *Peṭavika-vārika, Uttarakulika-vārika, Kalvapāla-vārika*), *reṣa* (?), *utkṛṣṭi* (Sanskrit *utkrośa*, wailing), *dhārmika* (probably, concessional rate of tax sanctioned by the Government in special cases), *chātra* (a constable), *saṁvadana* (probably, informing), *jayika* (the winning party), *bhāṣā* (written declaration), *phālāvana* (protection of a ploughed field), *ullambana* (probably, hanging), *vinaya* (fine), *tauṇḍika* (biting of crops with mouth), *avalokya* (probably, detection), *dosya* (possibly, clothes), *kāṁsya* (bronze utensils), *bharolaka* (possibly, distillery), *grahaṇaka* (possibly, custody), *daṇḍaka* (possibly, rule regarding the supply of the royal share of wine), *śoṭī* (pot for measuring liquids like wine), *cāturtha* (quarter of the standard measure), *ikṣu-vāṭa* (sugarcane plantation), *alla-vāṭa* (probably, ginger plantation, or low land), *yantra-kuṭī* (oil mill or manufactory), *śulk-ātiyātrika* (boundary-crossing tax), *bhāṇḍa-bhṛta-vahitra* (wagon or boat full of vessels), *mahiṣ-oṣṭra-bharaka* (a load on buffalo and camel), *poṭṭalikā-saṁkācitaka* (bundles suspended from loops), *ārdraka-lakaṭā* (dried ginger-sticks, or undried fire-wood), *kaṇikkā* (Sanskrit *kanikā*, cummin seed), *varṇikā* (Prakrit *vanniā*, a sample) *setikā* (Prakrit *seiā, seigā*, a measure equal to two *prasṛtis* or four *palas*), *paṭṭaka-dhārmika* (a case of transit legalised by passport), *madya-vahanaka* (a boat or vehicle full of wine), *chimpaka* (Prakrit *chimpaya*, a dyer of clothes), *padakāra* (shoe-maker, or hawker), *kolika* (Sanskrit *kaulika*, weaver), etc. See above, Chapter XIII, pp. 176ff.

20. G. Watt, *The Commercial Products of India*, 1908, p. 663.

21. W.H. Schoff, *The Periplus of the Erythraean Sea*, p. 172.

Indus.[22] Pliny (23-79 A.D.) says, "We have indicum, a substance imported from India...."[23]

The records of Viṣṇuṣeṇa, Samudrasena and Vidagdha would suggest that indigo was probably cultivated in Gujarat, Punjab and Chamba (Himachal Pradesh) in early times. The first and second of the three regions, it is interesting to note, are known to have continued indigo cultivation till recent times. As regards Gujarat, we are told, "in the 16th and 17th centuries, indigo, partly of local growth and partly brought from Upper India was one of the chief exports of Gujarat. Towards the close of the 18th century (1777), the cultivation, chiefly for local use, would seem to have been on a very considerable scale."[24] The Russian traveller Athanasius Nikitin (1468) speaks of Kanbat (Cambay in Gujarat) as growing indigo.[25] The production of indigo in Gujarat or in particular localities in the region, e.g., Cambay, Ahmedabad, Surat and Broach, is further mentioned by Linschoten (1598), Francois Pyrard (1601-10), Terry (1622), Mandelslo (1638) and Tavernier (1670).[26]

As regards the Punjab region, it is said that "the estimated area under indigo plantation in 1904-05 was 53,000 acres and the yield 9,900 cwt., and the most important districts for the production were then Multan, Muzaffarabad, Dehra Ghazi Khan and Rohtak."[27] Birdwood and Foster (1605-06) speak of Lahar (Lahore) as a place producing indigo.[28]

22. *Ibid.*, p. 38.

23. *Ibid.*, pp. 172-73; Pliny, XXXV. 25-27.

24. Watt, *op.cit.*, pp. 676-77.

25. *Ibid.*, p. 664. Garcia de Orta (1563) also speaks of the cultivation and manufacture of blue dye in Western India and of the *gālī* and *nīl* of Gujarat (*loc.cit.*).

26. See *ibid.*, pp. 664-66.

27. *Ibid.*, p. 676.

28. Cf. *ibid.*, p. 664.

VI

TRADERS' PRIVILEGES GUARANTEED BY KINGS

There is an interesting tale in Daṇḍin's *Daśakumāracarita* (Chapter II) in which a valuable article in the possession of a prostitute is found to be stolen property, and she is pressed by the king to divulge the source from which she had received it. The woman protested and pointed out that giving out the names of lovers is against the custom of her class and that a prostitute does not expect persons to spend at her place money earned only by righteous means.[1] But the king threatened her that the nose and ears of both herself and her mother would be cut off if she persisted in withholding the name of the person who had given her the article. Then under Dhanamitra's instructions, the prostitute gave out the name of the innocent merchant Arthapati as her lover who had given her the said article as a present. The enraged king then ordered the death of the culprit; but Dhanamitra said, *ārya, Maurya-datta eṣa varo vaṇijām=īdṛśeṣv=aparādheṣu n=āsti asubhir=abhiyogaḥ; yadi kupito='si, hṛta-sarvasvo nirvāsanīyaḥ pāpa eṣa iti*, "Sire, there is a privilege granted to the merchants by the Mauryas that they should not be punished with death in this kind of crime; in case you are angry, you may banish this wretch from the country after confiscating his entire property."[2]

The above tale has several interesting aspects. In the first place, it shows that there were certain crimes for which the punishment of the traders was lesser that that of ordinary criminals, and one of these was the possession of stolen property, which was generally regarded as theft. For this crime, the punishment of an ordinary criminal was apparently death; but a trader committing the same offence enjoyed a privilege granted by the Mauryas and was subject to the maximum

1. See *op. cit.*, ed. Jivananda, pp. 134-35 : *rājñ=ānuyukte ca n=aiṣa nyāyo veśa-kulasya yad=dātur=apadeśaḥ; na hi arthair=nyāy-ārjitair=eva puruṣā veśam=upatiṣṭhanti*, etc.

2. *Ibid.*, p. 135.

punishment of banishment from the area or the kingdom and confiscation of his property by the king. The reason underlying this concession is no doubt the fact that often a merchant might have to accept a stolen article from one, either in mortgage or for sale, because the person would solemnly declare the object to be his own, and it was not possible for the trader to conduct any business if all such objects are suspected to be stolen property. It is a matter of regret that, although the passage *īdṛśeṣv=aparādheṣu* suggests that a number of privileges were granted to the traders by the Mauryas, we are told of only one of them.

Before mentioning the other interesting aspects of the tale, a word may be said here about the expression *Maurya-datta* in the above tale. We have taken it to mean 'awarded by the Mauryas (i.e. the kings of the Maurya dynasty)', though it is sometimes interpreted as 'awarded by the Maurya (i.e. 'the son of Murā', meaning Candragupta, founder of the Maurya empire)'.[4] It is, however, significant that, while the early authorities use Maurya as the name of a family or clan,[5] it has been pointed out that only the late commentator of the *Viṣṇu Purāṇa* explains it as 'the son of Murā', and says that Candragupta was the Nanda king's son from a Śūdra woman named Murā, even though the correct form, in that case, should better have been *Maureya* and not *Maurya* which would mean 'the son of Mura (male).'[6] Really, Maurya is the Sanskrit form

3. Cf. Kane, *Hist.Dharm.*, Vol. III, p. 390.

4. Cf. Jivananda, *op.cit.*, p. 135, note 35.

5. On Pāṇini, V. 3.99 (*jīvik-ārthe c=āpaṇye*), Patañjali says, *Mauryair=hiraṇy-ārthibhir=arcāḥ prakalpitāḥ; bhavet=tāsu na syāt; yas=tv=etāḥ sam-prati-pūj-ārthās=tāsu bhaviṣyati.* It says that the Mauryas, who were greedy of gold or wealth, manufactured the images of Śiva, Skanda, Viśākha, etc., for sale, and such images would be called Śivaka, etc., but that images to be put up for immediate worship would not be so called. The Junagadh inscription of 150 A.D. (*Sel. Ins.*, Vol. I, 1965, p. 177) mentions both Candragupta and his grandson Aśoka specifically as *Maurya* (i.e. belonging to the Maurya clan). The historical sections of the Purāṇas use the word in the plural to indicate a dynasty or clan (Pargiter, *Purāṇa Text of the Dynasties of the Kali Age*, pp. 26 ff.).

6. See R.K. Mookerji in *The Age of Imperial Unity*, ed. Majumdar, p. 55. The commentator of the *Viṣṇu Purāṇa* says, *Candra-guptaṁ Nandasy=aiva patny-antarasya Murā-saṁjñāyāḥ putraṁ Mauryāṇāṁ prathamam* (Wilson, *The Viṣṇu Purāṇa*, trans., p. 375, note). Likewise Ḍhuṇḍhirāja, a late

of Pali *Moriya* which is the name of a tribe inhabiting Pipphalīvana in the sub-Himalyan region in the Buddha's age,[7] though the meaning of the name cannot be satisfactorily determined.

The second interesting fact in the *Daśakumāracarita* tale is that, whereas Daṇḍin, the author of the work, seems to have flourished in South India[8] about the seventh century A. D.,[9] the Mauryas ruled from their capital at Pāṭaliputra (modern Patna in Bihar) in c. 324-187 B. C. Thus the privileges

commentator of the *Mndrārākṣasa*, says that Candragupta was the son of Maurya from his Śūdra wife Murā (Mookherji, *loc. cit*), though the accounts of the two commentators do not tally. According to the earlier authority of the drama *Mudrārākṣasa* (c. sixth century A.D.), Candragupta was a *Maurya-putra* (II.6) and was brought up by the Nanda king and was called his son (II.8). *Maurya-putra* does not mean 'the son of Maurya' as is usually believed, but 'a scion of the Maurya clan' as in cases like *Śibi-putra*, *Bhoja-putra*, *Videha-putra*, *Guhila-putra*, etc. The same drama also suggests (III. 3)) that the Nanda king was Candragupta's *guru* (father), and (V.19) that Candragupta was the *svāmi-putra* (master's son) of the Nanda king's minister. Elsewhere in the work (Act IV), Candragupta is called *Nand-ānvaya* (descended from Nanda), and Nanda's minister is stated to have been Candragupta's *pitṛ-paryāy-āgata* (connected by ancestral succession). It is also said that the Nanda family was Candragupta's *pitṛ-kula-bhūta* (Act IV), i.e. as good as his paternal family. The *Mudrārākṣasa* (II.7; VI.6) also represents Candragupta as *kula-hīna* and a *vṛṣala* (Śūdra or outcaste) while Nanda is stated to have belonged to a highly respectable family. These facts appear to suggest that Candragupta was an illegitimate or adopted son of Nanda. But more reliable than these is the earlier Ceylonese chronicle (fifth century A.D.) tradition representing Candragupta as a scion of the Moriya clan. The Moriyas were apparently sub-Himalayan Mongoloids claiming the status of the Kṣatriya like the Licchavis and others, though they must have been regarded as outcastes by the orthodox leaders of society. It is difficult to say whether Candragupta was called Moriya because his mother belonged to that clan. See *Journ. Anc. Ind. Hist.*, Vol. V, pp. 242 ff.

7. See Malalasekera, *Dictionary of Pali Proper Names*, s.v. *Moriyā*. The commentary on the *Mahāvaṁsa* offers two fanciful explanations : (1) *Moriya* is a mistake for *Modiya* meaning 'rejoicing [in the prosperity of their city]', and (2) it is derived from the word *mora* (Sanskrit *mayūra*, 'a peacock'). These hesitant interpretations make it clear that the derivation of the name was unintelligible to the medieval writers. *Maurya* is associated with *mayūra* in the *Pariśiṣṭaparvan* or *Sthavirāvalīcaritra* (VIII. 229-31) by Hemacandra (1089-1172 A.D.), Candragupta being mentioned in it as a scion of a family of *Mayūrapoṣakas* (peacock-tamers).

8. Cf. Sircar, *Stud. Soc. Anc. Med. Ind.*, Vol. I, Calcutta, 1967, p. 202.

9. *Ibid.*, p. 203.

appear to have been continuously enjoyed by the merchants for about nine centuries even far away from the Maurya capital. It is of course well known that the Maurya empire extended over considerable parts of South India probably as far south as the district round Kāñcīpuram near Madras.[10] What is surprising is that even the southernmost areas of the vast empire of the Mauryas were under so much of their effective control that the concession granted by them to the traders remained in force at least for more than eight centuries after the fall of the Maurya dynasty about 187 B.C. This may be due to the fact that the mercantile community, at least in South India, was strong enough to be able to exact the concession from the State continuously throughout the centuries.

The third point of interest in the tale is that it recognises *rāja-śāsana* among the sources of law. In the early Indian legal literature, emphasis is usually laid on the *śāstra* in this connection. However, we have seen that Kātyāyana, as quoted by Devaṇṇa-bhaṭṭa, says—

deśasy=ānumaten=aiva vyavasthā yā nirūpitā |
likhitā tu sadā dhāryā mudritā rāja-mudrayā ||

śāstra-vad=yatnato rakṣyā tāṁ nirīkṣya vinirṇayet ||[11]

This refers to a partial recognition of *rāja-śāsana* in law, because the king is represented as entitled to recognise the customs of a particular locality, However, there is epigraphic evidence indicating the king's importance as a maker of law particularly in relation to the grant of concessions and privileges.

Thus one of the innovations introduced by Aśoka in the Maurya administration is that a respite of three days was granted to condemned men lying in prison under the sentence of death.[12] Likewise the Anjaneri (Nasik District, Maharashtra) plates (709-10 A.D.)[13] of Bhogaśakti and Tejovarman record

10. See Sircar, *Maski Inscription of Aśoka*, Hyderabad, 1958, p. 8.
11. *Smṛticandrikā*, Vol. III, Part I, p. 58; above, p. 183, note 2.
12. See Sircar, *Inscriptions of Aśoka*, 1967, p. 63.
13. *Ep. Ind.*, Vol. XXV, p. 237. The interesting passage of the inscription in question has already been quoted above and explained in connection with the charter of Viṣṇuṣeṇa, which also we shall have to refer to in the latter part of this Appendix. See below, pp. 280ff.

certain concessions granted in favour of the merchants of Samagiri, the first of which says that they would not have to pay any tax within Bhogaśakti's kingdom so long as the sun and moon endure. The traders of a particular town were therefore made permanently free from taxes. Besides that, a number of other privileges were also granted to the said merchants and these included freedom from *aputra-dhana* (confiscation of the wealth of a merchant dying without leaving an heir), *umbara-bleda* (entry of policemen into a merchant's house during his absence) as well as *āvāsaka* and *jemaka* (obligation for giving accommodation and food to royal officials visiting the town). In the same context, mention is also made of fines for certain offences, though it is not clearly stated whether they were concessional rates to be charged from the offenders if they belonged to the mercantile community or the merchants were allowed to realise fines for the particular crimes at Samagiri, i.e. in their own estate, at the prescribed rates. These included a fine of 108 *rūpakas* (silver coins) for the abduction of an unmarried girl (*kumārī-sāhasa*); 32 *rūpakas* for adultery (*saṁgrahaṇa*); 16 *rūpakas* for the mutilation of ears; 4 *rūpakas* for bruising one's head; and 108 *rūpakas* for a merchant's son having illicit connection with a female porter for a long time, though it was 8 or 16 *rūpakas* (as might have been fixed by the elders of the city council of merchants) for each such act of adultery. The reference to the fixation of the fines by the city elders probably suggests that the merchants were empowered to realise the prescribed fines. This seems also to be supported by the charter of Viṣṇuṣeṇa (Viṣṇubhaṭa) to be discussed below.

Another inscription[14] (1059 A.D.) from Sudi in the Dharwar District of Mysore, belonging to the reign of Cālukya Someśvara I Āhavamalla (1043-68 A.D.), registers the *śāsana-maryādā* granted to eight Śreṣṭhins and eighty households apparently of the merchant community living in the village. The privileges included freedom of the shops and households from payment of all taxes for two years. An interesting concession was that the guilt of the father would not affect the son, nor the guilt of the son affect the father. It is also said that,

14. *Ibid.*, Vol. XV, pp. 77ff. See above, p. 183 and note 1. For the gold Gadyāṇa (48 Ratis), mentioned in the record, see Sircar, *Stud. Indian Coins*, pp. 16-17. etc.

if a shop-keeper would strike a thief, robber, burglar, enemy or an evil-minded person in the veranda near the screen of the shop, there should be neither guilt nor fine, but that, if he would strike them elsewhere, he would be fined six gold Gadyāṇas. The record specifically states that the rules regarding the eight Śreṣṭhins should not apply to the country, nor those of the country to the said Śreṣṭhins.

There is an earlier copper-plate inscription[15] dated Vikrama 649 (592 A.D.), which says how king Viṣṇuṣeṇa (also called Viṣṇubhaṭa), apparently of the Gujarat region, was approached by the merchant community of a locality called Lohāṭā with the request of being favoured with the ruler's *ācāra-sthiti-pātra* which they could utilise in protecting and helping the members of their community (*loka-saṁgrah-ānugrah-ārtham*) and how the merchants were favoured with the king's *sthiti-pātra* which was used in the protection and settlement of the people of his kingdom (*janapadasya....parirakṣaṇa-sanniveśanāya*). This *sthiti-pātra* or *ācāra-sthiti-pātra*, in which the word *pātra* has the same meaning as *patra* or document, is elsewhere also called *anugraha-sthiti-pātra*, *sthiti-vyavasthā* and *sthiti-pātra-vyavasthā* and is actually a long list of regulations which look like prevalent customary laws without much modification and remind us of the opinion of Kātyāyana quoted above. At the end of the record, Viṣṇuṣeṇa further says that, in addition to the *ācāras* quoted in the document, he also approved of other *ācāras* that were handed down from ancient times (*pūrva-valamānak-ācārāḥ*). He concludes with the request that his *anugraha-sthiti-pātra* should be approved and followed by the future rulers of the land. The above document of Viṣṇuṣeṇa is followed by an endorsement, according to which *Sāmanta* Avanti of Darpapura issued an order, in Kalacuri 357 (605 A.D.), to his own officials informing them that he had given his assent to the *sthiti-vyavasthā* granted by king Viṣṇubhaṭa (Viṣṇuseṇa) to the community of merchants residing at Lohāṭaka-grāma (Lohāṭā) and that persons conducting their respective trades and following the above *sthiti-pātra-vyavasthā* should not be disturbed in any way.

15. *Ep. Ind.*, Vol. XXX, pp. 163 ff; above, Chapter XIII, pp. 176ff.

We have tried elsewhere[16] to explain all the seventy-two regulations in the charter of Viṣṇuṣeṇa, and it is not at all necessary to repeat the discussion on all of them here. It has, however, to be noticed that, the *sthiti-pātra* or *sthiti-vyavasthā*, obtained by the merchants of Lohāṭā or Lohāṭaka from king Viṣṇuṣeṇa contained certain rules followed in the administration of the kingdom and that the merchants obtained a copy of them for their own guidance expecially because some of the rules related to the merchantile community. It is, however, possible that some rules relating to the community indicated certain concessions to the traders.

Thus one of the rules is *varṣa-paryuṣitā vaṇijaḥ prāveśyaṁ śulk-ātiyātrikaṁ na dāpanīyāḥ; nairgamikaṁ deyam.* It says that merchants staying in the kingdom for the rainy season (or staying abroad for a year) should pay only the exit tax, but not the entry fee. This may have been a concession. Another rule of the kind is *para-viṣayāt kāraṇ -ābhyāgato vaṇijakaḥ para-reṣe na grāhyaḥ*, meaning that a merchant belonging to another district or kingdom and coming to another country or kingdom on business should not be apprehended for *para-reṣa* (doubtful; some offence alleged to have been committed by him elsewhere?). This also looks like a concession. Another rule is *bhāṇḍa-bhṛta-vahitrasysa śulk-ātiyātrike rūpakāḥ dvādaśa rū* 12; *dhārmike rūpakaḥ sa-pādaḥ* 1¼. It says that when a *vahitra* (probably, a large carrier) full of vessels (probably, manufactured articles) was going to cross the boundary of the kingdom, the crossing fee would be 12 silver coins and the concessional rate that may be approved in certain cases would be 1¼ of such coins. It is here difficult to be definite that the taxes mentioned do not indicate any concession in favour of the merchants. There are a good number of similar rules either relating to the merchants or to people including the traders in the charter of Viṣṇuṣena.

However, there are others which cannot be easily associated with merchants. One such is *prapāpūraka-gopālāḥ rāja-graheṇa na grāhyāḥ*, i.e. persons employed in filling the cisterns at watering stations as well as milkmen should not be apprehended or recruited for free labour on the king's behalf. This has no apparent relation to the merchants because the word

16. See above, pp. 183ff.; cf. pp. 186-87 (No. 16), 195 (Nos. 52-53).

gopāla seems to refer to the community of milkmen who are regarded as different from the mercantile community at least in most parts of our country. Likewise, rules like the following also do not appear to be particularly related to the mercantile community—(1) *lohakāra-rathakāra-nāpita-kumbhakāra-prabhṛtīnāṁ vārikeṇa viṣṭiḥ karaṇīyā*, i.e. the blacksmiths, carpenters, barbers, potters and others should be recruited for forced labour under the supervision of officers; (2) *gavāṁ tauṇḍike viṁśopakāḥ pañca, mahiṣyās=tad-dviguṇam*, i.e. the fine for one's cow grazing in another's corn-field was five *viṁśopakas* (i.e. $\frac{1}{4}$ of the silver coin called *rūpaka*) while for one's she-buffalo the fine was ten *viṁśopakas*, etc. Some of the rules appear to be general rather than applicable to the traders alone : e.g. (1) *puruṣ-āparādhe strī na grāhyā*, i.e. the wife should not be apprehended for the husband's guilt; (2) *śaṅkayā grahaṇaṁ n=āsti*, i.e. people should not be arrested on mere suspicion of a crime; etc. These may have been meant for guidng the merchants in the administration of their own estates under the king's permission.

There are also many other records in which remission of taxes on articles of merchandise is referred to. Thus the Kharepatan (Ratnagiri District, Maharashtra) plates[17] of the Śilāhāra *Mahāsāmantādhipati Mahāmaṇḍaleśvarādhipati Paścimasamudrādhipatt* Anantapāla, dated 1095 A.D. and addressed to the Hañjamana among others, records the release of certain tolls on carts coming to Sthānaka (Thana), Nāgapura (Nagaon near Alibag), Sūrpāraka (Sopara near Bassein), Cemūli (Chaul in the Kolaba District) and other sea-ports in the Koṅkaṇa-1400. In this case, the intention was no doubt to encourage export by the sea.

The above record of Viṣṇuṣeṇa and Avanti and the later documents of Bhogaśakti and Tejovarman and of the time of Someśvara I suggest that one of the Maurya kings of Pāṭaliputra, probably Candragupta, or Aśoka issued a similar document for the benefit of the mercantile community pursuing trade in various parts of the vast Maurya empire.

17. *Ind. Ant.*, Vol. IX, p. 33; *Bomb. Gaz.*, Vol. I, Part II, p. 543.

INDEX*

*This has been prepared by Sm. K. Bajpeyi, M.A., to whom the author's thanks are due.